# Sociology and

F. E. PEACOCK PUBLISHERS, INC.
Itasca, Illinois

# Everyday Life

DAVID A. KARP
Boston College

WILLIAM C. YOELS
University of Alabama, Birmingham

DEDICATION

For my wonderful daughters,
Joanna and Leandra Yoels

—*William C. Yoels*

For my family

—*David Karp*

Photo, page 6, © Alex Webb, Distributed by Magnum. All other photos by Lee Pellegrini

Copyright © 1986
F.E. Peacock Publishers, Inc.
All rights reserved
Library of Congress Catalog
Card Number 85-062183
ISBN 0-87581-317-8
Printed in the U.S.A.

# CONTENTS

PREFACE vii

PART I DEVELOPMENT OF THE PERSPECTIVE 1
1. Culture and the Organization of Everyday Life 5
2. Socialization and the Construction of Social Reality 35
3. Communication and Interaction 59

PART II ESTABLISHING SOCIAL ORDER 91
4. Contacts among Strangers: Everyday Urban Relations 95
5. Contacts among Intimates: Constructing Social Relationships 125
6. Power and Stratification in Everyday Life 161
7. Everyday Life in Bureaucracies 187

PART III DISORDER AND CHANGE IN EVERYDAY LIFE 217
8. Deviance in Everyday Interactions 221
9. Aging and the Life Cycle 249
10. Social Change and the Search for Self 277

INDEXES 305

# PREFACE

During the course of our teaching careers we have become increasingly dissatisfied with the focus of most introductory-level textbooks. Nearly exclusively, they are structured around macrosociological, institutional issues. If everyday interaction is treated at all, it is usually dealt with as a subheading in chapters on socialization, culture, or small-group study.

This is a serious omission for two reasons. First, the study of social interaction has always been a central concern of the sociological enterprise. Second, as we have come to learn very well, students taking introductory sociology courses are intent on learning something *immediately applicable to their everyday lives*. We have written *Sociology and Everyday Life* for those instructors who want to ground their treatment of traditional introductory topics in the stuff of daily life. In this book, which is an expanded version of our text originally published as *Symbols, Selves, and Society*, we have added three new chapters dealing with bureaucracy, deviance, and the life cycle. We have also updated the other material, featured certain topics, defined the key concepts, and prefaced each chapter with an outline showing how the material is organized.

A key assumption underlying this book is that the value and vitality of sociology depend on its ability to provide fresh insights into events and situations that students might ordinarily take for granted. In each chapter we show that there are underlying patterns to everyday life. These patterns become "obvious" only when we begin to look very hard at everyday phenomena and then apply sociological concepts to them. While our focus is fundamentally on processes of interaction, we are careful to indicate the mutually transformative connections between social structures and everyday face-to-face encounters.

To accomplish our goals, the book has been divided into three main parts. Part I, consisting of three chapters, introduces key concepts in sociology (culture, socialization, roles, power, self, and the like) as well as the theoretical perspective that is maintained throughout the book. Most of our analysis of everyday life is derived from the symbolic interaction perspective, though the studies we refer to were done from a variety of sociological viewpoints. The first three chapters, like all those in the book, are filled with examples that are resonant with the daily experiences of college students. Part II centers on the construction and maintenance of order in social life. This section includes chapters on urban life and relations among strangers, the construction of intimacies, the distribution and use of power in daily life, and everyday life within bureaucracies. Part III speaks to questions of deviance and change in everyday life. It includes chapters on deviance, aging, and contemporary social movements, including the search for self.

We have constructed the book so that the topics parallel those discussed in most introductions to sociology courses. Instructors will find that it can be used flexibly, in conjunction with other core texts or as the central book in the introductory course, along with a number of shorter texts.

## Acknowledgments

Several people provided us with their help, insight, and criticism during the preparation of this book. Darleen Karp, Mark LaGory, and Paul Romjue will no doubt see versions of their ideas on the following pages. Peter Hall of the University of Missouri and Louis Zurcher of the University of Texas carefully and most professionally reviewed early drafts. Their sophisticated knowledge of symbolic interaction and their sensitivity to the subtleties of everyday life helped us in expanding and clarifying our thoughts. Our long association with the late Gregory P. Stone of the University of Minnesota also had an important influence on the development of the ideas in this book.

The expanded text in the present version was reviewed by Del Samson, Montana State University; John Stimson, William Paterson College; and Jack Kamerman, Kean College.

We also want to express appreciation to Kathleen Crowell, Helen Dees, and Martha Roth who typed several drafts of this book with their usual skill, patience, and good humor. Robbie Reardon Hochgesang typed the edited versions. Last, we want to extend a special note of thanks to Gloria Reardon, our editor at F. E. Peacock. Her general knowledge, careful editing, and extraordinary capacity for organizing materials greatly improved our work.

September 1985                                                                    David A. Karp
William C. Yoels

# PART I  Development of the Perspective

| | |
|---|---|
| CHAPTER 1 | CULTURE AND THE ORGANIZATION OF EVERYDAY LIFE  5 |
| | Cultural Expectations and Everyday Interactions  8 |
| | Social Conventions as Guides for Social Order  9 |
| | Beyond Social Conventions: The Interpretation of Everyday Life  18 |
| | The Individual-Society Relationship  22 |
| | The Sociology of Everyday Life  25 |
| CHAPTER 2 | SOCIALIZATION AND THE CONSTRUCTION OF SOCIAL REALITY  35 |
| | Symbolic Communication  38 |
| | Development of the Self through Interaction with Others  44 |
| | Social Reality and Nonconformity  50 |
| CHAPTER 3 | COMMUNICATION AND INTERACTION  59 |
| | The Need for Communication in Role-Taking  61 |
| | Gathering and Processing Information about Others  64 |
| | Controlling Information and Managing Impressions  79 |

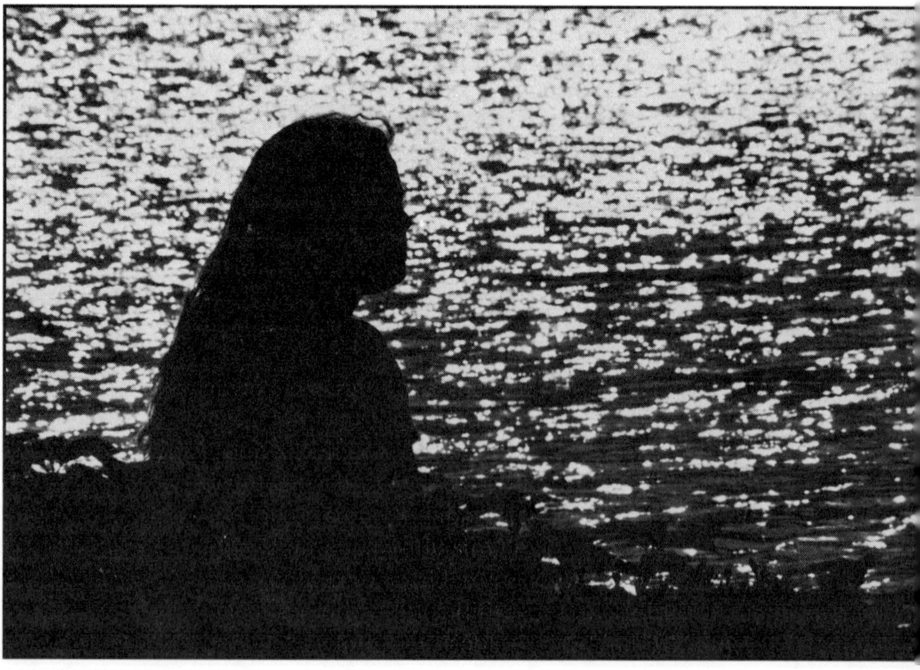

# PART I

THE FOCUS OF THIS BOOK is on everyday life. Our work is based on the belief that a key measure of sociology's value and vitality is its ability to provide insight into the underlying structure of day-to-day life. Certainly, sociology should provide you with a way to understand how society as a whole is organized and ordered. At the same time, a sociological way of looking at things should be immediately applicable to your everyday lives. We propose to show that there is an order and predictability to everyday life which becomes visible once you begin to look very hard at behaviors and situations that you might otherwise take for granted. Sociological analysis has the power to let you see everyday behaviors and situations in a fresh way. Talking, using space, waiting, relating to members of the opposite sex, choosing clothing, presenting images of yourself to others, touching, behaving in classrooms, and meeting strangers are all behaviors which happen in culturally predictable ways.

The first part of this book, consisting of three chapters, is designed to accomplish three broad goals:

To introduce the study of everyday life as a legitimate concern in the study of sociology.

To provide you with knowledge of some of sociology's key concepts.

To lay out the theoretical perspective that is most helpful in analyzing everyday events.

While close observation is required in order to comprehend how daily life is organized, you also need some tools to help you know what to do with your observations. Concepts and the theories that are built from them provide a blueprint for identifying underlying patterns in social life. In the first three chapters you will learn how such standard sociological concepts as culture, norms, values, roles, status, power, socialization, self, impression management, and interaction both direct the analysis of daily life and provide insight into its management.

In these chapters we also elaborate on a theoretical perspective in sociology called symbolic interaction. We will employ this theoretical view throughout the text as we investigate the various contexts of everyday life.

Chapter 1 presents a rationale for the study of everyday behavior. The notion that clear cultural expectations underlie daily activity is illustrated with examples of regularities in the use of time, space, and gesture. Beyond this, we emphasize how people's interpretations and definitions of social situations direct their behaviors. The question of how individuals give meaning to various social situations is central to the perspective of symbolic interaction. An additional concern in Chapter 1 is to show the significance of everyday behavior in studying how society itself is ordered. By the time you finish the first chapter you will possess several helpful ideas for looking at daily life in new ways.

Social life would be impossible without people's ability to define situations in shared ways. Chapter 2 elaborates on the important notion that human beings are symbol-using animals who collectively give meaning to the objects, events, and situations that make up their lives. We consider in detail the human capacity to symbolize, the socialization processes through which "selves" emerge, and the crucial importance of role-taking in human communications. The ability to engage in symbolic communication, we argue, not only makes social order possible, it also constitutes a continual source of nonconformity in social life. Chapter 2 can give you a deeper understanding of the symbolic interaction perspective and a better ability to use it yourself.

Chapter 3 shows how the assessment of meaning in interaction depends on information about others. Here we describe the kinds of information used to evaluate the people you physically encounter. We explain how such master attributes as sex, age, and race affect everyday relations and describe how people interpret each others' clothing, body type, and gestures. The chapter concludes by describing a view of interaction which stresses how individuals control information and foster impressions of self in everyday life. Chapter 3 builds on some of the key principles learned in earlier chapters.

# CHAPTER 1
## Culture and the Organization of Everyday Life

I. Cultural Expectations and Everyday Interactions
II. Social Conventions as Guides for Social Order
    A. Spatial Conventions
        1. Appropriate distances in everyday interactions
    B. Time Conventions
        1. Time concepts in contemporary societies
        2. The power to make others wait
    C. Posture and Gesture Conventions
        1. Avoiding communications
        2. Rules for physical contact
    D. A Blueprint for Everyday Life
III. Beyond Social Conventions: The Interpretation of Everyday Life
    A. Assessing Meanings and Formulating Behaviors
    B. Interpretation in the Acting Situation
IV. The Individual-Society Relationship
    A. Understanding Freedom and Constraint in Social Life
        1. The approach of the authors
    B. The Dynamic Interplay of Expectations and Interpretations
V. The Sociology of Everyday Life
    A. Why the Study of Interactions Has Been Neglected
    B. What the Study of Interactions Should Accomplish
        1. Discovering underlying social forms
        2. Developing sociological skepticism
VI. Conclusion

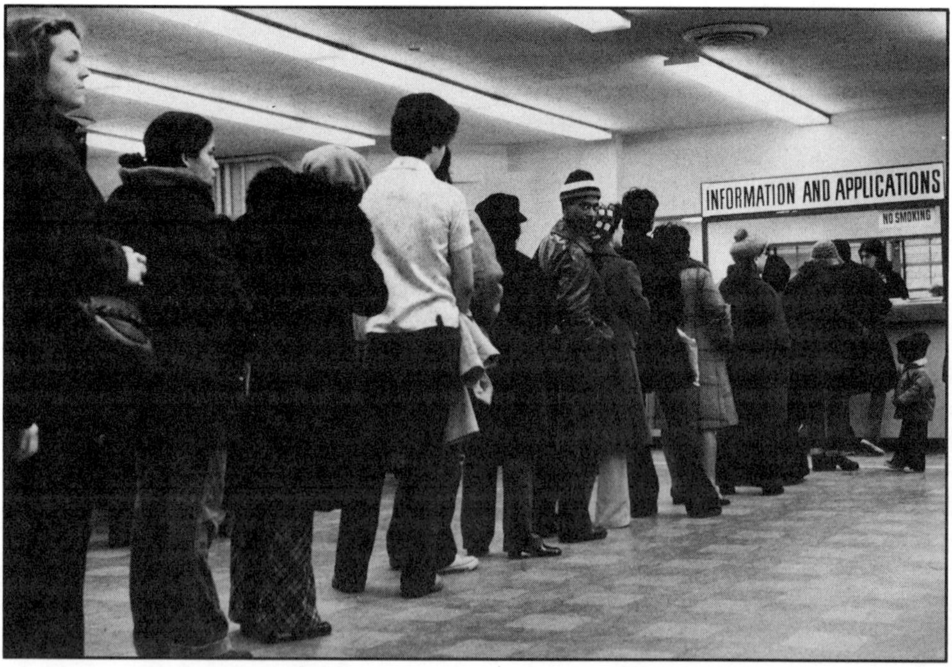
INFORMATION AND APPLICATIONS
NO SMOKING

# CHAPTER 1

A STORY IS TOLD about a man who became a fixture on the streets of Edinburgh, Scotland. He would stop people on Princes Street, a main thoroughfare, and ask them whether they were sane. "If any replied Yes, he would retort—ah, but can you *prove* it? And, if they could not, he proceeded triumphantly to show them that *he* at any rate could prove his sanity, by producing his own certificate of discharge from a mental hospital" (Gellner, 1975:431). This little anecdote raises significant questions about how we show that we are sane and the criteria we use in deciding whether others are insane. Even those who claim expertise in these matters—psychiatrists and other mental health professionals—have been unable to agree on any set of definitions of mental illness or insanity.

At the root of this difficulty is the fact that people's behaviors can only be seen as appropriate or inappropriate in terms of the societies and situations in which they take place. In the Jalé tribe of New Guinea, for example, people waiting for a meal, preparing the oven, tending the fire, or just standing around, would carefully appraise the victim destined to be the main course: "A healthy, muscular body is praised with ravenous exclamations, but a lesser grade body is also applauded" (Koch, 1974:198). In certain Eskimo tribes, a woman might wash her hair to make it smooth, rub tallow into it, grease her face with blubber, and scrape herself clean with a knife, "to be polite" (Reusch, 1951:87). At the turn of the century, the Arunta tribe of Australia considered the size of a girl's breasts a community concern:

To promote the growth of the breasts of a girl, the men assemble in the men's camp where they all join in . . . an exhortation to the breasts to grow . . . . At daylight one of them goes out and calls her to a spot close to the men's camp to which she comes accompanied by her mother. Here her body is rubbed all over with fat by her mother's brothers who then paint a series of straight lines of red ochre down her back and also down the center of her chest and stomach. A wide circle is painted around each nipple. (Spencer and Gillin, 1899:459–460)

Odd behaviors? Surely anyone in American society who engages in cannibalism, thinks rubbing fat on the face will make them more appealing, or has their breasts painted in public in hopes of increasing their measurements would shortly find themselves undergoing psychiatric examination. But members of the societies where these behaviors were practiced would be considered strange and possibly insane for *not* engaging in them.

## ■ CULTURAL EXPECTATIONS AND EVERYDAY INTERACTIONS

As Americans, we are born into an exceedingly complex **culture.** By culture we mean the totality including knowledge, beliefs, customs, and morals which is shared by members of a society. Our culture becomes so familiar to us at an early age that we tend to take it for granted. We normally do not question what we do and why we do it. Everyday life appears to be a reality which rarely requires explanation. It simply exists. The social world confronts us as an ordered and intelligible fact. We generally know which behaviors are proper and which would be improper in a given situation. Indeed, social life would be chaotic if we had to question at length the meaning of every behavior before we engaged in it. When we pull up beside a car at a red light we know we should not stare at the occupants. When we meet a person for the first time we do not need to ask ourselves how long we ought to shake hands. We do not expect new acquaintances to reveal their life problems to us. We would be likely to fear a stranger who boarded a nearly empty bus or train and deliberately sat next to us.

There are, in short, an extraordinary number of **cultural expectations** which we learn virtually from birth and which lend order and organization to our daily interactions with others. Such "background expectancies," as the sociologist Harold Garfinkel (1964) calls them, constitute the fundamental rules in accordance with which persons normally act. These rules, sometimes difficult to specify, reflect our mutually held assumptions about proper and conventional behavior.

The central goal of this book is to analyze **everyday interactions** or

9   *Culture and Organization of Life*

communications from a sociological point of view. This first chapter provides a rationale for the study of the routine social encounters in which everyone participates. The authors will also begin to outline the theoretical perspective that we consider to be most valuable in exploring how transactions with others are accomplished. This is the **symbolic interaction perspective,** which centers attention on how individuals interpret and give meanings to the daily interactions which make up their **social worlds.**

To begin our presentation of this perspective, we will first consider the numerous social conventions which serve as guides for human behaviors and the maintenance of social order. Beyond that, they also serve as the basis on which everyday interactions are analyzed and interpreted by individuals. They therefore have a bearing on both the power of society to influence individuals' behaviors and the power of individuals to change or manipulate society.

## ■ SOCIAL CONVENTIONS AS GUIDES FOR SOCIAL ORDER

There are thousands of cultural expectations which guide the minute details of our everyday interactions with others. These expectations are expressed as social conventions or **norms,** which make up the rules for acceptable behaviors. Several volumes would be needed to describe all the norms in American society, ranging from proper table manners to the enormously complex regularities of verbal discourse. Together these norms make our daily encounters reasonably predictable, so we know what is expected of us and what to expect of others. Conventions such as those governing use of space, time, and posture or gesture also provide indications of the relative power, prestige, and status among the individuals taking part in interactions.

The authors of this book maintain that social life would be utterly unmanageable if there were no broadly shared consensus about how members of the society ought to conduct themselves in the myriad situations encountered in daily life. Social conventions or shared norms based on cultural expectations make everyday life possible and, by extension, constitute the basis for order in the society.

### Spatial Conventions

The study of spatial conventions or norms regarding space between persons in everyday behaviors has been labeled **proxemics** (see LaFrance and Mayo, 1978). According to Robert Sommer (1969), we all have an invisible circle drawn around us which marks off our **personal space.** With few exceptions, we do not allow others to violate this personal territory.

There is evidence of **territoriality** (Lyman and Scott, 1967) in numerous types of daily encounters. Students in many classrooms soon develop a proprietary interest in their seats, for example. They lay claim to particular seats which they thereafter feel they own, for all practical purposes. They will challenge anyone, including a visiting professor, who happens to sit in their selected spot.

### *Appropriate Distances in Everyday Interactions*

Spatial conventions serve as an ordering device which sets rules and limits for most everyday interactions. In American society, normal conversational distance is about 2 feet, for example. We become increasingly uncomfortable should anyone come closer. Imagine how you would react if a stranger came up to you and began to talk to you with his face only inches from yours.

The conventions about appropriate distance often work in conjunction with use of the eyes. In an elevator in a public building, for example, the occupants may avoid eye contact with one another by looking either at the floor or at the flashing numbers over the door. A plausible explanation is that eye contact is an invitation to verbal contact, and we do not wish to make verbal contact with strangers in a situation where our personal space might be violated.

Four common distances used in interpersonal communication were distinguished by Edward Hall, an anthropologist. He used observation and interviews with middle-class adults, mainly in the northeastern United States, as a basis for categorizing the spatial conventions that

### Personal Space and the Middle East Crisis

In the complex, closely interconnected world of the late 20th century, cultural conceptions of space and personal territory can affect international relations. Edward Hall found that cultural variations in conceptions of space are reflected in such ways as differences in various people's felt need for privacy or their tolerance for population density and crowding. He points out that "Perceiving the world differently leads to differential definitions of what constitutes crowded living, different

govern the distances people maintain between themselves in their communications with one another.

The closest encounters, according to Hall (1969), take place at 0 to 18 inches, or within **intimate distance.** They include activities such as lovemaking, wrestling, or whispering which involve either actual body contact or very close proximity. At this distance, Hall says, "the presence of the other person is unmistakable and may at times be overwhelming because of the greatly stepped-up sensory inputs. Sight (often distorted), olfaction, heat from the other person's body, sound, smell, and feel of the breath all combine to signal unmistakable involvement with another body" (p. 116).

Encounters at 1½ to 4 feet take place at **personal distance,** in Hall's terms. The space between individuals at this distance can be thought of as "a small protective sphere or bubble that an organism maintains between itself and others" (p. 119). Most daily conversations take place within this range. Encounters which occur from 4 to 12 feet apart are said to take place at **social distance.** Casual social gatherings such as college mixers operate within this range. Encounters more than 12 feet apart are said to occur at **public distance,** "well outside the circle of personal involvement." In political addresses or theatrical performances, for example, "the voice is exaggerated and amplified, and much of the communication shifts to gestures and body stance" (p. 106).

In different cultures there are different expectations about the appropriate distances to be maintained between people who are communicating with one another. Much of Hall's work details cultural variations in the use of and response to space. He shows that perceptions of private territory, conversational distances, and public distances maintained by Americans, Germans, the French, Japanese, and Arabs are quite different (see box).

---

interpersonal relations, and a different approach to both local and international politics" (Hall, 1969, pp. 154–163).

Hall notes that olfaction (the sense of smell) is an important distance-setting mechanism for Arabs. Arabs breathe directly on one another while talking. They find it pleasant and desirable to experience each other's body odors. It follows that Arabs typically maintain a closer conversational distance than Americans do.

Unlike Germans, who seem to have a strong need for the kind of closed-in privacy provided by walls and doors, Arabs hate to be hemmed in. In terms of territory and ownership of space, Arabs have no real conception of boundaries. In the United States, "ownership" of public territory (a seat on a bus, for example) is determined by the party who first occupies the space. For Arabs, the ownership of space is determined by which person first began to move toward the unoccupied space, regardless of who arrives there first. In addition, for the Arab there is no such thing as an intrusion in public. According to Hall, for Arabs:

Public means public.... For example, if *A* is standing on a streetcorner and *B* wants his spot, *B* is within his rights if he does what he can to make *A* uncom-

In American society, conceptions of appropriate distance and personal space expand and contract, depending on the situation. How close to one another two people stand often is considered evidence of the degree of intimacy between them. Business conversations are carried out at one distance, talks between friends at another, and intimacies between lovers at still another. The relative status or position of different people also can be inferred from the spatial distances they maintain. The distance between the teacher and students in a classroom, for example, is a mark of the differences in their power and prestige. As the traditionally rigid status distinctions between teacher and student have been reduced in recent years, the way space is planned and used in classrooms also has changed. In many schools raised platforms and fixed rows of seats have been replaced by movable chairs and circular arrangements, in hopes of facilitating more direct and informal interactions between students and teachers.

Spatial conventions constitute only one aspect of the cultural expectations which lend order and predictability to everyday interactions. Inferences about differences in power, prestige, and status among individuals which are based on their use of personal space must be confirmed or rejected by other aspects of their behavior, such as regard for time, facial expressions, posture, and verbalization.

## Time Conventions

Seconds, minutes, and hours are not simply measures of time with a constant meaning. They assume different symbolic values in different contexts, different circumstances, and in front of different audiences (Hall, 1959). The meanings we attach to time are specific to particular situations and may, like spatial conventions, attest to differences in

fortable enough to move. In Beirut only the hardy sit in the last row in a movie theatre, because there are usually standees who want seats and who push and shove and make such a nuisance that most people give up and leave. (p. 156)

Knowledge of how the Arabs employ fluid boundaries to mark out territory and possess space obviously would be an advantage in business negotiations. It could even shed light on the struggles for political stability in the Middle East. The lessons to be learned from sociological study of everyday interactions thus can have global significance.

---

power, prestige, and status among persons. Students place a greater subjective value on a professor's time than on their own, for example. Entering a professor's office, students often begin their conversations with the declaration "I know you're probably busy, but . . . ," and during the conversation they look for cues to determine whether they are exceeding an "appropriate" time limit in the office.

While time is measured in such absolutely defined units as seconds, minutes, and hours, each interval is not experienced in an identical fashion. The time spent on an important job interview will carry a different meaning from the same amount of time spent on the tennis court, for example. Albert Einstein once commented on the relativity of time by saying that two minutes in an uncomfortable situation seem like two hours. Like all other features of any culture, time is experienced subjectively.

### *Time Concepts in Contemporary Societies*

There are clear understandings about most time conventions in American society. Imagine the reaction if you shook someone's hand for 60 seconds instead of the conventional 4 to 5 seconds, for example. Americans often plan their behavior to occur in a particular time sequence (see box). As with other social conventions or norms, however, there is considerable variation in expectancies about time within the society, depending on circumstances and the individuals involved.

A simple example is expectations about punctuality. In many social circles it is mutually expected that guests invited to a reception scheduled for 8:00 p.m. ought not to arrive until 8:30 or 9:00. The same punctuality rule would not apply to an appointment for a job interview. In other cultures less value is placed on strict punctuality. In South America, for

*13*

example, it is not considered unusual to arrive more than an hour late for an appointment. Late arrivers offer no explanation for being tardy, since their conception of time is much looser than in the United States. To be an hour late is not considered improper.

Temporal (time-related) conventions and perceptions are linked to a society's level of urbanization and industrialization. The more complex,

---

### On Timing a Farewell: Here's Looking at You, Kid

One of the great lines of all times was spoken by Humphrey Bogart to Ingrid Bergman in the climactic scene at the airport at the end of *Casablanca*. "Here's looking at you, kid," Bogart's toast to Bergman, was his way of convincing her at that point that their affair was over. The seemingly offhand comment signaled the end of a dramatic sequence of events which moved inevitably to a farewell heightened by the dangers and uncertainties of war.

Erving Goffman (1971) used a similar example of a person seeing a close friend off at the airport to illustrate how we time our behaviors to fit a particular sequence. The highly ritualized farewell is timed so that its effusiveness increases in intensity as the time of the departure gets closer. It reaches its emotional high point with tearful embraces just prior to departure time. The display of emotion cannot occur too early or too late.

A great deal of interactional work is necessary in the case of a "failed farewell," when the plane fails to take off. The scenario might be as follows: We have reached the climax of our farewell only to hear that because of some technical difficulty our friend's plane will be delayed. Through no fault of our own, our farewell has failed and we must now go through the awkward process of restructuring the timing of our behaviors. We must backtrack from the intimate situation of high emotional involvement to an earlier stage of nonaffective, nonemotional talk. We must then begin to move once more through the expected time sequence leading up to yet another emotional display. Imagine how difficult this restructuring process would be if there were no reliable information as to how long the plane would be delayed, or if, as in the case of Bergman and Bogart, the farewell represented the end of an interrupted love affair.

15   Culture and Organization of Life

rationalized, bureaucratized, urbanized, and industrialized a society is, the more rigorous, concrete, and linear its conception and treatment of time will be. In a highly developed urban-industrial society, precision of timing is of great importance. Virtually all Americans, including many children, consider it essential to have a wristwatch, and accuracy is the sign of excellence in timepieces. Americans often must know *exactly* what time it is.

The city dweller's constant preoccupation with time and punctuality has been identified as a central characteristic of urban life. Indeed, it has been observed that:

Without a meticulous devotion to punctuality on the part of most of the metropolis' inhabitants, the metropolis would become a bedlam. The very necessity of arranging a schedule for transportation to and from one's place of work, for example, heightens the significance of punctuality for the urban dweller. The interlocking activities of varied businesses in the urban area also reinforce a respect for punctuality so as to maximize operating efficiency. (Karp, Stone and Yoels, 1977:29)

Another aspect of the ways many people experience time in contemporary societies is boredom. One explanation is that modern life, especially work, has become so rationalized and simplified that there are no surprises. According to Jeffrey Nash, boredom is an inevitable consequence "as work becomes standardized and as place and time become situationally defined" (1985:338). Recognition of the routinization of everyday life has led some social scientists to speculate on how imagination and fantasy are used to combat boredom (Weigert, 1981; Fine, 1983; Farberman, 1980).

### The Power to Make Others Wait

Bureaucracy, a predominant influence in modern society (see Chapter 7), demands that much time be spent waiting for others or for goods and services. Barry Schwartz analyzes the nature, meaning, and uses of waiting time in a provocative book titled *Queuing and Waiting* (1975). The study of delay in a mass consumption society is a significant area of sociological inquiry because so much time must be spent waiting.

In the most immediate sense, delay may be caused by the relations between supply and demand for goods and services. Analysis of waiting, however, uncovers delay strategies used to exercise power and status in social interactions. The scarcity or monopolization of valued services creates situations which allow workers to exercise power over clients and customers, for example. Bureaucrats have notoriously abused their power to make people wait. They might not themselves possess anything of value, but in their work roles they control access to resources people need. We cannot even drive our automobiles without first acquiring licenses and registration papers from bureaucrats who, in fact, have low status within their organizations.

Others may keep us waiting because of the perceived importance of the services or knowledge they have to offer. Doctors usually have patients waiting for them, but a patient who fails to show up for an appointment will be charged for the unused time. Executives may regularly keep visitors waiting, "cooling their heels" in an outer office. Schwartz observes that "In general the more powerful and important a person is, the more others' access to him must be regulated. Thus, the least powerful may always be approached at will; the most powerful are seen only 'by appointment' " (1975:19).

## Posture and Gesture Conventions

Social conventions also can regulate the meanings conveyed by people's gestures and postures. **Kinesics,** the sociological study of body movement and gesture, is concerned with the shared cultural meanings attached to nonverbal behaviors. Consensus about the significance of postures, gestures, and expressions enhances our ability to explain and predict our own and others' behaviors in daily interactions.

Ray Birdwhistell (1952, 1970), a pioneer in this field, maintains that the majority of interactions utilize **nonverbal communication.** We give cues to our meanings by the way we stand, our facial expressions, and the position of our heads. We control most of these expressions and consciously use them to express a range of emotions from anger to disappointment to love. All communicative expressions are not easily controlled, however. We find it hard to control such physiological responses as a red face in an embarrassing situation or involuntary hand tremors during high anxiety. Often we look for these expressions in others with whom we are interacting as a check on their emotions or attitudes.

Studies have found that the pupils of a person's eyes dilate and constrict in response to particular stimuli, and these changes correspond to the degree of interest in the stimuli (Hess and Polt, 1960, 1964). Photos of nude women make males' pupils dilate more than females' do, and the finding is reversed when pictures of nude males are shown. Astute observers can use information of this sort for their personal advantage. Chinese jade dealers in the Far East are said to monitor how the size of their customer's pupils changes, for example, in order to gauge their interest in the gems and willingness to pay a high price for them.

The simplest nonverbal gestures can communicate a great deal. Think of a skier or skater who falls and then exaggerates the effect by lying on the cold ground longer than necessary with arms and legs flung out.

Through such exaggeration the person may wish to communicate: "I know I look kind of silly, but understand that I am really a quite competent person and you should not take this momentary awkwardness very seriously." Sometimes gestures of this sort are used in conjunction with verbal utterances, as when a woman runs headlong to catch a bus or elevator before it leaves, only to have the doors close in her face. At this point she might stand, hands on hips, moving her head from side to side, muttering. Her comments are supposedly made to herself, but they also may be meant to be heard by anyone within earshot. They might be intended to communicate: "Understand that although this has happened I remain fully in control of myself."

### Avoiding Communications

While conventions dictate that strangers in public situations should not make prolonged eye contact, there are also strategies to break this rule. A man who wants to look at a woman without seeming to stare on a subway, for instance, must choose a "correct" seat. This is accomplished by sitting across from the woman and pretending to be reading the advertisements over her head. Such a seat is preferable to one directly beside the woman, from which he would have to turn his head 45 degrees in order to see anything.

People often use props as an aid in such situations. We would be hard-pressed to explain why some people wear sunglasses on the subway, for example, unless we considered their use in shielding the "improper" use of eyes. Other props such as newspapers—Goffman (1963) calls them "involvement shields"—are also used to avoid any kind of contact with others. Avoidance may itself be a form of social interaction—we must sometimes communicate to others that we do not wish to communicate. Particularly in urban interactions with strangers, we must systematically take one another into account in order to avoid unwanted encounters (see Chapter 4).

### Rules for Physical Contact

There are also clear conventions regulating actual physical contact between persons. A commonplace behavior such as hand holding is a highly regulated activity, for example. A few questions suggest the range of these regularities: Who can hold hands with whom? Is it more appropriate for women to hold hands in public than it is for men? Why? Is there an age-related factor influencing who can hold hands with whom? Would a female in her 20s feel uncomfortable holding her father's hand while walking down the street? Would a male of the same age feel self-conscious holding his mother's hand in a restaurant? (See Henley, 1973.)

We share clear expectations about who may touch whom, on what part of the body, and in what context. Different meanings and symbolic significance are attached to different parts of the body. On the field athletes pat each others' bottoms after significant plays or outstanding personal efforts, but this same behavior elsewhere would hardly be interpreted as a display of male camaraderie. You might seek others' attention by lightly tapping them on the shoulder, but you would not grab them by the thigh. Sometimes it is considered appropriate for one person to touch another, but not vice versa. A teacher may, while explaining a point to a student, touch the student's shoulder. The student would hesitate to do the same to the teacher. Sometimes even the slightest touch (touching another's foot under a dining table, for example) requires an immediate apology.

### A Blueprint for Everyday Life

This section has described only a small fraction of the types of rules and expectations that constitute a critical part of any culture. As the members of a society together acquire knowledge, beliefs, art, customs, morals, and other capabilities and habits, the culture evolves over time. A pattern of norms or conventions about what one can and cannot do in a given society emerges. A society is possible only because its members share these standards and cultural expectations.

Commonly held ideas about how one ought to behave provide members of the same culture with a blueprint for conducting their everyday lives. Knowledge of cultural rules and social conventions is not itself enough to ensure social order, however. Human beings constantly interpret and negotiate such rules.

## ■ BEYOND SOCIAL CONVENTIONS: THE INTERPRETATION OF EVERYDAY LIFE

The sociologist's job—to explain human behavior—would be quite simple if behaviors were the product only of the types of social conventions we have mentioned. Were that the case, we would only have to set about cataloging all of the rules to which people in American society normally conform. Alas, things are not quite so simple! It would be more accurate to say that these conventions or shared norms constitute the *boundaries* within which people interact. Alone they are not sufficient to explain how daily encounters are managed. Beyond knowledge of background rules, successful interaction requires engaging in a **process of interpretation** through which a situation is assessed and meanings are assigned to a person's own behaviors and those of others.

## Assessing Meanings and Formulating Behaviors

It may very well be true that you know what to do when entering a new classroom for the first time because you have learned from an early age the general rules applicable to classroom behavior. You are unlikely to sit down in the chair behind the desk at the front of the room, for example. You have learned not to speak unless directed to do so by the teacher. Should you want to talk, you would probably raise your hand and wait to be acknowledged by the teacher. And so on. Knowledge of these rules alone, however, will not allow you to predict fully the meanings and patterns of behavior that will become central in any particular classroom. That is, the rules which govern classroom behavior will be products of ongoing actions by the particular teacher and students involved, all of whom must constantly take the others' actions into account when formulating their own lines of action (Karp and Yoels, 1976).

As in any other setting, participants in the classroom will be engaged in an ongoing assessment of each others' actions. Students will soon define the situation as to whether in a particular class the teacher *really* wants discussion, whether it is safe to make one's opinion known, whether one ought to laugh at the teacher's jokes and, if so, how raucously. Decisions of this sort cannot be anticipated or determined only through knowledge of the general and learned conventions applicable to most classrooms.

## Interpretation in the Acting Situation

In this sense, behavior is always produced via interpretation in **the acting situation.** The expectancies surrounding behavior in any situation always emerge from the interaction itself. They may be in a state of continual transformation. According to Herbert Blumer, "In the flow of group life there are innumerable points at which participants are *re*defining each others' acts" (1962:184).

Suppose someone approaches you and asks for a light for a cigarette. This is an apparently simple request, but in fact, it is not immediately clear how you would respond. You probably would believe the other person's motives to be different under different circumstances. What situational factors or variables might influence the meaning you attach to this request? Would the gender of the person make any difference in your interpretation? Would you possibly attribute different motives to a stranger and a close friend making the same request? Would it make any difference where the request was made (at a friend's house or a bar)? What role might such factors as the time of day, the age of the requester, or his or her dress, race, demeanor, and facial expression play in your interpretation of the request? Even the most apparently simple human transactions may call forth quite different meanings which we confer on them by piecing together bits of information in the situation.

Virtually all our behaviors depend on our ability to assess features of the situation in which we are acting and then define it. Some situations may require more extensive interpretation than others, however. In some situations we realize that we must be quite strategic in formulating our

### Reducing the Risks in Looking for Mr. Goodbar

Judith Rossner's novel about a New York schoolteacher's persistent search for male companions in singles' bars, *Looking for Mr. Goodbar*, focused on the physical dangers involved in close contacts with strangers. Other risks are involved in such encounters, however. For both women and men the attempt to develop an ongoing relationship with a stranger of the opposite sex can have negative outcomes. As in any interaction, there is a risk that a person's identity will be found unacceptable by others or that the interaction the person is promoting will somehow be disrupted. The risk of loss of face, when the identity a person presents is rejected, is especially great in the singles' bar situation. Other potential risks include boredom, loss of time, and the possibility of generating obligations that one is not prepared to meet. Many of the behaviors of men and women in singles' bars can be understood in terms of their risk-reducing utility.

For example, a man in such a situation, spotting a likely woman at some distance across a room, seldom walks directly toward her in a straight-line fashion to initiate the encounter. If he takes the straight-line approach, there is a certain risk involved. It would be clear to any onlooker that he intends to approach the woman, and if she refuses his offer to dance or converse, his failure and loss of face would be highly apparent. The preferred approach is a zigzag pattern, which can consume a good deal of time because the male stops for an appropriate period at several points in his apparently casual, nonpurposive meander about the room. If he is skillful enough, he will finally reach a position where he "just happens" to be beside the woman he wishes to meet. The zigzag pattern also has other advantages. The man can check out the woman at each point in this journey, assessing whether she is alone and if there are signs of her openness to interaction.

At some point the couple must begin to talk to each other. They will

behaviors. In these situations we might engage in extensive mind work or mental gymnastics prior to acting. We might consciously try to manipulate those with whom we interact in order to control the definition of the situation they will come to have. These may be situations which we consider risky or in which we perceive obstacles to the realization of our goals. The interactions between single males and females often take on this character (see box).

---

not discontinue their careful assessment of each other, however. The opening conversation is usually quite ritualized ("Hi, can I buy you a drink?") and serves to create an appropriate amount of "empty time" at the outset of the encounter during which both parties can safely evaluate each other without making any sort of commitment. One function of ritualistic, impersonal, or cold conversation at the outset of an interaction between previously unacquainted persons is to inject an appropriate time interval in which they can make a preliminary judgment about each other's suitability.

Those who seek to develop an ongoing interaction must progressively warm up the cold, impersonal talk. Those who become too personal too early in a meeting are met with suspicion, however. They may have some questionable motive which causes them to dispense with the normal rituals, so they are not to be trusted. Newly acquainted persons attempt to navigate this initial encounter in such a way that they can easily withdraw from the interaction if it becomes apparent to them that the costs of continued interaction are going to outweigh the benefits.

It is often the task of the woman who has been approached by a man to establish a line of behavior that indicates her willingness to continue the interaction for the time being, while not committing herself to it. At the beginning of the interaction she is likely to respond to his overtures noncommittally and give only brief answers to his questions. At the same time she indicates the possibility that her involvement will become greater. She tries to communicate to him, in effect, that he ought to keep working on it. To that end, the woman may continue the conversation, nodding or smiling at regular intervals, while she simultaneously scans the room with her eyes to show that her future involvement is still very much an issue. She must be careful to create the proper blend of interest and noninvolvement. A show of too great interest may find her committed to an unwanted encounter, but a show of too little involvement could end one that is potentially rewarding.

## ■ THE INDIVIDUAL-SOCIETY RELATIONSHIP

The social conventions described in the preceding section lend support to a central idea in the symbolic interaction approach to the study of sociology: The capacity of humans to interact and communicate effectively with each other is a truly extraordinary ability and worthy of in-depth investigation. The explanation of how social conventions reflect the social order and influence the interpretation of everyday events has brought out a number of general points. First, although we may not think much about it, there is a clear ordering to our everyday lives. There are underlying dimensions to everyday social life that can be discovered. Second, the coherence of everyday life depends on our possession of a truly remarkable range of knowledge. Third, our behaviors are a product of our ability to interpret social situations and confer meanings on them. Fourth, rather than being regarded as a given, social order should be considered a human accomplishment which requires explanation. Fifth, if we seek to understand how, in the broadest sense, a society is possible and how it operates as an ongoing concern, it is a good strategy to begin by exploring how we carry out our day-to-day interactions.

This approach also supports an even more general sociological theme: the relationship between the individual and the society. We live in a society which significantly influences our behaviors through numerous social conventions. At the same time, we exercise substantial freedom of action. It is a paradox of human existence that while societies influence human behaviors, humans sometimes also transform societies. We must entertain simultaneously the apparently contradictory thoughts that humans are social products and society is a human product.

### Understanding Freedom and Constraint in Social Life

The abiding theoretical questions of sociology flow from consideration of the individual-society connection: How do individuals become functioning members of a society? How and why do they become responsive to the demands of a society? Why do they conform to society's rules? How is it that some persons refuse to do so? To what extent is behavior determined by **social structure?** Just how much can individuals change societies?

Nearly all the great classical social theorists were intrigued by these questions. On the whole, their theoretical work may be read as attempts to understand the nature of the **social bonds** existing between persons and the bonding of persons to the society. Those who are considered the founding fathers of sociology—Karl Marx, Emile Durkheim, Georg Sim-

23   *Culture and Organization of Life*

mel, Max Weber, Ferdinand Tönnies, and William Graham Sumner, among others—all broached questions of order and disorder, change and stability, deviance and conformity. These questions, of course, do not allow for single, definitive answers. They still are the guiding questions for sociological work, and sociologists collectively are still in the business of trying to understand just how societies and individuals influence one another. One thing seems clear, however. Comprehension of everyday life requires a conception of the individual-society relationship in which primacy is placed on neither the society nor the individual.

## *The Approach of the Authors*

The authors of this book are convinced that any attempt to understand the operation of society that neglects the processes governing social interaction will be theoretically unsatisfying. Ultimately a society is composed of persons interacting with one another. All explanations of human behavior must in some way account for individuals' intentions, motives, and subjective understanding of the situation in which they act. All human behavior is constructed from everyday, **shared meaning structures.** As one writer (Douglas, 1970:11) has put it, "Any scientific understanding of human action, at whatever level of ordering or generality, must . . . be built upon an understanding of the everyday life of the members performing those actions."

This is not to suggest that sociologists should give up the study of social structure in favor of the study of human interaction. Instead, we believe the most fruitful sociological inquiries are based on an integration of the two levels of analysis, society and the individual. Too much sociology, we think, makes the mistake of accepting the **reification** of social structures, regarding them as having a life of their own independent of individuals. Much sociological work is based on the supposition that institutions are more than the sum of their parts and, once created, exert a force on individuals over which they have little control.

There is no question that institutions exert a strong force on individuals. Ample evidence of this can be found in the bureaucratic systems which provide a structure for the lives of college and university students. There are certain things you are required to do if you wish to remain within the system. You must show up for exams, you must pay your tuition, you must follow certain course registration procedures, and so forth. In that sense the structure is real, powerful, and has an obdurate quality that transcends the existence of any particular student. The university has an independent life in the sense that it existed as an institution before any of you were born and will, in all likelihood, continue to exist after you are dead.

Does this mean that your behaviors are utterly controlled by the academic bureaucracy? Does it mean that sociologists need not be concerned with the interactions among persons within the institution and the definitions and meanings they give to their lives in it? Of course not! It should not come as news that students manipulate academic institutions. Through interaction with others, you determine just how hard you will work in your courses. You and your fellow students could collectively choose to make life difficult for your instructors by such strategies as choosing not to participate in class discussion or conning them into letting you turn in late term papers.

We are committed to the idea that in large measure, human beings act according to the *interpretations* they make of social life. Individuals are not merely puppets pushed around by forces over which they have no control. Substantially, they make their own worlds. Unlike atoms, molecules, or stable elements of the physical universe, they think, construct meanings, and respond creatively to their environments. Consequently, the social world is in a state of continual process, change, and production. Values and attitudes change. Behaviors once thought taboo become incorporated into the repertoire of conventional behaviors. New social forms are created to meet needs better, and unpredictable fads are devised.

Humans thus experience choice and discretion in their everyday lives. But it would be misleading to minimize the significance of the constraints within which they must act. The dramas of daily life occur within larger historical and institutional settings. Because people are born into a world that is itself a product of the actions of previous generations, many areas of social existence have already been staked out for them. There are understood limits on their behavior. Societies have moral as well as geographical boundaries. And every society has its caretakers (e.g., police, judges, psychiatrists) who are entrusted with the responsibility for maintaining the integrity of those boundaries and the power to do so.

## The Dynamic Interplay of Expectations and Interpretations

In our view, therefore, human behavior must not be seen exclusively as either the product of the social structures enveloping persons or a matter of individual will and choice. There is a dynamic interplay between society's expectations for individuals and their own responses in situations.

The nature of the relationship between individuals and social structures is beautifully captured in a statement by a sociologist, Wendell Bell. Some people, he says, rather than following along like rats in a maze, view the social structure as tentative and proceed by experimentally testing to learn what parts of it can be manipulated. In his words,

> At the extreme, such persons may decide that the social structure, the maze itself, is subject to some extent to their will and may decide to shape it, as best they can, to suit themselves. . . . Usually in cooperation with others, some people try to manipulate the real world to conform more closely to their images of the future; push out some walls, add some new openings, widen the passageways, create some new opportunities. (1968:163)

Thus, while society sets the ground rules within which we act, we do not unthinkingly respond to society's expectations. Behavior is also partially the result of our personal, subjective interpretations of the situations we face. The most appropriate conception of daily life, therefore, requires that we understand human behavior as an ongoing interchange, or a *dialectic*, between freedom and constraint.

## ■ THE SOCIOLOGY OF EVERYDAY LIFE

The authors of this book advocate the study of everyday interactions as a central area of sociological study *in its own right*. We believe sociologists cannot afford to neglect the study of everyday life. On theoretical grounds, we maintain that the study of such interactions is necessary in order to understand social order and change in society. In a still broader sense, as we analyze various aspects of everyday lives in later chapters, we will be exploring the limits and potentialities of human beings' relations with each other. This is, by any standard, an important endeavor.

You may wonder, if the study of everyday interaction is as important as we believe it to be, why it is necessary to argue for its merits as an area of sociological investigation. The fact is that the processes governing everyday life and accounting for its order have been largely ignored by many sociologists who consider them as, at best, only the starting point for their own broader, more **macrosociological** investigations of large-scale processes and social structures. Much sociology, in this respect, leaves wholly unattended the grounds on which it is constructed. The sociologist Harold Garfinkel (1968:36) makes this point when he says that "Although sociologists take socially structured scenes of everyday life as a point of departure they rarely see, as a task of sociological inquiry in its own right, the general questions of how any such commonsense world is possible." Garfinkel is arguing that efforts to understand society as a whole depend upon **microsociological** investigations of individuals' daily interactions.

## Why the Study of Interactions Has Been Neglected

A central reason why sociologists have failed to study everyday interactions systematically is their concern for conventional methods of scientific inquiry. Virtually since sociology's inception in the 19th century, sociologists have modeled their discipline after the natural sciences. They have been intent on using the same tools the natural scientist uses in their investigation of human behavior. This has meant a central concern with the establishment of causal laws about human society.

Moreover, social scientists have frequently embraced a version of scientific inquiry in which precise measurement of variables and the rigorous testing of propositions is the standard for judging scientific work. The notion that there is only one proper form of scientific inquiry is a somewhat naive conception of science, in our view. It immediately restricts the range of phenomena that may be investigated to those variables that are clearly quantifiable and hence measurable. Such a bias is reflected in the definition of a true *behavioral scientist* as a person who, when asked if he loves his mother, replies that he cannot answer until he has done an analysis of their correspondence.

We surely would not argue with attempts to measure accurately the variables of interest to social scientists. But the demand that social scientists be concerned only with observable, quantifiable, and measurable phenomena has directed attention away from basic processes of human communication which often defy precise measurement. Our idea of interactions is that people act in awareness of each other and mutually adjust their responses in light of the actions of others. We therefore want to consider such factors as their motives, their goals, the meanings they confer on the gestures of others, their identities, their self-concepts, and the processes through which they define social situations. These necessary elements for understanding social interaction are resistant to precise measurement. We must be concerned with what goes on in persons' heads, their mind work, so to speak.

An appropriate metaphor might be the operation of a clock. We cannot fully comprehend how a clock works by looking only at the outside casing, or examining only the regularity of the minute, hour, and second hands. Certainly it is easier to describe these visible outer mechanisms, just as it would be simpler only to document and measure actual behaviors. The study of interaction requires more: concern with the inner dialogue that people have with themselves before they act.

A second reason why sociologists have generally neglected the study of routine, everyday social encounters may be their long-standing preference for investigations of issues which have social policy implications.

Sociologists have shown a preference for research areas which might persuade the public that sociologists have something to say about "important" issues. Understandably, they have concentrated their efforts on areas where they are likely to receive funding for their study. Such "social problems" as juvenile deliquency, poverty, race relations, health delivery systems, aging, prostitution, drug addiction, and homosexuality have always been issues for sociological study. These areas provide much rich information on day-to-day interactions, but they have not typically been investigated with this goal in mind.

## What the Study of Interactions Should Accomplish

If the analysis of everyday interactions is to be accepted as a central area of sociological study, it must be able to accomplish specified goals. Our explanatory efforts ought to produce some type of new knowledge about human behavior.

### *Discovering Underlying Social Forms*

The facts of everyday life are by definition obvious. For that reason, our goal is never simply the accumulation of data. The data are always there, accessible to everyone. What, then, can we learn by studying routine behaviors? Our task in studying everyday behaviors and processes is to develop explanations of how the data make sense in the first place. If we are successful, our analyses will let us see a familiar set of facts from new angles, and this will add new dimensions to our understanding. Another way to express the same thought is that our analyses should "penetrate" the obvious and thereby reveal underlying aspects of social life.

Ever since the first trees bore fruit, it has no doubt been obvious to everyone that apples fall from trees. Before Sir Isaac Newton purposely observed this event, however, no one had ever related the falling of apples to the motion of the planets. Newton's contribution was the conceptual breakthrough that revealed the laws of gravity. Once that underlying dimension of the physical world was uncovered, the fact that apples fall from trees became somewhat insignificant. Newton's law allowed scientists to understand the behavior of any falling body. The discovery of underlying dimensions that reveal commonalities in a whole *class* of events is the real task of scientific inquiry. Scientists are less concerned with the content of events than with the common forms taken by apparently dissimilar events.

The "obvious" empirical facts of social life are important in the same way. It is our job to make plain how the facts of everyday life reflect underlying social forms or dimensions. To illustrate the point, Georg Simmel (1950) suggested that social scientists interested in a phenomenon such as religious devotion should not just investigate what goes on in churches. They would do well to study also such seemingly diverse phenomena as labor union meetings and behaviors on national holidays. Were he alive today, Simmel might mention football games and punk rock concerts as events that could also be understood as expressions of religious devotion. The same intensity and reverence associated with religious rituals underlie these phenomena. Clearly, contexts or situations which differ widely in content (the content of church services is quite unlike the content of football games) can nevertheless display common social forms.

A phenomenon such as embarrassment is interesting, but we do not suggest studying it only to describe embarrassing situations. Our broader intention is to use these descriptions as a starting point for thinking clearly about more general issues such as risk, identity, performances, and deviance in interaction (see Chapter 8). To use an earlier example in this chapter, we might be interested in detailing conventions of "touching" behavior in order to gain insight into patterns of intimacy in society, elements of body image, and power relations.

If we wish to investigate how people behave in stressful, anxiety-related, or uncomfortable situations, we could focus on contexts where we expect them to experience stress, anxiety, and discomfort. We might choose to observe people as they visit severely ill patients in the hospital, for example. It would be true that we were observing behaviors in a hospital, but we would not be concerned with the context per se. We would be motivated to study hospital visiting behavior as a convenient context in which to develop an analysis of stress in interaction. This analysis has significance far beyond the hospital ward itself. Sociological analysis must always carry us beyond the specific context we are investigating. The specific case of visiting behavior becomes as incidental as apples falling from trees once we discover underlying elements of how humans behave under stress.

### Developing Sociological Skepticism

A somewhat more difficult goal is to teach you how your everyday interactions relate to this type of analysis. Unfortunately, there is no set of rules we can give that will allow you to discover the underlying forms of social life. What we can do in this book is to let you see how social scientists think about everyday phenomena, the particular imagination or consciousness they bring to the study of everyday events, and the kinds of questions that guide their analyses. The production of good ideas is not a mechanical process, as Stansilav Andreski notes:

> The so-called methods of induction are in reality methods of verification; they tell us how to test hypotheses *but not how to arrive at them*. Indeed, the latter process is just as much a mystery as it was in the days of Socrates: all that is known is that, *in order to conceive fruitful original ideas, one must have talent, must immerse oneself in the available knowledge, and think very hard* (emphasis added). (1972:108)

In the chapters that follow we will familiarize you with the ideas of those who have written about everyday behaviors and share the knowledge they provide. We will also continue to detail the elements of the theoretical perspective—symbolic interaction—that we consider most useful for analyzing everyday events. The central goal of this volume, however, is to force you to begin thinking very hard about how your daily interactions are organized and made sociologically intelligible.

At the risk of sounding too dramatic, we want to develop in those who read this book a kind of sociological skepticism. Good sociology demands a degree of skepticism. It is the sociologist's obligation to question those features of reality that appear quite obvious. Sociologists must strive to become strangers to the events and phenomena in their daily lives that they most take for granted. As a sociologist, therefore, you must step outside your "normal" roles as a member of the society and ask how your behaviors are structured and endowed with meaning. Good sociology requires you to be skeptical enough to believe that things are not always as simple as they appear to be.

We presume, in other words, that those things "everybody already knows," those apparently obvious aspects of the society that you have grown up with from infancy, can be subjected to sociological analysis. It is, we will show, an analysis which provides insight into the way people produce and construct their everyday existences. In this respect, we take on the professional obligation of questioning aspects of social life that may seem obvious and unproblematic. Our subject matter does not have anything mysterious about it—we certainly grant that. The questions we ask about familiar life phenomena and the analyses deriving from these questions are intended to advance and deepen your understanding of the sociological topics to be discussed in the following pages.

## ■ CONCLUSION

The focus of this book is on the application of sociological principles, concepts, and ideas to your everyday life. It begins with the assumption that the value and vitality of sociology is in large degree measured by its ability to provide fresh insight into events and situations that might ordinarily be taken for granted.

Spatial, time, and gesture and posture norms are examples of the underlying patterns in everyday life. These patterns become obvious only when we begin to look very hard at everyday phenomena. Moreover, social order persists only because we share knowledge of an extraordinary range of cultural expectations. Beyond knowledge of the norms or social conventions based on these expectations, however, the meanings we attach to behaviors vary from context to context. Social norms only provide the boundaries for our encounters. We must, in addition, interpret the meanings our behaviors have in a particular setting.

While much of the analysis in this book concentrates on face-to-face interaction, we also point out that the dramas of daily life are played out within larger institutional and historical settings. As members of schools, families, churches, and a multitude of other bureaucracies, we are obliged to behave in certain ways. Social structures certainly diminish personal choice and discretion. At the same time, people manipulate social structures. Human behavior therefore is the product of neither the social structures enveloping individuals nor the individual's free will and choice. Rather, it is the result of a dynamic interplay between cultural expectations and people's interpretations of situations.

The notion that people must define and interpret the meanings of both their own and others' behaviors is basic to the perspective which guides our inquiry in this book—symbolic interaction. An important idea in this perspective is that individuals collectively shape, mold, and refashion their social worlds through the process of communicating with others and responding to their communications. Because the analysis of interaction must be based on some clear set of ideas about human encounters and communication, our development of this perspective continues in the next chapter with consideration of the following issues:

1. What is the significance of interpretation in human interaction and communication?
2. How do objects take on meaning?
3. How do individuals come to evaluate the meaning of their own and others' acts?
4. What are the sources of innovation and unpredictability, and thus of nonconformity, in social life?

# Definitions

**Culture.** The complex whole which includes knowledge, beliefs, art, customs, morals, and any other capabilities and habits acquired and shared in common by the members of a society. A group's culture provides a blueprint for living which is transmitted to future generations.

**Cultural expectations.** Broad and widely shared cultural rules that reflect mutually held assumptions about proper and conventional behaviors in different social contexts.

**Everyday interactions.** Those patterns of communication with others that regularly comprise our everyday lives.

**Symbolic interaction perspective.** A theoretical perspective in sociology which focuses attention on the processes through which persons interpret and give meanings to the objects, events, and situations that make up their social worlds.

**Social worlds.** The totality of the various social locations individuals occupy in a society. Members of different classes and racial, religious, and ethnic groups inhabit different social worlds.

**Norms.** The range of rules, both written and unwritten, which dictate appropriate ways of acting in different social situations. Most social norms are unwritten and once learned are followed virtually automatically. *Laws* are norms of sufficient importance to society that they are written down. *Social conventions* are synonyms for shared norms in a society.

**Proxemics.** A field of inquiry in the social sciences in which the rules that govern people's use of space in their everyday relations are studied.

**Personal space.** The space that immediately surrounds a person's body. Others normally do not violate this space without permission. People's sense of personal space varies in different cultures and may expand or contract in different social situations.

**Territoriality.** The space which individuals or groups feel they "own." Groups will take measures to protect their territory from "invaders." Studies of animal groups show that they too operate within territories which they protect from outsiders.

**Intimate distance.** The area around a person within which the most intimate encounters take place. In American society intimate distance is between 0 and 18 inches.

**Personal distance.** The space maintained between a person and others during most routine interactions (such as conversations with friends). In American society personal distance is between 1.5 and 4 feet.

**Social distance.** The space maintained between a person and others during such casual gatherings as cocktail parties. In American society social distance is between 4 and 12 feet.

**Public distance.** The space maintained between an individual and the audience for presentations such as public speeches. Public distances are those beyond 12 feet.

**Kinesics.** A field of inquiry in the social sciences in which people's communication through body gesture and posture is studied.

**Nonverbal communication.** Any of the modes of communication (such as gesture or facial expression) other than verbal language.

**Process of interpretation.** The internal dialogues people have with themselves about the meanings of their own or others' behaviors in various acting situations.

**The acting situation.** The immediate place or circumstances of an interaction (for example, a classroom) considered by individuals as they give meanings to their own and others' behaviors.

**Social structure.** The totality of social institutions such as government, the family, and religion which influence how individuals behave in a society.

**Social bonds.** The connections of individuals to their societies which create feelings of loyalty, belongingness, and integration.

**Shared meaning structures.** The range of meanings about the world which is held by consensus of the members of a group or society. A shared meaning structure constitutes a group's view of reality.

**Reification.** Conceiving of social structures as if they had a life of their own, independent of the individuals that ultimately create those structures.

**Macrosociological investigation.** Social science research which centers attention on the ways social structures function or society as a whole operates.

**Microsociological investigation.** Social science research which centers attention on the ways in which people's daily, face-to-face communications are organized.

# Discussion Questions

1. Do you agree that there are no behaviors which are intrinsically deviant, that what we mean by deviance, mental illness, or insanity is a thoroughly cultural product?

2. What are some of the background expectancies concerning space, time, and gesture that operate in the classroom for this course?

3. Under what kinds of conditions do you feel people become most *strategic* in formulating their behaviors? What do they have to gain or lose in such situations?

4. In which aspects of your own life do you feel you have greatest freedom of choice, and in which areas do you feel most constrained by social structures? How much do you think people, individually or collectively, can change institutions such as universities?

5. What is your definition of science? What special problems does the social scientist studying human communication face?

6. Suppose your instructor asked you to observe behaviors in a local bar frequented by college students. What kinds of behaviors might it be important to record? What kinds of things might you be able to learn about interaction by observing behavior in a context like this? What general issues about human behavior could be examined by observing bar behavior? Where else might you investigate these same issues?

# References

Andreski, S. 1972. *Social Sciences as Sorcery.* New York: St. Martin's Press.

Bell, W. 1968. "The city, the suburb, and a theory of social choice." In *The New Urbanization*, ed. Scott Greer et al. New York: St. Martin's Press.

Birdwhistell, R. 1952. *Introduction to Kinesics.* Louisville: University of Louisville Press.

Birdwhistell, R. L. 1970. *Kinesics and Context.* Philadelphia: University of Pennsylvania Press.

Blumer, H. 1962. "Society as symbolic interaction." In *Human Behavior and Social Processes*, ed. Arnold Rose. Boston: Houghton Mifflin.

Douglas, J. 1970. *Understanding Everyday Life.* Chicago: Aldine.

Farberman, H. 1980. "Fantasy in everyday life." *Symbolic Interaction* 3 (Spring): 9–23.

Fine, G. 1983. *Shared Fantasy.* Chicago: University of Chicago Press.

Garfinkel, H. 1964. "Studies of the routine grounds of everyday activities." *Social Problems* 11 (Winter):225–250.

Garfinkel, H. 1968. *Studies in Ethnomethodology.* Englewood Cliffs, N.J.: Prentice-Hall.

Gellner, E. 1975. "Ethnomethodology: The re-enchantment industry or the California way of subjectivity."*Philosophy of Social Sciences* 5:431–450.

Goffman, E. 1963. *Behavior in Public Places.* New York: Free Press.

Goffman, E. 1971. *Relations in Public.* New York: Basic Books.

Hall, E. T. 1959. *The Silent Language.* New York: Doubleday.

Hall, E. T. 1969. *The Hidden Dimension.* New York: Doubleday.

Henley, N. 1973. "The politics of touch." In *Radical Sociology,* ed. P. Brown. New York: Harper & Row.

Hess, E. H., and J. M. Polt, 1960. "Pupil size as related to interest value of visual stimuli." *Science* 132:349–350.

Hess, E. H., and J. M. Polt. 1964. "Pupil size in relation to mental activity during simple problem solving." *Science* 143:1190–1192.

Karp, D. A., and W. C. Yoels. 1976. "The college classroom: Some observations on the meanings of student participation." *Sociology and Social Research* 60 (July):421–439.

Karp, D. A., G. P. Stone, and W. C. Yoels. 1977. *Being Urban: A Social Psychological View of City Life.* Lexington, Mass.: D. C. Heath.

Koch, K. 1974. "Cannibalistic revenge in Jalé warfare." In *A Slice of Life,* ed. L. Brown. New York: Holt, Rinehart & Winston.

LaFrance, M., and C. Mayo. 1978. *Moving Bodies.* Belmont, Cal.: Wadsworth.

Lyman, S., and M. Scott. 1967. "Territoriality: A neglected sociological dimension." *Social Problems* 15 (Fall):236–249.

Nash, J. 1985. *Social Psychology: Society and Self.* Minneapolis: West.

Reusch, H. 1951. *Top of the World.* New York: Pocket Books.

Schwartz, B. 1975. *Queuing and Waiting: Studies in the Social Organization of Access and Delay.* Chicago: University of Chicago Press.

Simmel, G. 1950. "The study of societal forms." In *The Sociology of Georg Simmel,* ed. K. E. Wolff. Glencoe, Ill.: Free Press.

Sommer, R. 1969. *Personal Space.* Englewood Cliffs, N.J.: Prentice-Hall.

Spencer, B., and F. Gillin. 1899. *The Native Tribes of Central Australia.* London: Macmillan and Co.

Weigert, A. 1981. *Sociology of Everyday Life.* New York: Longman.

CHAPTER 2

# Socialization and the Construction of Social Reality

I. Symbolic Communication
   A. The Difference between Symbols and Signs
   B. Can Animals Communicate?
      1. Language as an aspect of human culture
   C. The Liberating Effects of Symbolic Communication
II. Development of the Self through Interaction with Others
   A. Role-Taking
   B. The Socialization Process
      1. The play stage
      2. The game stage
   C. Components of the Self: The I and the Me
      1. The interdependence of self and society
III. Social Reality and Nonconformity
   A. Sources of Nonconformity
      1. The ability to symbolize
      2. The existence of multiple social realities
      3. The nature of generational differences
IV. Conclusion

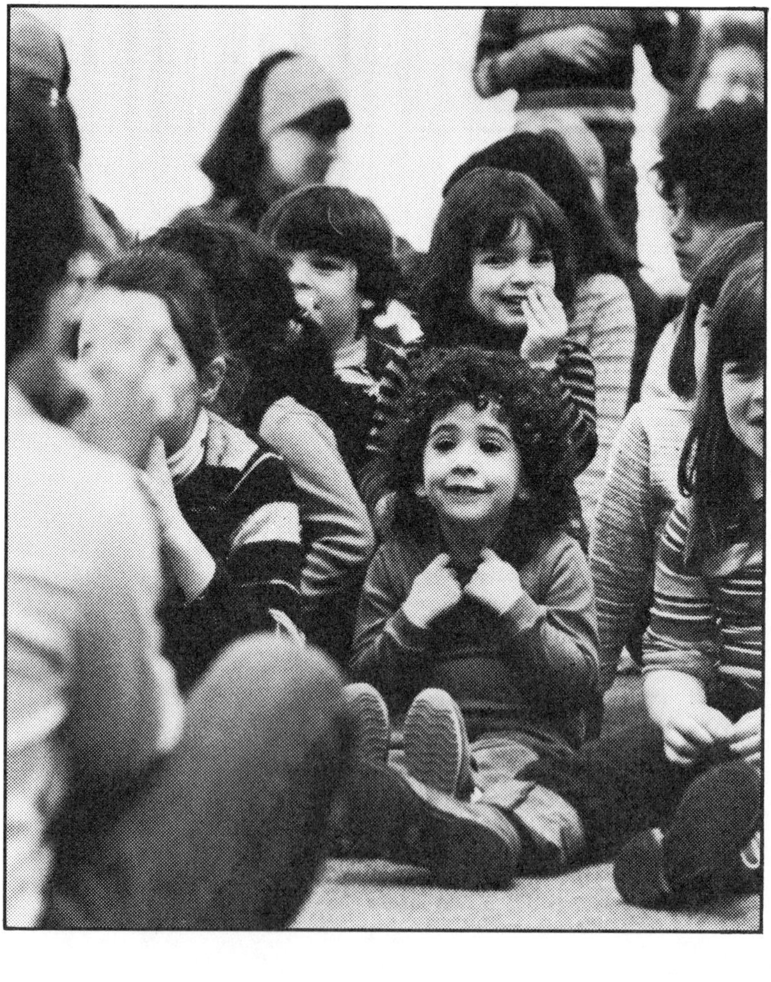

# CHAPTER 2

THE DYNAMIC INTERPLAY between cultural expectations and individuals' interpretations which governs everyday interactions and communications was described in Chapter 1 to introduce the idea that humans are not simply rule-following creatures. Norms or social conventions set the boundaries within which human interactions may occur, and situations are grounded in cultural expectations that the participants will interact in conventional ways. Through the process of interpretation, however, individuals constantly redefine the situations in which they are acting or will act in the future and reinterpret the behaviors expected of them. The symbolic interaction perspective provides a picture of social life which neither reifies social systems nor sees individuals as perfectly free to fashion society (Stryker, 1981).

The sense or intelligibility of interactions depends on the meanings individuals attribute to their environments. The perceived meanings of behaviors are always liable to revision as individuals piece together information about themselves and others and the arenas in which they interact. The social world cannot be seen as independent of people's definitions of it. A good summary of these ideas is Herbert Blumer's (1969:2) enumeration of the central premises of symbolic interaction:

1. Human beings act toward things or situations on the basis of the meanings that the things or situations have for them.
2. These meanings are derived from or arise out of the social interactions individuals have with others.
3. These meanings are handled or modified through the interpretative

process used by individuals in dealing with the things or situations they encounter.

These three premises (the first one in particular) call attention to the fact that things, as such, have no inherent meaning. Whatever meanings they have derive from the responses individuals make to them. It is in this sense that humans live in a world of symbols and interact through **symbolic communication.**

The sociological study of everyday interactions must attempt to explain how the varied meanings individuals attach to a thing or situation are constructed and used. The existence of shared meaning structures or a common definition of **social reality** must be assumed, but everyone does not construct an identical version of reality. Behaviors which deviate widely from what is expected become defined as **nonconformity.** In this chapter we will examine how symbols or meanings are used in the construction of multiple social realities. Particular reference will be made to the process of socialization by which individuals learn which behaviors are expected and which are considered deviant in the society.

## ■ SYMBOLIC COMMUNICATION

You may be sitting on a chair while reading this book. In order to know the meaning of a chair you might reasonably rely on the definition of it as an object "on which you sit." That is what a chair is—something to sit on. An object's meaning, in other words, is defined in terms of the uses to which it may be put. But there is nothing inherent in the object called a chair that dictates you must respond to it by sitting on it. Indeed, there are other uses; in western movies, for example, chairs are used as weapons in barroom brawls.

Our range of responses to an object is dependent on the social and cultural circles in which we live our daily lives. Should strangers from a planet where chairs are nonexistent land on earth, they would have difficulty figuring out that this object called a chair is something to sit on. We have to learn such meanings through symbolic communication with others.

### The Difference Between Symbols and Signs

A **symbol** should be understood as an object to which any meaning can be assigned, so it can have any kind of form:

Its meaning is derived from its [sociohistorical] context and cannot be derived from either its physical qualities or the sensory experience that it may cause. Thus the color yellow is in one context an order not to cross into the traffic lane on one's left, and in another context is an accusation of cowardice. (Hartung, 1960:237)

The physical characteristics of symbols can even be irrelevant to their meaning. To Christians, a crucifix has meaning because it represents (or better, re-presents) a historical event, the crucifixion of Christ, which has been designated as a divine event. Whether a crucifix is made of gold, iron, or wood is irrelevant to Christians, who define it as a holy object and respond to it reverently. As in the example of the chair, however, if strangers from another culture, never having heard of Christianity, were to happen upon a crucifix, there is no way that the physical characteristics of the object would indicate to them what it represents. They would have to learn that through communication with others. The crucifix also evokes a different response (that is, has a different meaning) for members of groups with alternative religious views, such as Jews, Moslems, or atheists.

In the world inhabited by humans, they alone assign meanings to things. Symbols mobilize their responses to their environment and help them bring together, or conceptualize, aspects of it. In contrast, animals live in a world of signs. A **sign** differs from a symbol in that its meanings remain constant. Its meaning is identified with its physical form and may be grasped through the senses (Becker, 1962:20). To use an analogy suggested by Leslie White, a noted anthropologist, "Man, with symbolism, can give [messages] as well as receive; animals, with signs, can only receive. An animal can be likened to a radio receiving set, but a man, with symbolism, is similar to the radio station that can send messages as well as receive them" (Hartung, 1960:238). Animals, in short, can respond to their environments only in terms dictated by their physiology. Humans alone, through symbolic behavior, are able to transcend the limits of their bodies through the development of such phenomena as technology and science. In so doing, they transform their environment through the meanings which they collectively confer on it. As Becker puts it: "Nature provided all of life with $H_2O$, but only man could create a world in which 'holy' water generates a special stimulus" (1962:20).

The claim that human beings' capacity for symbolization distinguishes them from the lower animals is often disputed (see box). This is even more true in regard to animals higher in the evolutionary scale, such as chimpanzees and other primates.

## There's No Such Thing as a Bad Dog

You may have had success teaching your dog to sit or to bark when it wants to go outside, but this does not mean you have an obedient pet. At the same time, a dog which ignores the command to sit or soils the carpet is not being disobedient. The reason is that the lower animals cannot be held responsible for either following rules or breaking them.

Teachers often find it difficult to convince students that animals have no regard for rules. The following dialogue from one of our classes illustrates the rationale for the argument that animals react to the physical properties of objects (signs) without endowing them with the meanings attached to them (symbols).

*Teacher:* Let me try to illustrate this distinction between animal and human behavior by asking you this question: Can animals be deviant?

*Student A:* Sure, don't we punish animals for doing things we don't like? I have a dog that used to urinate in the house. After I gave the dog a few whacks with a rolled-up newspaper, he stopped doing it. Now all he's got to do is see the paper and he runs under the bed.

*Teacher:* But is the dog really responding to your commands in terms

## Can Animals Communicate?

One of the most interesting and hardest-to-solve puzzles in the social sciences is whether primate animals are capable of any form of symbolic communication. While researchers concede that animals are incapable of human language, studies show that, after painstaking work, chimpanzees can be taught a vocabulary of several hundred signs (Fleming, 1974). Perhaps the most famous "speaking" animal was an ape named Washoe. In the 1960s two researchers, Beatrice and Allen Gardiner, realizing that chimps in the wild appear to communicate mainly through gestures, began to teach Washoe the sign language used by the deaf to communicate. The Gardiners never used verbal speech in Washoe's presence, only sign language. They reported that by the age of five Washoe

*40*

of symbols? Or is it merely responding to a particular physical stimulus without giving it any meaning?

Let me try to make myself clear on this. You can get a dog to stop at a red light, a traffic light, by physically punishing it if it doesn't. But you must understand that that red light, like your rolled-up newspaper, can never be more than a sign to the dog. When we stop at a red light, on the other hand, we could think about the meaning behind the light. Why is it there? What would happen were it not there? You see, we understand the necessity for stopping at the red light. We recognize that people's safety depends on it. That's the essential difference.

*Student B:* I still don't understand why it's not possible for a dog to be deviant. The dog *is* breaking rules. Isn't that deviance?

*Teacher:* Deviance itself is a symbolic phenomenon. I mean, what is deviance? Is there any social act that is intrinsically deviant? Like anything else, it's human beings who confer the label "deviance" on a particular act. After all, people establish the social rules in the first place, and the departures get labeled as deviance. Can animals establish those rules?

Most students eventually acknowledge that animals neither make nor break the rules governing their conduct.

had acquired a vocabulary of 160 signs and could put together "words" to form new "sentences" (Gardiner and Gardiner, 1969).

The most prominent advocate of the view that animals are capable of abstract thought processes is a biologist, Donald Griffin. In his book *Animal Thinking* (1984) he offers numerous examples which appear to indicate intelligent animal behavior, including the following:

Chimpanzees which seem to show a sense of self-awareness. The chimps were given mirrors to play with and then anesthetized while researchers drew a large dot on their foreheads. When the chimps awoke, they looked in the mirror, saw the dot, and immediately reached to touch their foreheads.

Dolphins which appear to have a rudimentary grasp of grammar. Dolphins can correctly distinguish the difference between the commands "Bring the ball to the surfboard" and "Bring the surfboard to the ball."

Sea otters which often eat while floating on their backs, holding a shellfish against their chests with one paw while cracking it open with a rock or even a beer bottle. An otter may keep a particularly good rock tucked under an armpit while swimming or diving.

While data of this sort are certainly intriguing, they do not resolve the question whether animals are self-aware in the way we are. The debate is not whether animals can learn. The ongoing controversy is whether animals are capable of picturing the future, planning, improvising, and symbolically communicating with each other. There is no doubt that animals have managed to learn a code that includes some of the characteristic features of human communication. Nevertheless there remains an unbridgeable gap between human language and communication of the sort demonstrated in research studies. Chimps can use relatively few symbols to communicate with their trainers, not with each other. Moreover, the animals are essentially limited to the symbols they have been taught. This is, of course, very different from the manner in which humans learn and then employ verbal language.

### *Language as an Aspect of Human Culture*

One way to put this argument is to say that only human beings possess a culture, or collectively shared ideas, concepts, beliefs, and knowledge which can be transmitted to succeeding generations (see Chapter 1). Lower animals may be said to operate within *social structures* in the sense that there is an order and predictability to their behaviors. This is a consequence of biological instinct, however. Culture, in contrast, is a symbolic creation, and language has an important role in its construction.

In one of a series of early studies, Wolfgang Köhler (1927) placed a stack of bananas outside a chimpanzee's cage, just beyond its reach. He also placed a number of sticks inside the cage that could be fitted together to make a longer stick, thus enabling the animal to reach the fruit. Now it might be said that when, after much trial and error, the monkey fits the sticks together to reach the bananas, it has at that moment gained insight into a very abstract idea—the concept of addition. But (and this is the important point) without verbal language the monkey cannot transmit that abstract idea to others of its species. If a particular monkey has discovered the principle of addition, it remains, without language, forever its individual possession. It never becomes a collective, cultural possession that can be elaborated on to produce new mathematical principles and eventually such revolutionary discoveries as computers. In this respect, language reflects and is part of human culture. Language is also essential to the continuance of a culture and ongoing changes in it.

We are not suggesting that animals do not communicate. They do. For example, bees can, with great precision, communicate the location of food via physical movement, and sea animals (whales and dolphins) communicate danger warnings over long distances. Such communications are rooted in instinct, however. There is never any variation or elaboration of the available messages that can be transmitted. The content of the messages is genetically determined.

In contrast, it is the essence of human communication that there is no intrinsic or built-in meaning to the words constituting the language used. The very same words can carry different meanings for different persons and groups, and certain words, used in particular contexts, can be considered either obscene or acceptable. The meanings of words are constantly subject to change. A good example is *gay*, which now is more apt to mean homosexual than happy and excited, an earlier definition.

## The Liberating Effects of Symbolic Communication

Symbolic communication (or symbolic behavior) also permits humans to in effect liberate themselves from the physical constraints of time and space. If we create a word, or verbal symbol, such as *house* to refer to the physical object called a house, we are free to talk about, think about, and refer to houses without the necessity of having a house in sight. It is possible to refer to houses that existed in the past as well as to conjure up houses that might exist in the future, not just in the United States, but elsewhere—even on other planets! The range of possible habitats for humans is limited by our imaginations rather than our physiology, as space trips to the moon and experiments in living under the oceans have demonstrated.

The use of symbols not only permits humans to step outside the particular physical setting in which they find themselves. More important, it permits them to step outside themselves. We can look at ourselves from the standpoint of others, put ourselves in their place, and anticipate how they are going to react to us. We can, in effect, look at ourselves as if we were objects and anticipate how others are going to respond to those objects. Verbal symbols (language) are critical in this situation, since the spoken word is heard simultaneously by both the speaker and those to whom it is addressed. The speaker can react to the word while monitoring the responses of others to what is being said.

The ability to evaluate our own behaviors objectively, from the perspective of others, is necessary if we are to become "normal," functioning members of society. Once we acquire that ability, we possess what George Herbert Mead, a major formulator of the interactionist perspective, calls **the self.** This conception of self underlies the symbolic interaction perspective.

## ■ DEVELOPMENT OF THE SELF THROUGH INTERACTION WITH OTHERS

In the same way symbolic communication requires an audience to which communications can be directed, the self is formed and transformed through interaction with others. You were not born with a preformed self. Through the use of symbols you have learned to take on the attitudes, values, and moods appropriate to the particular social circles in which you participate. Through the reflected appraisals of others, you have come to define yourself as a certain kind of person.

In fact, you have many identities which are established and validated (or invalidated) through the responses others make to you. The psychologist William James suggested in 1892 that humans have as many

---

### Put Up Your Hands! (Know What I Mean?)

In order for two people to interact or communicate, each must understand the point of view of the other. This may mean you have to put yourself in some unlikely positions. If a robber tells you to put your hands in the air, for example, you have to think like the robber as well as the victim in order to behave as you are expected to. If you don't you may save your wallet but not your skin.

Herbert Blumer (1969) suggests that a robbery can only occur if both the robber and the victim can put themselves in the place of the other person. The robber, for example, can only understand the logic of his own demand for the victim to put his hands in the air by being able to imagine what it means to face the barrel end of a gun. In fact, the robber could not even make the verbal demand ("Put your hands up in the air") unless he understood the meaning it would have for the victim. The victim, likewise, "has to be able to see the command from the standpoint of the robber who gives the command; he has to grasp the inten-

selves as they have memberships in various social groups. Individuals belong to numerous social circles simultaneously—the family, a church, friendship cliques—and adjust their behaviors to take into account the particular situations and the others with whom they are interacting. Others do the same with them. One does not act in a classroom, for example, as one does in a morgue—at least, most of the time! As Mead notes:

> We carry on a whole series of different relationships to different people. We are one thing to one man and another thing to another. We divide ourselves up into all sorts of different selves with reference to our acquaintances. We discuss politics with one and religion with another. There are all sorts of different selves answering to all sorts of different social reactions. (1934:142)

## Role-Taking

The capacity to adjust one's behavior in response to particular social situations is termed **role-taking** by Mead. From the symbolic interaction perspective, the development of the self is inextricably bound up with the capacity to take the role of others (see box). Every act of role-taking simultaneously involves a person's anticipation of the responses that others are going to make toward him or her and the person's evaluation of his or her own behavior in terms of others' anticipated responses.

---

tion and forthcoming action of the robber" (p. 10). Interaction is always oriented to the future, to what the other person will do, and the only way to anticipate the future is through this kind of mutual role-taking.

A newspaper account told how robbers broke in on a party and demanded that everyone turn over their valuables. The guests, thinking it was a put-on, refused to cooperate and dismissed the situation as a harmless spoof. They told the robbers to cut it out and stop joking, while they continued to joke about it themselves. The robbers, faced with this totally unexpected reaction, were stymied in their efforts and finally fled the party empty-handed. They were arrested later trying to break into another house. Still confused, they told the police of their experience at the party.

Thus, even robbers must count on the mutual understanding of their victims if they are to make a success of their way of life. When the victim refuses to validate the robber's identity as a robber and defines him instead as a prankster, the robber must be willing to assume a new identity—even that of murderer—if the robbery is to succeed.

Such expressions as being proud of yourself or being ashamed of yourself illustrate the principle of role-taking. There is no way to experience such reactions as shame or guilt without appraising our own behavior from the perspective of others. It is in this sense that the self is both the subject and the object of our own acts. We engage in a behavior and then subjectively evaluate the meaning of that behavior to others through the responses they make to it.

There is an important difference between role-taking and role-playing. Role-taking, the process of imaginatively putting yourself in another's place and considering what they expect of you, or how they might respond to behaviors you are thinking of enacting, precedes role-playing. It is on the basis of role-taking that we fashion the roles we actually play and the role performances we undertake.

## The Socialization Process

The process through which individuals learn societal expectations of their behaviors is called **socialization.** According to Mead, the development of the self occurs in childhood in two distinct phases of this process: the play stage and the game stage. Mead's writings on childhood play are probably the most important interactionist statement on self-development.

### *The Play Stage*

The **play stage,** according to Mead, is the period in which children develop the ability to actually take on the characteristics associated with others in particular roles. They become able to look at themselves from the point of view of others. During this stage, a girl, for example, learns to put herself in the role of mommy, doctor, teacher, or TV star. She is able to cast herself as a social object and then respond in the role of others to that object. In playing doctor, for example, she may talk to others as she interprets how a doctor might actually talk to her. During this period the child also realizes that there is a direct linkage between a person's status (mother, father, police officer, and so on) and behavior. The importance of "child's play" in creating durable male and female roles has been noted by several social scientists (Henslin, 1985; Oakley, 1981).

For Mead, the most important quality of the role-playing engaged in by children during the play period is its unorganized character. During this period children pass from playing one role to another in a very inconsistent and erratic fashion. They have proceeded beyond sheer imitation of others' behaviors, but they do not yet have any *unified* conception of themselves. In referring to the play stage, Mead notes:

The child is one thing at one time and another at another, and what he is at one moment does not determine what he is at another. That is both the charm of childhood as well as its inadequacy. You cannot count on the child; you cannot assume that all the things he does are going to determine what he will do at any moment. He is not organized into a whole. The child has no definite character, no definite personality. (1934:159)

In the play stage children may be able to take the roles of particular others toward themselves, but as yet they fail to see how the behavior of others toward them represents the expectations of larger social groups. They are unable to view themselves from the point of view of the community or, even more abstractly, the society. They may understand, for example, what mommy means when she tells them to be good. They will learn later that it is not only mommy who expects them to be good, but others in the neighborhood, the school, and the larger society as well.

## *The Game Stage*

After children have mastered the ability to take the roles of particular others, they are presented more and more with the task of responding to the expectations of several persons simultaneously. According to Mead, it is participation in the **game stage** which equips the child for this task. Games are distinguished from play by the presence of an organized body of *rules* to which the participants must orient their responses. Rather than reacting to particular individuals, as in the case of play, children must now begin to see themselves in relation to all the roles played by the other participants.

In order to play baseball, for example, a boy must know how his position (third base, let us say) relates to those of every other person on the team. When a ball is hit to him, he must realize that he should throw it to first base, not because he likes the person on first base but because that is what the rules of the game dictate. He must also conceptualize how his team stands in relation to the opposing team. He must throw to first base to put the batter out. That is what the game is all about.

In effect, in order for the game of baseball to be played, all the participants must have a conception of how to act vis-à-vis their own team and the opposing one. In doing so each player develops a conception of how a particular position is really part of a larger social organization called "the team." Mead observes that in the game stage, "a definite unity . . . is introduced into the organization of other selves." In the play stage, in contrast, there is "a simple succession of one role after another" (1934:158–159).

If you think of the baseball game as a metaphor for the organization of society in general, you can see that we are truly functioning members of a social order only when we know the basic ground rules and can organize our actions with reference to the whole group. Mead's terms for all of those countless others whose behaviors and expectations are considered and interpreted by individuals in formulating their own behaviors is the **generalized other.** In the case of the baseball game, the team constitutes the most important generalized other to which the players must orient their actions.

The socialization process through which the child eventually comprehends societal expectations can be illustrated by an example from Peter Berger and Thomas Luckman's book, *The Social Construction of Reality* (1967). They note that

> . . . there is a progression from "Mummy is angry with me now" to "Mummy is angry with me *whenever* I spill the soup." As additional significant others (father, grandfather, older sister, and so on) support the mother's negative attitude toward soup-spilling, the generality of the norm is subjectively extended. The decisive step comes when the child recognizes that *everybody* is against soup-spilling, and the norm is generalized to *"One* does not spill soup"—"one" being himself as part of a generality that includes, in principle, *all* of society insofar as it is significant to the child. (Emphasis in original; pp. 132–133)

## Components of the Self: The I and the Me

If we were to look at Mead's conception of the socialization process and the development of the self uncritically, we might be led to believe that all our behaviors are totally determined by others, leaving no room for us to do anything but conform completely to their expectations. This robotlike image does not square very well with either our knowledge of people or our own life experiences, however. Although we are certainly constrained by society, we do have some freedom of action. Mead takes this into account in his socialization theory by introducing the idea that the self has two components—the I and the me.

In Chapter 1 we emphasized that everyday life must be analyzed in a way that takes into account both the expectations of society and the unique, individual interpretations of our responses to their worlds that individuals make. On the one hand, we formulate our behaviors in terms of the attitudes of others, or in terms of the generalized other. Ultimately a society is possible only because the individuals in it carry around a picture of that society in their heads. Behaviors constructed in terms of that picture reflect what Mead termed *the me*. **The me** represents the more conventional aspect of the self—the aspect that responds to social conventions. At the same time, because we are self-conscious, reflective, conceptual beings, we can never completely predict what our own responses will be in any situation. **The I,** in contrast to the me, consists of those particular idiosyncratic, personal factors that enter into our communications with others.

In the example of the baseball game, the third baseman, like every other player on the team, no doubt wants to play well. He wants his team to win. In that sense he organizes his own behaviors from the perspective of the team and, in so doing, tries to meet the expectations of fellow team members. But just how well he will play in a game cannot surely be predicted in advance. His mind may wander, for example, and he may drop an easy pop-up. He might get angry enough at the umpire to show it and get thrown out of the game. The range of such unanticipated, novel, subjective responses reflects the operation of the I.

Development of the self thus is a process in which we act in response to continuous conversations we have with ourselves. These conversations have two components. We ask ourselves: What does society want *me* to do in this situation? and How do *I* personally respond to this situation? We are, in sum, only partially the product of the roles we learn from childhood on. Our behaviors are affected not only by all our various learned social roles, but by our personal, subjective interpretations of the situations we face. The relationship between the I and the me is nicely captured in this example:

. . . a little boy growing up in American society is taught certain things that supposedly are appropriate to little boys, such as fortitude in the face of pain. Suppose he bangs his knee and it starts to bleed. The *I* is registering the pain and, we might imagine, wants to scream its head off. The *me*, on the other hand, has learned that good boys are supposed to be brave. It is the *me* that makes our little boy bite his lip and bear the pain. (Berger and Berger, 1975:65)

### The Interdependence of Self and Society

Mead's conception of the self refers, in the fullest sense, to the interdependence of the individual and the society. He locates the self in society. The development of the self is an ongoing process which emerges from the person's interactions with others in society. There is a point in the creation of the self at which the person can view himself or herself from the perspective of others. At this point the person is able to treat the world as a symbolic entity—to endow the world with meaning. This capacity for symbolic behavior makes it possible for humans to modify and sometimes to substantially transform society. The self is simultaneously a reflection of society as it exists and a source of change in it.

Our daily lives are describable in terms of these theoretical distinctions. Everyday behaviors represent a combination of conformity and novelty, of response to the expectations of others and more impulsive personal reactions to situations. In any situation, we cannot know ourselves just how we will act. We know the parameters within which we are expected to act, but such knowledge does not guarantee complete predictability of behavior. In a fundamental way we really do not know how we are going to respond in any situation until we actually begin to act. We cannot, for example, fully anticipate feelings and expressions of anger, pleasure, relief, indifference, confusion, and the like as we move through even the most routine day-to-day situations.

Human behavior, in Mead's terms, is constructed through the interchange of the two aspects of the self—the I and the me. While the me encourages conformity to societal expectations, the I permits personal interpretations which allow for nonconformity and the construction of multiple social realities.

### ■ SOCIAL REALITY AND NONCONFORMITY

Social reality should not be thought of as a "thing" which exists objectively "out there" in the world. Rather, reality is something that human beings constantly negotiate, recreate, alter, and disagree on. In a very real sense reality is the product of a political process in which different individuals and groups vie to have their idea of reality become accepted as *the* reality for everyone (see Chapter 6). From this perspective, reality is in a continual state of process and production. The fluid nature of reality ensures the emergence of multiple realities, some of which will be labeled and responded to as deviant by those in positions of power. At the same time, the versions of reality produced by different groups must agree or overlap to some extent, or we will not be able to get on with the business of everyday living.

In all our daily activities, we assume that we are responding to the same realities as others. Suppose, for example, that the clock-radio wakens you with a news report. Simply in order to understand the news, you must assume that the words being used to describe the events mean roughly the same thing to the newscaster as they do to you. The newscaster makes the same assumption. In reporting some catastrophe such as an earthquake or tornado, for example, it is assumed that the listener knows what the phenomenon is. Rarely does a newscaster attempt to define such words as *tornado* or *earthquake*.

Having been bombarded with the morning's scoreboard of human misery and unhappiness, you probably still have enough fortitude to leave your home and go out, entering the world of anonymous others. Consider the assumption of trust you must make in order to navigate your way through the day's activities. In going to your job or class, for example, you must assume that others share your understanding of the social conventions relating to personal safety. As a pedestrian, you assume that others know how to move their bodies or control their cars so they avoid bumping into you. Other pedestrians or drivers make the same assumption about you. If you are driving, you must assume that other drivers also know the meaning of green lights, stop signs, railroad crossings, and so forth. Think what driving in any metropolitan area would be like without such understandings!

While smooth daily functioning depends on the assumption of a commonly shared social reality, there is also an element of uncertainty in the construction of reality. You must anticipate that your own version may not be totally shared by others. You also cannot be sure how you and others will behave in an anticipated or ongoing interaction. In any social situation, allowances must be made for the unexpected behaviors of the participants.

## Sources of Nonconformity

When behaviors seriously deviate from societal expectations, they are defined as deviance (see Chapter 8) or nonconformity. In the interactionist perspective, nonconforming behaviors can be explained in terms of the human ability to symbolize and the existence of multiple social realities within the society. Generational differences also encourage the existence of deviant or nonconforming behaviors.*

---

*The discussion which follows was developed in William C. Yoels and David A. Karp, "A social psychological critique of 'oversocialization': Dennis Wrong revisited," *Sociological Symposium*, Fall 1978, pp. 27–40.

## The Ability to Symbolize

From the interactionist perspective, society is formed through the symbolic communication occurring between two or more persons. Since, as we have noted, there is no inherent meaning in an object, it is always possible for these persons, through their symbolic activity, to redefine objects in ways that challenge existing definitions of reality. The transformation of the meaning of *Negro* to *black* in racial terms provides dramatic evidence of this. As a consequence of the 1960s civil rights movement, blacks began to think of the former term as having been imposed on them by whites. The label *black*, carrying the meaning of racial pride and a rich cultural heritage, now is universally used. Similar changes have occurred in the definitions of male and female gender roles as a result of the women's movement.

Symbolic behavior makes it possible to reject the symbols used by those in one's immediate physical surroundings and to identify with symbols used by others elsewhere. A person's **reference groups** (those groups providing standards for the person's behaviors) need not be confined to others who are physically present. In that sense, the ability to symbolize provides humans with a continual source of nonconformity. Ward Abbott illustrates how symbolic activity can lead to nonconformity with the following statement concerning the relationship of the artist to the state:

> The artist is doubly subversive in that only a bullet can stop him. He feeds on changes as others shy away from them. Josip Brodsky, exiled in Siberia, infuriated officials by *enjoying his life there*. Unlike a banker, the artist carries his work in his mind. To express it, he needs only a stub of pencil and a scrap of paper, or charcoal and any surface. One of the last acts of Gaudier-Brezka in the trenches of World War I, surrounded by death and desolation, was to carve, out of a bit of blown-up rifle butt, a splendidly Brezkian sculpture. (Italics added; 1975:89)

The example of the subversive artists suggests that individuals are, to a substantial degree, responsible for determining their environments. The environment, like any object, derives its meaning from our conception of it. There are, however, real limits to our capacity for determining what the nature of our immediate environments will be. However much the artists Brodsky and Gaudier-Brezka were able to redefine their lives in Siberia and World War I trenches, they still had to cope with the physical demands of their surroundings. Thus we both determine the environment and are determined by it.

Despite the physical and social constraints we face, the self-reflecting character of interactions makes nonconformity possible. To use Jean Paul Sartre's terms, it is "bad faith" to claim that we are utterly without choice in a particular situation. Even an individual being tortured decides when, or indeed whether, to give in to her or his tormentors. The choice in an extreme situation might be death, but it *is* an available choice.

## The Existence of Multiple Social Realities

In highly diverse, stratified societies such as contemporary American society, several realities exist concurrently. People at different levels or locations in the society, possessing more or less power, prestige, status, and wealth, have very different images of the world. The definition of reality adhered to by a person is influenced by his or her position in the social structure, as Berger and Luckman (1967) and, most notably, Karl Mannheim (1952) have suggested. Various racial, ethnic, and religious groups also make different responses, and therefore give different meanings, to their worlds. Moreover, individuals develop commitments to their distinctive values, attitudes, and lifestyles. They may even take action against those representing alternative or contrary versions of reality, particularly if the others' reality is perceived as threatening to their own.

Influence over the morality, the values, and therefore the behaviors that are deemed to be socially acceptable is related to differences in power. Everyone does not have an equal role in the development and maintenance of society's dominant or official versions of reality. Psychiatrists have exercised substantial power in debates about whether homosexuality is an illness or a legitimate lifestyle choice, for example. A referendum of the membership of the American Psychiatric Association in 1974 upheld the declaration of the Board of Trustees that homosexuality "by itself does not necessarily constitute a psychiatric disorder," and it was later dropped from the definitive *Diagnostic and Statistical Manual of Mental Disorders*. The ability of psychiatrists to influence public policy and public opinion affecting the daily lives of homosexuals suggests that when it comes to ideological conflicts, "he who has the biggest stick has the better chance of imposing his definition of reality" (Berger and Luckman, 1967:109).

There are always some people who are unwilling to accept others' notions about proper behavior. If they seek each other out and agree to act collectively, they may decide to challenge the dominant version of reality. Sometimes these challenges are successful, and new expectations for behavior become institutionalized over time. The women's movement, for example, influenced legislation prohibiting gender-related discrimination in jobs and education, and it has altered in many ways the relations of men and women as friends, lovers, and colleagues. More often, however, challenges to established reality fail. Those with a strong investment in the status quo react quickly, vigorously, and sometimes violently to any threat to their reality. In every society, agencies (such as prisons and mental hospitals) and roles (witch doctors, psychiatrists, clergy, police officers) are created to manage reality disruptors.

Erving Goffman, in his numerous works (1959, 1961, 1963, 1971), describes the construction of social realities as a fluid affair. The maintenance of these realities is subject to the continual negotiation of the participants. If the term *subversion* were stripped of its political and negative connotations, it could be applied more broadly to everyday interactions. Individuals constantly bend or subvert established rules and expectations to their own purposes. They include students who turn in papers late and pedestrians who jaywalk, as well as drug users who steal to maintain their habit.

A continual source of nonconformity in society is the actions of persons and groups seeking to have their versions of reality either accepted by others or translated into the accepted version of reality. Deviance and nonconformity arise from the variety of perspectives produced in different social worlds. We could say that when a person raised in one social world, equipped for travel on a particular symbolic highway, enters another world's symbolic thoroughfare, the result could be a multisymbol accident!

### *The Nature of Generational Differences*

Another source of nonconformity, in social terms, is the different viewpoints of the various generations in a society. Biologically, a generation may be thought of as a group of persons who were born at about the same time. Sociologically, a **generation** should be thought of as persons who have experienced similar *historical* events at similar points in their lives. Others who have not undergone such experiences at the same time in their own lives find it difficult to understand the meanings conferred on particular events by those who have. Depending on the nature of the historical situation, members of different generations may be thought of as inhabiting different social worlds and recognizing different social realities.

The development of different generational styles is one reason the socialization process is not perfectible. New generations do not adopt the behaviors expected of them by society without question. Because they have not themselves had a hand in the creation of the reality they are expected to appropriate as their own, they are bound to experience it differently than older generations do. The older generations are confronted with the problem of legitimating their reality to the new generations, and the newcomers may well challenge the assumption that they will accept it. Not being satisfied with the explanations of their elders, they may proceed to subvert that reality—through symbols of dress, music, language, and so on—in the course of their daily lives. At some point they may succeed in constructing a new reality which they must then legitimate to their own children, and so on.

The concept of generation calls attention to a socially derived process related to the "rhythm" of social life. Because of its effects on the construction of social reality, it represents another continual source of nonconformity and change in society.

## ■ CONCLUSION

Our concerns in this chapter have been primarily theoretical, and the discussion has been somewhat abstract. To conclude that there is no relationship between the issues discussed and your everyday life would be to miss an important point, however. You cannot begin to understand how associations with others are ordered and made predictable and sensible unless you have some theoretical understanding of human relations.

As we noted in Chapter 1, sociological analysis, particularly the analysis of everyday events, requires more than simple description. To get beyond description and discover underlying forms of social interaction, sociologists adopt different theoretical perspectives. The authors of this book have adopted the perspective of symbolic interaction. In this chapter we have introduced the central concepts in the interactionist perspective: symbolic communication, the emergence and development of the self through interaction, the process of role-taking, the existence of multiple social realities, and the sources of nonconformity in social life. We believe that these ideas provide a foundation for an understanding of human interaction and communication, and we will make references to them throughout this volume.

The intelligibility of our interactions or communications with others depends on the meanings we attribute to our environment. According to the central premises of symbolic interaction set forth by Herbert Blumer, individuals act toward things or situations on the basis of the meanings that the things or situations have for them. These meanings are derived from the social interactions individuals have with others and are modified through the interpretive process individuals use in dealing with the things or situations they encounter.

Symbolic communication provides a means of interaction in a world where things and situations have no fixed meanings. Symbols mobilize individuals' reactions to their environment and help them conceptualize the social world in which they live. By conferring meanings, they can transform their environment.

The symbolic interaction perspective stresses the interconnections between individuals and society. As originally conceived by George Herbert Mead, it provides a picture of social life in which individuals make their own interpretations of the situations in which they are involved, while they also take societal expectations into account. Analytically, this idea is expressed in Mead's description of the collaboration between the I and the me. The two components of the self operate together to maintain a balance between conventional behavior and nonconformity. The social self thus both reflects society as it exists and provides a means of change in it.

Any social encounter requires role-taking, or understanding the position of the other person. In order to role-take successfully, we must continually assess available information about others. We cannot engage in meaningful communication with others without first identifying *who* they are. Knowledge of others' social attributes, such as their age, sex, and occupation, strongly affects our judgments about the type of people they are. In the next chapter we will examine the central role of information in role-taking efforts.

## Definitions

**Symbolic communication.** Communication which involves people's ongoing interpretations of each others' actions. In nonsymbolic communications such as those among animals, responses to actions are fixed and not endowed with meaning.

**Social reality.** The totality of meanings about the world on which the members of a group or society agree. It is possible that different individuals and groups will hold quite different pictures of reality. In any complex society there are multiple realities.

**Nonconformity.** Behaviors that deviate from generally held cultural expectations or social norms.

**Symbol.** An object to which any meaning can be assigned. The meanings assigned to symbols can be arbitrary and are not determined by the physical characteristics of objects or the sensory experiences they may cause.

**Sign.** An object to which a fixed, unchanging response is made. In contrast to a symbol, a sign is characterized by the fact that its meaning is identified with its physical form. Animals respond to objects as signs, not as symbols.

**The self.** The view of oneself derived from the ability to evaluate one's behaviors from the point of view of others, ultimately from the point of the standards of society as a whole.

**Role-taking.** The process through which individuals imaginatively put themselves in the positions of other people in order to evaluate how others see them and their behaviors. Individuals ordinarily modify their behaviors on the basis of their role-taking efforts.

**Socialization.** The process through which people learn the behaviors required by their cultures. It is also the process through which culture is transmitted from one generation to the next. Without the process of socialization, society could not exist.

**Play stage.** The stage of the socialization process during which children learn certain roles by playing at them, as when they play doctor, nurse, police officer, and so on.

**Game stage.** The stage of the socialization process during which children become able to understand the morality of their own behaviors. The game stage is distinguished from the play stage in that children orient themselves to a body of rules which spell out proper behavior.

**Generalized other.** All of those persons whose behaviors and expectations are considered by individuals in formulating their own behavior. In the most abstract sense, the generalized other is society as a whole.

**The me.** One of two aspects of the human self. It is that part of the self that is conventional, the conforming, rule-following part.

**The I.** One of two aspects of the human self. It is the spontaneous, creative, unpredictable part of the self. The I consists of subjective, idiosyncratic, and unanticipated factors that enter into our communications with others.

**Reference groups.** Any social group used by an individual as a standard for evaluating his or her behavior. One need not officially belong to a group to have it as a reference group.

**Generation.** A group of persons who have experienced similar historical events at similar points in their lives. Members of different generations inhabit different social worlds and recognize different social realities.

capacity? What does it imply about the distinctiveness of human communication that we can discuss this and other questions in class?

2. Can anything you do (or think, for that matter) have any meaning apart from your assessment of how some other people are likely to evaluate your behaviors?

3. Reflect on your activities during a typical day. To what extent do your behaviors represent a combination of conformity and novelty, of your responses to the expectations of others and more impulsive reactions to situations? In which kinds of situations is it hardest for you to anticipate just how you will behave? In which situations is it easiest?

4. Think of a time when you did *not* conform to some person's or group's expectations. Now think of a situation in which you did not want to conform to the expectations of others but did so anyway. What distinguished the two situations? In what way were your behaviors constructed in response to symbols?

5. What is the relationship between the kinds of games people play as children and the kinds of roles they later perform in adult life?

6. The authors suggested that every generation of persons is confronted with the problem of legitimating its view of reality to the next generation. In what areas do you feel that your own conception of reality is fundamentally different from that held by your parents? Describe some of the symbols that reflect the different generational realities.

# Discussion Questions

1. Do you agree with the authors that human beings are uniquely different from other animals because of their symbol-using

# References

Abbott, W. 1975. "Begin by shooting the poet." *The Nation* 221 (August 2):88–89.

Becker, E. 1962. *The Birth and Death of Meaning.* Glencoe, Ill.: Free Press.

Berger, P., and B. Berger. 1975. *Sociology: A Biographical Approach*. New York: Basic Books.

Berger, P., and T. Luckman. 1967. *The Social Construction of Reality*. New York: Doubleday.

Blumer, H. 1969. *Symbolic Interactionism: Perspective and Method*. Englewood Cliffs, N.J.: Prentice-Hall.

Fleming, J. 1974. "The state of apes." *Psychology Today* 7:31–38.

Gardiner, R., and B. Gardiner. 1969. "Teaching sign language to a chimpanzee." *Science* 165:664–672.

Goffman, E. 1959. *The Presentation of Self in Everyday Life*. New York: Doubleday.

Goffman, E. 1961. *Asylums*. New York: Doubleday.

Goffman, E. 1963. *Behavior in Public Places*. New York: Free Press.

Goffman, E. 1971. *Relations in Public*. New York: Basic Books.

Griffin, D. 1984. *Animal Thinking*. Cambridge, Mass.: Harvard University Press.

Hartung, F. 1960. "Behavior, culture, and symbolism." In *Essays in the Science of Culture*, ed. G. E. Dole and R. L. Carneiro. New York: Thomas Crowell.

Henslin, J. 1985. "On becoming male: Reflections of a sociologist on early childhood and socialization." In *Down to Earth Sociology*, ed. J. Henslin. New York: Free Press.

Köhler, W. 1927. *The Mentality of Apes*. New York: Harcourt Brace.

Mannheim, K. 1952. *Essays on the Sociology of Knowledge*. London: Routledge & Kegan.

Mead, G. H. 1934. *Mind, Self, and Society*. Chicago: University of Chicago Press.

Oakley, A. 1981. *Subject Women*. New York: Pantheon Books.

Stryker, S. 1981. "Symbolic interactionism: Themes and variations." In *Social Psychology: Sociological Perspectives*, ed. M. Rosenberg and R. Turner. New York: Basic Books.

Yoels, W. C., and D. A. Karp. 1978. "A social psychological critique of 'oversocialization': Dennis Wrong revisited." *Sociological Symposium* (Fall): 27–40.

CHAPTER 3 | Communication and Interaction

I. The Need for Communication in Role-Taking
   A. Failed Communications
   B. The Importance of Information
II. Gathering and Processing Information about Others
   A. Information Provided by Social Attributes
      1. The master attributes
      2. Processing master attributes
      3. The ongoing search for information
   B. Information Provided by Physical Attributes
      1. Appearance and attraction
      2. Appearance and character assessment
      3. Effects of clothing on appearance
   C. Information Provided by Discourse
III. Controlling Information and Managing Impressions
   A. Presenting the Right Impression
      1. Mutual protection
   B. Performance Aspects of Interaction
      1. Conformity
      2. Cynicism and sincerity in role-taking
   C. Modifying the Situational View of Self
IV. Conclusion

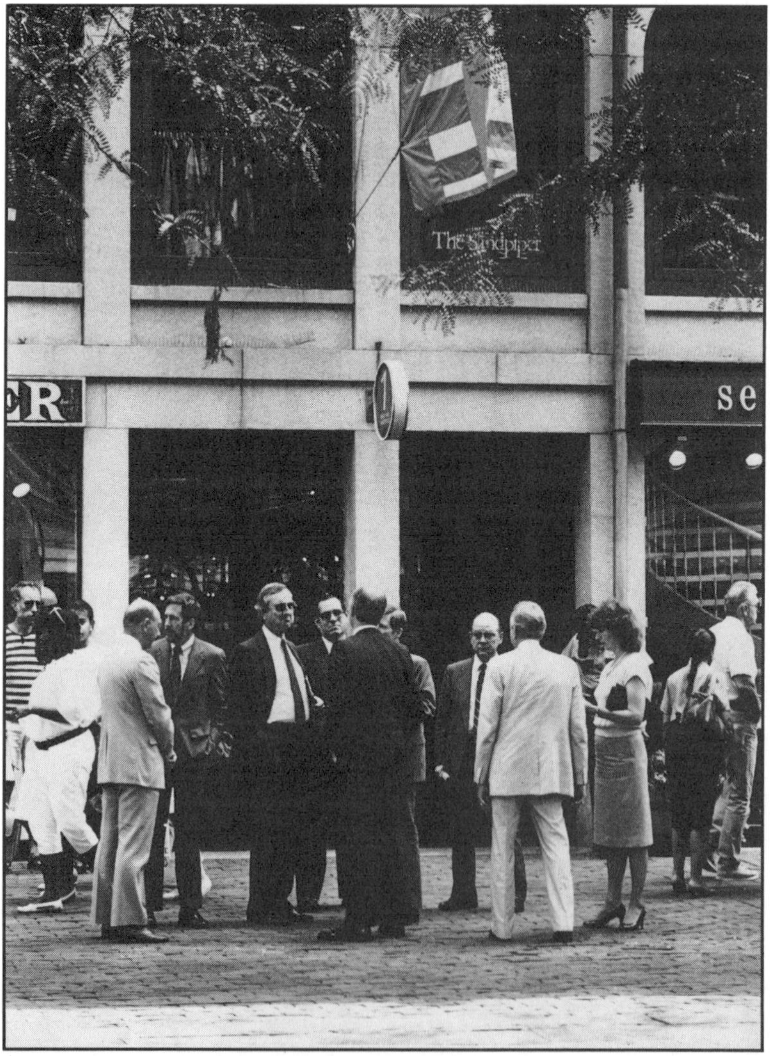

The Sandpiper

# CHAPTER 3

LIVING IN a modern society, engaging in everyday activities, involves virtually constant interactions in a variety of settings and with a multitude of different persons, each of which may demand a different posture. A person's attempts to get along with others or to get her or his own way with them in these various social arenas can require an astounding amount of practical and social knowledge. There also must be reasonable agreement among the persons involved on their view of social reality. Otherwise human communication—and society itself—would be impossible.

## ■ THE NEED FOR COMMUNICATION IN ROLE-TAKING

The process through which we act in awareness of others and continually adjust our own behaviors in accordance with the way they are acting depends on our distinctively human ability to role-take, as we noted in Chapter 2. In order to infer correctly the intentions, motives, and goals of others, and therefore to predict their future behaviors, we must put ourselves in their place and attempt to view the situation as they do. We cannot gauge the meanings of others' acts and then respond appropriately unless we achieve some understanding of the way others are interpreting and making sense of the situation. Such role-taking is, of course, mutual. All persons in any particular interaction are simultaneously formulating their behaviors in accordance with their assessments of the perceptions and expectations of others.

## Failed Communications

This does not mean that the capacity for role-taking necessarily ensures that all interactions occur smoothly and without difficulty. In many everyday encounters, role-taking leads to incorrect inferences about others. We frequently find it difficult to understand why others act as they do. There is the possibility that our attempts at role-taking will lead us to formulate a definition of the situation that varies from the definition held by those with whom we are communicating. When this happens, a **failed communication** can result.

The college classroom is a setting which offers numerous possibilities for failed communications. Teachers often proceed under one set of assumptions about "intellectual work," while students operate under another. Teachers tend to value critical thinking. They may respond critically to comments made by students and push students to defend their own points of view. The teacher's goal—to help students think more analytically—may be misperceived by the students, however. They may consider the teacher to be flaunting his or her superior knowledge or, worse still, to be putting the students down. The authors have identified this situation as "the beginning of a vicious circle of sorts. The more that teachers try to instill in students a critical attitude toward their own ideas, the more students come to see faculty members as condescending" (Karp and Yoels, 1976:434). In the classroom, as elsewhere, a host of misunderstandings may arise when different persons define the situation differently.

The most difficulty in assessing the meanings of another's actions ordinarily arises in those situations where we know very little about the other person. Differences in experiences, biographies, and cultural backgrounds increase the likelihood that two persons will not understand one another. Those who have traveled in foreign countries should recognize the difficulty of role-taking with cultural strangers. In our own country, we tend to regard with caution the members of ethnic, class, or racial groups whose patterns of speech, grooming, dress, and demeanor vary from our own. Ferdinand Braudel (1981), writing from a historically informed vantage point, argues that the most visible cultural differences between the elite, or ruling classes, and the masses have always involved speech, etiquette, protocol, and even body language. Poor persons who manage to achieve high rank may still find it difficult to overcome cultural barriers which exclude them from full membership in higher social circles. They may not immediately know how to talk, walk, and generally act "correctly."

Differences in the inventories of symbols that distinguish groups are often responsible for misunderstandings between their members. Gerald Suttles describes how the distinctive meanings attached to gestures by ethnic and racial groups can be responsible for faulty communication:

> The other ethnic groups think it odd that a group of Mexican men should strike a pose of obliviousness to other people, even their nearby wives and children. Puerto Ricans, on the other hand, are disparaged because they stand painfully close during a conversation and talk in such a voluble manner as to "jabber." Whites say that Negroes will not look at them in the eye. The Negroes counter by saying that Whites are impolite and try to "cow" people by staring at them. (1972:38).

We can never experience exactly what another person is experiencing because we cannot be that person. We can only approximate through imagination what it must be like to be a given person in a given situation. Moreover, everyone is not equally able or willing to see the world as others do. In some cases the persons involved are simply insensitive. In other situations they make little effort to take others' roles. In Chapter 6 we will elaborate on the apparent unwillingness of many people to role-take with those in less powerful positions.

## The Importance of Information

In theoretical terms, role-taking requires us to distinguish between identification *with* and identification *of* others (Stone, 1962). In role-taking, one person tries to identify *with* another person or group—tries to imagine how others are seeing and conceiving a given situation. Before such an identification with others can be made, however, it is necessary to place, categorize, or define them. Knowledge or identification *of* others' social class, gender, age, race, and the like is a requisite of the role-taking process. In other words, successful role-taking is heavily dependent on the *information* we pick up about others during the course of our interactions with them.

The building up of information is essential to the continuance of interactions. If we incorrectly assess both the information we possess about others and the amount and nature of the information they possess about us, the communication is likely to fail. That is, both persons in an interaction may incorrectly judge how much information of the other they actually possess. Further, the information they believe they have may be wrong. In either case, the result could be a "fractured interaction," as individuals act either out of ignorance or on the basis of incorrect information. Such interactions may result in embarrassment or, in the extreme case, the alienation of persons from one another.

This chapter explores more deeply the relationships among information, role-taking, and the attribution of meanings in interactions. We will consider in detail the categories of information employed in assessing others, the manner in which information is processed, and the ways in which these assessments of others affect daily interactions. We will also consider how information is controlled to create favorable definitions of self in various situations.

## ■ GATHERING AND PROCESSING INFORMATION ABOUT OTHERS

When we confront others, particularly those about whom we have little biographical information, we form a total picture of them—a kind of gestalt—by considering simultaneously and fitting together a number of highly visible cues or clues about them. The specific meanings we attach to any attribute of a person may be modified as we assess it in conjunction with the person's other attributes. In most situations, we identify or form a more or less definite picture of others by taking into account their social attributes, such as age, gender, and race; their physical attributes, such as attractiveness, posture, facial expressions, and body type; their clothing; and their discourse, or what they say.

### Information Provided by Social Attributes

Meaningful social interaction is rooted in the definitions of ongoing situations arrived at by the persons involved in them. Participants in any encounter must be mutually oriented to the social expectations concerning the setting, to the purpose of their communications, and to any available information about others. Certain **social attributes** have informational significance because they help to define the identities of self and others.

Individuals bring with them to all social encounters their own expectations about what to anticipate from other persons with certain attributes. As a result of the socialization process Americans have experienced, for example, we have learned the significance in our society of being male or female, black or white, young or old. We have learned how to deal with these categories of persons and, on occasion, how to manipulate them. Our interactions depend on our images or categorical conceptions of persons possessing such social attributes. For better or worse, we begin our interactions with culturally given conceptions of the ways that women, blacks, Jews, and old persons, to name a few categories, are likely to behave.

A large number of attributes may define a person socially or indicate a person's **social status.** A woman might, for example, simultaneously occupy the statuses of mother, Republican, member of the Better Business Bureau, Phi Beta Kappa, divorcee, and so on. Sociologists make a useful distinction in discussing the properties of social attributes by differentiating between ascribed and achieved statuses. **Ascribed statuses** are those which are acquired at birth (such as gender and race), and **achieved statuses** are acquired during the course of a person's life (such as educational, organization, and occupational statuses). This distinction alone, however, does not indicate the relative importance of the many statuses a person may occupy.

## *The Master Attributes*

Some statuses are substantially more central than others, both to the way persons view themselves and the way others view them. Such highly visible, essentially unalterable attributes as race, gender, and age sharply define a person in any situation. These statuses tend to supersede any other definitions of self that an individual might present to others. When a black person becomes a doctor, for example, many other persons will, even in medical settings, relate to him or her first as a black and only second as a doctor. In this case, ascribed racial status takes precedence over achieved status. Attributes which powerfully define persons, and therefore significantly affect the course of their interactions with others, have been described as **master attributes.**

The information provided by such master attributes as gender, age, and race is so familiar that we can easily lose sight of its importance for the conduct of our everyday affairs. We may recognize just how dependent we are on such knowledge only when we are confronted by a situation where it is not available. Our interactions with others would be considerably complicated if their gender suddenly became unclear, for example. Our role-taking ability depends heavily on our ability to assess others' genders, and we would become disoriented in the absence of this information (see box).

## Relating to Ronald/Ronnie/Rachel: A Weird Experiment?

At the beginning of the academic year, faculty members may be asked if they want to have a graduate student work with them as a teaching assistant. A sociology professor welcomed Ronald, a new graduate student in his department, in this role. The assistant was assigned to teach small discussion sections in an introductory sociology course.

The professor's first encounters with Ronald were uneventful. After a couple of months, however, the professor became aware of a change in Ronald's dress, demeanor, and appearance. He had let his hair grow, and there was something about the obvious care with which he groomed it that gave him a distinctly feminine appearance. He began wearing frilly blouses, plaid pants, and very shiny patent leather shoes. It also became apparent that Ronald's voice had assumed a softer tone. His general demeanor and posture became more feminine, and his beard was much less apparent than it once was.

Then Ronald announced that he preferred to be called Ronnie. The adoption of a gender-neutral name further increased the confusion about the identity he was presenting. At this point, the professor found himself becoming more confused and uncomfortable each time Ronald appeared in his office. He believed Ronald to be a man, but it was becoming increasingly difficult to relate to him, as he was not acting in a predictably masculine fashion. The professor soon realized that the confusion he felt was shared by others. After Ronald left his office, the secretaries in the outer office would ask, "What is it?" "Is he crazy?" "Is he a man or a woman?"

*The case of transsexualism.* The overwhelming significance of gender as a strategic piece of information in guiding interactions is illustrated by transsexualism. In such a case, a person who is genetically of one gender mimics the opposite one, even to the point of having the sex organs modified surgically. Much early socialization is directed toward recognizing the significance of gender and the proper behaviors associated with sexual differences. Conceptions of manhood and womanhood are cultural products acquired through interaction with others. Gender is one attribute that is ordinarily considered to be fixed and unchange-

Soon students started appearing in the professor's office to express their concern, discomfort, confusion, and anger about Ronnie. They indicated that they simply did not know how to relate to the teaching assistant with questions and comments such as: "Is this some kind of weird experiment you're doing in class?" "Is Ronnie a he or a she?" "Should we refer to Ronnie as Ms. or Mr.?" The students were not sure how to act in front of him/her. There was a vague sense that they were being fooled or tricked. The fact that they were unable to place Ronnie into one or another of two mutually exclusive categories—male or female—made their interactions with that person unclear and unpredictable. What was the proper way to speak? What spatial distances ought to be maintained? What topics of discussion were proper? What kinds of eye contact were permissible and what kinds were not? How should they shake hands with such a person?

The dilemma of these students supports the assertion of James Spradley and Brenda Mann that in every society, the biological differences between female and male create "a special kind of reality" in feminine and masculine identities:

Cultural definitions are imposed on nature, creating a vast array of different identities from one culture to another. Male and female become linked to specific roles, attitudes, feelings, aspirations, and behavior patterns. What it means to be a woman, what it means to be a man—these are intimately linked in every culture. Femininity often becomes the antithesis of masculine virtues and vice versa. (1975:144)

The professor later learned that Ronnie was a transsexual in the process of preparing for a gender change operation. She now calls herself Rachel and lives as a woman.

able. This piece of identity information pervades our lives in countless ways. It is questioned only in the unusual case of persons who seek to alter that status.

Transsexualism also highlights the significance of name as a central feature of a person's identity. Like gender, name is a piece of information which grounds the person's identity in the eyes of society. Both gender and name are "identity pegs" which become a part of a person's official, documented identity:

Whether an individual's biographical life is sustained in the minds of his intimates or in the personal files of an organization, and whether the documentation of his personal identity is carried on his person or stored in files, he is an entity about which a record can be built up. . . . He is anchored as an object for biography. (Goffman, 1963b:62)

Imagine the complexity of changing those definitions of self that have become institutionalized in literally hundreds of records. The transsexual soon realizes the difficulty of obtaining name and sex changes on such official documents as social security cards, insurance forms, identification cards, draft cards, birth certificates, and driver's licenses.

Studies of transsexual populations (Kando, 1972; Morris, 1974) have demonstrated the extent to which gender and name "anchor" biographies and social identities. When Deborah Feinbloom interviewed a number of transsexuals, one of them reported being pleased with a new name and new identification until it was necessary to look for a new job:

. . . . the first place I went they gave me a long form to fill out with places for school, other jobs, medical history, etc. I froze. I just hadn't stopped to realize that I really do have a past that I had to do something about and that the name change alone was nothing. My new name had no transcripts, no references, no awards, no pension plan . . . no nothing. (1976:123)

The unusual case of transsexualism illuminates the extraordinary importance of gender as part of our self-definitions, the definitions that others have of us, and the implications these normally mutual definitions have for the way we order our encounters.

### *Processing Master Attributes*

Much the same case can be made with regard to the other master attributes, age and race. Like gender, they are aspects of others upon which we rely in making judgments about the kinds of persons they are, the kinds of behaviors we might expect of them, and the attitudes and values they are likely to hold. Therefore, they help us judge the kinds of behaviors in which we might properly engage in our encounters with others.

The manner in which we use the information revealed by these attributes to formulate our behaviors is somewhat complicated. It is not simply a matter of attributing significance to these attributes *one at a time*. We do not consider them singly and in isolation from each other. Instead, we formulate a conception of persons based on a **configuration of attributes,** or the statuses they simultaneously occupy. People are not just male or female, they are *young* males, *old* males; *young* females, *old* females; *young, black* males, *young, white* females; and so forth. Each of these different combinations calls forth a somewhat different conception of others. Because these statuses are possessed in combination, the number of categorical conceptions we must store in our minds is quite large.

If we consider only the master attributes of gender, age, and race, and consider each in dichotomous terms (that is, male/female, young/old, black/white), we can generate eight categories of persons based on different combinations of attributes. These categories are:

| | |
|---|---|
| Young, black male | Young, black female |
| Old, black male | Old, black female |
| Young, white male | Young, white female |
| Old, white male | Old, white female |

With such a simple example, you could conjure up in your mind a different picture of the kind of person represented by each of these eight types. We have purposely chosen the simplest case, treating each of the three statuses as a dichotomy, or two mutually exclusive groups. Such an assumption is reasonably safe with respect to gender. With the exception of such unusual cases as transsexuals or hermaphrodites, a person is either male or female. It would be an oversimplification to treat age and race as dichotomies, however.

Our conceptions of age, for example, are more specific than just young or old. If we only add the frequently used category of middle-aged, the number of combinations of age along with race and gender becomes 12. The issue is further complicated because age is a continuous variable with values which can range from 0 to over 100 in a series of steps. Our assessments of others' age are therefore quite sophisticated. A matter of even a few years can influence our judgments about what a person can and cannot or should and should not do (see Chapter 9).

There are also many racial distinctions within the black-white dichotomy. Distinctions are made between light- and dark-skinned blacks in the United States, for example, and in countries such as South Africa even finer distinctions constitute the basis for racial oppression. Since, like age, race is also a continuous variable, the number of possible combinations of the attributes of gender, age, and race is very large.

## *The Ongoing Search for Information*

We can very quickly make inferences about people who possess different configurations of these master attributes. In the presence of other persons for the first time, we assess virtually instantaneously their age, gender, and race, and on this basis we form some preliminary judgment about them. Our evaluation of these attributes sensitizes us to what we can generally expect from such persons. The judgments we make after picking up this **face information** cannot be final, however. Our preliminary conceptions of others may prove incorrect as the interaction proceeds, and we must be prepared to make continuous revisions in light of their actual behaviors.

The search for salient or conspicuous information about other persons does not begin and end with assessment of the master attributes, therefore. Once we make a preliminary judgment about others based on these attributes, we begin to search out additional information to help us confirm, reject, or modify these early decisions concerning the kinds of persons with whom we are dealing. In most encounters other central sources of information are available from which we can make inferences about these persons. The information provided by social attributes is complemented by information from such attributes as physical appearance and clothing, which are easily observed and therefore serve as important cues for role-taking.

## Information Provided by Physical Attributes

Advertising attests to the enormous emphasis placed on physical appearance in American society. If our teeth are not white enough, our haircut is not in the latest style, our bodies do not have an agreeable odor, we weigh too much or too little, or our complexion is not clear, we are told that we are unattractive and our interactions with others will suffer. We may be convinced that if our appearance is unattractive or incorrect we will be denied any reasonable opportunity for intimacy with others.

Physical appearance—height, weight, facial characteristics, posture, mannerisms, and grooming—certainly plays a large part in nearly all social interactions. These features of self provide cues as to what we can expect from others and they from us. Like age, race, and gender, **physical attributes** also serve as a basis for judging the kinds of persons others are or appear to be.

The importance of physical attributes in our assessments of self and others emphasizes the significance of symbols in the person perception process. In Chapter 2 the distinction between signs and symbols was described in terms of a crucial difference between fixed and socially conferred meanings. We do not respond to the attributes of others merely as signs. It is not, for example, the physical characteristics of clothing as such that we respond to, but the meanings which have been given to certain types of clothing. In the same way, no intrinsic meaning is attached to shortness, tallness, thinness, or fatness. The meanings conferred on these physical attributes are culturally and historically established, and there are wide variations in the values attached to them.

### Appearance and Attraction

Body image and physical appearance affect our perceptions of ourself and others, as well as our interactions with one another (see box). Our

---

## Do Blondes Really Have More Fun?

The old saying "Beauty is only skin deep" may provide psychological comfort to those who could not be called beautiful people. Research suggests, however, that physical attractiveness affects our perceptions of ourselves and others, as well as the quality of our social relationships. The following findings are typical:

1. Physical appearance is strongly related to the likelihood of attracting a mate, and this is especially true for women in American society. (Berscheid et al., 1971)

2. Persons who view themselves as unattractive have more difficulty establishing relationships with others, particularly persons of the opposite sex. (Brislin and Lewis, 1968)

3. Men and women of equal levels of physical attractiveness (and so equal levels of "social desirability") tend to pair off in courtship and marriage. (Berscheid, Walster, and Bohrnstedt, 1973)

4. All other things being equal, one's chances for economic and occupational success are strongly related to one's physical attractiveness. (Feldman, 1975)

5. Persons who are dissatisfied with the level of their own physical attractiveness report themselves as generally less happy than persons satisfied with their body image. (Berscheid, Walster, and Bohrnstedt, 1973)

6. Overall, women show greater dissatisfaction with their bodies than men do. (Berscheid, Walster, and Bohrnstedt, 1973)

7. The more physically attractive persons are judged to be, the more they are perceived as intelligent, personable, and likable. (Miller, 1970)

awareness of the influence our physical appearance has on others' perceptions of us is illustrated in the care and preparation involved in the way we present ourselves in public. Before we enter any social encounter, we normally make rather extensive assessments of our physical readiness for it. Men, for example, prepare for potential involvements with others by making sure their hair is combed, ties are straight, zippers are zipped, faces are shaved, and so on.

Erving Goffman points out how mirrors are used in this sort of preparation:

> In many business offices . . . one can find half shielded washstands where a secretary can look into a mirror to apply make-up, comb her hair, examine the effect her face is creating, and the like, being able here to engage in a degree of auto-involvement not elsewhere permitted. Mirrors are important objects to study when considering the problem of managing auto-involvements. In American society, apparently, the temptation to make use of nearby mirrors is very difficult to resist. . . . (1963a:66)

This suggests that we respond to mirrors as if they represent an unseen audience. The reflected appraisals of ourselves which we get from mirrors allow us to anticipate the responses others may make to us. In terms of the discussion in Chapter 2 of the self as both the subject and the object of our actions, we present ourselves to the mirror and then stand outside this presented object, trying to view it from the perspective of others. Often mirrors are strategically placed in relatively private areas where people can check their appearance out just before they enter a public setting.

The extent to which people worry about their physical appearance is, to some degree, a function of the situation. In some contexts physical appearance affects the nature of interactions more than in others. The competition involved in developing relationships in such situations as college dances and singles' bars calls for considerable care to present as attractive an appearance as possible. Joan Fischel and Natalie Allon quote one woman on this point:

> I get very nervous before I go into a single's bar. I know I'm relatively attractive and have a good figure, but so do so many other girls there that I worry whether I'll even be noticed. Sometimes I wish I had blonde hair. Blondes always stick out in a crowd. (1973:36)

The emphasis on appearance contributes to students' "fear and loathing" of college mixers, as Pepper Schwartz and Janet Lever point out:

> The men first ask pretty women or those with a good figure to dance; women usually prefer handsome men or men with some sort of "cool." Being "cool" is

not necessarily based on looks for a man. It means that somebody "puts himself together" well, that he walks or talks with some authority, or that he looks "interesting" or at ease. The *participants know that the appearance criterion is inadequate and demeaning, but they use it.* . . . (Emphasis added; 1976:419)

While there cannot be complete agreement in any society as to standards of beauty and ugliness, research has indicated fairly wide cultural consensus in evaluations of others' attractiveness (see Iliffe, 1960). When study participants are shown photographs of various persons and asked to rate them on their relative attractiveness, there is a high degree of consistency in the ratings. Some interesting and revealing variations have been reported by researchers, however. In one study (Razran, 1950), participants were asked to rate the attractiveness of a number of women. When they were given no information other than photographs of the women, they substantially agreed in their ratings. Then the researcher showed the same pictures to another group, identifying each woman with a fictitious Italian, Irish, Jewish, or "old American" name. The participants' judgments of each woman's beauty varied significantly, depending on the ethnicity of the rater and the presumed ethnic identification of the women. This shows how powerfully our perceptions of others can be colored once we acquire certain kinds of information about them.

## *Appearance and Character Assessment*

Not only do we discriminate or rank people in terms of their physical attributes, we also make inferences about the "kinds" of people who display particular physical attributes. That is, we make inferences about others' personalities and even their *moral* characteristics as we assess them physically. Warranted or not, we form preliminary conceptions of others as confident, strong-willed, prudish, sentimental, withdrawn, happy, jolly, evil, tough, honest, sincere, dangerous, intellectual, stupid, and the like.

Our evaluation of others' facial expressions is especially crucial in our "reading" of their attitudes and emotions (Ekman and Friesen, 1979; Cook, 1979). One writer (Birdwhistell, 1970) has estimated that humans' facial muscles allow some 250,000 different expressions. Our assessment of others' faces is central to the view we come to have of them for two reasons. First, in most interactions we spend a good deal of time looking directly at faces. Second, facial expressions, purposely or unwittingly, express an enormous variety of attitudes and emotions. Much attention is given to politicians' facial expressions in assessing their character, for example. In the 1984 presidential election, writers speculated whether

Table 3.1
Stereotyped Responses Relating Characteristics to Body Image

| Endomorphic | Mesomorphic | Ectomorphic |
| --- | --- | --- |
| Dependent | Dominant | Detached |
| Calm | Cheerful | Tense |
| Relaxed | Confident | Anxious |
| Complacent | Energetic | Reticent |
| Contented | Impetuous | Self-conscious |
| Sluggish | Efficient | Meticulous |
| Placid | Enthusiastic | Reflective |
| Leisurely | Competitive | Precise |
| Cooperative | Determined | Thoughtful |
| Affable | Outgoing | Considerate |
| Tolerant | Argumentative | Shy |
| Affected | Talkative | Awkward |
| Warm | Active | Cool |
| Forgiving | Domineering | Suspicious |
| Sympathetic | Courageous | Introspective |
| Soft-hearted | Enterprising | Serious |
| Generous | Adventurous | Cautious |
| Affectionate | Reckless | Tactful |
| Kind | Assertive | Sensitive |
| Sociable | Optimistic | Withdrawn |
| Soft-tempered | Hot-tempered | Gentle-tempered |

*Source:* Reprinted with permission of authors and publisher from: Wells, W. D., and Siegel, B. "Stereotyped Somatotypes," *Psychological Reports*, 1961, 8, 77–78.

the face Ronald Reagan presented in his public "performances" truly reflected his private beliefs. An earlier example was the popular poster showing Richard Nixon's face with the caption, "Would you buy a used car from this man?"

We also consider the general demeanor and body type of those with whom we are interacting. One study (Wells and Siegal, 1961) examined whether different qualities are attributed to persons with three different body types: **endomorphs,** persons whose body type tends toward softness, roundness, or fatness; **mesomorphs,** those whose body type is more muscular and athletic; and **ectomorphs,** those whose body type is tall and thin. Participants were shown silhouette drawings of these three body types and asked to rate each on a set of 24 characteristics (intelligent/unintelligent, lazy/energetic, and so forth). The participants shared the same stereotyped responses to body build, as shown by the list of characteristics attributed to each one in Table 3.1.

Other physical characteristics such as posture and gesture are also used as a basis for inferences about others' emotions, attitudes, and character. People are viewed as being more or less open, accessible, aloof, rigid, and so forth, depending upon their gestures and stance.

*The case of obesity.* The stigma attached to obesity in American society makes it abundantly clear that assessments of others' morality and general worth are made on the basis of their appearance. The growth of dieting workshops, plans, and organizations, as well as low-calorie food industries, in which Americans yearly spend billions of dollars, is persuasive evidence of the general concern with weight. A rigid cultural value is placed on thinness, and those who are very noticeably overweight are evaluated quite negatively. They may be judged by others as lacking in willpower, self-indulgent, and even morally unfit (Millman, 1980).

Natalie Allon refers to obesity as "a central target for human vindictiveness and puritanical zeal." She says, "The public condemns and scorns the overweight, who are viewed as handicaps to themselves" (1971:217). A number of studies on public reaction to obesity support the idea that obese persons are held in low esteem, criticized, and stigmatized precisely because they are considered responsible for their own condition. Overweight is viewed as a voluntary condition because such persons are thought to have control over the condition of their own bodies. One study found that:

. . . even if the reputed association between leanness and longevity were demonstrably false . . . fatness would still be assessed negatively as unaesthetic and as an indication of self indulgence. In a society which has historically been suffused with a Protestant Ethic, one characteristic of which is a strong emphasis on impulse control, fatness suggests a kind of immorality which invites retribution. . . . (Maddox, Back, and Liederman, 1968:288)

The stigmatization of obese individuals comes full circle when they accept the legitimacy of others' negative definitions of them. Overweight persons are in a peculiarly disadvantaged position because: (1) they are discriminated against, (2) they are made to feel that they deserve such discrimination, and (3) they come to accept their treatment as just (Cahnman, 1968).

## *Effects of Clothing on Appearance*

The way people dress also provides information about them. Popular writers (for example, Molloy, 1976) have capitalized on the significance of clothed appearance with "how to dress" advice for aspiring executives, female as well as male. Politicians often employ consultants to advise them about the right clothes to wear for various occasions and in different settings. The fashion industry exploits the desire of Americans to be considered up-to-date and to be acknowledged by others as sophisticated, interesting, important, or successful.

We make assessments of the ethnicity, social class, occupations, social values, moods, emotions, and even political ideologies of those we encounter on the basis of their clothing. The ways others are dressed provides a cue we can use in formulating our behaviors toward them (see box). Clothing also is a prop which helps us project the images of ourselves that we choose to present. It provides a way to manipulate the images we publicly present of ourselves which is simpler than that provided by other physical and social attributes. Gender and race, for example, are difficult if not impossible to modify.

## Information Provided by Discourse

The necessary information for role-taking in interactions is not acquired solely by observing others' social (or master) and physical attributes. Interactions are accomplished through both appearance and discourse, which is the actual "text" of the communication or the conversation

---

### Dressing for Success: How to Get a Little Respect

Ben Jonson's 17th-century observation, "Apes are apes, though clothed in scarlet," to the contrary, we tend to judge others by their outward appearance. Clothing provides one of the easiest ways to convey an impression of authority and respect. You can instantly change from easygoing student to serious job candidate, for example, by changing from jeans and tee shirt to suit and tie or heels and dress.

The significance of clothing in assuring a positive response to requests was examined in a series of studies by Leonard Bickman. One of his studies (1971) began with the question, "Will a person's clothes-categorizing system affect his degree of honesty in a chance encounter?" Bickman and his colleagues, dressed in either high- or low-status clothing, entered phone booths in Grand Central Station and Kennedy Airport, placed a dime on the shelf, and left. Then they observed those who subsequently entered the phone booth, where the dime was in clear sight. Virtually all pocketed the money. The experimenter then tapped on the phone booth and said, "Excuse me, I think I might have left a dime in this phone booth a few minuts ago. Did you find it?" The gender, age, or race of the experimenter *made no difference* in the number of people who returned the money. However, the experimenter's *dress* did make a significant difference. The dime was returned to the well-dressed ex-

between persons. Gregory P. Stone suggests that appearance and discourse must have at least equal significance in any theory of human communication:

> Appearance and discourse are in fact dialectic processes whenever people converse or correspond. They work back and forth on one another, at times shifting, at other times maintaining the direction of the transaction. . . . In all cases, however, discourse is impossible without appearance which permits the requisite identifications with one another by the discussants. (1962:91)

The information on others provided by social and physical attributes sets the stage for verbal encounters. Before we can talk to people with different attributes, we use the information we have to decide what we can expect from them. This lends some predictability to our encounters.

---

perimenter in 77 percent of the cases, compared to a 38 percent return to the poorly dressed person.

In another experiment, Bickman (1974) showed that students' dress was a significant factor in gaining the cooperation of the people they approached to sign a petition. He also found that certain uniforms confer power and legitimacy on those wearing them. In this study (1974), the experimenters were dressed in one of three types of clothing: sports jacket and tie, milkman's uniform, or guard's uniform. They stopped people on the street and authoritatively made certain requests. In one variation the researcher, indicating a confederate in the experiment standing beside a car at a parking meter, told bystanders, "This fellow is overparked at the meter but doesn't have any change. Give him a dime!" People were most obedient to the guard, the highest authority figure, as they were in all variations of this experiment.

These experiments were conducted around relatively simple demands. They affirmed a previously documented relationship between authority and obedience (Milgram, 1963) and extended earlier findings by specifying the role of dress in this relationship. Bickman was also concerned with how the findings might extend to potential real-life situations: "If people were willing to respond to trivial requests from a guard, how would they react to more serious or perhaps deadlier demands from policemen or military personnel?" (1974:51)

78  Development of the Perspective

We make reasonable guesses about others' future behaviors. However, as you have no doubt learned through your own interactions, we cannot rely solely on such guesses. We must be prepared to modify our images of others as the interaction proceeds.

Much of the information considered important for predicting others' behaviors must be ferreted out during verbal discourse. The search for relevant information and the corresponding role-taking occur throughout the interaction process. Such aspects of others' identities as their occupation, social class affiliation, ethnicity, marital status, educational level, religion, prejudices, and political beliefs cannot be fully determined through observation alone. Verbal discourse furthers the search for such aspects of others' identities.

Many of our inquiries about others are designed to elicit this information. Consider the information-seeking intentions that lie behind the following types of verbal probes, which are often heard in the course of conversation:

*Question Asked:*                                      *Possible Information Sought:*

Does your wife work?                                   Are you married?
Did you belong to a fraternity                         What is your education?
  in college?
Where do you live?                                     What is your social class?
Did your kids learn about that                         What is your religion?
  in church?
Do you find enough time away                           What is your occupation?
  from your job to do that?
What do you think about politician                     What are your political attitudes?
  X's position on that issue?

We not only seek out information about others, we frequently find it useful to provide selective information about ourselves. We deliberately present certain images of ourselves by the way we stand, our dress, and our general demeanor. We also provide selective information about ourselves in our verbal communications. At a party where children were present, the hostess openly warned her husband to watch the children carefully to prevent spills on the $600,000 budget he had been preparing. This communication served a dual purpose: to actually protect her husband's work, and to make clear to everyone that her husband was quite an important businessperson.

Examples of such information being "given off" abound in everyday communications:

79  Communication and Interaction

| Statement Made: | Possible Information Provided: |
|---|---|
| We plan to spend a month at our ski chalet in Switzerland. | I am financially well off. |
| I took a course on that subject while I was at Harvard. | I am a well-educated person. |
| As vice-president of the company, I must do a lot of traveling. | I hold an important position. |

These examples suggest an important point about the interaction process: Human beings are capable of manipulating the information they provide others in order to present certain self-images. We conceal, control, and give off certain bits of information about ourselves in order to realize certain desired ends in our transactions with others. Since we carefully monitor the information we provide others, we must presume that those with whom we interact are doing the same. This knowledge certainly complicates our interactions, as we must sometimes question whether and to what extent others are presenting authentic or deceptive images of themselves.

## ■ CONTROLLING INFORMATION AND MANAGING IMPRESSIONS

The communication and interaction process we have been describing in this chapter takes the following form. Two persons come into each others' presence and immediately begin to assess one another. Each begins to pick up as much information as possible about the other's physical and social attributes. This information is important if each person is to have some degree of control over the interaction and to elicit a response from the other person that can be considered favorable. As the encounter proceeds, however, the participants do more than rely on the cues gleaned from one another. Beyond that, they begin to put on a performance and try to project certain identities of themselves. This part of the process is called **impression management**.

The idea that individuals systematically control the information they provide others about themselves in order to manage the impressions they are presenting is basic to a view of human interaction called the **dramaturgical view.** This view of interaction is most closely associated with the writings of Erving Goffman, who is sympathetic to the idea we have presented that individuals must be capable of assigning meanings to their own and others' behaviors in order to communicate. Goffman's work falls within a symbolic interaction frame of reference because he agrees that individuals must learn to interpret through role-taking the transactions with others in which they find themselves and to formulate the meanings of their encounters. However, in Goffman's work certain aspects of this process are emphasized. The dramaturgical view of interaction sees individuals not simply as *role-takers* but equally as **role-makers** (Turner and Shosid, 1976). They do not merely interpret meanings, they also purposely create and manipulate meanings.

In the analogy suggested by the dramaturgical view of interaction, the essential reality of life is a series of fabricated roles, and society is a theater in which everyone is an actor engaged in a perpetual play. Goffman's view of human behavior indicates he takes seriously Shakespeare's claim that "All the world's a stage and all the men and women merely players."

## Presenting the Right Impression

In the dramaturgical view, individuals construct their **presentations of self** in a calculated and often contrived way. They do this not only to give a favorable impression of themselves but to establish specific definitions of the acting situation. Goffman reads a Machiavellian kind of manipulation into human interactions:

When an individual appears before others his action will influence the definition of the situation which they will come to have. Sometimes the individual will act in a thoroughly calculating manner, expressing himself in a given way solely in order to give the kind of impression to others that is likely to invoke from them a specific response he is concerned to obtain. (Goffman, 1959:6)

By fabricating impressions, we try to control the definition of the acting situation others come to have, and in so doing we set the future course of the interaction. If we succeed in this, we can achieve significant control over others.

The dramaturgical view also assumes that humans are approval-seeking animals. We wish to be applauded by others for the self-images we present. We are anxious to receive approval for our behaviors, opinions, and attitudes. We want to be seen as worthwhile, social, proper persons, so we try to present our "best face" to others. To accomplish this end, we seek out information about others and systematically control information about ourselves. We particularly strive to exclude information we perceive as damaging to ourselves.

Sometimes we go to great extremes to conceal biographical information about ourselves. This is so if we believe the hidden information would somehow taint our identities. Some persons seek to disavow their ethnic or racial statuses, for example. Jews may find it necessary to present an impression of non-Jewishness so they can participate freely in social settings where they might be excluded if their true attributes were known, since discrimination is still a reality in American society.

Other kinds of information may also be concealed. In order to present an integrated, consistent, and proper impression of ourselves in everyday situations, we carefully monitor our actual behaviors. We make use of various devices to conceal our participation in improper or unconventional activities. Goffman describes the "involvement shields" people use to give the impression of being properly involved, though they are not strictly conforming to the obligations of a social setting. They might use their hands to cover their eyes if they cannot keep them open when attention is demanded, or use a portable shield such as a newspaper to stifle a yawn. They may use their hands to cup a cigarette in places where smoking is not allowed. They sometimes sustain a pose of deep interest when they are, in fact, uninterested in a conversation. You no doubt have, at one time or another, nodded agreement to something you did not hear or understand.

Contrary to a number of psychological models of the human being, Goffman does not view persons as having one identity. Rather individuals have **multiple identities,** a repertoire of identities, and can choose from among these available identities the one that they judge best suits the expectations of a given audience. Goffman describes humans as persons of *appearance.* It matters little what we actually are, therefore. What most matters is what we appear to be. And this is inevitably true because it is on the basis of our appearance, on the basis of the images, identities, impressions, and information we provide others about ourselves, that others will formulate their conceptions of us.

### *Mutual Protection*

While we conceal certain aspects of ourselves so others will think of us as proper, there is another way in which information control is related to the appearance of propriety. The preservation of orderly interaction depends on the mutual protection of the individuals involved. The ultimate display of social morality is a person's attempt to protect the social images of others. Life therefore should not be viewed as an endlessly competitive struggle in which individuals aggressively protect only their own interests.

A basic feature of social interaction is that individuals tend to conduct themselves in encounters in such a way that both their own image and those of the other participants are protected. Both the construction of a favorable personal impression and the protection of others' fabricated impressions involve information control. In Goffman's terms, individuals "show respect and politeness, making sure to extend to others any ceremonial treatment that might be their due. They employ discretion; they leave unstated facts that might implicitly or explicitly contradict or embarrass the positive claims made by others" (1967:16).

## Performance Aspects of Interaction

The dramaturgical view of humanity and society has been characterized as follows:

... Goffman's image of social life is not of firm, well-bounded social structures, but rather of a loosely stranded, criss-crossing, swaying catwalk along which men dart precariously. In this view, people are actors and gamesmen who have, somehow, become disengaged from social structures and are growing detached even from culturally standardized roles. They are seen less as products of the system, than as individuals "working the system" for the enhancement of self. ... (Gouldner, 1970:379)

Such an image involves the issues of conformity and sincerity in interactions.

### *Conformity*

In the usual sociological view of conformity, when individuals internalize social norms, their behaviors conform to societal expectations. Society, in effect, gets inside their heads. The price of nonconformity, under the condition of internalization, is not simply the scorn of one's fellows but, more important, scorn for oneself. Individuals conform because not to do so engenders guilt. From this perspective, norms are not merely guidelines. They assume a moral force.

Goffman provides an alternative view of conformity, at least implicitly. The dramaturgical analyst sees most human behavior as highly stylized and ritualized. It is performed in accordance with the rules, but not necessarily motivated by a *belief* in the rules. As individuals move from one setting or situation to another, they may simply adopt the interactional posture most appropriate for this situation.

### *Cynicism and Sincerity in Role-taking*

If we do not believe in the rules but conform merely because we are expected to do so in the situation, the honesty and sincerity of our behaviors may be suspect. In the dramaturgical view, society is viewed as a stage on which the actors, with premeditations, manipulate and withhold information about themselves and sometimes offer false information. The question is to what extent the role-players or performers are being consistent with their own image of self. Indeed, the dramaturgical model raises the question of just where to locate the person's "real" self or even whether there is a real self. When you act one way in front of your same-sexed friends and an entirely different way in the company of the opposite sex, which of the two behaviors reflects your true self more accurately? When you display thoroughly proper table manners at a formal affair and the next day at dinner gruffly demand that your roommate "pass the goddamn butter," which of the two performances best reflects the kind of person you really are? Or are you both kinds of persons, simply alternating in a chameleon-like way from one situation to the next?

In a book titled *The Managed Heart* (1983) Arlie Russell Hochschild notes that in postindustrial society more and more jobs are requiring workers to manage their feelings. Occupations such as flight attendant require constant smiles and cordial behavior, even when customers become nasty or abusive. Hochschild warns that the "emotional labor" required in the growing number of service occupations will take a heavy psychological toll from workers who are required to put on cynical role performances as a matter of course.

It would be a mistake to assume that everyone is always being cynical in the performance of her or his roles, however. The issue is not, we think, whether a person puts on performances, plays roles, or manipulates others. We all do that. The question of sincerity or cynicism in role-taking turns rather on whether performers *believe in their own performances.* We may think of role performances as sincere when individuals present themselves to others as they really believe themselves to be. Only when they rationally set out to deceive others by presenting false information about themselves can it be called a cynical role performance.

An observer of another's behavior cannot always determine whether the performance is cynical or sincere. Only the person producing the act knows whether he or she is being dishonest. Two different persons could put on concretely identical performances, one of which would be sincere and the other cynical. As an example, a cynical sweetheart could quite consciously behave ineptly as a lover in order to convince a man that she is inexperienced, and he is the first person she has ever really loved. But a sincere sweetheart who really is inexperienced might also behave ineptly. The two would put on identical acts—both performing ineptly as lovers—yet one performance would be cynical and the other sincere.

The only time a cynical performance can be uncovered as such is when it fails—when it falls through, and the person's true intentions are therefore made plain. If at a dinner party a businessman is passing himself off as, let us say, an upper-level manager in some organization, and without warning a fellow worker appears and proceeds to identify him as a low-level bureaucrat, the man's cynical performance will have failed.

A person may eventually come to believe in a performance that was originally cynical. For example, young people may act intellectually in order to gain the status associated with being considered intellectuals in some situation. At the outset they may sustain this performance even though they do not believe themselves to be intellectuals. If they are accorded the status of an intellectual by others and recognized for their intellectual performance, however, at some point they might come to believe in their own originally cynical performance. The music they once listened to, the books they once read, and the museums they once attended only to provide props for this particular performance become over time true sources of pleasure. Their image as intellectuals has been incorporated into their conception of self.

## Modifying the Situational View of Self

The concept of self appears throughout this book. In Chapter 2 we described Mead's conception of self as a process in which persons objectively evaluate their behaviors from the perspective of the generalized other. This implies that a person presents quite different selves in different situations. To employ Mead's term, a person has not one me but a number of me's, each corresponding to a situationally proper role.

Goffman also offers a highly situational view of the self. As persons move from one acting situation to another, their self presentations change, often dramatically. R. H. Lauer and W. H. Handel suggest that "In theoretical terms, the others in a situation act as an audience for one's performance, evaluating and responding to its adequacy" (1977:431). In this interactionist view, individuals construct and perform roles in terms of both the norms governing particular situations and the specific responses they want to invoke from others. According to dramaturgical theorists, individuals remain detached from the roles they perform, "coolly alternating" (Berger and Luckman, 1967:172) presentations of self each time they enter a new situation.

Critics have charged that the dramaturgical metaphor is committed to an overly fluid, changeable notion of the self. They have questioned whether the self is always discrete, called forth only by the situation and the audience. These critics suggest that there are order and stability in the self, as well as some consistency in presentations of self, which transcend particular settings. Some organizing attribute or unifying principle in the self keeps a person from being only a bundle of situationally constructed roles.

Personality theorists such as Sigmund Freud, Abraham Maslow, Harry Stack Sullivan, and Erik Erikson argue for the development of a personality structure that controls or coordinates situational presentations of self. Although they frequently stress different themes and processes, all understand human beings as developing a distinct, bounded, identifiable conception of themselves (a personal identity, if you will) that has continuity through time.

Through interaction with others we appear to develop early in childhood a conception of ourselves—perhaps as intelligent, shy, confident, physically attractive, or clumsy. If persons do develop an overriding, independent, and relatively stable view of themselves, we must somewhat amend or revise the situationalist stance of the dramaturgical model. We need not reject Goffman's emphasis on the performance features of interaction. We simply have to acknowledge that basic and pervasive elements of self-conception may lie behind and motivate the particular performances individuals choose, the images they project, and the manipulations they attempt. A complete explanation of behavior must incorporate both the immediate character and requirements of social situations and the unique, subjective conception of self that individuals bring to every situation.

## ■ CONCLUSION

In the first three chapters we have been asking: How do individuals organize, interpret, and give meaning to their own and others' behaviors? To answer this question we have been analyzing how individuals build up a conception of others to make judgments about their interests, motives, values, attitudes, and character. They also try to manage the impressions of themselves that they present in order to control social situations and appear proper.

Information gathering is an important part of the person perception process and the basis for the theoretical idea that *identification of* others precedes *identification with* them. From the interactionist perspective, information is critical to role-taking and so to meaningful human communication and interaction. The master attributes—gender, age, and race—are especially significant in the definitions individuals come to have of others. The absence of these key pieces of information can create confusion and uncertainty in daily interactions.

Preliminary evaluations of others based only on these attributes may be incorrect, however. Individuals therefore continue to seek out information to refine their conceptions of others before and during their interactions. Elements of physical appearance such as height, weight, facial characteristics, posture, grooming, and clothing, as well as discourse, are noticed carefully. Beyond such information, which is immediately observable, verbal communications can provide knowledge of others' attitudes and values by seeking out information on their educational levels, occupations, and religions.

The dramaturgical model of interaction stresses the manner in which information is controlled to create definitions of situations. The idea that persons present manufactured selves to each other, striving to appear proper in each other's eyes, rings true as a general statement about interaction. But presentations of self vary with particular settings. Some situations in everyday lives require more extensive interpretation, calculation, and "self-work" than others do. There are some contexts in which individuals become especially concerned with the effects of their performances on others. In the following chapters we will examine how our relations with strangers and intimates involve us in different configurations of self, meaning, and informational analysis.

# Definitions

**Failed communication.** An instance in which those interacting respond to each other on the basis of fundamentally different definitions of the situation.

**Social attributes.** Those aspects of self that define an individual's locations in society. Among social attributes are race, gender, ethnicity, occupation, and religion. We build up a picture of others based on our knowledge of their various social attributes.

**Social status.** An individual's position in society based on social attributes including the ascribed statuses of race, gender, and age as well as achieved statuses such as wealth, education, and occupation. Status indicates the degree of prestige, esteem, and power conferred on persons because of these attributes.

**Ascribed statuses.** Those social statuses possessed by individuals over which they have no control (for example, race, gender, age, and circumstances of birth).

**Achieved statuses.** Those social statuses that are acquired during the course of individuals' lives and over which they may exert some control (for example, occupational level, educational attainment, or marriage into a higher social position).

**Master attributes.** Those statuses that are most central both to the way persons view themselves and the way others view them. Race, gender, and age are three attributes that sharply define a person in any situation and tend to supersede other definitions of self that an individual might present to others.

**Configuration of attributes.** The whole range of attributes about other persons that we take into account as we try to assess the kinds of persons they are and the behaviors we might expect from them.

**Face information.** Information about aspects of a person's identity that can be gleaned simply by observing them. Race, gender, demeanor, and clothing, for example, are normally visible as soon as we encounter another person. It is on the basis of face information that we make preliminary judgments about the likely behaviors of others.

**Physical attributes.** Those aspects of self that define an individual's physical appearance. Height, weight, expression, posture, gesture, and so on provide cues to the expected behaviors of others.

**Endomorphs.** Individuals whose body type tends toward softness, roundness, and fatness.

**Mesomorphs.** Individuals whose body type is muscular and athletic.

**Ectomorphs.** Individuals whose body type is tall and thin.

**Impression management.** The process through which individuals consciously try to foster particular images of themselves in order to gain control of a situation or the approval of others.

**Dramaturgical view.** A perspective that uses theatrical metaphors to describe and analyze social interaction. The basic idea is that individuals present themselves to others in a manner analogous to a stage actor's presentation of a role to an audience.

**Role-makers.** All human beings are role-makers to the extent that they do not unthinkingly act out socially prescribed roles. In addition, humans create and manipulate meanings through the roles they choose to perform.

**Presentations of self.** The ways in which individuals present themselves to others in order to evoke a favorable impression and control definitions of situations.

**Multiple identities.** According to the dramaturgical view of interaction, individuals have several identities from which to choose in staging a particular performance. From the repertoire of identities at their disposal, they ordinarily choose to present the identity that in their opinion best suits the expectations of a given audience.

# Discussion Questions

1. Think of a time when your attempts to role-take with another did not succeed. What happened to the interaction? How did it proceed? Why did you have difficulty role-taking? In what kinds of situations generally do persons have the most difficulty assessing each others' meanings?

2. Which of your social attributes or statuses do you consider as most centrally defining your identity? Describe how you think those attributes affect the way others respond to you.

3. Describe some of the ways in which you feel that individuals' physical attractiveness influences their own behaviors and the behaviors of others toward them. Do you think that physical appearance affects the lives of men and women differently in American society? If so, how do you account for this difference?

4. Devise some simple experiments to demonstrate for yourself the significance of the clothes you wear in determining how others treat you in a variety of settings. Would you be treated differently by clerks in department, specialty, or discount stores, depending on your clothing, for example? What kind of experiment would you construct? Where would you conduct it? How would you alter the type of clothing worn by the experimenters? Which reactions would you particularly want to record?

5. Do you agree or disagree with Erving Goffman's picture of humans as strategic, manipulative, sometimes insincere managers of impressions? In what ways might contrived performances be necessary for maintaining social order?

6. Is there such a thing as a "real" self, or are we only a bundle of situationally constructed roles? What do you think is the linkage between persons' "stable" personality attributes and the particular selves they present in a given situation?

# References

Allon, N. 1971. "Group dieting interaction." Unpublished Ph.D. dissertation, Brandeis University.

Berger, P., and T. Luckman. 1967. *The Social Construction of Reality*. New York: Doubleday Anchor Books.

Berscheid, E., K. Dion, E. Walster, and G. W. Walster. 1971. "Physical attractiveness and dating choice: A test of the matching hypothesis." *Journal of Experimental Social Psychology* 7:173–189.

Berscheid, E., E. Walster, and G. W. Bohrnstedt. 1973. "Body image, physical appearance, and self-esteem." Paper presented at the Annual Meeting of the American Sociological Association.

Bickman, L. 1971. "The effect of social status on the honesty of others." *Journal of Social Psychology* 85 (October):87–92.

Bickman, L. 1974. "Social roles and uniforms: Clothes make the person." *Psychology Today* 7 (April):48–53.

Birdwhistell, R. 1970. *Kinesics and Context*. Philadelphia: University of Pennsylvania Press.

Braudel, F. 1981. *The Structures of Everyday Life*. New York: Harper & Row.

Brislin, R. W., and S. A. Lewis. 1968. "Dating and physical attractiveness: A replication." *Psychological Reports* 22:976.

Cahnman, W. 1968. "The stigma of obesity." *Sociological Quarterly* 9 (Summer):283–299.

Cook, M. 1979. "Gaze and mutual gaze in social encounters." In *Nonverbal Communication*, ed. S. Weitz. New York: Oxford University Press.

Ekman, P., and W. Friesen. 1979. "Measuring facial movement." In *Nonverbal Communication*, ed. S. Weitz. New York: Oxford University Press.

Feinbloom, D. 1976. "Transsexualism: A study of individual and social response to identity change." Unpublished Ph.D. dissertation, Boston College.

Feldman, S. D. 1975. "The presentation of shortness in everyday life." In *Life Styles: Diversity in American Society*, 2nd ed. Boston: Little, Brown.

Fischel, J., and N. Allon. 1973. "Urban courting patterns: Singles' bars." Paper read at the 68th Annual Meeting of the American Sociological Association.

Goffman, E. 1959. *The Presentation of Self in Everyday Life*. New York: Doubleday Anchor Books.

Goffman, E. 1963a. *Behavior in Public Places*. New York: Free Press.

Goffman, E. 1963b. *Stigma*. Englewood Cliffs, N.J.: Prentice-Hall.

Goffman, E. 1967. *Interaction Ritual: Essays on Face-to-Face Behavior*. New York: Doubleday Anchor Books.

Gouldner, A. 1970. *The Coming Crisis in Western Sociology*. New York: Basic Books.

Hochschild, A. 1983. *The Managed Heart: Commercialization of Human Feeling*. Berkeley, Cal.: University of California Press.

Iliffe, A. H. 1960. "A study of preference in feminine beauty." *British Journal of Psychology* 51:267–273.

Kando, T. 1972. "Passing and stigma management: The case of the transsexual." *Sociological Quarterly* 13 (Fall):475–483.

Karp, D. A., and W. C. Yoels, 1976. "The college classroom: Some observations on the meanings of student participation." *Sociology and Social Research* 60:421–438.

Lauer, R. H., and W. H. Handel. 1977. *Social Psychology: The Theory and Application of Symbolic Interactionism*. Boston: Houghton Mifflin.

Maddox, G. L., K. Back, and V. R. Liederman. 1968. "Overweight as social deviance and disability." *Journal of Health and Social Behavior* 9 (December):287–298.

Milgram, S. 1963. "Behavioral study of obedience." *Journal of Abnormal and Social Psychology* 67:371–378.

Miller, A. G. 1970. "Role of physical beauty in impression formation." *Psychonomic Science* 19:241–243.

Millman, M. 1980. *Such a Pretty Face*. New York: W. W. Norton.

Molloy, J. T. 1976. *Dress for Success*. New York: Warner Books.

Morris, J. 1974. *Conundrum*. New York: Harcourt Brace.

Razran, G. 1950. "Ethnic dislike and stereotypes: A laboratory study." *Journal of Abnormal and Social Psychology* 45:7–27.

Schwartz, P. and J. Lever, 1976. "Fear and loathing at a college mixer." *Urban Life* 4 (January):413–432.

Spradley, J., and B. Mann. 1975. *The Cocktail Waitress: Woman's Work in a Man's World*. New York: John Wiley & Sons.

Stone, G. P. 1962. "Appearance and the self." In *Human Behavior and Social Processes*, ed. A. Rose. Boston: Houghton Mifflin.

Suttles, G. 1972. "Communicative devices." In *Down to Earth Sociology*, ed. J. Henslin. New York: Free Press.

Turner, R., and N. Shoshid. 1976. "Ambiguity and interchangeability in role attribution: The affect of alter's response." *American Sociological Review* 41 (December):993–1006.

Wells, W., and B. Siegal. 1961. "Stereotyped somatypes." *Psychological Reports* 8:77–78.

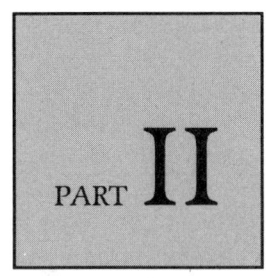

# PART II Establishing Social Order

| | |
|---|---|
| CHAPTER 4 | CONTACTS AMONG STRANGERS: EVERYDAY URBAN RELATIONS  95 |
| | Sociological Definitions of the Stranger  97 |
| | The Paradox of Doubt and Trust  99 |
| | The Structure of Everyday Public Behaviors  102 |
| | The City as a World of Strangers  109 |
| | Establishing Relationships with Strangers  116 |
| CHAPTER 5 | CONTACTS AMONG INTIMATES: CONSTRUCTING SOCIAL RELATIONSHIPS  125 |
| | Intimate Relationships in Contemporary Society  128 |
| | The Interactionist Perspective on Intimacy  130 |
| | From Strangers to Intimates: The Construction of Love Relationships  139 |
| | Alternatives to Marriage  147 |
| CHAPTER 6 | POWER AND STRATIFICATION IN EVERYDAY LIFE: THE POLITICS OF INTERACTION  161 |
| | Power Relations in the Macro and Micro Worlds  164 |
| | The Relationship of Power to Role-Taking  170 |
| | The Subtle Faces of Power in Everyday Interactions  177 |
| CHAPTER 7 | EVERYDAY LIFE IN BUREAUCRACIES  187 |
| | The Pervasive Effects of Bureaucracy  189 |
| | The Bureaucratization of Modern Life  192 |
| | Thinking about Bureaucracy  195 |
| | Work in Bureaucracies  200 |

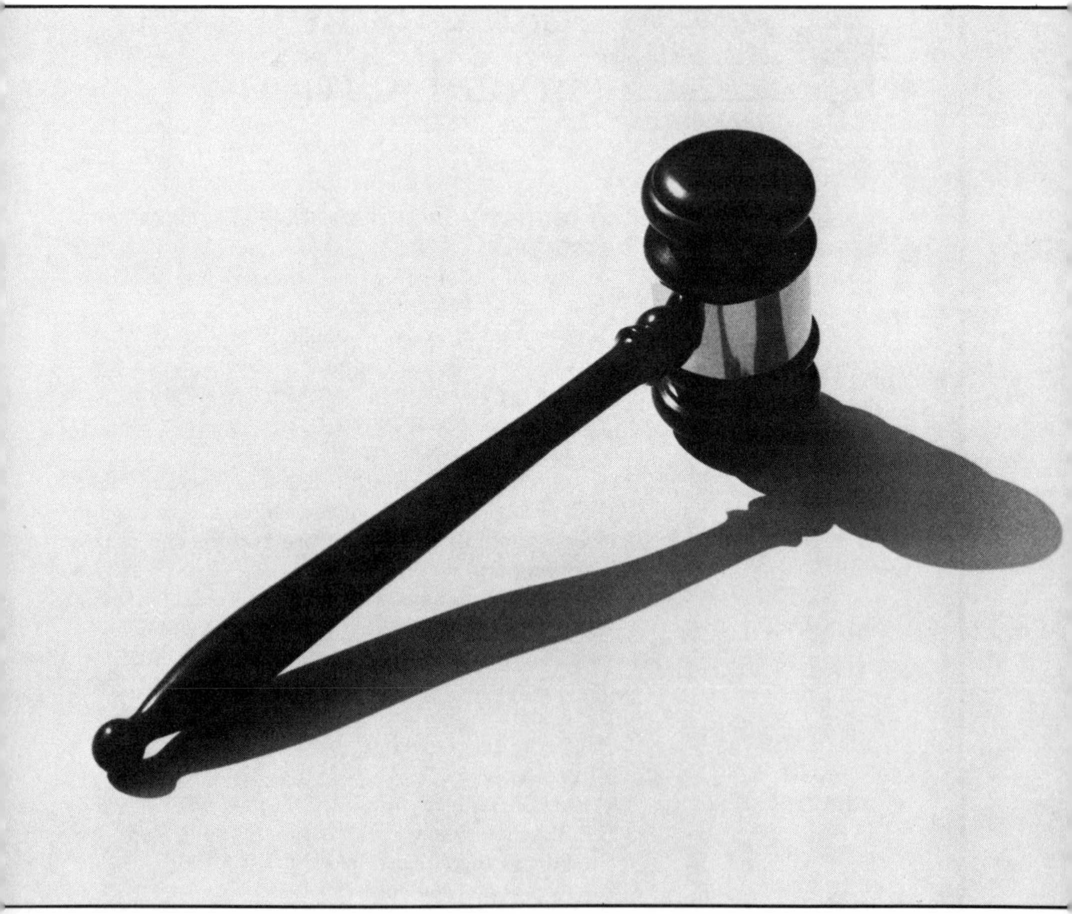

# PART II

P ART II DEMONSTRATES how the elements of face-to-face communication can be employed to analyze aspects of everyday life. Our concern centers on the ways in which people establish predictable, meaningful patterns of behavior in a wide variety of daily settings. The three contexts discussed in this part are contacts between strangers, or urban public encounters; contacts between intimates; and relationships in the world of work in bureaucracies. We also consider the definitions of the situations people create through their participation in various social arrangements, and we examine how power and status differences affect face-to-face encounters. The chapters in Part II will help you understand that the meanings of any human relationships are socially constructed; that is to say, people establish meanings through their daily communications with one another.

Chapter 4 is concerned with how people perceive and interact with others in anonymous public places. Our analysis proceeds from the observation that people in public places are strangers to one another. They employ various adaptations to cope with the huge volume of stranger contacts experienced in cities and may adopt strategies to avoid direct communication. The consideration of stranger relations in Chapter 4 describes the connections between information, trust, and risk in *any* interaction.

The substance of Chapter 5 is intimate relations. This chapter begins with the argument that intimacy is a socially constructed, symbolic phenomenon. The meanings of intimacy vary both historically and in terms of individuals' personal attributes. The building of relationships is an ongoing process, and strangers go through typical stages in their transformation into intimates. The last section of Chapter 5, which looks at the literature on living together and staying single, gives you some idea of recent changes in the meanings given to intimacy, commitment, and sexuality.

In our analyses of relations among strangers and intimates, we touch on questions of power only briefly. Chapter 6 provides an important addition to our treatment of social interaction by stressing the differences in access to decision-making processes for various individuals and groups. As a result of these differences, some individuals are in more strategic positions than others to have their definitions of the situation translated into actuality. There is also a relationship between role-taking ability and the power accorded the positions occupied in society. You will see that such daily behaviors as staring, pointing, crowding, touching, and interrupting others' conversations are all functions of power differentials between people.

Chapter 7 expands on the importance of the positions a person occupies in the social order by focusing more specifically on everyday life in bureaucratic organizations. Contacts between persons in modern societies are increasingly mediated by the intervention of third-party agencies such as insurance companies, government bureaus, and the courts. Our treatment of bureaucratic life emphasizes the concepts of multiple realities, the processes of negotiation, and the symbolic foundations of social structures. You will be shown how people's locations in the organizational hierarchy of a work organization shape their conceptions of their jobs. You will also learn how workers strive to achieve some degree of autonomy over their work lives.

# CHAPTER 4

# Contacts among Strangers: Everyday Urban Relations

I. Sociological Definitions of the Stranger
   A. Biographical and Cultural Strangers
II. The Paradox of Doubt and Trust
   A. Uncertainty in Interactions with Strangers
      1. How cabdrivers size up strangers
      2. The case for being uncertain about strangers in public places
III. The Structure of Everyday Public Behaviors
   A. Efforts to Remain Anonymous
   B. Efforts to Assure Public Privacy
      1. Abiding by the rules
   C. Impression Management with Strangers
   D. The State of Involved Indifference
IV. The City as a World of Strangers
   A. The Volume of Interactions in Cities
   B. Behaviors in Urban Settings: Selectivity and Noninvolvement
   C. Tolerance for Strange Lifestyles
      1. Social contracts among groups
      2. The spatial ordering of city activities
V. Establishing Relationships with Strangers
   A. Effects of Social Settings and Situations
      1. Definitions of behaviors
      2. Information about others
   B. How Strangers Meet
VI. Conclusion

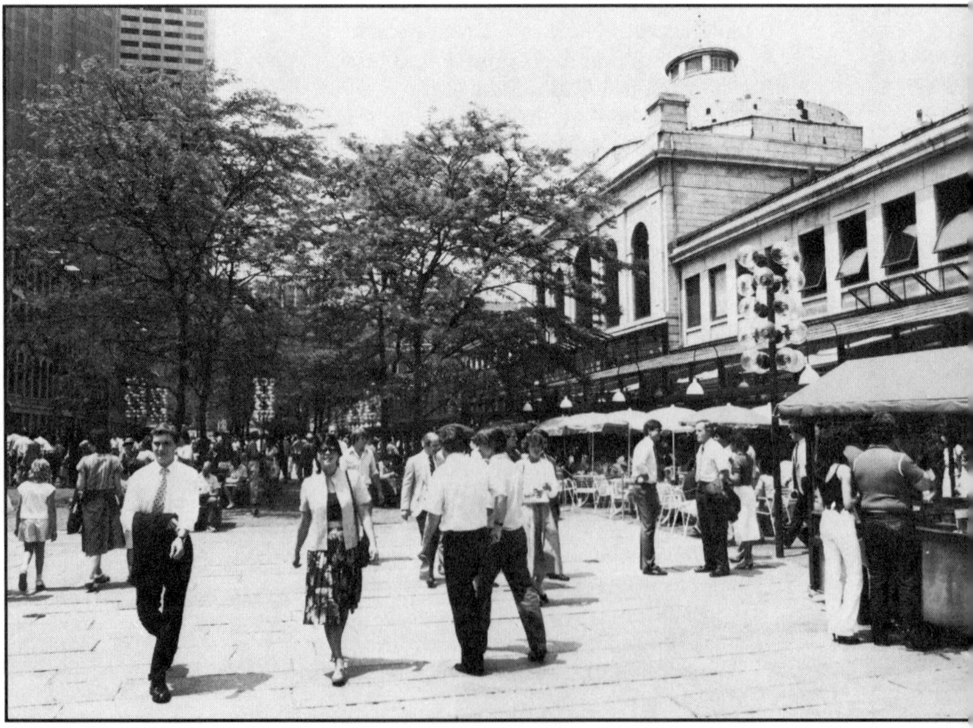

# CHAPTER 4

When we were children, we were taught to avoid strangers and even fear them, for our own protection. Who knew what a stranger might really want who stopped you on the street asking for directions, approached to sell you something, or chose a seat next to you on a bus? Because we cannot know for sure what the motives of strangers are, we learn to regard them with suspicion.

Strangers are strange precisely because we know little or nothing about them. Their lives may be guided by symbol systems that are different from our own, and they may not share our concept of social reality. In such a case the essential meanings they give to objects, events, and situations will be different from our own. This difference is what makes communication and interaction with strangers so difficult.

## ■ SOCIOLOGICAL DEFINITIONS OF THE STRANGER

The stranger has always intrigued sociological theorists. Georg Simmel, for example, was concerned not with one-to-one relationships between strangers but with new relationships between an individual and a larger social system (a group, an institution, a community). Simmel (1950b) conceived of the special quality of the stranger status as always remaining peripheral or marginal to groups with which interactions are being sought. The best example is the successful trader or merchant who has direct dealings with a number of groups but does not seek assimilation into any of them. The stranger's distinctive position is to be near and distant to a group at the same time.

In American sociology, the stranger as a social type has often been equated with what Robert Park referred to as **marginal man.** He applied the idea to immigrant racial and ethnic groups in the city who remain marginal members of urban society because they are in the process of giving up their old cultures without having fully assimilated the culture of the new. The marginal man stands between the two cultures as "one who lives in two worlds, in both of which he is more or less a stranger" (Park, 1928:892). The wandering Jew, historically without a homeland, was the best example of the stranger or marginal man by Park's definition. Everett Stonequist (1937) extended the ideas of Park, who had been his teacher, by exploring the social processes that could result in greater numbers of marginal persons in a society.

Alfred Schutz (1960) also speaks of the stranger in terms of an individual's relationship to organized group life. His analysis focuses on the definition of the stranger as one who is not knowledgeable about the cultural pattern of the group to which admission is sought. For a stranger approaching a group, the relevancies of everyday life are not the same as for the group's members. The stranger therefore is not sure how to interpret social situations, events, and behaviors. The stranger, puzzled by the apparent incoherence and inconsistency of the group's cultural pattern, is likely to question elements of group life that fullfledged members take for granted. In Schutz's words, "The cultural pattern of the approached group is to the stranger not a shelter but a field of adventure, not a matter of course but a questionable topic of investigation, not an instrument for disentangling problematic situations but a problematic situation itself and one hard to master" (1960:104). For Peter Berger and Hansfried Kellner, an essential element of the concept of strangeness is the fact that unacquainted individuals come from different face-to-face contexts and **areas of conversation,** with different biographies and life experiences. Their pasts have a similar structure, but because they do not have a shared past they are likely to define situations quite differently (1970:54).

## Biographical and Cultural Strangers

Sociologists have defined the stranger concept in very specialized ways. We will adopt a more conventional use of the term and differentiate between those who are **biographical strangers,** because we have never before met them and have no information about their pasts, and those who are **cultural strangers,** because they occupy symbolic worlds different from our own. We are cautious in the presence of both, those whom we have never met before and those who do not share our values, attitudes, or lifestyles.

Much of a person's time is spent in front of an audience of strangers. Public thoroughfares are crowded with people who are biographical and often cultural strangers to one another. Each time you enter a subway, stand in a line, go jogging in a city park, attend a concert, or shop in a discount store you are in effect performing in front of an audience of people you have never seen before and who, in all likelihood, you will never see again.

When biographical or cultural strangers confront one another, they typically put on a performance which reflects the uncertainties in such encounters. In this chapter we will explore the uncertainties which accompany relations with strangers and the strategies which can be employed to take them into account. Patterned and predictable presentations of self are necessary if individuals are to manage and make sense of their daily lives in public places.

## ■ THE PARADOX OF DOUBT AND TRUST

Social life could not proceed in an orderly fashion if a **norm of trust** did not underlie our behaviors with others (Lewis and Weigert, 1985). By and large, we trust that others' spoken words and actions really represent the kinds of individuals they are. Each day we face situations that demand such trust. For example, in dealing with bank tellers, store clerks, or waitresses, there is a moment when we hand them our money and must trust them to complete the transaction honestly by returning with the proper change. What could you do in a restaurant if the waitress claimed you gave her a $10 rather than a $20 bill? Normally we must, in order to get through the day, trust that others mean us no harm, that we are not being purposely misled in our encounters with them. Social life would be intolerably complicated if we had to routinely suspend the norm of trust.

While trust is essential in order to maintain an ordered social life, there is always some measure of doubt about the true motives, goals, and intentions of others. This is because role-taking efforts can never be perfect; we can never identify absolutely with others. All social interactions, even those between intimates, therefore involve some measure of doubt or risk. Our inability to suspend doubt fully in our social interactions presents the paradox that we must doubt and trust others at the same time. It is true that ordered interaction proceeds on the general assumption of trust, *but we can never be certain that such an assumption is perfectly safe.* James Henslin describes the co-existence of trust and distrust this way:

> Trust is a fundamental aspect of "anyday/everyday life-in-society." We deal with trust all the time. It is with us each day as we go about our regular routines, but it is one of those "taken-for-granted" aspects of "life-in-society" that we seldom analyze. At times we may be sharply aware of our distrust of others and be quite verbal in specifying why. At other times we may be only vaguely aware that we are uneasy and distrustful in the presence of certain persons. (1972:21)

## Uncertainty in Interactions with Strangers

We are most likely to distrust others, as a general rule, when they obviously have different social attributes than we do. An old man who tries to talk to a little girl in a park may well be regarded as a dirty old man, for example, and an unshaven, slovenly man approaching a woman who does not know him on a dark city street could be accused of being a mugger. Those who try to initiate encounters when there are discrepancies in their attributes are likely to find their motives misinterpreted. We depend heavily on immediate observation of others to determine whether we can trust them and whether interaction with them is therefore permissible. We carry around pretty clear expectations about the appropriateness of interactions between people with particular attributes.

Encounters with strangers pose special trust problems because we have no information about them, other than face information, or that which is obtainable through immediate observation. Sometimes a person's general appearance or location can tell us a good deal about them. In the presence of strangers, however, information of this sort is usually incomplete and possibly unreliable. To judge with assurance the genuineness of others' performances and the meaning of their behaviors, we must know about their areas of conversation, as Berger and Kellner (1970) put it. The more we know about others' biographies and life experiences, the better we are able to role-take with them. To illustrate the point, knowing that a woman is diabetic helps us to interpret what she is doing injecting some substance into her arm with a hypodermic needle. If we have knowledge of her biography, the interpretation "maintaining her health" is a far more credible explanation of her behavior than "maintaining her habit."

### *How Cabdrivers Size up Strangers*

The relationship between face information and trust is especially crucial in some interactions with strangers. City cabdrivers, for example, who must be in continual contact with strangers, adopt certain strategies to assess which ones to accept as passengers. Henslin (1972) has documented the informal criteria cabdrivers use in sizing up the trustworthiness of passengers. He conceptualizes trust in dramaturgical terms: "trust consists of an actor offering a definition of himself and an audience being willing to interact with the actor on the basis of that definition" (p. 22). Like everyone else, cabdrivers must determine the conditions under which they have reason to question the performances put on by others. In deciding whether a passenger is to be trusted, they consider: (1) the setting in which the person is picked up, (2) the characteristics of the person as judged by their appearance, and (3) the individual's behavior. In other words, cabdrivers simultaneously consider the characteristics of the *persons* they pick up, the *places* where they pick them up, and the *poses* adopted by their passengers.

Cabdrivers ordinarily accept a person's self-definition as a passenger who wishes to be taken to a particular destination. Sometimes, however, they have reason to distrust a person's performance as a legitimate passenger. Each time a passenger approaches the driver must decide if it is safe to make the trip. The driver's trust judgments are made on the basis of the individual's age, race, general demeanor, and social class; the neighborhood and the time of the day of the pickup; and the announced destination of the passenger. When the configuration of these factors indicates the need for distrust, the prudent driver usually decides to pass up the potential passenger.

The decisions of cabdrivers to trust or distrust a stranger rely heavily on commonly accepted stereotypes about social classes and groups in American society. The results of Henslin's study indicated that drivers expect comparatively less trouble from passengers in upper- and middle-class areas, females, whites, and the very young or very old. Passengers who sit in the rear or directly behind the driver, rather than in the front or diagonally behind, also are more likely to arouse suspicion.

## *The Case for Being Uncertain about Strangers in Public Places*

Mutual strangeness puts limits on people's role-taking capacity and therefore on the ways they can and will relate to each other. The following propositions sum up the reasons why interactions between strangers have a large element of uncertainty in them.

1. There is a measure of uncertainty attached to *any* interaction, since we can never be completely certain of another's motives.
2. The uncertainty of risk decreases as we acquire more information about others, since the accuracy of our role-taking increases.
3. Strangers in public places possess no biographical information about each other.

4. It follows that public relations between strangers carry particularly great uncertainties.

## ■ THE STRUCTURE OF EVERYDAY PUBLIC BEHAVIORS

Public behaviors seldom require more than a passing acquaintance, and strangers typically confront each other in highly anonymous situations.* While the ability to remain anonymous increases the potential for individual freedom of action, it does not decrease the constraints imposed on individual behaviors by society. In fact, anonymity must be created

*This section is based on material in David A. Karp, Gregory P. Stone, and William C. Yoels, *Being Urban: A Social Psychological View of City Life* (Lexington, Mass.: D. C. Heath, 1977).

### Pedestrians and Other Strangers: Avoiding a Collision Course

When you walk down a busy city sidewalk, common courtesy demands that you do not push or shove others or rush headlong into passing pedestrians. The tactics you use to avoid such behaviors, however, are seldom the result of conscious decisions. You would have to observe the interactions from some vantage point in order to interpret your movements and those of the others on the scene.

Michael Wolff (1973) set up a videotape camera on a building on 42nd Street in New York City in order to study how pedestrian behavior is orchestrated and coordinated. Analysis of these tapes indicated that "the most outstanding characteristic of pedestrian behavior that has emerged is the amount and degree of *cooperation* between persons on the streets of the city" (p. 48). The research showed a number of consistent patterns of accommodation made by passersby on the sidewalk. Among these were the following:

*The step-and-slide.* As people pass one another, they do not try to totally avoid physical contact. There is a "slight angling of the body, a turning of the shoulder and an almost imperceptible sidestep—a sort of step-and-slide." While pedestrians do not make a totally clean pass, they cooperate with one another by pulling their hands inward and twisting their bodies so as to minimize the amount of physical contact. As a test of the operation of the step-and-slide the experimenters purposely did not cooperate. Wolff says the pedestrians responded with such comments as "Watsa madder? Ya blind? Whyn't ya look whea ya going? Ya crazy?"

and maintained through social relationships, and this is itself a social effort. Rather than being a state which is independent of social relationships, therefore, anonymity must be produced by people interacting with one another. The structure of public behaviors between strangers is reinforced by efforts to maintain the **norm of anonymity.**

One way to study the structure of everyday public behavior is to challenge the norms guiding it and observe how people behave when their normal routines are disrupted. Research which combines careful, naturalistic observation and the purposive manipulation of social settings can reveal a great deal about how everyday life is constructed, ordered, and typically carried off. This is demonstrated, for example, in studies on pedestrian behavior which have shown how strangers in anonymous street situations take each other into account (see box).

---

*The head-over-the-shoulder pattern.* When walking behind a person less than 5 feet away, a pedestrian tries to see "over the shoulder" of the person in front. This accommodation serves two purposes. It allows individuals to see clearly what is occurring in front of them and makes it less likely that they will stumble into the feet of those in front.

*The spread effect.* In order to maximize efficiency on the street, people walking in one direction on a sidewalk distribute themselves to the fullest width that the natural boundaries will allow.

*Detouring.* Pedestrians forced to detour around an object or person attempt to regain their original path once the detour has been accomplished.

*Avoiding perceptual objects.* People tend to treat perceptually distinct parts of the pavement, such as a grating, as obstructions to be avoided or circumnavigated when possible.

*Monitoring.* Pedestrians are continually monitoring the environment in order to avoid collisions as well as to evaluate the potential behaviors of others. They take into account the expressions of those approaching them on the street, for example. If the oncoming pedestrians appear to be fixating in the same direction and, more important, are expressing surprise, fear, or general excitement, this is taken to be a cue to make a full head turn, stop for a full checkout, or both. In this sense, pedestrians use other pedestrians as a "rear-view" mirror.

Thus pedestrians' movements, a set of behaviors which we largely take for granted, are really quite well organized. In this case the norm of anonymity is supplemented by a distinctive norm of cooperation among strangers.

## Efforts to Remain Anonymous

When Michael Wolff (1973) studied pedestrian behaviors on 42nd Street in New York City, his goal was to uncover the social conventions ordering this commonplace behavior in an anonymous situation. His research was conducted on one of the busiest sidewalks in the country, those bordering 42nd Street in New York City. A male or female experimenter approached pedestrians on a direct collision course under one of two conditions: low density, with 5 to 15 people in the immediate vicinity, or high density, with 16 to 30 people in the area.

Wolff was primarily interested in discovering the yield distance, at which those approached would alter their course in order to avoid colliding with the experimenter. He found that there were very significant regularities in the behaviors of those approached. Under low-density conditions, they consistently yielded at a distance of about 7 feet, and in high-density conditions they yielded at about 5 feet. When the experimenter was the same sex as the approaching person, the yield distance was slightly shorter than when their sexes differed. In another variation of this experiment, a stationary object was placed on the sidewalk so pedestrians had to detour around it. In this situation they began to alter their course and prepare to get around the object at a considerably greater distance—16.5 feet.

Systematic observation of behaviors in subways also has shown how people indicate they do not wish to be communicated with (Levine, Vinson, and Wood, 1973). In this face-to-face situation a premium is placed on avoiding unnecessary encounters. As in many other public contexts, individuals engage in what Erving Goffman (1963) has described as **civil inattention** when they are forced to recognize others' presence while trying to minimize the possibility of a "focused" interaction with them. In other words, they try to minimize the interactional claims that others might make on them.

This interactional effort is, of course, reciprocal, as all the individuals in the situation are doing the same thing. Subway passengers choose seats that maximize their distance from fellow travelers. They limit their visual attention to props that they may have with them (books, magazines, newspapers) or to advertising over the windows; they take great pains to avoid physical contact once the subway car begins to get crowded, and the like. These regulations, shared and known about by all participants, are designed to limit the accessibility of unacquainted individuals to one another.

## Efforts to Assure Public Privacy

The order of public life is clearly demonstrated in situations where a person's moral identity is called into question. David Karp (1973) studied the behaviors of customers of pornographic bookstores and movie theaters in Times Square, the ultimate example of the anonymous public place. He found that the people engaging in unconventional behaviors in a typically anonymous sector of the city were quite concerned with being considered social or proper, even by total strangers. The individuals were not engaged in direct verbal interaction, but they were very much taking each other into account.

Karp describes a number of strategies employed in these settings to assure a kind of **public privacy.** Once in the store, shoppers maintain a strict impersonality toward one another. Under no circumstances do they make physical or verbal contact, and the clerks quickly eject anyone who interferes with the privacy of other customers. The normative structure appears to demand silence and careful avoidance of any focused interaction.

Patterns of behaviors also are engaged in by purchasers of pornographic materials. Customers adopt techniques that allow them to complete their purchases as quickly and unobtrusively as possible. They are more likely to make a purchase if left alone. A store manager described how customers look, without touching, at the "highline," a long table in the middle of the room on which are displayed the most current, most expensive items:

> These guys make a circle around the table, never touching anything. Then they go to the back of the store and spend a little time there. They aren't really interested in what's in the back. On their way out they make their selections . . . 1, 2, 3, 4, 5. You can't say a word to these guys or you will lose a sale. (Karp, 1973:442)

The goal of the maneuvers clearly is to minimize the amount of time that must be spent in making the purchase. In this way customers appear as uninterested as possible.

Such settings encourage a highly structured social situation in which privacy norms are standardized and readily understood. The system works so that each person's bid for privacy is complemented by the behaviors of others in the store. Even in anonymous public places such as Times Square, people are very much constrained in the production of their behaviors. Despite the impersonality and anonymity of daily life, and despite the fact that actions in the public domain are overwhelmingly performed in front of strangers, it is necessary to constantly engage in impression management. When it comes to maintaining a proper image of ourselves, everyone else counts.

## Abiding by the Rules

Another situation where strangers adopt elaborate strategies in order to maintain a distinctive public privacy is in sexual encounters between homosexuals. In a book entitled *Tearoom Trade* (1970), Laud Humphreys analyzed the behaviors of homosexuals meeting in public toilets (known as "tearooms"). He describes these settings as well-organized places where the participants strictly abide by the rules. The activities of approaching the room, positioning oneself inside it, signaling one's availability, contracting for the nature of the sexual exchange, completing the sexual act, coping with intrusions, and finally leaving the situation are carefully patterned. Nearly all of these negotiations occur without any verbal interaction between the participants.

The importance of Humphreys's study goes far beyond description of the particular behaviors he documented. The fact that these kinds of behaviors can be accomplished at all serves as a broader commentary on the orderliness of everyday public activities. In Humphreys's words:

> Analysis of the highly structured patterns that arise in this particular situation increases our understanding of the more general rules of interaction by which people in routine encounters of all kinds manage their identities, create impressions, move towards their goals, and control information about themselves, minimizing the costs and risks in concerted action with others. (1970:ix)

### Step by Step to Interactions with Strangers

When you first arrived on campus in the midst of a crowd of strangers, you no doubt were aware of the impression of yourself you were presenting. The orientation period for new students is a unique setting in which the techniques of self-management must be quickly mastered under the scrutiny of others. You may not have been aware, however, of the pattern of behaviors you were following in your interactions with others in the planned events and casual encounters of that experience.

Lyn Lofland (1971a) found a step-by-step pattern of behaviors when she studied the strategies used by strangers in public places. The three steps followed in routine encounters are:

*Step 1: Checking for readiness.* People prepare themselves before en-

## Impression Management with Strangers

The patterns of behavior followed in the situations described above not only maintain the norm of anonymity and assure public privacy. They also are designed to protect personal identities, minimize social risk, and give the appearance of propriety. Thus they are examples of the impression management techniques people use to foster particular images of themselves in their interactions with others (see Chapter 3). They also are examples of the **self-management** techniques people use to control the identities of themselves that they present to others and to protect their selves when in the presence of strangers.

The self-management techniques used by strangers in their everyday interactions were studied by Lyn Lofland. She takes an interactionist perspective with the assertion that "If a person is to exist as a social being, as an organism with a self, there must be some minimal guarantees that in interaction with others he will receive the affirmation and confirmation of himself as 'right' " (1971a:95). The risk for the self in confronting strangers in public places is that they may be unable to provide this confirmation. An encounter with a stranger may even *disconfirm* the other person's "rightness."

As we noted at the beginning of this chapter, the uncertainties which result when strangers interact stems from their lack of knowledge about one another. Lofland is concerned with the ways people compensate for these uncertainties in their everyday experiences (see box).

---

tering a potential encounter situation by checking their appearance, making sure their hair is in place, their clothes are in order, and so on.

*Step 2: Taking a reading.* People essentially stop to take stock of the social setting. They may briefly delay entering a room until they have had a chance to scan it with their eyes, noting the placement of furniture and the like.

*Step 3: Reaching a position.* The final step in this sequence is to reach a stopping point. People seek to enter the situation as inconspicuously as possible—to minimize the time they are under the social spotlight. Once having decided on the spot or territory they wish to occupy, they may make a no-nonsense, direct approach or approach slowly and by degrees, stopping briefly at various points until the destination is reached.

There are also patterns to the self-management styles adopted by people once they have positioned themselves in a public setting (Lofland, 1971b). In a setting such as a waiting room or a bus stop, people characteristically assume a posture which closes them off from interaction with others, such as refusing to make eye contact or making a little movement away from the spot they have chosen. At the beach, many people choose a particular spot to nest in, spreading their belongings

## The State of Involved Indifference

In their efforts to maintain anonymity and protect public privacy, strangers in public places adopt elaborate strategies to avoid one another. This does not mean that they are entirely uninvolved with one another, however. Strangers in public places also adopt mechanisms to produce ordered relationships. Even the **avoidance behaviors** engaged in by strangers is a highly coordinated social activity which demands some degree of cooperation. To suggest that humans are like atoms anonymously floating around each other at random is not a very satisfying description of the public relationships of strangers. It fails to account for the means by which public life is managed and ordered. While strangers rarely talk with one another or exchange information of a private nature, it is nevertheless clear that public life is ordered rather than chaotic.

The authors of this book suggest that there is a fragile balance between noninvolvement and cooperation in the structure of public relationships. Strangers try to avoid involvement with others in order to protect themselves from unwanted and risky encounters. At the same time, they orient their behaviors toward others and cooperate enough to ensure some degree of order and sense in their everyday lives. Like the pedestrians on the sidewalk, they systematically take each other into account in public places in order to avoid unwanted encounters.

In sum, we are offering a mini-max description of public encounters. Strangers are obliged both to *minimize involvement* and *maximize order*. They must take each other into account while simultaneously protecting their own and others' privacy. The idea of **involved indifference** as a basis for interactions with strangers may seem contradictory. We use this term to communicate that although strangers may not engage in direct verbal interactions, they nevertheless produce their behaviors from a careful assessment of those around them. Everyday public life "works" because of the subtle blending of involvement, indifference, and cooperation that is produced in public places.

around in a way that marks off their territorial boundaries. At a college mixer or in a singles' bar, a common strategy is to investigate the setting by moving around but being careful not to offer strangers an invitation for social interaction. Such self-management techniques become almost unconscious responses to the implied threat of encounters with strangers. They allow individuals to keep distance between themselves and others and help maintain the order of public encounters.

## ■ THE CITY AS A WORLD OF STRANGERS

The volume of contacts between strangers is greatest in anonymous city places.* According to Lofland, "The urbanite, whenever he ventures forth into the public sector of the city, is . . . plunged into a world peopled by many strangers and alien others" (1973:97).

### The Volume of Interactions in Cities

By definition, cities are places where large numbers of individuals with varied backgrounds live crowded together in a limited space. Urban areas are no longer limited to cities, however. They include the surrounding towns and suburbs in metropolitan areas and megalopolises, in which several adjacent cities are merged. Along the East Coast, for example, an unbroken metropolitan area with more than 100 people per square mile stretches from Kittery, Maine, to Quantico, Virginia. This megalopolis of over 40 million people, popularly known as Boswash, includes the cities of Boston, New York, Philadelphia, Baltimore, and Washington, D.C.

American society has become predominantly urban—it was 73.7 percent urban (places of 2,500 or more) and 26.3 percent rural in 1980, according to the Census Bureau (U.S. Bureau of the Census, 1983, Table 26). With modern transportation and communication, very few small towns are still considered rural. In large cities, however, the density of the urban population greatly increases the number of possible contacts between persons. Around New York City, for example, the number of people encountered in a 10-minute walking distance varies from 11,000 in Nassau County, to 20,000 in Newark, New Jersey, to 220,000 in midtown Manhattan (Palen, 1975). In midtown Manhattan you probably

---

*The discussion on urban relationships draws on David A. Karp, Gregory P. Stone, and William C. Yoels, *Being Urban: A Social Psychological View of City Life* (Lexington, Mass.: D. C. Heath, 1977).

would not know intimately any of the thousands of people who would pass you by.

Social scientists have constructed explanations of everyday interactions based on the volume of potential interactions in anonymous urban settings. Georg Simmel argued that because urban dwellers are bombarded with far more stimuli than they can possibly manage, they must maintain superficial, impersonal relationships with fellow urbanites. He contrasts urban and rural life in this respect:

> With each crossing of the street, with the tempo and multiplicity of economic, occupational and social life, the city sets up a deep contrast with small town and rural life with reference to the sensory foundation of psychic life. The metropolis exacts from man as a discriminating creature a different amount of consciousness than does rural life. Here [in rural life] the rhythm of life and sensory mental imagery flows more slowly, more habitually and more evenly. . . . [T]he sophisticated character of metropolitan psychic life becomes more understandable as over against small town life which rests upon deeply felt and emotional relationships. (Simmel, 1950a:410)

For Simmel, a central difference between the resident of the metropolis and the resident of the small town is the former's more *rational* response to the world. In his essay "The Metropolis and Mental Life" he described the urban person as reacting "with his head instead of his heart." In order to cope with the shower of highly varied stimuli characterizing urban life, individuals must be selective in terms of the stimuli to which they will respond. As the social psychologist Stanley Milgram (1970) put it, urban persons, facing **stimulus overload,** must develop very clear norms of noninvolvement.

### Somebody Ought to Do Something . . .

An incident which took place over 20 years ago has been widely publicized as an example of the apathy and indifference of city people and their failure to get involved when help is needed. Kitty Genovese, returning to her home in Queens, New York, shortly after 3:00 a.m., was attacked by an assailant with a knife. In response to her screams, "Oh my God, he stabbed me! Please help me!" lights went on in a number of apartments and people peered out. One man called out, "Let that girl alone!" But no one called the police, though 38 people later testified that

## Behaviors in Urban Settings: Selectivity and Noninvolvement

Because of the stimulus overload and the constant presence of biographical strangers in urban public places, urbanites must learn to set priorities for the events and persons to which they will pay attention. Certain situations, in fact, become effectively invisible. Few people passing through an inner-city area pay much attention to the homeless down-and-outers on the street. They cannot, because if they stopped to get help for every such person they could accomplish little else. Milgram observes that the **norm of noninvolvement** is so strong in relationships between strangers that "men are actually embarrassed to give up a seat on a subway to an old woman" (1970:1464).

Urbanites also use mechanisms to block off or filter out certain encounters with strangers before they have a chance to occur. Living in an apartment house with a uniformed attendant to monitor who goes into and out of the building and having an unlisted phone number are two ways to do this.

The mechanisms of selectivity and noninvolvement adopted by city dwellers in their daily interactions in a world of strangers are sometimes used as an explanation for their alleged detachment in public relationships. The popular stereotype of urbanites is that they are cold, indifferent, brusque, and generally uncaring. We question whether people who live in the city really have colder personalities than those who live in the country, however. The often-cited failure of people in the city to offer help to someone in trouble has been found to be due less to their indifference than to the **diffusion of responsibility** that results when there are many bystanders who *might* intervene (see box).

---

they had heard her screams. The attacker was scared off but returned twice to finish the murder.

The assumption that these bystanders had failed to intervene because of their alienation or apathy to urban life was challenged by two sociologists, John Darley and Bibb Latané. They conducted laboratory experiments in which the participants were led to believe that someone was being victimized or in trouble and then their offers to help—or failure to offer it—were observed. Darley and Latané's results were summarized in a book entitled *The Unresponsive Bystander: Why Doesn't He Help?* (1970).

In one of their ingeniously conceived studies (Darley and Latané, 1968), participants were placed in separate rooms and allowed to communicate only by microphone. In this way they could hear other study volunteers but could not see them. At some point the investigators played a recorded, staged tape of a person experiencing an epileptic seizure. The study participants believed the person heard on the tape was another volunteer. In one experimental variation each person was led to believe that she or he alone had heard the seizure. In other cases everyone was made to believe that a number of others also heard the individual in trouble. The findings confirmed that subjects were far more likely to help when they thought no one else had heard the incident. Indeed, the greater the number of persons who were thought to have heard it, the less likely each individual was to help.

---

Interactionists, in fact, question the existence of unique rural and urban personality types as an explanation of behavior. They believe instead that people everywhere respond more coolly and with greater distrust to others they do not know. Any observed differences in the public behaviors of urban and rural residents can be understood in relation to the fact that urbanites are confronted much more often by strangers. As Milgram says, "Contrast between city and rural behavior probably reflects the responses of similar people to very different situations rather than intrinsic differences in the personalities of rural and city dwellers. The city is a situation to which persons respond adaptively" (1970:1465).

While there is a situational basis for public behaviors, in most situations urbanites abide by the norms of noninvolvement. They rarely implicate themselves in each others' public lives. Strangers in public places appear, by and large, to avoid one another. In most public settings in American society we close ourselves off from interaction with others. We typically avoid excessive eye contact since we do not want to encourage others to talk to us. We make use of such portable props as newspapers to insulate ourselves from those around us. We try to maximize our personal space as we travel on buses, sit in waiting rooms or theaters, stand in lines, or simply walk along the street. Indeed, most of our interactions are brief and highly impersonal. They are interactions constructed around a question asked and an answer given, an accidental bump and an "I'm sorry." These are, we might say, interactions without a "career." They have no past and virtually no possibility of a future. We can understand these patterns of avoidance in terms of the need for

These and similar studies by Darley and Latané offer strong support for the proposition that the *more* bystanders there are in an emergency, the *less* likely any one bystander is to intervene to provide aid. Each person, aware that others are witnessing the event, assumes that one or more of these others will take the responsibility to intervene. The result of this "pluralistic ignorance" is that no one steps forward. Darley and Latané suggest that this is how Kitty Genovese could have been murdered while others listened and looked on. It also helps explain how smashing windows of women motorists and grabbing their purses in full view of a crowd of onlookers, or extorting gradeschoolers' lunch money on a busy playground can become everyday interactions for some ghetto youths.

---

city dwellers to protect themselves from stimulus overload and the uncertainties of interactions with strangers.

## Tolerance for Strange Lifestyles

The city not only provides the most opportunities for contacts with biographical strangers. It also is the context in which individuals are likely to have the most contact with cultural strangers, or members of groups which do not share their beliefs, attitudes, ideologies, or values. An urban society supports a great diversity of class, ethnic, racial and **alternate lifestyle groups** such as homosexuals or the drug culture. In managing their involvements with one another, members of culturally different groups must take into account the uncertainties and intolerance that arise when information about others is biased or incomplete.

There are many instances of intolerance in cities. Political groups quarrel, homosexuals face discrimination, and racial conflicts flare up. Around certain issues, whether in rural or urban areas, it is difficult for groups to sustain a tolerant attitude toward other groups they have defined as adversaries. This is especially so where the members of a group perceive, correctly or incorrectly, that their economic interests are threatened. Such a perception is a dominant factor in the animosity between the ethnic and racial groups that abound in the city. When whites see blacks climbing the socioeconomic ladder, they may fear that they will be displaced in jobs and put at a disadvantage in the competition for scarce resources.

The city also fosters tolerance for differences in behavior and group lifestyles, however. Urban people are comparatively more sophisticated about lifestyle diversity. Robert Park, an early urban sociologist, commented that while the small community tolerates eccentricity, the city rewards it: "Neither the criminal, the defective, nor the genius has the same opportunity to develop his innate disposition in a small town that he invariably finds in a great city" (1925:41).

## Social Contracts among Groups

Evidence that urban tolerance is based on a specific type of interaction between members of different groups was found in a study of San Francisco lifestyles by Howard Becker and Irving Horowitz (1972). They suggest that members of diverse groups strike a silent unwritten bargain, a kind of social contract. The essence of this bargain is that members of a minority group will moderate their behaviors in certain ways to make them acceptable to the other groups around them. There are implicitly agreed-upon behavioral boundaries beyond which the several groups "promise" not to go.

According to Becker and Horowitz, each group seeks to maximize its opportunities for a peaceful, free, ordered life. In order to accomplish this, members of different groups learn to keep their moral and value judgments to themselves. They do not try to impose their own behavior standards and values on each other. It is a true reciprocity, as each group is willing to give something up in order to maximize social order. The police do not break up congregated groups on street corners, and members of these groups police themselves to prevent behaviors that could be interpreted as troublesome, for example. An accommodation is developed between the police and group members.

There is an element of self-fulfilling prophecy in such a social contract. As different urban groups conform to the agreement and work together, they begin to recognize the inaccuracy of the stereotypes and images of each other they may have held. There is a socialization process which helps members of the conventional community understand that gay persons are not child molesters, for example. The level of civility toward the different groups in the city increases, and the city becomes known as a desirable location for those who want freedom for their personal lifestyles. Such individuals gravitate toward the city as a place where they will be relatively unharassed and their behaviors will be less likely to be considered erratic or undesirable. The result is greater tolerance in the city.

Becker and Horowitz apparently have only a *positive* notion of tolerance, however. They imply that tolerance exists in cities because the different groups involved consciously value it and agree to ensure it. While this is undeniably often so, it may equally be the case that tolerance in cities is a by-product of avoidance. That is, city people may develop social procedures that minimize the probability that they will come into intimate contact with those with whom they do not agree.

## The Spatial Ordering of City Activities

Social ecologists provide a picture of the city in which different groups are segregated and have little contact with one another. There are clear territorial groupings composed of persons with similar characteristics, such as homosexuality or various national backgrounds, who restrict their activities to well-defined areas.

In this view there is a **spatial ordering** to city activities (LaGory and Pipkin, 1981). Properly socialized urbanites know that certain types of persons will be found in specific areas of the city. According to Lofland (1973:69), people learn about "the meaning of locations, about what is expected to go on where and who is expected to be doing it." They can choose to be in areas of the city where they will come into contact with people engaging in certain behaviors or practicing different lifestyles, or they can choose to avoid such contact. They have, in other words, **controlled contact** with various lifestyles or marginal groups. If, for example, they want to avoid contact with prostitutes or those selling pornography, they can simply avoid those areas of the city where such persons are likely to be found.

Tolerance is contingent on this controlled contact. The spatial segregation of groups and activities provides a comforting predictability in encounters with cultural strangers. It follows that tolerance is likely to break down when the conditions for controlled contact are not met. A public clamor is likely when members of certain groups begin to appear in areas where they "don't belong." In many cities, for example, a section of the downtown area is informally designated as an "adult entertainment area." Those who earn their living by supplying sexual services are pretty much left alone as long as they restrict their activities to the designated area.

Of course, we do not always wish to avoid those whom we perceive as having unusual lifestyles. We may welcome the opportunity to observe the behaviors of cultural strangers or to participate in ethnic or neighborhood festivals. Every city has certain public parks or areas where representatives of a range of lifestyles and social types can come into contact and become familiar with one another. Ruth Love (1973) analyzed why so many people frequent a particular park in Portland, Oregon, which attracts a wide diversity of persons, for example. "People watching" was given as a reason for going to the park by about half of all visitors.

The spatial ordering of activities in cities allows urbanites to maintain a limited level of intimacy with cultural strangers. By being able to control the place and timing of contacts with others and by knowing what kinds of behaviors to expect of people in different city areas, they can monitor the extent of their involvement with cultural strangers.

## ■ ESTABLISHING RELATIONSHIPS WITH STRANGERS

While the city provides a setting in which strangers can protect themselves from the intrusion of others, too much emphasis can be placed on their lack of direct interaction with one another. There are occasions when strangers come together and freely interact. There are situations in which people can begin to dissolve the strangeness between them. The usual conception of risk and uncertainty in interactions with strangers can be reduced in certain circumstances.

### Effects of Social Settings and Situations

As casual observation indicates, strangers are more likely to meet and begin relationships in some settings or situations than in others. In some settings, such as cocktail parties, such meetings are very likely, and in others, such as bus stops, they are very unlikely. Between these extremes there is a range of contexts where the likelihood of strangers meeting is greater or less (classrooms, ballgames, plays, laundromats, and so forth). Why is it easier for strangers at a baseball game to strike up conversations than those in, say, an elevator? To answer this question we will briefly consider the effects of settings, contexts, or situations on interactions with strangers.

Settings cannot be defined only in physical terms. A bookstore is a place with a lot of books, salespersons, a cash register, and so forth, but such a description would not capture the distinction between a college bookstore and a pornographic bookstore. Even if someone were to describe the contents of the books, we would not fully appreciate how the two places differ. A more accurate way to define these places would be in terms of the social conventions governing the nature of the interactions that occur in them.

## Definitions of Behaviors

We cannot understand the meaning of another's behavior without considering the setting in which it occurs. For example, in order to assign a meaning to the behavior of one person striking another with a fist, we would have to know whether it happens in a neighborhood bar, the middle of Times Square, or a ring in Madison Square Garden. The very same behavior can assume quite different meanings in different places.

We tend to excuse others for acting improperly with the explanation that they have never been in the situation before. In essence, we are saying, "He should be excused because he does not know the rules here. He does not know the meaning his behavior carries in this setting." More directly still, "He thinks he knows the meaning of his behavior, and he is correct that it is the meaning of his behavior somewhere else, but he does not know that the same behavior carries a different meaning here." We also use the phrase "acting out of place" to describe an impropriety. The immigrant who acts out of place is, in this respect, the prototype of the cultural stranger.

Extraordinary events can change the character of settings. When the normal character of a setting becomes abnormal, or an ordinary setting becomes somehow extraordinary, and all involved recognize that fact, definitions of behavior change. It may be perfectly appropriate to begin conversations where ordinarily this would be considered improper. Conversations between strangers become allowable in stalled subway trains or elevators or when motorists are stuck in traffic, for example. Goffman notes that:

During occasions of recognized natural disaster, when individuals suddenly find themselves in a clearly similar predicament and suddenly become mutually dependent for information and help, ordinary communication constraints can break down. . . . What is occurring in the situation guarantees that encounters aren't being initiated for what can be improperly gained by them. And to the extent that this is assured, contact prohibitions can break down. (1963:36)

## Information about Others

The context of a situation not only provides information which helps define the meaning of behavior. It also may indicate certain aspects of individuals' identities or details of their biographies which can make it easier to initiate interactions. Sometimes a person's mere presence in a setting gives out a good deal of information about that person. When you encounter a group of strangers in a university classroom you can safely assume a good deal about them, such as their social class and values. Seeing a crowd of people standing on a street corner waiting for a red light to change would tell you very little about such strangers, however.

The difference that the social setting or context makes in an interaction is related to the amount of information it provides about the individuals taking part (see Chapter 3). Some contexts provide more information about those in them than others do. In fact, an anonymous place can be thought of as one that provides little or no information about the people in it. *The likelihood of strangers meeting and beginning interactions is greatest in those settings that provide the most information.* The more information we possess about another, the more easily and correctly we can assess whether those with whom we begin a transaction will reciprocate in an acceptable fashion. Some settings give off enough information about the persons in them to substantially reduce the uncertainties normally accompanying interactions with strangers.

## How Strangers Meet

Once people decide to begin an interaction, they must find some way to initiate it. In the usual case, talk is preceded by a series of nonverbal gestures indicating the individuals' openness to interaction. This preparatory stage preceding verbal interaction is in effect a risk-reducing mechanism. Without directly committing themselves to an interaction, people use nonverbal communications to obtain a reading of others' willingness to respond. At this stage the level of their involvement is very slight, and if their own gestures are not positively responded to, they may gracefully discontinue their invitational efforts.

People who want to engage in interaction can let this be known with various types of nonverbal gestures. In full view of those around them and in a quite deliberate fashion, they may make a point of removing territorial markers (clothes, books, and so forth) from areas close to them. Thus they indicate that their personal space will not be violated should someone choose to approach them. They may engage others in eye contact and smile, or make a show of not being involved in any activity that demands all of their attention.

On occasion, people go beyond these purely nonverbal gestures by making statements aloud, ostensibly to themselves but clearly directed to those around them. The following report of an occurrence in a laundromat is a typical example:

> One girl sat down next to me and started biting her nails. A few minutes later she opened a textbook of New Testament something or other and flipped through it. She put the book down, as if really bored with it, and she got up and read the notices on the wall. Then she blurted out to no one in particular "They (the machines) take forever."

Another laundromat conversation began this way:

> I sat down next to a guy who was reading something and I began reading an essay in *Time* magazine. Every once in a while this fellow would start to laugh out loud to himself. At one point he started to laugh very hard.
> "All right *now*, what's so funny? What are you reading?"
> "*Finnegan's Wake*. It's so full of puns. . . ."

According to the norm of noninvolvement, the usual procedure for strangers in public places is to communicate systematically that they do not wish to become involved in an interaction. These kinds of nonverbal and verbal initiatives, which are also based on the commonly understood rules of noninvolvement, are designed to communicate just the opposite. They communicate to others an openness for interaction. When these moves for opening up interaction succeed, they do so precisely because the procedures for closing oneself off from interaction are so widely used and understood.

When conversations are begun, very ordinary issues such as weather, work, traffic, or the price of food are typical opening topics. No one can pretend ignorance of such things. People are normally constrained to respond when such issues have been raised, and just mentioning them is taken as an indication of openness for interaction. These openings are specifically used and understood as ritualized throwaway lines whose only purpose is to initiate conversation. Such topics also serve as vehicles for probing the willingness of others to engage in conversation. Should they decline, their reluctance can be communicated without personally discrediting or embarrassing those making the probe.

One strategy for those who wish to begin an encounter is to make things go wrong purposely. People may pretend to be lost when they are not; they may show puzzlement about what is happening around them; or they may purposely bump into another person, so some kind of remedial interaction is necessary. These strategies are used to create a situation where the ordinary becomes extraordinary and interaction is more acceptable.

## ■ CONCLUSION

The manner in which people manage their public encounters is determined by the fact that public places are almost exclusively populated by persons who are strangers to one another. They are biographical strangers who know nothing of each others' pasts, cultural strangers because they live in different social worlds, or both. Relationships between strangers pose special role-taking problems which make them uniquely risky and uncertain.

Every interaction carries a measure of uncertainty and risk. There is the chance that the images a person presents to others will be found unacceptable or that events will cast an unfavorable light on the individual. It also is never possible to be absolutely sure of others' attitudes, goals, and motives. The probability of doubt is greater in public encounters, since strangers, as they try to role-take, must rely solely on information they can acquire through observation. Sometimes this face information is sufficient to persuade individuals that they can or cannot, should or should not, try to communicate directly with others. More typically, though, it is recognized as an incomplete basis for making these decisions.

City dwellers are confronted with public situations in which the number of potential encounters with strangers is enormous. They adapt to the volume of possible contacts and the role-taking problems inherent in urban relationships by structuring their public lives in ways designed to minimize the chances of unpleasant or unwanted encounters. More important, they adopt norms of noninvolvement that insulate them from unnecessary contact with strangers.

People in anonymous public settings adopt certain strategies to communicate their desire to maintain public privacy. Avoidance behaviors do not fully explain the complexity of ordered public life, however. People also are constrained to follow the norm of anonymity. They mutually orient their behaviors in order to construct a situation in which others' actions are intelligible, their own self-images are protected, and risky contacts are reduced. In public life, people seek to maximize order while minimizing involvement with others. They create a delicate balance between indifference and cooperation in their public transactions.

Unacquainted persons may also adopt strategies to open up interactions. In some contexts, people relax their noninvolvement stance, enjoy communicating with others, and begin to establish long-lasting relationships. Situations vary in their capacity to support relationships among strangers.

Strangers comprise only one part of our social worlds, however. Relationships with strangers stand at one end of an interaction continuum, with intimate relationships characterized by deep commitment and trust at the other end. As Stanford Lyman and Marvin Scott have observed, a relationship is not established completely until the individuals involved "reciprocally regard one another as persons whom they know 'fully' and for whom they have sincere affection, deep trust, and broad commitment" (1970:48). In the next chapter we will explore the processes involved in the transformation of strangeness to intimacy.

# Definitions

**Marginal man.** A person who participates in the social activities of two different social groups without identifying completely with either group. A marginal person in a society is a stranger.

**Areas of conversation.** Topics of mutual interest to both participants. The participants also share a common understanding of the meaning of such topics.

**Biographical strangers.** Persons who have no knowledge of one another's life histories.

**Cultural strangers.** Persons who have no shared frameworks for interpreting social reality. They occupy different symbolic worlds.

**Norm of trust.** A shared expectation that others will act in the ways we expect them to, and vice versa.

**Norm of anonymity.** A shared expectation that individuals will not intrude on each other's privacy.

**Civil inattention.** The act of appearing to be uninvolved in the affairs of others. Individuals engage in this behavior when they are forced to recognize the presence of others but want to avoid interaction with them.

**Public privacy.** A situation in which strangers in public places try to maintain a strict impersonality in their interactions with one another.

**Self-management.** The manner in which individuals present themselves to others. With self-management techniques, people try to match the identities they present to others with the expectations others have of them.

**Avoidance behaviors.** The ways in which strangers seek to avoid involving themselves in the affairs of others.

**Involved indifference.** A way of taking others' presence into account but avoiding intrusion in their affairs. Strangers are obliged to minimize involvement while they maximize public order.

**Stimulus overload.** Bombardment with more stimuli than people can possibly respond to. Urbanites must develop very clear norms of noninvolvement to deal with the excess of stimuli they encounter.

**Norm of noninvolvement.** A shared expectation that strangers will not intrude on the activities of one another.

**Diffusion of responsibility.** A phenomenon of behavior whereby no member of a group is regarded as clearly responsible for taking action in a situation which seems to demand it.

**Alternate lifestyle groups.** Groups whose members exhibit a lifestyle which differs in significant ways from that adopted in mainstream, conventional society.

**Spatial ordering.** The ways in which various groups are associated with particular geographic areas. In the city, certain types of people and activities can be found in certain neighborhoods.

**Controlled contact.** The manner in which members of one group regulate the contact they have with members of other groups.

# Discussion Questions

1. How do you interpret the authors' claim that we must simultaneously doubt and trust others as we interact with them? Would social life be impossible if it were not rooted in a general norm of trust? Under what conditions do you become most distrustful of others?

2. Suppose you are asked to try establishing a relationship with a stranger. In what settings would you find it easiest to do this? In what kinds of settings would you be unwilling to try meeting someone? Why? What characteristics or attributes of an-

other would make a difference in your willingness to approach them? Why? What would you consider the biggest risks in carrying out such an assignment?

3. Do you think there is such a thing as a distinctive urban personality?

4. Describe some of the techniques you use to protect your privacy in public places. To what extent do you take others into account in formulating your own behaviors, even though you have no direct verbal communication with them?

5. Do you feel that cities provide greater freedom to practice unusual lifestyles than small towns do? If so, what is it about cities that fosters greater tolerance for strange lifestyles? When is such tolerance most likely to break down?

6. What behaviors can you think of that would constitute transgressions of noninvolvement norms in anonymous settings? How do you imagine people would react to such rule infractions?

# References

Becker, H., and I. Horowitz. 1972. *Culture and Civility in San Francisco.* New Brunswick, N.J.: Transaction Books.

Berger, P., and H. Kellner. 1970. "The social construction of marriage." In *Recent Sociology*, ed. H. P. Dreitzel. Toronto: Collier Macmillan.

Darley, J., and B. Latané. 1968. "Bystander intervention in emergencies: Diffusion of responsibility." *Journal of Personality and Social Psychology* 8:377–383.

Darley, J., and B. Latané. 1970. *The Unresponsive Bystander: Why Doesn't He Help?* New York: Appleton-Century-Crofts.

Goffman, E. 1963. *Behavior in Public Places.* New York: Free Press.

Henslin, J. 1972. "What makes for trust?" In *Down to Earth Sociology*, ed. J. Henslin. New York: Free Press.

Humphreys, L. 1970. *Tearoom Trade.* Chicago: Aldine.

Karp, D. 1973. "Hiding in pornographic bookstores: A reconsideration of the nature of urban anonymity." *Urban Life and Culture* 4 (January):427–451.

Karp, D., G. Stone, and W. Yoels. 1977. *Being Urban: A Social Psychological View of City Life.* Lexington, Mass.: D.C. Heath.

LaGory, M., and J. Pipkin. 1981. *Urban Social Space.* Belmont, Cal.: Wadsworth.

Levine, J., A. Vinson, and D. Wood. 1973. "Subway behavior." In *People in Places: The Sociology of the Familiar*, ed. A. Birenbaum and E. Sagarin. New York: Praeger.

Lewis, J., and A. Weigert. 1985. "Trust as a social reality." *Social Forces* 63 (June):967–985.

Lofland, L. 1971a. "Self-management in public settings, Part I." *Urban Life and Culture* 1 (April):93–117.

Lofland, L. 1971b. "Self-management in public settings, Part II." *Urban Life and Culture* 2 (July):217–231.

Lofland, L. 1973. *A World of Strangers.* New York: Basic Books.

Love, R. 1973. "The fountains of urban life." *Urban Life and Culture* 2 (July):161–208.

Lyman, S., and M. Scott. 1970. "Game frameworks." In *A Sociology of the Absurd*, ed. S. Lyman and M. Scott. New York: Appleton-Century-Crofts.

Milgram, S. 1970. "The experience of living in cities." *Science* 167 (March):1461–1468.

Palen, J. 1975. *An Urban World.* New York: McGraw-Hill.

Park, R. 1925. "The city: Suggestions for the investigation of human behavior in the urban environment." In *The City*, ed. R. Park et al. Chicago: University of Chicago Press.

Park, R. 1928. "Human migration and the marginal man." *American Journal of Sociology* 33:888–896.

Schutz, A. 1960. "The stranger: An essay in social psychology." In *Collected Papers:*

*Studies in Social Theory*. The Hague: Martinus Nijhoff.

Simmel, G. 1950a. "The metropolis and mental life." In *The Sociology of Georg Simmel*, ed. K. Wolff. New York: Free Press.

Simmel, G. 1950b. "The stranger." In *The Sociology of Georg Simmel*, ed. K. Wolff. New York: Free Press.

Stonequist, E. 1937. *The Marginal Man*. Chicago: University of Chicago Press.

U.S. Bureau of the Census. 1983. *Statistical Abstract of the United States, 1984*. Washington, D.C.: Government Printing Office.

Wolff, M. 1973. "Notes on the behavior of pedestrians." In *People in Places: The Sociology of the Familiar*, ed. A. Birenbaum and E. Sagarin. New York: Praeger.

# CHAPTER 5 Contacts among Intimates: Constructing Social Relationships

I. Intimate Relationships in Contemporary Society
II. The Interactionist Perspective on Intimacy
    A. Intimacy as a Social Construction
        1. The social meanings of sexuality
    B. Historical Changes in the Meaning of Intimacy
        1. The parent-child relationship
    C. Social Status and the Meaning of Intimacy
        1. Gender differences
        2. Effects of social class
III. From Strangers to Intimates: The Construction of Love Relationships
    A. The Romantic Love Ideal
        1. The ideal and the real
    B. The Process of Falling in Love
        1. Rapport and self-revelation: "You think you know me, but you don't"
        2. Mutual dependency and commitment: "All I ever need is you"
IV. Alternatives to Marriage
    A. Premarital Sex
    B. Living Together
        1. Reasons for cohabitation
        2. Problems of cohabitation
        3. Role-making and the new morality
    C. Staying Single
        1. Pros and cons
        2. The single's search for intimacy
V. Conclusion

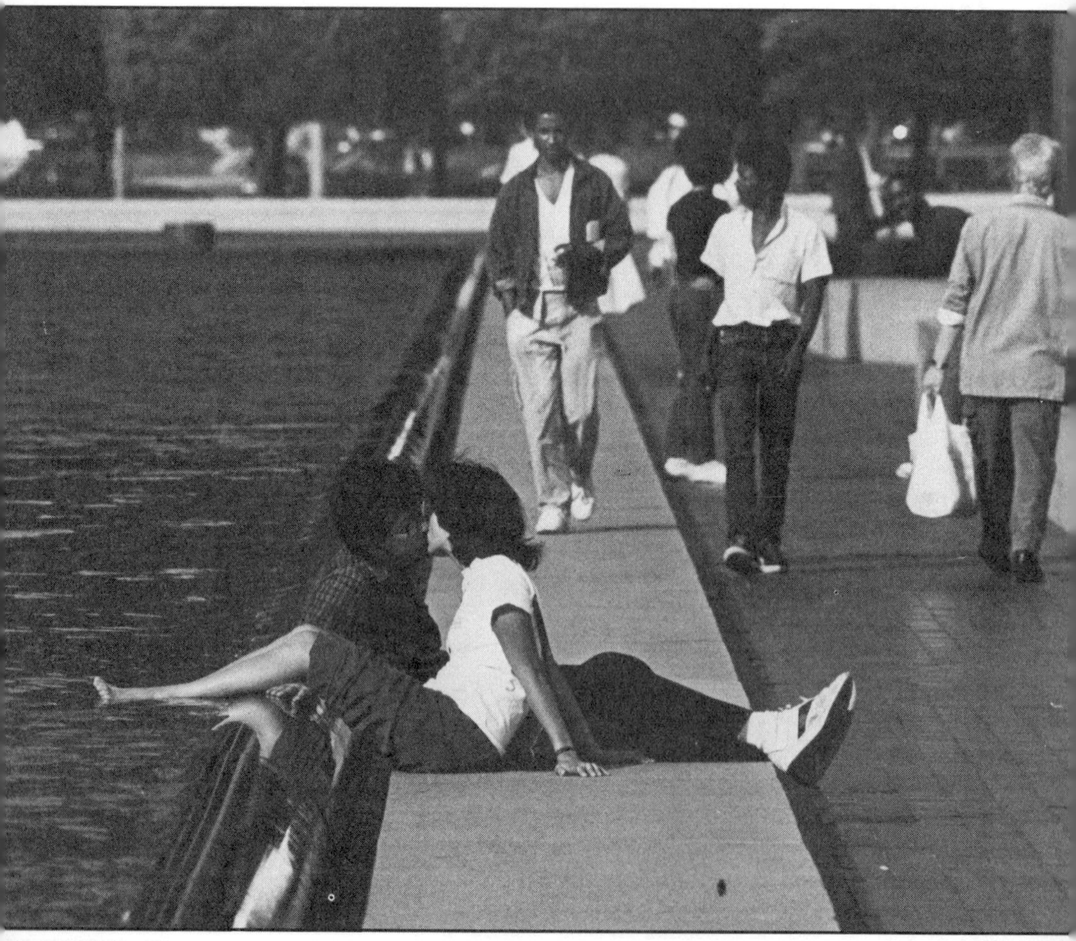

# CHAPTER 5

THE NEED FOR intimate relationships is so strong it has given rise to an industry devoted to helping compatible singles make contacts with one another. This industry provides such facilities as singles' bars and apartment complexes, as well as dating services and other operations designed to bring people together.

Operation Match, the first computer dating business in the United States, was organized by a Harvard sophomore some 20 years ago. The response was overwhelming, and thousands of college students happily spent $3 each on the chance that they would meet others whom they would find attractive and who would be attracted to them. The process has become more sophisticated and more costly as the intimacy industry has become more legitimate. Now it costs up to several hundred dollars to acquire the names of others who may have the physical and social attributes, tastes, attitudes, and interests that would fit a lonely person's romantic ideal. It also has become specialized, offering services for specific groups such as young singles, divorcees, middle-age persons, professionals, or single parents. Some services make videotapes of clients to make it easier to assess the characteristics and sample the personalities of prospective dates before committing to an actual meeting. This reduces the risks normally associated with blind dates: boredom, loss of time, and, most important, possible rejection.

Young people, particularly, devote considerable time to thinking about, worrying about, analyzing, developing, or trying to end intimate relationships. The advice columns of daily newspapers, television programming, and popular fiction all indicate the extent to which the quality of our relations with family, friends, and lovers occupy our time and thoughts.

## ■ INTIMATE RELATIONSHIPS IN CONTEMPORARY SOCIETY

The idea that human beings require identity-sustaining relationships with intimate others is not new. The **need for affiliation** (Schacter, 1959) is a theme that has always been present in social science literature. In 19th-century sociological theory, concern was expressed that industrialization and urbanization were destroying intimate bonds between individuals. Theorists such as Ferdinand Tönnies and Emile Durkheim sought to explain the effects of the transformation of the social setting from small preurban or peasant communities to large cities. Although the theoretical conceptions of these writers vary, their ideas generally reflect agreement on these points:

1. Modern society is characterized by increased rationality and individuality.
2. People are less well integrated into modern society than they were in preurban communities.
3. Relationships between people in modern society become more contractual, artificial, and contrived.
4. Ties to primary groups (family, neighborhood, and friendship groups) are weaker in modern society.

Other social science literature has called some of these propositions into question (Fischer, 1984; Karp, Stone, and Yoels, 1977). Nevertheless, there can be no doubt that contemporary society does impose a variety of unique pressures on human relationships. Both social science literature and the popular media have discussed the changing character of human relations in the 20th century. Rapid social change, the urge toward achievement and social mobility, and the weakening of community associations are said to have produced a pervasive rootlessness in modern people. The failure to sustain intimate relationships is often cited as a serious shortcoming in urban-industrial society (see box).

## Alone in the Lonely Crowd

Americans live lonely lives in the midst of a crowd of lonely people, according to David Riesman. In a book titled *The Lonely Crowd*, he proposes that the American character has changed from the *inner-directed personality* of the 19th century, motivated by an internalized set of achievement goals, to the *other-directed personality* of the 20th century, motivated by a desire for the approval of peers and associates. The modern personality is sensitive to cultural expectations and responds to the cues others give about the behaviors they expect. Such persons find it difficult to establish lasting intimate relationships with others because they have no firm values to base them on. Riesman describes the other-directed person as "at home everywhere and nowhere, capable of a rapid if sometimes superficial intimacy with and response to everyone" (1950:25).

The difficulty of establishing intimate relationshps in such a society is suggested by the following examples, drawn from a variety of sources:

*Item 1.* From the diary of a man in his mid 40s recently separated from his wife:
I want to call again but I know it is no good. She'll only yell and scream. It makes me feel lousy. I have work to do but I can't do it. I can't concentrate. I want to call people up, go to see them, but I'm afraid that they'll see that I'm shaky. I just want to talk. I can't think about anything beside this trouble with Nina. I think I want to cry. . . . The only thing I seem to be able to do is to write this. As long as I'm concentrating on how I feel, I feel almost all right. (Weiss, 1975:48).

*Item 2.* From the "personal" column of the *Free Paper:*
What must a guy do to get a little attention? Maybe scream or weep a little? I am lonely and seek correspondence with anyone willing to reach out and take my hand.

*Item 3.* From a *Los Angeles Times* news story:
An 84-year-old woman wrote the *Los Angeles Times* saying she was so lonely she wanted to die and please wouldn't somebody call or write. She enclosed a dollar bill and some stamps.

*Item 4.* From a *Boston Globe* news story:
According to the *Boston Globe* several prominent psychiatrists recommend that

*Silent Night* and *I'm Dreaming of a White Christmas* be banned from the radio. People living alone might find them dangerously depressing.

*Item 5.* From a survey of women:
In a recent survey a majority of women rated eating alone in a restaurant more unpleasant than asking for a loan or having a gynecological examination.

---

Intimacy thus not only dominates our everyday consciousness; it is also a yardstick against which we can evaluate the quality of our everyday lives. The level of intimacy that we perceive exists in any encounter affects our presentations of self, impression management, and the kinds of information about ourselves we reveal to others. In general, the configuration of expectations, obligations, and reciprocities that govern any relationship is bound up with the degree of intimacy that exists between the persons involved. The ways we allocate our time and the social circles we enter and leave cannot be understood apart from the networks of intimate relationships we sustain. Inquiry into the structure and operation of everyday life therefore demands serious consideration of the manner in which we define, interpret, and give meaning to relations of intimacy.

## ■ THE INTERACTIONIST PERSPECTIVE ON INTIMACY

Students often resist sociological analyses of personal relationships. When asked to describe some of the social factors that might account for the way intimate relationships are conducted in American society today, students in our courses have argued that it is impossible to generalize about intimacy. Among other things, they say: "It all depends upon the individual." "No two people relate to one another in the same way." "You can't define what love is."

To some degree the students are correct: No two relationships are the same, even when the social characteristics of the participants are very similar. Each relationship emerges out of the unique context in which the individuals encounter one another. They are also correct that any attempt to provide an absolute, clear, permanent definition of intimacy, love, or friendship would be fruitless. We agree that a relationship is intimate only when the participants in the relationship define it that way. At the same time, we maintain that the criteria used in arriving at such a definition are *social* in origin.

## Intimacy as a Social Construction

As we noted in Chapter 2, social life would be impossible if there were no general consensus concerning the meanings people give to objects, events, and situations in their lives—if people were not generally agreed on the meaning of symbols. The definitions given to intimacy depend on both the general values of the society in which individuals live and the more specific values of the groups to which they belong or with which they identify.

These roots in socially shared definitions are what allow us to carry our analysis of intimacy beyond the assertion that each human relationship is unique. Relationships of love and friendship can only be understood as symbolic or **social constructions** which by themselves have no intrinsic meaning. You are friendly or in love with another person because you have given the relationship that interpretation. This point is illustrated by Elaine Walster (1974), who suggests that in order to experience passionate love it is first necessary to have learned the proper meanings associated with specific physiological feelings.

Consider what you might feel on some enchanted evening should you see across a crowded room a stranger to whom you are immediately attracted. Your eyes meet the stranger's, you smile warmly at each other, and as you approach one another, oblivious to others in the room, you experience increased heart and respiratory rates, flushing of the face, dryness of the mouth, and slight body tremors. Aware of these physiological responses, you may decide that you are experiencing love at first sight. You have learned from your peers, from television, and from books and magazines that such feelings can be interpreted as love.

The feelings we have described do not *have to be* interpreted as love, however. If we did not know the context in which the feeling occurred and simply knew that an individual had experienced higher heart and respiration rates, flushing, dry mouth, and body tremors, we could make a variety of interpretations concerning what was happening. It could be that the individual was high on drugs, suffering from the flu, or experiencing any one of a number of quite diverse emotions—fear, anger, anxiety, jealousy, embarrassment, or love. Our emotional states are symbolic states. As such, they require interpretation and labeling to establish their meaning. As Walster says, "One can experience love only if (1) he is physiologically aroused, and (2) concludes that love is an appropriate label for his aroused feelings" (1974:278).

## The Social Meanings of Sexuality

Much the same point can be made concerning the meanings attached to sexuality. The ways in which individuals pursue and engage in sexual relationships reflect the social attitudes of both society as a whole and the groups with which the individuals are affiliated. Our capacity for intimate sexuality is in part a function of biological maturity, but we become sexual through a learning process. John Gagnon and William Simon (1973) point out that what we think of being sexual, what turns us off or on, and even the belief that we are "horny" as a result of sexual deprivation, all reflect culturally defined and learned ideas about sexuality.

The extraordinary variation in human responses to sexuality affirms the symbolic nature of this activity. Clearly individuals must define a situation as sexual before sexual activity will occur. The social meanings attached to sexuality are illuminated in the very vocabulary we use to describe sexual behaviors:

> We often evaluate people by their choice of sexual objects. If they appear to show no discrimination, we think them licentious. If they prefer their own sex, we deem them queer. If they have what we think are too many sexual encounters, they are promiscuous; if too few, they are prudes. Those who are compulsive in their sexual behavior we regard as attempting to prove their masculinity. We categorize sexual behavior, if money is exchanged, as prostitution. And the presumed proficiency, style and attitude of the participants, too, reflect on their more general moral character. (Cavan, 1976:57)

The participants in sexual relationships are judged not only by the frequency, variety, and financing of their intimacies, but also by the sex and age of their partners. We generally share very rigid ideas concerning who may have an intimate sexual relationship with whom, for example. Discrepancies in age are deemed critically important in this respect. In the cult classic film *Harold and Maude*, a young man pursues an intimate relationship with an old, dying woman. Humorous scenes are constructed around the attempts of Harold's mother to distract him from this relationship by providing women nearer his age as suitable replacements for Maude. But sexual relations in what are considered inappropriate couples are not always viewed with humor. It is common to speak of romantic relationships between persons with a significant age gap as "robbing the cradle" or "May-December" romances. Although we do not refer to "dirty old women," the portrayal of Mrs. Robinson in *The Graduate* would fit such a description. The audience is moved to cheer when Benjamin rejects middle-aged Mrs. Robinson for a more appropriate partner—her daughter.

Definitions of intimacy vary because they are social constructions with no fixed meaning. They have their roots in both general societal values and the more specific values of the groups and persons with whom an individual frequently communicates. The meanings also vary historically and according to the social attributes of the participants.

## Historical Changes in the Meaning of Intimacy

The social conventions concerning intimacy in a society have been different in various historical periods. In *Gone with the Wind*, Rhett Butler sweeps the protesting Scarlett O'Hara off her feet and carries her to an upstairs bedroom. According to Civil War era definitions of appropriate male-female relationships, the acceptable interpretation of Butler's behavior would be intense passion. Men could plausibly disregard women's attempts to rebuff their sexual advances because men were expected to be aggressive in such situations and women were expected to protest. With the exception of black males, who could be lynched for improprieties as slight as looking the "wrong" way at a white woman, it would be unthinkable to define behaviors like Rhett's as rape.

Today there are quite different interpretations of such male-female interactions. A feminist documentary—*Rape Culture*—shows the same scene from *Gone with the Wind* following a number of very descriptive confessions of convicted rapists. In the context of present values and women's raised consciousness, Butler's behavior would be unlikely to be interpreted as mad passion or romantic devotion. It might be defined as illicit, even as rape.

### *The Parent-Child Relationship*

The clearest examples of historical change in the quality and nature of intimate relations are the norms governing the relationships between parents and children. Although expectations about parent-child relationships vary with the ethnic, religious, and social class characteristics of families, most parents today seek to be friends with their children and try to foster mutual respect for all family members' behaviors and opinions. The family circle typically resembles a democracy in which the children have the right to participate in the decision-making process. It is, however, an imperfect democracy. Because parents have full responsibility for their offspring, they have authority over them and are expected to exert strong control over their lives.

In the Middle Ages, in contrast, children were considered to be small adults. The equality of their relationship with adults was reflected in numerous customs. Parents and children wore similar clothing, participated in identical work and play activities, and even exchanged sexual jokes. The social invention of childhood began to emerge in the 17th century (see Chapter 9). As the dominant form of the family institution changed from the **extended family,** including several generations of a kinship network, to a **nuclear family,** composed only of a father, a mother, and their children, the father assumed absolute control over both mother and children. The extent of such domination is reflected in the laws of the period. In Massachusetts, children over 16 were subject to the death penalty for cursing or striking their parents or refusing to obey their orders (Aries, 1962). Historical analyses reveal similar changes in expectations concerning appropriate behaviors between siblings, friends, and lovers.

## Social Status and the Meaning of Intimacy

The meanings attached to family, friendship, and love relationships also vary with a person's social status (see Chapter 3). At various levels of the social structure of American society there are variations in the definitions and meanings assigned to these relationships.

Friendships, for example, are distinguished from family relationships by their voluntary character. The saying, "You can pick your friends but you can't choose your relatives" contains much truth and has significant sociological implications. First, we expect friendships to be less binding than family relations. Indeed, one way we describe "close" friendships is to invest them with a familial status. A woman might affirm the closeness of her friendship with another woman by saying, "She is like a sister to me." "Kindred spirits," a quaint phrase in Victorian literature, carries the same sentiment as the more current phrase, "going for brothers" used by black men to describe friendships based on trust and mutual responsibility. Friendships, of course, vary in intensity. A range of terms is used to describe gradations of nonkin intimacy, from acquaintance to friend, close friend, and best friend.

The meanings we give to friendship and other intimate relationships reflect a person's social attributes, including the ascribed statuses of age, race, and gender, as well as achieved statuses such as occupation, education, and social class (see Chapter 3). We will consider how two of these attributes, gender differences and social class, affect the maintenance of intimate relationships among friends and in the family.

### *Gender Differences*

The social science literature on **gender roles** has generally supported the idea that women are better able than men to maintain intimate friendships with persons of the same sex. This is so, the argument goes, because the traditional gender-role socialization of women emphasizes sensitivity to interpersonal relationships and allows the expression of affection and the revelation of weakness, whereas men are socialized to avoid signs of affection toward other men.

Male relationships are said to be characterized by competition and an impersonal quality; their conversations are supposedly confined to such relatively nonintimate matters as sports and business. Marc Fasteau comments that most men do not talk personally to one another, and those who do have problems which have gotten the best of them. Told they have to choose between expressiveness and manly strength, men avoid talking about themselves. Communication among males is also limited by obsessive competition, according to Fasteau:

> Competition is the principal mode by which men relate to each other—at one level because they don't know how else to make contact, but more basically because it is the way to demonstrate, to themselves and others, the key masculine qualities of unwavering toughness and the ability to dominate and control. (1974:11)

There has been evidence that men, compared to women, are less willing to reveal personal information in interaction, more willing to express aggression, and substantially more fearful of being latently homosexual. Deborah David and Robert Brannon sum up these and similar findings with their description of four masculine gender-role "core requirements" in American society (1976:13):

1. *No sissy stuff.* The stigma of all stereotyped feminine characteristics and qualities, including openness and vulnerability, must be avoided.
2. *The big wheel.* Success, status, and the need to be looked up to are recognized.
3. *The sturdy oak.* A manly air of toughness, confidence, and self-reliance is respected.
4. *Give 'em hell.* An aura of aggression, violence, and daring is to be projected.

As these characteristics suggest, men are expected to control their feelings in a much more restricted way than women are. Women usually have to encourage men to talk about their deepest feelings. Lillian Rubin calls this situation "the single most dispiriting dilemma of relations between men and women":

> He complains, "She's so emotional, there's no point in talking to her." She protests, "It's him you can't talk to, he's always so darned rational." He says, "Even when I tell her nothing's the matter, she won't quit." She says, "How can I believe

him when I can see with my own eyes that something's wrong?" He says, "Okay, so something's wrong! What good will it do to tell her?" She cries, "What are we married for? What do you need me for, just to wash your socks?" (1983:71–72)

Gender roles have been changing, however, as women have entered the labor force in increasing numbers. About 48 million women were employed in the civilian labor force in 1982, compared to about 23 million in 1960 (U.S. Bureau of the Census, 1983, Table 671). In 1982, also, women comprised about 42 percent of the total work force. It is important to note, however, that women's work is still largely confined to low-status, low-paying positions in the white-collar clerical and service sectors of the economy—areas which Florence Howe (1977) has termed "pink-collar" ghettoes. They still have a long way to go to assure equal positions with men in the family and in the society (see Chapter 6).

Changes in female employment patterns have important consequences for marital relationships. When both marriage partners work outside the home, critical questions are raised about who should do what everyday household tasks, for example. These kinds of questions can lead to intense feelings of resentment on the part of the wife, who often must assume two demanding, virtually full-time jobs. Recent studies have affirmed the fact that paid employment saddles the wife with additional work without lessening her household or child-rearing responsibilities (Hofferth and Moore, 1979; Pleck, 1981). Intimate relations within the home are bound to be affected by wives' efforts to negotiate an equitable distribution of household chores, as well as their desire to be recognized as equal partners in the rights and responsibilities of the marriage.

## *Effects of Social Class*

Social class position also influences the meanings attached to friendship. There is, for example, a strong relationship between **social mobility** and the maintenance of friendship ties. Some people maintain very strong allegiances to the same friends throughout their lives, while for others friendships are much more transitory and entail few obligations. Position in the occupational structure has a lot to do with the processes of friendship choice and development, the social contexts in which friends are made, the influence of social mobility on friendship ties, and the significance of the workplace for friendship development. Howard Robboy (1983), for example, has studied night shift workers to assess the effects of irregular working hours on family and friendship relations.

"*Corner boys.*" Sociological studies have found that for lower- and working-class men, friendships require substantial commitments and the fulfillment of an extensive set of mutual obligations. Indeed, the requirements of friendships in these classes are said to be so extensive and morally binding that they can stand in the way of occupational and educational achievement.

In his classic study of a Boston slum community, *Street Corner Society* (1955), William Foote Whyte explained how the friendship loyalties of a group of "corner boys" (actually men in their 20s and 30s, mostly second-generation immigrants) restricted their social mobility. He described them as so tied to their group through a network of reciprocal obligations and so unwilling to sacrifice their friendships that they failed to get ahead. For example, friends were expected to share whatever money they had. Such a friendship norm prevented these young men from adopting the middle-class values of thrift, savings, and investment and made the eventual financing of a college education or business career impossible. A leader of the corner gang—a man named Doc—expressed his feelings about his friends when he told Whyte:

I suppose my boys have kept me from getting ahead. . . . But if I were to start over again—if God said to me, "Look here, Doc, you're going to start over again and you can pick out your friends in advance," still I would make sure that my boys were among them—even if I could pick Rockefeller and Carnegie. . . . Many times people . . . have said to me, "Why do you hang around these fellows?" I would tell them, "Why not? They're my friends." (p. 180)

This group distinguished different levels of friendship, ranging from an inner circle of individuals who were "up tight" with one another to others who remained at the periphery of a network of personal relationships. To be up tight with another person required trusting that person like kin, with the usual claims, obligations, expectations, and loyalties that such a status implies. The result was a contradiction between the requirements of friendship and the desire to get ahead. More recent interviews with working-class members suggest that this contradiction still exists and can be a source of acute strain or tension.

*Organization men.* The friendship model of lower- and working-class men contrasts sharply with the ways upper-middle-class men in managerial occupations construct and define their friendships. In his book *The Organization Man* (1956), William H. Whyte described the friendships of career-oriented, rising young executives as short-lived and largely utilitarian. Friends were frequently *cultivated* for their potential value in career advancement. Such friendships were often dissolved or forgotten when the aspiring executive moved up the corporate ladder or left the area. Breaking off friendship ties when they posed an obstacle to mobility did not create moral dilemmas for these men. They clearly recognized the need for an extensive network of the "right" friends, and who these friends were could change at each point in their career development.

The transitory character of friendships among corporate officials is partly a function of their geographic mobility. In his book *A Nation of Strangers* (1972), Vance Packard estimated that the average corporate manager moves every two and one-half years. Such a transient lifestyle works against lasting friendships for the executive's whole family. One executive's wife, commenting that sooner or later, every executive's family has to decide whether money and possessions or roots is more important, said:

> For me, family and friends—*old* friends—mean a great deal. I am sorry my children will never know the same kind of family closeness that I did. Travel and new experiences are good for children. All the ladies' magazines keep telling us the good outweighs the inconvenience. I don't buy this anymore. I think the security of having a real home with family and friends I don't have to say goodbye to again means more to me than the security of a bigger pay check. (Packard, 1972:146)

*Working women and working-class wives.* Problems associated with career moves are magnified in the case of the increasing number of two-career families, where both husbands and wives have considerable psychological investments in achieving success at work. In many cases the opportunity to advance the career of one partner in the marriage leads to the necessity of living apart. Such a decision poses a serious problem for the maintenance of intimacy, as a respondent in a recent study by Harriet Engel Gross noted:

> We knew that neither of us was willing to give up the course we were going on so we couldn't ask the other to. Yet implicit in that was the realization that somehow you are making the statement that at least some aspect of your career is more important than being together. I think that's a real issue for today. I get really angry and feel like why do I even have to make these choices, one against the other. It doesn't seem right. There's obviously still a lot of pain. (1984:181)

Our treatment of the social class-friendship relationship has been limited to males because there have been no similar social science studies of the ways in which social class affects female friendships. Some recent research, however, does suggest that for women, too, class plays a critical role in the formation of intimate relations. Lillian Rubin's (1976) study of working-class wives shows that it is extremely difficult for husbands and wives to develop joint friendships with outsiders. As a result, for these women, neighbors and extended family are the prime sources of sociability outside of the marriage. Feminist writers have also pointed out that the exclusion of women from male-dominated informal occupational networks has hindered middle-class women in their professional goals (Chafetz, 1984).

## ■ FROM STRANGERS TO INTIMATES: THE CONSTRUCTION OF LOVE RELATIONSHIPS

Despite the variability in the ways individuals construct, maintain, and change the quality of their relationships with family members, friends, and lovers, it is possible to identify an **intimacy process** with certain common elements. This section is concerned with one part of that process, the construction and development of love relationships. It explores the steps through which two strangers typically become intimates—meeting, dating, becoming committed to each other, falling in love, and usually, marrying. While the specifics of the process through which strangers are transformed into lovers may vary widely, the socially prescribed benchmarks or stages of these relationships are much alike.

We share certain expectations about the appropriateness of intimate relationships. We expect to fall in love, have sex, and get married within well-recognized time frames. Adults typically define teenagers' first attempts at establishing intimate relationships as infatuation or "puppy love"; they are considered too young to experience the real thing. At the other extreme, people who remain unmarried past their late twenties may be considered "problems" by parents, relatives, and friends. Similarly, sexual relationships between teenagers could be considered improper if not immoral, but status as a virgin after the middle to late twenties could be a source of embarrassment.

In American society the completion of formal education seems to be a key point in intimacy time conceptions. High school students who do not go on to college are more likely to marry soon after graduation. For others the college years are thought to be an appropriate time to fall in love. Indeed, because college students constitute a readily accessible sample of participants for research studies, most of the generalizations concerning the process through which individuals fall in love come from studies of college students. To understand this process, we must first appreciate the conception of love that guides the construction of our intimate relations.

### The Romantic Love Ideal

The idea that love is the only basis for marriage is typically American. Some years ago a Korean graduate student who was becoming visibly distressed as she neared the completion of her master's degree work confided she had been receiving letters from her parents indicating that she would be married upon her return to Korea. Throughout her education in the United States she had known that she would eventually be expected to marry the person her parents chose for her. Now, however, she did not want to return to Korea, and she certainly did not want to marry someone she had never met. She knew it would be a breach of cultural tradition to refuse her parents' wishes, but she had adopted American values which consider love to be the only reasonable basis for marriage.

The **romantic love ideal,** formulated in France and Germany during the 12th century, filtered down from the nobility to the lower classes over the centuries. In its pure form the ideal of romantic love involves the notion that there is only one person in all the world that we are meant to love; although "love is blind," we will recognize our "true love" at first sight. The role of *fate* in this process is a strong feature of the romantic ideal. We are expected to "fall in love" and to believe that "You were meant for me." From adolescence on, we wait for that moment when "That old black magic has us in its spell."

## *The Ideal and the Real*

While love ought to be the sole basis for marriage, according to the romantic ideal, most of us recognize the discrepancy between ideal and real. We may generally subscribe to the romantic ideal, but we also know that life rarely corresponds to ideals, that people do not and ought not to marry *only* because they are in love. Most young people are socialized to believe that love is necessary for marriage but not always a sufficient reason to marry. We have a negative view of anyone who would marry *exclusively* for money, status, prestige, or security. But we also consider anyone foolish who would marry a poor person rather than a wealthy one, other things being more or less equal.

Studies have found differences between men and women in the weight they give to love as a condition for marriage. Willard Waller, who made the most perceptive analysis of dating patterns among young people (particularly college students), found that contrary to popular belief, men are more likely than women to hold to the romantic ideal. In other words, women are *less* romantic than men (Waller, 1938:243). Because of women's traditional dependence on men, in Waller's view, the process of mate selection is of much greater consequence to them. Women therefore have been comparatively less idealistic and more rational and cautious in love relationships.

## The Process of Falling in Love

You probably have known people who claim to have fallen in love at first sight—perhaps you have yourself. For most people, however, the development of a love relationship is a gradual process. Ira Reiss (1960) has proposed what he calls the **wheel theory of love,** in which the four stages of a love relationship—rapport, self-revelation, mutual dependency, and need fulfillment—are represented by the spokes of a wheel diagram (see Figure 5.1). According to Reiss, we proceed through these stages one at a time and in order. Before we are willing to reveal significant identity information about ourselves to another person, we must first have achieved a certain level of rapport with that person. Self-revelation then sets the stage for a sense of mutual dependency. The final stage in this process is the belief that the other person fulfills our basic needs.

Research conducted on various aspects of mate selection and marriage suggests that there is indeed considerable regularity and rationality to the process. Using Reiss's wheel theory, as shown in Figure 5-1, as a general guide, we can analyze the movement from rapport to self-rev-

Figure 5.1
The Wheel Theory of the Development of Love

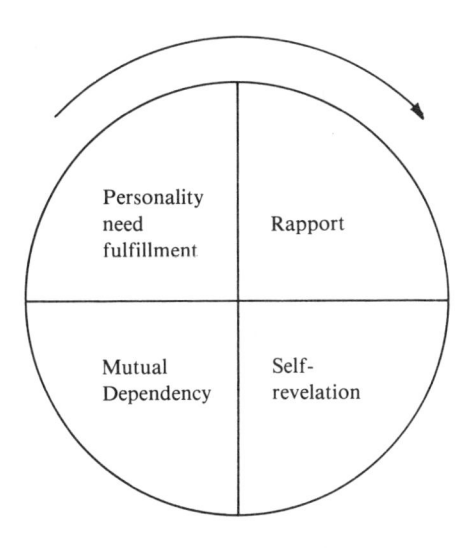

*Source:* Ira Reiss, "Toward a Sociology of the Heterosexual Love Relationship," *Marriage and Family Living,* 22 (May 1960):143. Copyrighted 1960 by the National Council on Family Relations, 1910 West County Road B, Suite 147, St. Paul, Minnesota 55113. Reprinted by permission.

elation to commitment and marriage, as well as the factors that sometimes hinder such movement.

### Rapport and Self-revelation: "You Think You Know Me, but You Don't"

Meeting a stranger—at a party, through the introduction of mutual friends, in a class or church group—usually starts with casual conversation and the exchange of superficial biographical information. College students meeting at a party engage in fairly ritualistic conversation: "What year are you in? What is your major? Where are you from?" If one of the participants has no desire to continue the conversation, this incipient relationship is easily ended. If, however, the individuals wish to pursue the relationship, the conversation becomes progressively less superficial and more far-reaching, as each person seeks to learn more about the other.

Physical attractiveness is a critical factor in determining whether people want to see each other again after an initial meeting. Research has found significant gender differences in the importance attached to this factor, however. When Don Byrne (1970) asked study participants to rank a variety of factors concerning their attraction to others, 90 percent of the male respondents ranked physical attractiveness as most important. This was not true for women. Although they certainly ranked attractiveness high, they considered it more important for the males with whom they might develop an ongoing relationship to share their attitudes and values. For 92 percent of the female respondents, value and attitudinal similarity was more important than physical attractiveness. Such a finding supports Bertrand Russell's well-known remark that women tend to love men for their character, while men tend to love women for their appearance.

*The impression management stage.* Once two people have begun to interact, their primary goals typically are to determine the issues on which they agree and disagree and to assess the significance of their similarities and differences. Complicating the information assessment during the initial stage of a relationship is the deliberate impression management engaged in by both parties. Individuals may be so intent on establishing a relationship that they systematically present attitudes and values that they believe will be acceptable. Each will be careful to feel out the other person before expressing an opinion that might be disliked enough to bring an end to the relationship. Identity information is manipulated to present the proper first impression. This may change on further acquaintance, causing one of the participants to observe, "I thought I knew her (or him), but I didn't" (see box).

## Somehow You've Changed . . .

Courtship is a unique period in the love relationship in which each person typically offers an idealized image of herself or himself and is willing—even eager—to accept the idealized image the other person presents. When the couple learns more about one another it comes as a surprise if the original presentations of self turn out to have been deliberately manipulated to create a favorable impression. One of the lovers has to be willing to take on a lifelong commitment to live up to the expectations such an impression has created in the other, or the relationship runs into trouble.

What happens when one participant in a romance recognizes the results of the others' impression management is suggested in the following example from a book entitled *Pairing: How to Achieve Genuine Intimacy*, by George Bach and Ronald Deutsch (1970):

*Doug:* I don't understand why you don't want to take the weekend backpack trip with Hal and Gwen. You know it's been three months since we've been in the woods or the mountains? I really miss it.
*Helen:* Well, I was never that much of an outdoor woman after all. I mean, I love the scenery, but camping out is pretty hard on a woman. It's different for a man.
*Doug:* But don't you remember what you said when we met on that Sierra Club Hike?
*Helen:* What did I say? That I loved the scenery? That I loved nature? Of course, I do. But carrying a pack is really exhausting for me.
*Doug:* It seems so much like part of us—being alone in the wilderness. Remember how we slipped away, the two of us? Cooked our meals together?
*Helen:* Well, what do you want me to say?
*Doug:* I don't know. You seem different now, somehow. It just isn't the same. That's why I want to get into the mountains with you again, bring it back, bring you back. (p. 175)

As we noted in Chapter 3, people manage impressions of themselves by systematically concealing information they consider potentially damaging in the encounter, at the same time they seek out information about the other person. It is relatively easy to manipulate information about attitudes and values. Other items of identity information, however, are difficult to hide or conceal, such as the ascribed attributes of ethnicity, race, religion, and social class. These social class attributes also serve as **relationship filters.** If people discover that others' ethnic, religious, or class affiliations are very different from their own, they are likely to end the relationship at an early stage.

Supplied with the information the participants have provided about themselves and the symbols defining their social worlds, the couple must then decide whether the worlds they respectively inhabit are close enough that they will eventually be able to produce and sustain a common reality. Social science studies have found that if two persons' biographies are very dissimilar, they will be unlikely to produce such a reality. It is the obvious disparity in biographies that forms the substance of such legends as Cinderella, for example. *Cinderella* is a fairy tale precisely because it relates the story of a successful love relationship despite vast differences in the individuals' biographies.

When a relationship endures beyond the point of self-disclosure and the participants are dating each other "seriously," they begin to try to interpret their level of commitment to the relationship. Murray Davis (1973) draws this analogy: "Intimates, like college professors, want tenure. And in order to guarantee that their relationship will continue, they must make a commitment to each other. After a probationary period, intimates, again like academics, go 'up or out' " (p. 192).

### *Mutual Dependency and Commitment: "All I Ever Need Is You"*

If the love relationship persists eventually it reaches the point where the participants' everyday lives are much intertwined. At the stage of mutual dependency, the couple's relationship has ceased to be their private affair. The individuals have probably been publicly defined as a couple. Once this **public definition** has been applied, their relationship becomes more exclusive, and they are bound in a complex web of expectations. Not only do the participants have new expectations of each other, so do their friends and family. The couple is issued joint invitations; one is expected to accompany the other to social gatherings; and when they are apart, each partner is expected to be able to account for the other's ideas, attitudes, and whereabouts. The partners signal the seriousness of their relationship to each other, family, and friends by engaging in a variety of activities which are generally understood to indicate a growing level of commitment. Such symbolic gestures may include spending time together every day rather than just on weekends, introducing the partner to relatives, bringing the other person to such important family events as weddings and annual gatherings, and purchasing expensive gifts for each other.

The point of mutual dependency is a time when the relationship may undergo severe tensions and stresses. These difficulties are often related to the growing intensity of commitment demanded in the relationship. Their own and others' expectations for the couple may cause one or another to feel smothered by the pressure to make a permanent commitment. In the past, there often were gender differences in the meanings attached to commitment. Traditionally, males have been socialized to view the acceptance of a long-term relationship as a surrender of their freedom and independence, while females have been socialized to seek the security of a permanent commitment. Now women also are becoming wary of losing their identity in a relationship. Many women refuse to subordinate their interests to those of their male partners and would not hesitate to dissolve a relationship in which they are treated as only an appendage to the male.

For some lovers, graduation from college precipitates a **commitment crisis.** Time and again students come to teachers and counselors with much the same problem:

I think that I am in love with him, but he has been accepted to graduate school and I don't want to go there. I have my own career to think about. But I am pretty sure that if we go our separate ways now, it will in all likelihood spell the end of our relationship. This whole situation is driving me crazy and I don't know what to do.

In years past, many women in this situation would have subordinated their own career plans in order to sustain the relationship. Today, many relationships founder at this point unless arrangements can be made for both persons to pursue their own career goals in the same geographical area.

There are other reasons for breaking up a relationship at this stage (see box). One frequent cause is that parents or friends dislike or disapprove of the dating partner. A woman's friends, for example, may demand to know what she sees in her companion when they meet him. In college, as in high school, students place a great deal of weight on the evaluations of their peers. Many students also form friendships with slightly older persons, such as seniors, graduate students, or young faculty members, who can offer guidance in the place of their parents. Conflicts with parents can easily threaten a developing relationship. If a father who has dreamed of sending his son to medical school perceives his son's intimate relationship with a girl as a potential threat to this plan, for example, he may demand: "Stop seeing her or I will stop paying for your education." Parents' control over students' financial welfare can easily extend to control over their love lives.

## Breaking Up Is Harder to Do in Certain Circumstances

The popular stereotype of a love relationship that ends before marriage pictures poor pitiful Pearl pining away for a lost love. Such endings actually are harder on men, however, according to a study of breakups before marriage by Charles Hill, Zick Rubin, and Letitia Peplau (1977). This study distinguishes between "his breakup" and "her breakup." His breakups are more devastating because men find it more difficult to believe that they are no longer loved. The difference might be explained by women's greater practicality in love relationships. As one of the female respondents in the survey for this study noted, "I don't think I ever felt romantic about David—I felt practical. I had the feeling that I'd better make the most of it."

The partners in a lasting relationship are likely to share equal commitments to it, according to Hill, Rubin, and Peplau. Their data indicate that only 23 percent of equally involved couples broke up, compared to 54 percent of those in relationships where one person was more committed than the other.

Because the couples studied were college students, Hill, Rubin, and Peplau found that relationships tended to break up at clear demarcations in the school year: May–June, September, December–January. Understandably, the person interested in terminating the relationship found it easier to suggest just before vacation, "It might not be a bad idea for us to date others while we are apart." Also, as might be expected, each partner's conception of the terminated relationship differed according to whether he or she had acted in the role of "breaker-upper" or "broken-up-with." There is a tendency for each partner to claim to have initiated the breakup. It is obviously preferable to define a situation as one in which you have exercised power and controlled another person's behavior, rather than the other way around.

Many relationships end in the face of such pressures, but many partners also develop a commitment to a relationship just because it has continued for a long time. Intimate relationships often develop a momentum of their own as a result of sheer endurance. Investing time and energy in their own relationship while foregoing them with others commits people; often they remain in the relationship even when it becomes a painful one.

Whatever the dynamics of a relationship that leads two persons to declare their commitment to one another, the next step in their intimacy normally is plans for marriage. One of the best predictors of eventual marital success is how couples manage conflicts as they plan for their weddings, according to Katherine Knafl (1975). This is the first time during the idyllic period of courtship that the couple must make some of the practical social and economic decisions that will later typify their married life. The couples interviewed for this study:

. . . associated the staging of the wedding with an explicit shift in the nature of their relationship. While respondents typically described courtship as an essentially carefree time characterized by numerous shared, pleasurable experiences, questions concerning their wedding plans elicited a very different kind of response. Typically the respondent's tone of voice changed and comments focused on the multitude of problems being faced. (p. 8)

Today, however, it is not uncommon for individuals to decide to live together without marriage or to remain single. For some, living together represents a satisfactory alternative to marriage; for others it is viewed as an additional opportunity to test out their relationship. The number of people making such choices dramatically increased in the 1970s. There have also been steady increases in the numbers of men and women between the ages of 20 and 34 who remain single. Because of the magnitude of these changes, the meanings of commitment, intimacy, sexuality, and marriage have changed accordingly.

## ■ ALTERNATIVES TO MARRIAGE

In the last few years there has been much discussion in both the popular press and academic literature about the perception that a sexual-moral revolution has occurred. Sociologists and the public agree that there have been significant changes in sexual norms and behavior, but they disagree on the specific nature of these changes, when they began, or whether they are tapering off. Evidence based on self-reports of behavior suggests that the rate of premarital sexual intercourse among male college students did not change much after World War I, remaining at a constant 65 percent. Between 1965 and 1980, however, the incidence of college women reporting intercourse rose from 29 to 54 percent (Robinson and Jedlicka, 1982). The obvious inferences from this are that sexual consciousness among women has been raised, and the double standard by which premarital sex was approved for males but not for females has been largely discarded.

## Premarital Sex

Sociologists generally agree that major changes in sexual activity among unmarried persons did not begin in the 1960s, as many presume. Rather, if there was a sexual revolution, it originated in the 1920s. John Cuber suggests that it was during this period that "premarital chastity began to lose its force as a guiding moral precept of the young. The motorcar and not the pill opened the floodgates" (1975:80). The most significant "revolution" in sexual relations in recent years has involved changes in attitudes:

> The last generation—a sizable minority of it—broke the rules of sexual morality and in particular the rule of premarital chastity, but clandestinely and with great guilt. The members of this generation—a good many of them—simply do not accept the rules any longer. Whether they themselves wish to engage in the forbidden acts is immaterial. Many of them don't wish to. But they challenge the validity of the law—and that is revolution. (Cuber, 1975:80)

The general acceptance of the legitimacy of premarital sex by today's college generation does not mean that their sexual lives are trouble-free. Students face a great deal of stress related to the degree of sexual intimacy they will permit. According to Gagnon and Simon (1979), young people "still experience losing their virginity as an identity crisis; a nonvirgin is something they did not expect to be." The first sexual experience may well be a response to peer pressure. One college junior had this to say: "My virginity was such a burden to me that I just went out to get rid of it" (p. 79).

Other problems stem from inadequate communication between males and females because explicit talk about sex is still not acceptable, and such feelings must be expressed indirectly. When the Boston Women's Health Book Collective was compiling the book *Our Bodies—Our Selves* (1974), a group of college students was asked how they let someone know they wanted to go to bed with them. The responses included:

> By the eyes—the way you look at each other, you know.

> I ask her if she wants to come to my room and smoke a joint.

Such indirect communications easily can lead to misunderstandings. The students surveyed said they sometimes engage in sex even when they do not want to, largely because such behavior is expected.

> I've been in that situation and couldn't say no even though I didn't want intercourse.

> There have been times I didn't feel like sex—holding hands and a good-night

kiss were fine, and yet I felt the girl expected it, and the guys I live with expected it, so I had sex.

Difficulties of this sort persist, despite the acceptability of premarital sex. It is generally agreed, however, that unmarried persons who engage in sexual intercourse should not feel any guilt about it. These attitudinal changes have allowed substantial growth in the number of unmarried couples living together.

## Living Together

In her much-cited study of the practice of living together by unmarried college students, Eleanor Macklin (1972) defined **cohabitation** as "having shared a bedroom and/or bed with someone of the opposite sex (to whom one was not married) for four or more nights a week for three or more consecutive months" (p. 463). After reviewing available studies on the subject, she found that college campuses varied widely in the percentage of student cohabiting, ranging from a low of 10 percent to higher than 33 percent. Such variation was related to the geographical location of the college, its housing and parietal (visiting regulations for the opposite sex) regulations and their enforcement, the college's male/female student ratio, and the definition of cohabitation used in the study. Macklin's own sample of 200 students (half male and half female) was drawn from Cornell University.

In comparing the 31 percent of her sample who were presently cohabiting or had done so with those who had never engaged in this activity, Macklin found few differences of a demographic sort. Her finding that cohabitors did not significantly vary from other students in terms of family and community background, social class, college major, occupational goals, and grade-point average is consistent with evidence from other studies (Macklin, 1974; Arafat and Yorburg, 1975). Cohabitors were, however, found to be less likely to attend church or hold traditional religious views and more likely to identify with liberal lifestyles and to use drugs.

Statistics from noncollege populations are harder to obtain. According to census data, in 1982, 1.9 million unmarried couples were sharing the same household (U.S. Bureau of the Census, 1983, Table 59). The number of unmarried couples grew most rapidly in the 1970s, as Figure 5.2 shows. In the one-year period from 1977 to 1978 alone there was an increase of 19 percent. The number of unmarried couples with children who are living together has changed more slowly.

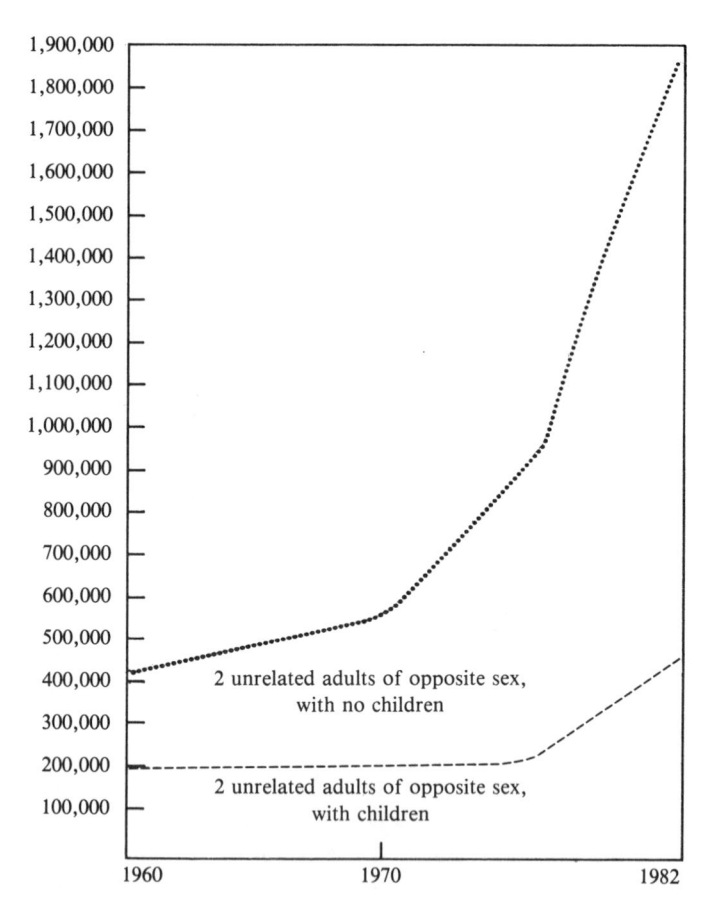

Figure 5.2
Unmarried Couples Sharing Same Household, United States, 1960–1982

[Chart showing two lines from 1960 to 1982. "2 unrelated adults of opposite sex, with no children" rises from about 400,000 in 1960 to about 1,850,000 in 1982. "2 unrelated adults of opposite sex, with children" stays near 200,000 until mid-1970s then rises to about 450,000 by 1982.]

*Sources:* Population Bulletin, no. 5, vol. 32 (Washington, D.C.: Population Bureau, Inc., 1977). Unpublished Current Population Survey data for June, 1975 (Washington, D.C.: U.S. Bureau of the Census, 1975). J. Ross Eshleman, *The Family*, Fourth Edition (Boston: Allyn and Bacon, 1985).

### *Reasons for Cohabitation*

The decision to live together is based on a variety of reasons. Many of the students questioned in various studies indicated that they would not consider marrying someone without first living with them. Three-quarters of Macklin's sample made such a claim, and many said their reason was a general disillusionment with marriage. Student comments of the following sort are quite common:

A wedding license is just a scrap of paper.

Marriage is just one of society's definitions.

I feel that if two people want to live together unmarried, they should because all the legalities in the world won't keep them together if they want out. So to save time and energy, do whatever comes natural—not legal. (Arafat and Yorburg, 1975:306)

I think marriage is a sort of dead end. I have seen so many couples who were very happy when they were just living together. Then they decided to get married and things really got to be a drag. (Thorman, 1973:250)

On the whole, the evidence suggests that the majority of couples who decide to live together are not perfectly certain of their motives for entering the relationship. This is not to say that they enter it lightly, since most report strong ties of affection and a sense of loyalty toward their partners as prerequisites of such an arrangement. The reasons for maintaining such relationships vary, however (see box).

## Living Together: Give Me One Good Reason Why

The reasons unmarried couples give for deciding to share a household involve varying degrees of intimacy and commitment. Eleanor Macklin's (1983) typology of cohabitation arrangements indicates the range of differences in these explanations.

1. *Temporary, casual convenience.* Two individuals share the same living quarters because it is expedient to do so.
2. *Affectionate dating—going together.* In this type of relationship, the partners stay together because they enjoy being with one another. They will continue as a couple as long as both prefer to do so.
3. *Trial marriage.* This type includes partners who are "engaged to be engaged" and those who are consciously testing the relationship before making a permanent commitment.
4. *Temporary alternative to marriage.* The individuals are committed to staying together but are waiting until it is more convenient to marry.
5. *Permanent alternative to marriage.* The individuals live together in a long-term committed relationship similar to marriage, but without the traditional religious or legal ties.

## Problems of Cohabitation

Unmarried couples living together experience many of the same problems as young married couples. For example, 71 percent of the students interviewed by Macklin (1972) reported that there was some discrepancy between their own and their partners' level of sexual interest; 62 percent reported fear of pregnancy; and 62 percent mentioned occasional failure of the woman to achieve orgasm as problems. The experience of couples living together as compared to married couples is unique in several respects, however. The most common problem reported by cohabiting individuals involves the opposition of parents or the tensions involved in keeping their relationship secret. Nearly half of Macklin's female respondents said that their parents did not know of their living arrangements, and more than one-fourth said they were troubled by such factors as "parental disapproval of the boy, fear of discovery, guilt because they were deceiving or hurting their parents, rejection by or ultimatums from parents, and, most frequently, sadness at not being able to share this important part of their lives with their parents" (1972:468).

For a number of attitudinal and structural reasons, the relationships of cohabiting couples are less stable than those of married couples. Three-quarters of Macklin's (1972) sample of cohabiting students continued to maintain separate residences. This was done not only to avoid confrontations with parents but to guard against identity loss and to give each person privacy and sufficient time with her or his own friends. Safeguarding their personal autonomy made it easier for the individuals to split up if they perceived that the relationship was not doing well.

Because unmarried cohabitants do not, by definition, go through any public commitment ceremony, their relationship is not labeled by either themselves or society as a permanent one. The importance of this labeling process cannot be overemphasized. Sociologists consider one of the requirements of a permanent, stable relationship to be that the participants and those around them publicly define it as demanding a long-term commitment. Apart from the obvious legal restraints of marriage, publicly promising and expecting to live together forever makes two individuals more likely to try to sustain a relationship through difficult times. More important, in response to a public announcement of marriage, the expectations of others may function as obligations to be fulfilled by the marriage partners. The public proclamation of marriage can knit couples more securely into the social fabric than a decision made in private to live together.

Pubic proclamations of marriage do not ensure harmonious long-term relationships, however, as studies of marital satisfaction over the life cycle reveal (Eshleman, 1985:443–445). In fact, such proclamations often help lock people into unfulfilling marriages that might best be ended were it not for pressures to please one's relatives or friends.

### Role-Making and the New Morality

The increasing acceptability of unmarried cohabitation is a prime example of the practice of role-making (see Chapter 3). During the last decade or so, young men and women have transformed the structure of their own intimate relationships; they have surely provided new meaning to the word *roommate.* It is too early to tell whether this social innovation will have long-lasting or permanent effects on later generations' views about intimacy, sexuality, and commitment, or whether young persons' disillusionment with marrige will grow or persist.

If there has been any new morality expressed by those living together, it is that love and marriage do not necessarily "go together like a horse and carriage," as the song goes. A principle of the emerging morality seems to be that it is right to live with someone you love, whether or not you are married. One respondent in a survey of attitudes on marriage, living together, and infidelity suggested that "The only real infidelity is living together with someone you don't love" (Karlen, 1972:99).

## Staying Single

In the past few years the stereotype of an unmarried person as a lonely eccentric, unable to find a mate, has given way to the image of an affluent, sophisticated, urban member of the singles' set whose life is an endless round of parties, tennis matches, vacations, and fulfilling but unrestrictive sexual encounters. The portrayal in the media of a "swinging singles" lifestyle in the 1970s chronicled a steady increase in the number of unmarried Americans.

Census reports indicate that the percentage of males 20 to 34 years old in the population who were never married increased from 28.6 in 1960 to 41.8 percent in 1982, and the percentage of never-married females that age went from 15.2 in 1960 to 29.4 percent in 1982 (U.S. Bureau of the Census, 1983, Table 57). There were 34.4 million single never-married persons of all ages in 1982. Today's singles also include a growing number of divorced persons—from 2.9 million in 1960 to 11.5 million in 1982. An even larger number of widowed persons (12.7 million) also could be considered singles (U.S. Bureau of the Census, 1983, Table 50).

Some additional statistics from the 1980 Census data were cited by Peter Stein (1981:2) to indicate just how the singles group is growing:

About 50 percent of all women between 20 and 24 years of age had never been married (compared to less than 30 percent in 1960).

The divorce rate more than doubled in 15 years, from 2.5 per 1,000 population in 1965 to 5.2 in 1980.

The number of individuals living alone increased by nearly 60 percent in the 1970s—to 1 out of 5 households.

### Pros and Cons

Many singles have a negative view of marriage which is a central factor in their decisions to avoid it. In another study by Stein (1977), respondents said that in their opinion marriage inhibits personal growth, provides inadequate emotional support, and promotes an unwelcome dependency on one's mate. They thought their single status gave them greater freedom, more opportunities to meet new people, and the chance to enjoy more and better sexual experiences. The women interviewed thought the psychological autonomy they enjoyed would be impossible within the context of marriage.

While the single lifestyle may offer advantages, American society remains couple-oriented, and singles face substantial problems. Beyond a certain age, they experience pressure from parents, friends, and colleagues to get married. Many report that they have few married couples as friends, and the circle of their friendship is generally restricted to other single persons. Loneliness is a distinctive problem for many single persons, who may look back on their high school or college days as a time when it was easy to make friends. Friendships with other singles are always considered secondary to a possible date. Many singles describe their greatest need as "networks of human relationships that provide the basic satisfactions of intimacy, sharing, and continuity" (Stein, 1977:534).

### The Single's Search for Intimacy

Unmarried persons go to great lengths to try to produce intimate, caring relationships. In singles' bars, for example, just being present signals receptivity to such a relationship, but the development of intimacy is no easy matter. There are fairly rigid social conventions governing behavior in this setting (see Chapter 1).

Suzanne Gordon (1977) found, for example, that Wednesdays and Fridays were the most popular evenings at singles' bars. Going to one on a Saturday night is equivalent to a public admission that one is unable to get a date elsewhere. Singles' bars habitués try to avoid the appearance of being "regulars." According to a waiter at Maxwell's Plum, a singles' bar in New York:

People tell me this is the first time they have been to a bar because they don't want people to know that they have to come to bars every night. . . . You want people to think you have things to do and that you're busy and worldly, and the last thing you want them to think is that you're in the bar every night. It's bad for the image. (Gordon, 1977:225)

It's bad for the image! That pretty well sums up why singles nearly uniformly dislike singles' bars. Such a high premium is placed on impression management and "scoring" that the players in this particular drama put on performances that would be considered outrageous elsewhere. Because of the crowded, noisy conditions, most conversation is directed at quickly determining the other person's salary, position, and marital status. Gordon gives instances of both men and women approaching strangers and, after only the barest and most superficial communication, asking them home for the evening.

The popularity of this uniquely urban setting has continued even though most participants expect to be disappointed. The atmosphere is often one of artificiality, enormous risks to one's self, and extraordinary insensitivity. One woman explains the self-fulfilling prophecy operating in these bars: "You know that you'll never meet any man that you'd really like because the kind of man you'd really like wouldn't be in a singles' bar. . . . But you get lonely and go anyway" (Gordon, 1977:230).

*Meeting in unexpected places.* Settings which cater to singles, taken together, are frequented by only a small percentage of single persons. To produce sustained relationships, they also use other settings that were not designed as meeting places for unmarrieds. Small stores, taverns, laundromats, clubs of various sorts, and church functions are all considered places in which potentially intimate relationships can be established.

Sociologists have long recognized that, along with the stated, obvious or **manifest functions** performed by an institution, setting, or organization, there may also be a number of unintended or **latent functions.** Single persons who wish to meet others under the most "natural" conditions possible may find such settings as evening education classes, museums, political club meetings, protest marches, and church groups preferable to bars. For many singles, the latent functions of these settings is *mating*. Indeed, some single persons strategically choose unexpected settings for the purpose of meeting others. One woman, fed up with the bar scene, reported that she occasionally visited San Francisco International Airport on weekends because "When a guy has to wait an hour between planes, he might as well sit around and talk" (Keyes, 1975:334).

In their systematic study of the ways recent college graduates adapt to city life, Joyce Starr and Donald Carns (1973) also minimize the significance of singles' bars, apartment complexes, and other such facilities for establishing social contacts. The respondents to their survey said work was the most significant institutional setting for making friends and eventually establishing intimate relationships. The connection between work and dating is, however, an indirect one. Starr and Carns describe a two-stage process:

> It is on the job that most graduates form friendships, much in line with the view of the city as a pattern of functionally, not spacially, interrelated people. They do not, by and large, date persons from the office for a number of reasons, among them, a lack of eligibles and the tendency to avoid social intimacy with persons one must face each day whether the relationship succeeded or failed. But through office friends, dates are arranged. It is, in short, a friend-of-a-friend pattern that provides the raw material out of which dating relationships are formed. . . .(p. 290)

This discussion of how singles take advantage of the latent functions of institutions such as work is not intended to serve as a survival guide for singles in the city. It does provide support for our view that human beings are capable of transforming their environments in important ways, however. People are not mere victims of their environments, as many sociologists would have it. We would not want to minimize the extent of many single persons' loneliness, but it seems a fair inference that they can tolerate only so much impersonality in their relationships. Perhaps at the height of their feelings of depersonalization and lack of integration, they will seek out alternatives in the environment to provide them with the kinds of relationships they seem to be denied. The fact that some singles purposively go to airports, laundromats, or public libraries to meet others reveals more than the ingenuity of a few individuals. As people's needs demand, they assign new meanings to and make different usages of existing institutions. We interpret the adaptive strategies of single persons as elegant evidence for our position that they are active participants in the construction of their social worlds.

## ■ CONCLUSION

This chapter began with the somewhat circular conception of intimate relationships as those which the participants define as intimate. Our goal has been to extend this idea by analyzing how people come to define their relationships as intimate. Relations of love and friendship are without intrinsic meaning and must be understood as symbolic constructions which are deeply rooted in social life. Individuals soon learn the values of the society and of their immediate reference groups concerning the meanings of love, friendship, and family relationships.

Like any symbol whose meaning by definition is not fixed, the concept of intimacy is subject to substantial historical and contemporary variation in meanings. The meanings of sexual relations and relations of parents and children have changed over time, for example. The meanings given to love and friendship also vary with such social attributes as age, occupation, race, ethnicity, gender, and social class. The substantial differences in the definitions given friendships by males and females and by persons in different social classes are particularly apparent in the connection between social mobility and the nature of friendship ties.

Intimate relationships are continually being interpreted and reevaluated by the participants in a regular, patterned process. The wheel theory of love describes the process through which strangers are transformed into intimates. The typical movement of such a relationship is from achievement of rapport to self-revelation to mutual commitment. The next step normally would be plans for marriage. In recent years, however, many young people have chosen to live together without marriage or to remain single. These efforts to refashion social ties have brought changes in the meanings given to intimacy and commitment.

Our treatment of intimate relations has been based on the assumption that individuals are joint participants in the construction of their social relationships. In most relationships, however, they are not equal participants. Some individuals have restricted choices about how they can respond to others and about the meanings conferred on objects, events, and situations. In the next chapter we will focus on the important issue of the distribution and application of power in everyday life.

## Definitions

**Need for affiliation.** The perceived need or desire for meaningful relationships with others.

**Social constructions.** Meanings of things and situations which are created by people through their interactions with one another.

**Extended family.** A household made up of husband and wife plus other relatives, often including several generations. The extended family includes a *kinship network* of persons related by birth or by marriage.

**Nuclear family.** A family consisting only of a husband, wife, and their children.

**Gender roles.** Societal and cultural expectations which regulate feminine and masculine behaviors.

**Social mobility.** The process by which people make changes in their occupation or social class.

**Intimacy process.** The ways individuals establish a relationship of emotional closeness with one another.

**Romantic love ideal.** The notion that the love of a man and woman for each other is the only basis for marriage.

**Wheel theory of love.** A metaphor used by Ira Reiss to describe the circular process by which two persons pass through phases of increasing intimacy with each other.

**Relationship filters.** Subtle devices by which individuals determine if they have anything in common with one another.

**Public definition.** The ways in which others in an immediate social circle define an individual. Two individuals who have been publicly defined as a couple become bound in a web of societal expectations.

**Commitment crisis.** A situation in which a person must make a decision about how important a relationship is to him or her.

**Cohabitation.** A situation in which unmarried heterosexual couples live together and share the same household.

**Manifest functions.** The explicit, or stated, purposes of an organization or institution.

**Latent functions.** The unintended consequences of the ways in which an organization or institution actually operates.

# Discussion Questions

1. Are you willing to agree with the authors' point of view that intimacy is a *social construction*—that relationships of love and friendship are symbolic productions and have no intrinsic meaning?

2. How would you describe the distinguishing characteristics of a love relationship? What are the distinctive obligations and expectations defining love relationships? How do such obligations and expectations differ from those defining friendship relationships?

3. Describe a relationship that you have had with a boy or girl friend. Did the relationship pass through discernible stages as it developed? Do these stages conform to those named in the chapter? Are there similar stages to the "breaking up" process?

4. How would you characterize the attitudes of your friends toward premarital sex? Has there been a sexual revolution? How would you explain the reported increase between 1965 and 1980 in the percentage of college women experiencing intercourse?

5. Would you interpret the recent increase in the number of unmarried persons choosing to live together as signaling basic shifts in the meanings people are giving to intimacy and commitment?

6. What do you think are the positive and the negative aspects of being single?

# References

Arafat, I., and B. Yorburg. 1975. "On living together without marriage." In *Intimate Life Styles*, ed. J. R. DeLora and J. S. DeLora. Pacific Palisades, Cal.: Goodyear.

Aries, P. 1962. *Centuries of Childhood: A Social History of Family Life*. New York: Vintage Books.

Bach, G., and R. Deutsch. 1970. *Pairing: How to Achieve Genuine Intimacy*. New York: Avon Books.

Boston Women's Health Book Collective. 1974. *Our Bodies—Our Selves*. New York: Simon & Schuster.

Byrne, D. 1970. "Continuity between the experimental study of attraction and real-life computer dating." *Journal of Personality and Social Psychology* 16:157–165.

Cavan, S. 1976. "Talking about sex by not talking about sex." In *The Social Psychology of Sex*, ed. J. Wiseman. New York: Harper & Row.

Chafetz, J. S. 1984. *Sex and Advantage*. Totowa, N.J.: Bowman & Allanheld.

Cuber, J. 1975. "How new ideas about sex are changing our lives." In *Intimate Life Styles*, ed. J. R. DeLora and S. J. DeLora. Pacific Palisades, Cal.: Goodyear.

David, D., and R. Brannon. 1976. *The Forty-Nine Percent Majority*. Reading, Mass.: Addison-Wesley.

Davis, M. 1973. *Intimate Relations*. New York: Free Press.

Eshleman, J. R. 1985. *The Family*. Boston: Allyn & Bacon.

Fasteau, M. 1974. *The Male Machine*. New York: McGraw-Hill.

Fischer, C. 1984. *The Urban Experience*. New York: Harcourt Brace.

Gagnon, J., and W. Simon. 1973. *Sexual Conduct: The Social Sources of Human Sexuality*. Chicago: Aldine.

Gordon, S. 1977. *Lonely in America*. New York: Simon & Schuster.

Gross, H. E. 1984. "Dual-career couples who live apart: Two types." In *Work and Family*, ed. P. Voydanoff. Palo Alto, Cal.: Mayfield.

Hill, C., Z. Rubin, and L. Peplau. 1977. "Breakups before marriage: The end of 103 affairs." In *Family in Transition*, ed. A. Skolnick and J. Skolnick. Boston: Little, Brown.

Hofferth, S., and K. Moore. 1979. "Women's employment and marriage." In *The Subtle Revolution: Women at Work*, ed. R. E. Smith. Washington, D.C.: Urban Institute.

Howe, F. 1977. *Pink Collar Workers*. New York: Avon Books.

Karlen, A. 1972. "The unmarrieds on campus." In *Contemporary Society*, ed. J. Perry and M. Seidler. New York: Canfield Press.

Karp, D., G. Stone, and W. Yoels. 1977. *Being Urban: A Social Psychological View of City Life*. Lexington, Mass.: D. C. Heath.

Keyes, R. 1975. "Singled out." In *Intimate Life Styles*, ed. J. R. DeLora and J. S. DeLora. Pacific Palisades, Cal.: Goodyear.

Knafl, K. 1975. "Preparing for marriage: A case of misrepresentation." Paper presented at the American Sociological Association Annual Meetings, San Francisco, California.

Macklin, E. 1972. "Heterosexual cohabitation among unmarried college students." *The Family Coordinator* (October):463–471.

Macklin, E. 1974. "Going very steady." *Psychology Today* 8 (November):53–59.

Macklin, E. 1983. "Nonmarital heterosexual cohabitation." In *Family in Transition*, ed. A. Skolnick and J. Skolnick. Boston: Little, Brown.

Packard, V. 1972. *A Nation of Strangers*. New York: David McKay.

Pleck, J. 1981. "The work-family problem: Overloading the system." In *Outsiders on the Inside: Women and Organizations*, ed. B. Forishe and B. Goldman. Englewood Cliffs, N.J.: Prentice-Hall.

Reiss, I. 1960. "Toward a Sociology of the Heterosexual Love Relationship." *Marriage and Family Living* 22 (May):139–145.

Riesman, D. 1950. *The Lonely Crowd*. New Haven, Conn.: Yale University Press.

Robboy, H. 1983. "At work with the night worker." In *Social Interaction: Readings in Sociology*, ed. H. Robboy and C. Clark. New York: St. Martin's Press.

Robinson, I., and D. Jedlicka. 1982. "Changes in sexual attitudes and behavior of college students from 1965 to 1980: A research note." *Journal of Marriage and the Family* 44 (February 1982):237–240.

Rubin, L. 1976. *Worlds of Pain*. New York: Harper & Row.

Rubin, L. 1983. *Intimate Strangers*. New York: Harper & Row.

Schacter, S. 1959. *The Psychology of Affiliation*. Stanford, Cal.: Stanford University Press.

Starr, J., and D. Carns. 1973. "Singles and the city: Notes on urban adaptation."

In *Cities in Change*, ed. J. Walton and D. Carns. Boston: Allyn & Bacon.

Stein, P. 1977. "Singlehood: An alternative to marriage." In *Family in Transition*, ed. J. Skolnick and A. Skolnick. Boston: Little, Brown.

Stein, P. 1981. *Single Life: Unmarried Adults in Social Context*. New York: St. Martin's Press.

Thorman, G. 1973. "Cohabitation: A report on the married-unmarried life style." *The Futurist* 7 (December):250–253.

U.S. Bureau of the Census. 1977. "Marital status and living arrangements: March 1976." *Current Population Reports* (Series P-20, no. 306). Washington, D.C.: Government Printing Office.

U.S. Bureau of the Census. 1983. *Statistical Abstract of the United States, 1984*. Washington, D.C.: Government Printing Office.

Waller, W. 1938. *The Family: A Dynamic Interpretation*. Hinsdale, Ill.: Dryden Press.

Walster, E. 1974. "Passionate love." In *Intimacy, Family and Society*, ed. A. Skolnick and J. Skolnick. Boston: Little, Brown.

Weiss, R. 1975. *Marital Separation*. New York: Basic Books.

Whyte, W. F. 1955. *Street Corner Society*. Chicago: University of Chicago Press.

Whyte, W. H. 1956. *The Organization Man*. New York: Simon & Schuster.

# CHAPTER 6

# Power and Stratification in Everyday Life: The Politics of Interaction

I. Power Relations in the Macro and Micro Worlds
   A. The Broad Contours of Power: Money and Jobs
      1. Family income and wealth
      2. Effects of ascribed-status characteristics
   B. Social Class, Power, and Self-Concept
      1. Men and work
      2. Women, work, and family politics
II. The Relationship of Power to Role-Taking
   A. The Less the Power, the Better the Role-Taking
      1. Ascribed-status differences in role-taking
   B. Conning Strategies of the Powerless
III. The Subtle Faces of Power in Everyday Interactions
   A. Power Talks: The Names People Use
      1. Affection for subordinates and respect for superiors
   B. Staring
   C. Touching
   D. Interrupting
   E. Crowding Another's Space
   F. Frowning, Looking Stern, Pointing
IV. Conclusion

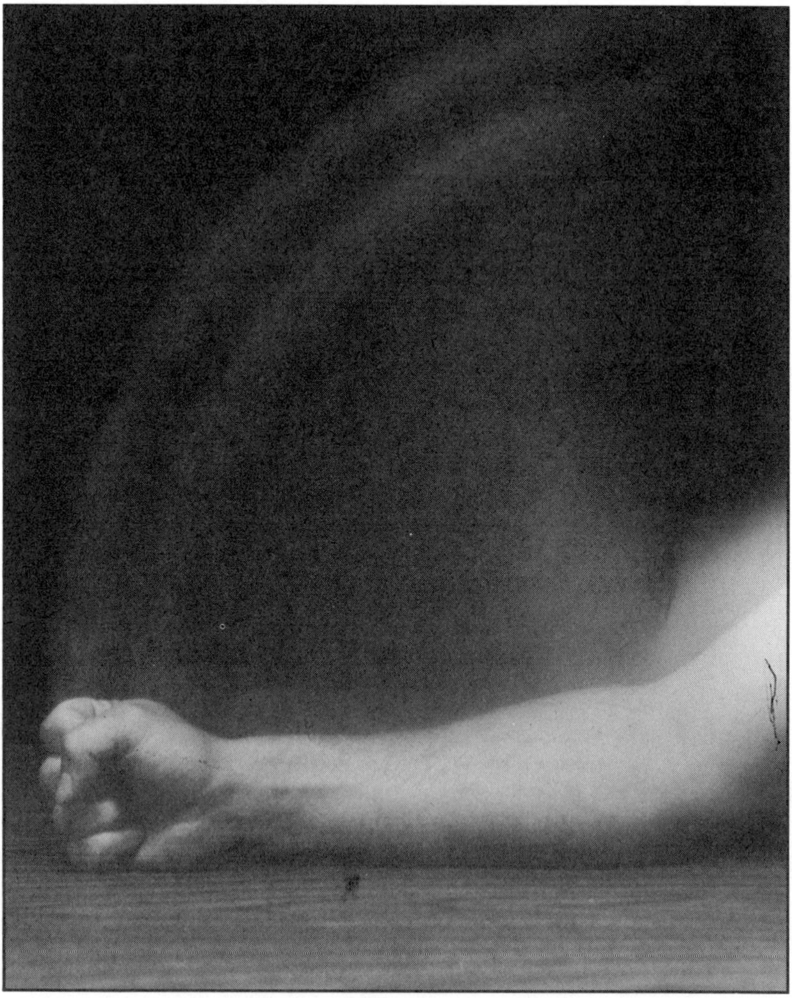

# CHAPTER 6

KARL MARX, a noted observer of human affairs, remarked long ago that "Human beings make history, but not under conditions of their own choosing." While symbolic interactionists would agree, they would put it that individuals jointly construct reality, socially and symbolically (see Chapter 2), but everyone in a society does not participate equally in the construction of social worlds. People with various ascribed and achieved attributes and members of different social classes have varying opportunities to gain access to the decision-making processes in a society. These differences are reflected in the system of social stratification which prevails in the society.

For many social scientists, **social stratification** is simply a ranking of the persons in a society from upper class to lower class, according to such measures as their income, education, or occupation. Symbolic interactionists believe it more appropriate to think of social stratification as a power phenomenon. That is, in discussing stratification we are really talking about the ways in which various individuals' opportunities or **life-chances** are distributed in a certain society. A person's access to such valued goals as well-paying jobs, positions of prestige and status, opportunities for a long and comfortable life, and even adequate health care are determined to a large extent by her or his *position* in the stratification system. It is in terms of these life-chances that the importance of history, as Marx suggested, becomes evident. We are born into a social world whose symbols have been prefabricated by the activities of previous generations. Their actions have resulted in the construction of social realities whose existence we, as newcomers, must acknowledge if we are to operate as "sane" and "normal" members of society. There is evidence of the social dialectic between freedom and constraint discussed in Chapter 1. We are free to make choices and decisions in our everyday lives, but the range of alternatives from which we choose is the result of historical and institutional factors beyond our control.

The distinction between ascribed and achieved statuses is particularly important in this regard (see Chapter 3). Ascribed statuses are those we acquire at birth, such as gender and race, while achieved statuses are those acquired (achieved) during the course of our lives, such as our organizational and occupational statuses. In contemporary American society, despite a great deal of official rhetoric to the contrary, our ascribed-status characteristics have much to do with the nature of our life-chances. One lesson of social science is that one must choose one's parents with great care!

## ■ POWER RELATIONS IN THE MACRO AND MICRO WORLDS

The **differential access** of various persons in a society to scarce and highly valued resources—such as jobs and money—confers on those who have comparatively greater access an advantage of power in everyday, face-to-face relations. Interactions between men and women, husbands and wives, even children and parents are inextricably bound up with the issue of power between **superiors** and subordinates, or **inferiors.** Face-to-face relations between members of different social classes, races, and genders must also be seen within the broader context of power relations. In this sense everyday interactions are political acts, and they can be studied within the frame of the *politics of interaction* which takes into account these power differentials.

This interface between individuals' daily lives and the organization of the society also shows clearly the manner in which personal biographies intersect with the larger arenas of history and social structure. As Peter and Brigitte Berger put it, we simultaneously inhabit different worlds, the **micro world** and the **macro world:**

First of all, crucially and continuously, we inhabit the *micro-world* of our immediate experience with others in face-to-face relations. Beyond that, with varying degrees of significance and continuity, we inhabit a *macro-world* consisting of much larger structures and involving us in relations with others that are mostly abstract, anonymous and remote. Both worlds are essential to our experience of society, and . . . each world depends upon the other for its meaning to us. (1975:8)

The Bergers suggest that any analysis of face-to-face behavior must consider it within the context of broader institutional arrangements. Similarly, any analysis of an institution, such as religion or education, must take into account its origins in the daily communications among its members. To use the terms introduced in Chapter 1, both macrosociological and microsociological investigation are necessary to the analysis of behavior. Moreover, interplay between the types of power exercised in the macro and micro worlds determines individuals' access to the rewarding incomes and occupations a society has to offer.

## The Broad Contours of Power: Money and Jobs

In contemporary American society, access to the means for the production and distribution of wealth is a crucial factor in a person's ability to establish a dominant position in the stratification system. To begin our analysis, we will sketch the broad outlines of how certain resources are distributed in American society.

### Family Income and Wealth

Table 6.1 presents data on the distribution of family income in the United States in the period 1950–1982, during which the concentration of income fluctuated slightly but remained virtually unchanged. The fifth of the population with the highest income, which accounted for 42.7 percent of the nation's total income in 1950, accounted for the same percentage in 1982. The percentage of income held by the lowest fifth rose only from 4.5 to 4.7 percent in this period.

Membership in the upper class, at the top of the stratification system, is determined by wealth, or total assets, rather than family income or

Table 6.1
Distribution of Family Income, United States, 1950–1982

| Year | Family Income Level ||||| 
|---|---|---|---|---|---|
| | Lowest Fifth | Second Fifth | Middle Fifth | Fourth Fifth | Highest Fifth |
| 1950 | 4.5% | 12.0% | 17.4% | 23.4% | 42.7% |
| 1960 | 4.8 | 12.2 | 17.8 | 24.0 | 41.3 |
| 1970 | 5.4 | 12.2 | 17.6 | 23.8 | 40.9 |
| 1980 | 5.1 | 11.6 | 17.5 | 24.3 | 41.6 |
| 1982 | 4.7 | 11.2 | 17.5 | 24.3 | 42.7 |

*Sources:* U.S. Bureau of the Census, *Statistical Abstract of the United States, 1982–83* (Washington, D.C.: Government Printing Office, 1982), p. 58, and *1984* (published 1983), Table 765.

earnings. In 1976, the wealthiest 1 percent of the population owned 18.3 percent of the personal wealth in the United States, as measured by such assets as real estate, corporate stock, bonds, and cash (U.S. Bureau of the Census, 1983, Table 795). The top 1 percent is composed of different persons over the course of time, but movement into the upper class is very slight, since membership is largely based on such ascribed-status characteristics as family background, race, and ethnicity (Tyree and Smith, 1978).

In *The Higher Circles* (1970), G. William Domhoff documents the exclusiveness and impermeability of upper-class social worlds. He also notes the gender distinctions in management of this wealth: "The American upper class is based upon large corporate wealth that is looked after by the male members of the intermarrying families that are its basis . . . [upper class women] participate in a great many activities which sustain the upper class as a social class and help to maintain the stability of the social system as a whole" (p. 56). It is the men who "look after" the wealth, however.

### Effects of Ascribed-Status Characteristics

To a dramatic extent, ascribed-status characteristics such as gender and race are embedded in the institutions of American society. The differential access to positions of power and prestige which results is built into the organization of the society, or the macro world. It is within this macro world that the stage is set for the daily dramas of the micro world in interactions between individuals.

*Women's occupational opportunities.* Women's access to better-paying jobs has been consistently restricted, though the earnings of women relative to those of men have increased slightly in recent years. The median wages for female workers with full-time jobs went from 62.2 percent of those of full-time male workers in 1970 to 64.9 percent in 1982 (see Table 6.2). As these figures indicate, however, women still earn only about two-thirds the wages of men.

The male-female gap is wider in some occupations than in others. Department of Labor statistics for 1980 indicate that in that year women professionals earned 66 percent of male professionals' earnings, women managers earned 55 percent of male managers' earnings, and women in sales earned 49 percent of male sales workers' earnings. Most female professionals are employed in traditional occupations such as elementary and secondary teaching, nursing, and library work. Women are not well represented in such professions as college teaching, medicine, and law. Indeed, the greater the prestige of a profession, the smaller the proportion of women in it. In 1982, for example, women held 71 percent of

Table 6.2
The Male-Female Earnings Gap,
United States, 1970–1982

| Year | Women's Median Earnings as Percent of Men's (full-time positions) |
|---|---|
| 1970 | 62.2% |
| 1975 | 61.9 |
| 1977 | 61.9 |
| 1978 | 61.2 |
| 1979 | 62.4 |
| 1980 | 63.3 |
| 1981 | 64.5 |
| 1982 | 64.9 |

*Source:* U.S. Bureau of the Census, *Statistical Abstract of the United States, 1984* (Washington, D.C.: Government Printing Office, 1983), Table 716.

the teaching positions in elementary and high schools in the United States but only 35 percent of the teaching positions in colleges and universities. Only 15 percent of physicians, dentists, and related practitioners and 15 percent of lawyers and judges were women in that year (Persell, 1984:304, 305).

*Black-white income differences.* There are also racial and ethnic differences in access to occupations, which largely determines family incomes. Table 6.3 compares median family income in the United States

Table 6.3
Median Family Incomes by Race of Householder, United States, 1950–1982

|  | Median Family Income in Current Dollars* | | |
|---|---|---|---|
| Year | White Families | Black Families | Black Family Income as Percent of White Family Income |
| 1950 | $ 3,445 | $ 1,869 | 54.3% |
| 1960 | 5,835 | 3,230 | 55.4 |
| 1970 | 10,236 | 6,279 | 61.3 |
| 1980 | 21,904 | 12,674 | 57.9 |
| 1982 | 24,603 | 13,598 | 55.3 |

*Current dollars are unadjusted for inflation.
*Source:* U.S. Bureau of the Census, *Statistical Abstract of the United States, 1984* (Washington, D.C.: Government Printing Office, 1983), Table 763.

for whites and blacks between 1950 and 1982. During this period the gap between black and white median incomes was very slightly reduced. Black median family income went from 54.3 percent of white family income in 1950 to 55.3 percent in 1982. Despite such changes, the income differences between white and black families have remained very large indeed. The data in Table 6.3 illustrate the influence of ascribed-status characteristics on an individual's life-chances.

## Social Class, Power, and Self-Concept

Perhaps no aspect of social position has a more fateful hand in the control individuals have over their own lives than their membership in a particular **social class.** Social classes are largely distinguished from one another in terms of the resources and power their members possess. Studies of lower-class and working-class members, for example, have demonstrated the effects of powerlessness on the self-concept. It is often a struggle for those at the lower end (the powerless end) of the stratification system to maintain feelings of self-worth, respect, and honor.

### *Men and Work*

Sociologists have analyzed the connection between the dominant values of American society and the specific values of male members of the lower and working classes. In one well-known study of black "street-corner men" in Washington, D.C., Eliot Liebow (1967) contends that their behaviors can be understood in terms of a social class position that renders them powerless and virtually ensures their failure to succeed by middle-class standards.

To protect themselves from the assaults on their self-conceptions which are created by repeated failures in work and family settings, these men construct what Liebow terms a "shadow system of values." He maintains that they actually subscribe to middle-class achievement values but are unable to realize them because of the constraints imposed by their ascribed class position. They therefore develop an alternative value system. Unable to sustain the breadwinner role, for example, the men respond by depreciating the value of family life. Reluctant to face unemployment or a demeaning job every day, they demean the value of work. Without the resources to raise their children as they would like, they limit their intimacy with them. In short, the street-corner man's behavior

> . . . appears not so much as a way of realizing the distinctive goals and values of his own subculture, or of conforming to its models, but rather as his way of trying to achieve many of the goals and values of the larger society, of failing

to do this, and of concealing his failure from others and from himself as best he can. (Liebow, 1967:222)

Liebow shows how the daily, face-to-face relationships of men with their wives, lovers, friends, and children relate to the broader configurations of power in the society. He also illustrates how the "hurts" of a powerless class position influence individuals' self-conceptions, which accounts for their patterns of adaptive behavior.

In another book with much the same theme, *The Hidden Injuries of Class* (1973), Richard Sennet and Jonathon Cobb present interviews which describe how working-class men create their own interpretations of dominant American social values. The emphasis in American society on achievement is continually reaffirmed in education and the mass media. Americans are socialized to measure a person's worth, honor, and respect in terms of individual achievement. It follows that those who fail to achieve in the work world suffer from feelings of self-doubt and shame.

Working-class men, near the bottom of the occupational scale, must somehow adapt to a society that measures their value in terms of occupational achievement. There is a sort of "catch 22" operating in this situation. Those who are born into a powerless, dependent, and subordinate social class position come to feel bad about themselves because they lack autonomy. A social sleight of hand occurs whereby the victims of a system of institutionalized inequality are socialized to blame themselves for that state of affairs. According to Sennett and Cobb, these men "know they are supposed to work hard, and do the best they can. They see that a few do 'make it,' but not, as far as can be seen, because of anything different about them. To keep going in the face of this riddle, a defense . . . is needed" (p. 201).

One such defense identified by Sennett and Cobb is to define work itself as meaningless—to view it as a sacrifice a man must make for his family. By defining work this way, the working-class male transforms his definition of self. Rather than focusing on his own poor work performance, he comes to view his work self-righteously, as a noble sacrifice. Moreover, the definition of work as sacrifice provides a solution to the problem of powerlessness. In return for this sacrifice, a working-class man can demand complete power within the family. He may be denied a power role within the larger occupational system, but he can exercise this role in his day-to-day relations with wife and children.

## *Women, Work, and Family Politics*

Working-class women also suffer from the "hidden injuries of class." Barbara Garson's (1977) study of such women, based on her own work experiences, dramatically reveals the extent to which they also feel trapped and demeaned by jobs that have little social worth and prestige in American society. Stuck in boring, routine jobs as clerical workers, sales personnel, or factory workers, the women interviewed by Garson tried to "humanize" their jobs by improvising various "play activities" to make their workdays bearable. One worker who had to deal with the isolation associated with work as a keypuncher told Garson that she and another girl who were both very good, high performers, but bored, used to race one another:

> I guess it was the only kind of entertainment you could have. Like I said, your hands were occupied, your eyes were occupied, you couldn't move your body, couldn't talk. You only had the numbers on the sheets and the sounds of the other machines. (1977:155)

As we noted in Chapter 5, increasing numbers of women are entering the labor force. The home itself often becomes a forum for family politics in which wives seek an equitable trade-off for the work they do outside the home (see the box on family politics in Chapter 9). Questions of power become critical in such situations. In working-class couples, the wife's decision to look for paid full-time work is often experienced by the husband as a threat to his masculinity and a challenge to his ability to perform in the role of family breadwinner. According to Lillian Rubin, both women and men become stuck in "a painful bind," with each blaming the other:

> She isn't the dependent, helpless, frivolous child-woman because it would be ludicrously inappropriate, given her life experiences. He isn't the independent, masterful, all-powerful provider, not because he does "dumb" or irresponsible things, but because the burdens he carries are too great for all but a few of the most privileged—burdens that are especially difficult to bear in a highly competitive economic system that doesn't grant every man and woman the right to work at a self-supporting and self-respecting wage as a matter of course. (1976:178)

## ■ THE RELATIONSHIP OF POWER TO ROLE-TAKING

If you think of the world in dramaturgical terms (see Chapter 3), as a Shakespearian stage on which everyone is a player of roles, then, in real life as in any play, some roles evoke much more respectful attention and applause than others. Some persons are able to elicit far more consideration and respect for their wants, desires, and needs than are others. Indeed, in daily encounters with others, this is the most basic face that power presents. The powerful *demand* attention and interest. They do it overtly through the resources at their disposal to punish people who ignore them. And they do it covertly through the way people are socialized by society's institutions—family, school, church, and so on—to respect those whom society deems most worthy.

Role-taking has been described as the basic process by which persons develop their selves (see Chapter 2). By putting themselves in the role (i.e., the "place") of others, individuals are able to view themselves from the perspective of others, while anticipating how others are going to respond to them. This is certainly accurate as a general statement about interaction, but something is missing. That missing ingredient, the authors suggest, is the acquisition and use of power.

Many learned treatises have been presented on the nature of power, but for our purposes it is sufficient to conceive of **power** as the English scholar R. H. Tawney defined it years ago:

Power may be defined as the capacity of an individual, or group of individuals, to modify the conduct of other individuals or groups in the manner which he desires, and to prevent his own conduct being modified in the manner in which he does not. (1931:229)

This definition indirectly acknowledges the necessity of taking the role of others in order to communicate with them meaningfully. But some persons face much less pressure to engage in role-taking than others do. Their power allows them to demonstrate insensitivity, callousness, or indifference to the desires of others. Others must respond sensitively and, above all, accurately, to the wishes of the powerful.

In the process of role-taking, the requirements for accuracy vary with the power of the position occupied by the role-taker. In Erving Goffman's terms (see Chapter 3), some individuals "make" the roles and others are constrained to "take" them; that is, some people's symbols evoke a more deferential response than others' do. An example of how the more powerful make the roles that the less powerful must take is the restricted movements and expressionless countenances and prudent behaviors traditionally expected of women in many everyday situations. If men tried to take the roles of women in this respect they would have to go through some difficult maneuvers (see Figure 6.1).

## The Less the Power, the Better the Role-Taking

Studies of the relationships between power and role-taking ability have generated an interesting body of findings. In one study, Darwin Thomas, David Franks, and James Calanico concluded that "role-taking ability varies inversely with the degree of power ascribed to social positions"

Figure 6.1
Role-Taking for Men: How to Put Yourself in the Place of Women

1. Sit down in a straight chair. Cross your legs at the ankles and keep your knees pressed together. Try to do this while you're having a conversation with someone, but pay attention at all times to keeping your knees pressed tightly together.

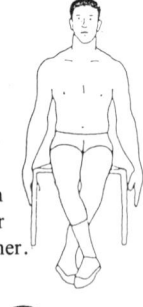

2. Bend down to pick up an object from the floor. Each time you bend remember to bend your knees so that your rear end doesn't stick up, and place one hand on your shirtfront to hold it to your chest. This exercise simulates the experience of a woman in a short, low-necked dress bending over.

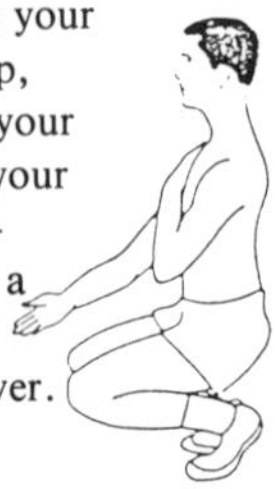

3. Run a short distance, keeping your knees together. You'll find you have to take short, high steps if you run this way. Women have been taught it is unfeminine to run like a man with long, free strides. See how far you get running this way for 30 seconds.

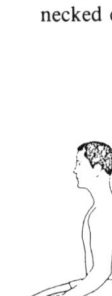

4. Sit comfortably on the floor. Imagine that you are wearing a dress and that everyone in the room wants to see your underwear. Arrange your legs so that no one can see. Sit like this a long time without changing your position.

5. Walk down a city street. Pay a lot of attention to your clothing: make sure your pants are zipped, shirt tucked in, buttons done. Look straight ahead. Every time a man walks past you, avert your eyes and make your face expressionless. Most women learn to go through this act each time we leave our houses. It's a way to avoid at least some of the encounters we've all had with strange men who decided we looked available.

6. Walk around with your stomach pulled tight, your shoulders thrown back, and your chest thrust out. Pay attention to keeping this posture at all times. Notice how it changes your breathing. Try to speak loudly and aggressively in this posture.

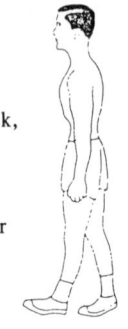

*Source:* "Exercises for Men," from Willamette Bridge (and Liberation News Service), 1971, (Portland, Ore.: Portland Scribe). Reprinted in Nancy Henley, *Body Politics* (Englewood Cliffs, N.J.: Prentice-Hall, 1977), p. 144.

(1972:612). In comparing the accuracy of people's predictions about the behaviors of others, they found that those in lesser positions of power have more accurate perceptions of their superior's behaviors than vice versa. The *position* the person occupies, not just within some organization but within society as a whole, is an important factor. The question of power is not simply a matter of individuals' personality characteristics. This is another demonstration of the importance of seeing the larger institutional order as the setting within which daily life occurs.

Thomas and his colleagues note that "role-taking not only socializes the individual but is used to control others' responses by pleasing them on their own terms" (p. 606). In their study of power relations within the family, for example, they found that "fathers are significantly less accurate role-takers than mothers and mothers significantly less accurate role-takers than their children" (p. 612). These findings generally supported their hypothesis, since fathers usually have more power within the family than mothers, and mothers have more power than children. The less powerful—mothers and children—were the more accurate role-takers.

In measuring role-taking accuracy, these authors presented the members of the families selected for their study with a series of test items posing hypothetical situations. Respondents were asked to indicate how they would advise the persons in the situation to act and how they thought other members of the family would advise them to act. The following example from their study used a situation which posed a dilemma for male college-age students before the military draft ended in 1973 and they faced the possibility of being drafted for service in the armed forces:

A young man about to graduate from college is opposed to military service but is sure he will be drafted shortly after he graduates. He is trying to decide whether to allow himself to be drafted and serve in the armed forces or to unlawfully resist the draft, thereby risking the chance of arrest and imprisonment.

a. I would advise this young man to allow himself to be drafted and serve in the armed forces.
1. no
2. probably no
3. probably yes
4. yes

b. In my opinion, my father would advise this young man to allow himself to be drafted and serve in the armed forces.

1. yes
2. probably yes
3. probably no
4. no

c. In my opinion my mother would advise this young man to allow himself to be drafted and serve in the armed forces.
1. no
2. probably no
3. probably yes
4. yes

(Thomas, Franks, and Calanico, 1972:608)

Each person's actual response to the questions was compared to the other's prediction of that response. Thus, if a wife predicted that her husband would choose option 4 on question *a* and he *actually* chose option 3, the wife's role-taking accuracy score was 4 minus 3 equals 1.

### *Ascribed-Status Differences in Role-Taking*

Studies such as the one described above have raised a number of interesting questions about how differences in ascribed status affect role-taking ability. If, as this study demonstrates, power and the ability to role-take are inversely related, we can hypothesize that women generally (not just wives) take the roles of men more accurately than men take the roles of women, since women have much less power than men in both the micro world of the family and the macro world of the society. Studies of nonverbal interaction have lent support to this and similar propositions (see box).

Shirley Weitz, for example, inquired into the relationship between the socially constructed roles of men and women and their sensitivity to nonverbal communications. A number of studies have merely demonstrated that women are more likely to smile than men are in heterosexual encounters. Weitz questions the "meaning" of the smile in such a situation. She cites evidence that, for women, "smiling tended to correlate with feelings of social anxiety, discomfort, deference, and abasement, while for men smiling correlated with measures of affiliation and sociability" (1975:4).

Weitz concluded that in the first moments of interaction with men, the nonverbal styles of women are closely attuned to male personality traits. Presumably these traits are transmitted by the male in the very early stages of the interaction and picked up by the female. Weitz's fe-

## Passing the PONS Test: Women's Advantage

If you saw a two-second film clip showing the face of a woman looking upset and saying something that sounds important, though the words aren't clear, could you figure out what she was talking about? According to Robert Rosenthal and Associates (1974), who developed a test to measure sensitivity to nonverbal messages, your accuracy in describing the scene would be better if you are a female than if you are a male. They suggested that the greater sensitivity of women to nonverbal cues may be due to the fact that "when one is powerless, one must be subtle" (p. 66).

The test, called *Profile of Nonverbal Sensitivity*, or PONS, measures a person's ability to understand two kinds of nonverbal communications—tones of voice and facial or body movements. A 45-minute film presents a series of scenes showing facial expressions or a person speaking a few phrases that are audible as sounds but not understandable as words. After each scene is shown, the test-taker is asked to choose one of two possible labels for the scene which are listed on a standardized form. In the example above, the labels might be "expressing jealous anger" or "talking about her divorce." For each scene presented, there is only one correct answer.

The test thus not only measures nonverbal communication understanding. It also provides a means of discrimination between those who can accurately put themselves in the role of the film actors and those who cannot. After administering the PONS test to more than 130 groups of people, Rosenthal and his colleagues concluded that females are more able than males to detect nonverbal cues: "Females of all ages, from third grade through adult, showed a small but reliable advantage over males" (p. 66).

For students of gender-role differences, it is particularly interesting that differences between male and female performances on the PONS test narrowed significantly and were even reversed for men in occupations that are considered to require "nurturant," artistic, or expressive behavior. According to Rosenthal et al., men who were "Actors, artists, interior and industrial designers, psychiatrists, clinical psychologists and the staff of mental hospitals, college students in visual studies courses and school teachers" all tended to score "like women" (p. 66).

male respondents were "not as attuned to female traits" as they were to male ones. She suggests that a possible explanation is that females pose little "threat" to other females in face-to-face encounters. Women can therefore exercise comparatively less interest in, attention to, or involvement with the behavior of other women.

Role-taking ability may also vary among racial groups—certainly an area in which there are substantial power differentials. In another study (Gitter, Black, and Mostofsky, 1972), 48 undergraduate students, both blacks and whites, were presented with a set of photographs. They were then asked to choose, from a list of seven emotions, the one they believed was being expressed by the person in each picture. The results indicate that "Negroes were superior both in terms of overall accuracy score as well as correct scores for the individual emotions" (p. 275).

## Conning Strategies of the Powerless

Studies of race and ethnic relations have demonstrated that when members of the dominant group and members of subordinate groups engage in face-to-face relations, the latter often must resort to indirect **conning strategies** to maintain their self-esteem. Niels Braroe's (1970) anthropological study of Indian-white relations in western Canada is one example. While these Indians are forced to play the roles that whites have made for them, behind the scenes, in what Goffman (1959) calls the **backstage** region, they brag about how they have "conned" the whites:

Jokes are made about the stupidity of whites and the ease with which they are taken in. Fine points of strategy are discussed. "The way to get off easy" according to one informant, "is to act like a dumb Indian in front of the magistrate." This way the punishment for being drunk and disorderly will be lighter than a white man would receive, and "credit" can be arranged—the magistrate will give the guilty Indian months to pay his fine. (p. 246)

As the book *Roots* by Alex Haley (1976) poignantly demonstrates, the **frontstage** performance of the slaves shuffling along saying "Yes, sir, massa," was a role brutally forced on them by the slaveholders. In the backstage regions, they could let their guards down and indicate their awareness of the roles they had been coerced into performing. The ability of the less powerful to take the role offered by the powerful can be a matter of life and death.

When the powerless are denied the opportunity to engage in overt confrontations with their superiors, they must resort to more subtle means of manipulation, conning, and evasiveness. If these words sound vaguely familiar, it may be because they are the same words that are often used to describe how women "naturally" behave in family and career situations. This is not to suggest that women inevitably engage in such behaviors, however. When they do resort to such poses, it has little to do with female biology and a great deal to do with female *destiny*—with the power position of women vis-à-vis men.

The "place" traditionally accorded women in society is similar to that occupied by other disenfranchised groups. Women's progress in entering prestigious occupations which have been traditionally dominated by men has been slow but steady in recent years. Between 1974 and 1980, for example, women's representation in the field of medicine grew from 9.8 to 13.4 percent, and in law it went from 7 to 12.8 percent. According to Jean Lipman-Blumen, "Women engineers were so scarce in 1974 that their percentage of the field was not even recorded in official government statistics; by 1980, they were 8.6 percent of all individuals employed as industrial engineers" (1984:169). As we noted earlier in this chapter, however, the percentages of women in professions are still very small, and they remain relegated to the less prestigious rungs of the professional career ladder (Fox and Hesse-Biber, 1984).

## ■ THE SUBTLE FACES OF POWER IN EVERYDAY INTERACTIONS

The pervasiveness of power in our daily affairs can be demonstrated by numerous examples of verbal and nonverbal interactions. Forms of address are powerful verbal symbols for affirming and reaffirming distinctions among people. A variety of nonverbal "gestures of dominance and submission," as the social psychologist Nancy Henley (1977) puts it, also mark the behavioral responses which acknowledge the power of others. These behaviors include staring, touching, interrupting, and crowding another's space, as well as the gestures of frowning, looking stern, and pointing.

### Power Talks: The Names People Use

The ways in which we address one another may on the surface appear to be merely forms of etiquette. On a deeper level, however, they can be viewed as inextricably bound up with questions of power.

Have you ever, for example, called a boss by her or his first name without asking permission to do so? And has your boss ever asked your permission to use your first name? Quite probably you address your boss in some titular fashion such as Mr., Ms., Doctor, or Professor, while the boss calls you by your first name. You call your parents Mom and Dad or Mother and Father, while they address you with your first name or some endearment. You might say, what else should we call them and they us? But why is that so "natural"? We suggest that there is a power dimension to such common forms of address.

As creatures in a symbolic world, we use terms to refer to ourselves and others which convey a great deal about who and what we are. Our very conception of self is intimately related to the names we use to describe ourselves. Does a man refer to himself, for example, as Robert or Bob? Does a woman want others to call her Margaret or Peggy? We self-consciously fashion our names, within limits, to achieve some agreement with our beliefs about who we are and hope to be.

The use of first names rather than titles like Mr. or Ms. in relations with others represents a particular form of association. The exchange of first names is a way of quickly establishing intimate relationships. We must be careful here, however, since the use of first names is frequently decided by those who have the most power in a relationship. They have the prerogative of intruding into the intimate details of others' lives, though the others are denied similar access to details of theirs. Superiors easily become personal and familiar with subordinates, but the latter are not permitted to get personal. The social psychologist Roger Brown (1965) noted that in English-speaking countries, first names are used by status equals in encounters with each other and by superiors in encounters with subordinates.

### *Affection for Subordinates and Respect for Superiors*

The symbolic communication of intimacy between equals and from superiors to inferiors reflects, as Zick Rubin suggests, "basic differences between the motives that underlie affection and those that underlie respect" (1973:43). We feel affection toward those who are like ourselves because we know them best and probably feel most relaxed and comfortable in their presence. We can assume that such people probably value the same things we do. We are certainly more secure and less anxious in the presence of equals than in the presence of superiors. Rubin says "this is often precisely the way we are made to feel by subordinates whom we look after—comfortable, secure, worthwhile, and certainly on top of things" (p. 43). We are not threatened by such people.

When we like someone we view as superior to ourselves, however, we have mixed responses—admiration, anxiety, or fear, for example. Thus, Rubin suggests, we *respect* our superiors but feel *affectionate* toward both our equals and subordinates. Likewise, our superiors feel affectionate toward their equals and inferiors. Rubin warns that, "As women, slaves, and members of other underprivileged groups are likely to discover, to be regarded with affection is often to be patronized. To receive affection one must stay in one's place and take care not to threaten one's superiors" (p. 44).

## Staring

In American society, one of the privileges of power is the ability to intrude upon another's personal space by prolonged staring without suffering the consequences. Should those of lower status engage in similar behavior, they might be asked to explain their insubordination or lack of respect for their superior's position. The term *insubordination* means precisely failure to acknowledge one's subordinate status in the presence of a superior.

Studies have indicated that women are more likely to look at men than vice versa and are more likely to avert their eyes first, thus breaking off contact, when they are confronted by men. Henley (1977) suggests that this apparent paradox—women both look more often and do not look sooner—might be explained by the "pull of contradictory demands on females—to avert the gaze and to be alert to what the male is doing" (p. 165). Similarly, children are often told—by adults—that it is not nice to stare. Such instruction is often phrased as a matter of etiquette, but it too is related to the question of power. Have you ever heard a child instructing an adult that it is not nice to stare, particularly at children? Probably not. Insofar as staring may be viewed as an invasion of one's privacy or personal space, the less powerful must acknowledge their superiors' "right" to enter that space.

## Touching

You have probably been in situations where a superior—a boss or teacher, for example—has approached and put his or her arm around you, perhaps to compliment you on something you had done. It is hard to imagine the positions reversed, however, with you putting an arm around a boss or teacher. The right to invade another's personal space through touching is another privilege of power and status. There is empirical evidence, for example, that males touch females more often than vice versa; older persons are more likely to touch younger people than the other way around; and people of higher socioeconomic status may touch those of lower socioeconomic status, but the opposite is unlikely (Henley, 1977; Heslin and Boss, 1975).

The power involved in touching others is particularly evident in male-female interactions. Girls are more likely to be touched by others than are boys, a difference which is established very early in life. Indeed, according to advertisements and the lyrics of popular songs, women are "meant" to be cuddled and held. The common use of the term *baby* by males to refer to females may not be coincidental.

The tragic extremes of the presumed "right" of men to touch women may be found in the sexual abuse of children. One study of this problem found that about 90 percent of the sexual offenses committed on children involve the abuse of young girls by older males, who are usually known to the victims (Rush, 1971).

## Interrupting

Interrupting others' conversations is another behavior which has to do with the exercise of power in everyday affairs. Think about your own experiences in talking with someone of higher status than yourself. Who would be more likely to interrupt, you or the other person?

Studies have shown that men not only speak more often and at greater length than women, they also interrupt other speakers more than women do. According to Henley (1977), "This finding applies to all kinds of social situations—alone, in single-sex or mixed pairs, and in groups; it has been found at all occupational levels; and it applies to 'real-life' couples (e.g., husbands and wives) as well as to experimentally created dyads and groups" (p. 74).

The data from one such study (Zimmerman and West, 1975) are quite dramatic. Female speakers accounted for only 4 percent of the interruptions in male-female conversations, while males accounted for the remaining 96 percent! These researchers suggest that males take the role of listener differently when they converse with females than they do with one another. The reason, they say, is that when men talk to one another, "continual or frequent interruption might be viewed as disregard for a speaker, or for what a speaker has to say" (p. 116). The rights of females to speak apparently are casually disregarded by males. Zimmerman and West also found that the silent intervals of women speakers are related to how long and how often they are interrupted by men.

## Crowding Another's Space

One of the prerogatives of privilege and power is the freedom to restrict others' access to one's property and to circumvent the activities of inferiors. Most suburban communities in the United States have enacted housing standards and zoning ordinances which make it very difficult for low-income people to live in such communities, for example. These restrictions by local governments prohibit the construction of low-cost housing and the location of apartment houses and businesses in residential areas.

The consequences of such policies for the quality of contemporary urban life have been noted by John Kasarda:

> Through zoning restrictions and discriminatory practices, the suburban populations have been able to insure that most of the low-income, poorly educated, and chronically unemployed people in the metropolitan area are confined in the central cities. Suburban residents are, therefore, able to avoid the costs of public housing, public health, and other welfare services which often impose a heavy burden on the operating budget of central cities. (1972:1123)

According to Lynn Lofland's (1973) insightful study of urban history, the introduction of zoning ordinances was related to the desire of the emerging middle class, beginning in the 19th century, to "separate itself from the 'dangerous' classes." As a result, "developers did their best, creating district after district of similarly valued homes, and 'protecting' those values through 'covenants' and 'gentlemen's agreements' " (p. 74).

A good example of the relationship between the use of space and power in daily encounters is Archie Bunker's old, homey chair in the TV comedy "All in the Family" which was eventually enshrined in the Smithsonian Institution. It was clear that this was not just any chair—it was Archie's chair. If his wife Edith had a chair also, it was never so designated. Anyone who tried to "usurp" that chair (throne?) from Archie was quickly put in her or his place about whose chair it was.

Such usage of private space beautifully illustrates the interplay between the organization of the institutional, macro world and the dynamics of face-to-face encounters in the micro world. Henley (1977) says:

> Our world is set up so that powerful humans own more territory, move through common areas and others' territory more freely, and take up more space with their bodies, possessions, and symbols. We yield space to them and they grab it from us, either openly or covertly as the occasion (and our acquiescence) allow. Even that corner of the world we call our own . . . will not gain us the resources, privileges, the pleasures, even the survival possibilities that come with the space of the powerful. This is what "position" means in life. (p. 42)

## Frowning, Looking Stern, Pointing

Power and status give superiors license to express their anger, outrage, and displeasure with subordinates. Think of how you might have to handle your own anger if you were particularly upset with something your boss did. Could you tell your boss right out how angry you are? Probably not. More likely, you would have to express your real feelings very diplomatically to avoid provoking the boss's wrath. If you were in your boss's place, it would be much easier to express your resentment, disappointment, or other negative feelings. The tendency for women to smile at men more often than men smile at women is often correlated with women's feelings of anxiety, discomfort, and deference, responses which are typical of the powerless.

The gesture of pointing at another person may also be seen as a power play. Children may be told by adults that pointing, like staring, is not polite. But you never hear an adult admonish another adult not to point at children for the same reason. People in power can point at others and order them forward, backward, and, if need be, even sideways with a simple movement of their fingers. The classic example would be that of the traffic officer in the middle of the intersection, directing traffic by gesturing or pointing in various directions. Needless to say, we usually obey such pointers. In a broader sense, as Michael Wolff (1973) suggests, we must orient our actions to avoid continually colliding and bumping into others, both figuratively and literally (see the box on pedestrian behavior in Chapter 4). Society provides us with authority figures, analogous to traffic officers, who have the license to point us in the "proper" directions.

## ■ CONCLUSION

The idea that social life represents a balancing of freedom and constraint, which is an integral part of the interactionist perspective, is related to humans' capacity for acting upon their surroundings, exercising choice, injecting new meanings into social life, and changing the world through the process of interaction. In this chapter we have been elaborating on the constraint side of the life equation. We have tried to show that opportunities for personal choice are not equally distributed throughout the social system. The plain fact is that some people are "freer" than others to control their personal destinies.

Whole categories of people can be distinguished in terms of the relative power they possess. Wealth is highly concentrated in the hands of a few, for example. Comparisons of men with women and whites with blacks along any power dimension reveal a patterned, institutionalized, culturally rigid system of superiors and subordinates. In each case, those with little power must pay deference to those with the resources to affect them directly. Studies illustrating the relationship between power and role-taking consistently have found that powerless persons must be more accurate role-takers than powerful persons.

The most comprehensive social groups with various levels of power are called social classes. People who are born into social classes at the lower end of the stratification system have little opportunity for occupational success and then are devalued because they do not succeed. We briefly traced some of the adaptations lower- and working-class men make to this situation, pointing out that the poses such men take on in their relationships with family and friends are a direct consequence of their social positions.

Power makes its presence felt throughout our daily lives. The way we look at people, what we call them, and where we travel all are instances in which we must be cognizant of our proper place in the social order. Staring, touching, interrupting, crowding another's space, frowning, and smiling are often *political* acts. Through such routine behaviors, power differences are expressed and maintained. Should we step out of line or forget our roles, the powerful will quickly respond. The *politics of interaction* operate in both the macro world of social structures and the micro world of face-to-face relations.

The general point made in this chapter is that people's daily interactions reflect the constraints of their particular social positions. It is possible to conceive of social positions in an even broader sense, however. We can consider a person's place in the organizations which characterize modern urban-industrial societies. In the following chapter we examine the nature of life in bureaucracies, the organizational setting which characterizes American society.

## Definitions

**Social stratification.** The hierarchical ordering of a society in terms of the income, education, or occupation of persons in it.

**Life-chances.** The ways in which a person's opportunities in life are related to her or his place in society. Examples would include the likelihood of living a long life, staying healthy as opposed to being sick, attaining a high-paying job, and so on.

**Differential access.** The various opportunities individuals have, depending on their place in society, to achieve positions of wealth, status, or power.

**Superiors.** Those whose status gives them power over others.

**Inferiors.** Those whose status makes them subordinate to the power of others. Another name for those in this position is *subordinates*.

**Micro world.** The world of everyday, direct face-to-face relations between individuals.

**Macro world.** The broader institutional and historical setting in which individuals' daily lives take places. Relations with others in this world are more abstract, anonymous, and remote, according to Peter and Brigitte Berger.

**Social class.** Groupings of people based on their common standing on rankings of education, occupational prestige, and income.

**Power.** The ability to get others to do what one wants, while preventing them from changing one's own behaviors.

**Conning strategies.** The subtle, indirect ways in which the powerless try to manipulate the powerful.

**Backstage.** Private areas of social life that are off limits to those who are not members of a group.

**Frontstage.** Public areas of social life in which those who are not group members can participate and affect the behavior of group members.

# Discussion Questions

1. Which of your ascribed attributes do you think have been or possibly will be important in determining your life-chances positively or negatively? From among those you name, which seem most influential? What do your answers to these questions suggest about the ideology that America is a land of equal opportunity?

2. Think about an occasion when you felt powerless and oppressed. In that situation, who do you feel was doing the most accurate role-taking, yourself or the more powerful person? Which of your own or the other person's behaviors illustrate this differential role-taking sensitivity? What strategies did you employ to cope with your powerlessness?

3. Elaborate on the idea that such behaviors as staring, touching, interrupting, smiling, and frowning are often *political* acts.

4. How would you respond to the arguments that lower-class members who are unemployed are simply lazy and do not want to work, or that such persons just do not hold middle-class achievement values?

# References

Berger, P., and B. Berger. 1975. *Sociology: A Biographical Approach.* New York: Basic Books.

Braroe, N. 1970. "Reciprocal exploitation in an Indian-white community." In *Social Psychology through Symbolic Interaction,* ed. G. P. Stone and H. Farberman. Waltham, Mass.: Ginn-Blaisdell.

Brown, R. 1965. *Social Psychology.* Glencoe, Ill.: Free Press.

Domhoff, G. W. 1970. *The Higher Circles.* New York: Vintage Books.

Fox, M., and S. Hesse-Biber. 1984. *Women at Work.* Palo Alto, Cal.: Mayfield.

Garson, B. 1977. *All the Livelong Day.* New York: Penguin Books.

Gitter, G. A., H. Black, and D. Mostofsky. 1972. "Race and sex in the communication of emotion." *The Journal of Social Psychology* 88:273–276.

Goffman, E. 1959. *The Presentation of Self in Everyday Life.* New York: Doubleday Anchor Books.

Haley, A. 1976. *Roots.* New York: Doubleday.

Henley, N. 1977. *Body Politics.* Englewood Cliffs, N.J.: Prentice-Hall.

Heslin, R., and D. Boss. 1975. "Nonverbal boundary behavior at the airport." Unpublished paper cited in Nancy Henley, *Body Politics.* Englewood Cliffs, N.J.: Prentice-Hall.

Kasarda, J. D. 1972. "The impact of suburban population growth on central city services." *American Journal of Sociology* 77 (May):1111–1124.

Liebow, E. 1967. *Tally's Corner.* Boston: Little Brown.

Lipman-Blumen, J. 1984. *Gender Roles and Power.* Englewood Cliffs, N.J.: Prentice-Hall.

Lofland, L. 1973. *A World of Strangers*. New York: Basic Books.

Persell, C. 1984. *Understanding Society*. New York: Harper & Row.

Rosenthal, R., et al. 1974. "Body talk and tone of voice: The language without words." *Psychology Today* 8 (September):64–68.

Rubin, L. 1976. *Worlds of Pain*. New York: Harper & Row.

Rubin, Z. 1973. *Living and Loving*. New York: Holt, Rinehart & Winston.

Rush, F. 1971. "The sexual abuse of children." *Radical Therapist* (December):9–10.

Sennett, R., and J. Cobb. 1973. *The Hidden Injuries of Class*. New York: Random House.

Tawney, R. H. 1931. *Equality*. London: Allen & Unwin.

Thomas, D., D. Franks, and J. M. Calanico. 1972. "Role-taking and power in social psychology." *American Sociological Review* 37 (October):605–615.

Tyree, A., and B. Smith. 1978. "Occupational hierarchy in the United States: 1780–1969." *Social Forces* 56:881–889.

U.S. Bureau of the Census. 1983. *Statistical Abstract of the United States, 1984*. Washington, D.C.: Government Printing Office.

Weitz, S. 1975. "Sex differences in nonverbal communication." Paper presented at American Sociological Association Annual Meeting.

Wolff, M. 1973. "Notes on the behavior of pedestrians." In *People in Places: The Sociology of the Familiar*, ed. A. Birenbaum and D. Sagarin. New York: Praeger.

Zimmerman, D. D., and C. West. 1975. "Sex roles, interruptions and silences in conversations." In *Language and Sex: Difference and Dominance*, ed. B. Thorne and N. Henley. Rowley, Mass.: Newbury House.

# CHAPTER 7 Everyday Life in Bureaucracies

I. The Pervasive Effects of Bureaucracy
II. The Bureaucratization of Modern Life
   A. From Mass Society to Organizational Society
   B. The Rise of the White-Collar Worker
      1. Effects on society
III. Thinking about Bureaucracy
   A. Weber's Model of Bureaucratic Organizations
   B. Perrow's View: Organizations as a Means of Power
   C. The Symbolic Interaction Perspective on Organizations
      1. The construction of organizations by their members
IV. Work in Bureaucracies
   A. The Protestant Ethic (Work) versus the Social Ethic (Managing)
   B. Leadership and Organizational Position
   C. The Lonely Manager
      1. Psychological isolation
      2. Physical and social isolation
   D. The Blue-Collar Worker's Search for Autonomy
      1. Getting around top-down control
      2. Negotiating a more satisfactory order
V. Conclusion

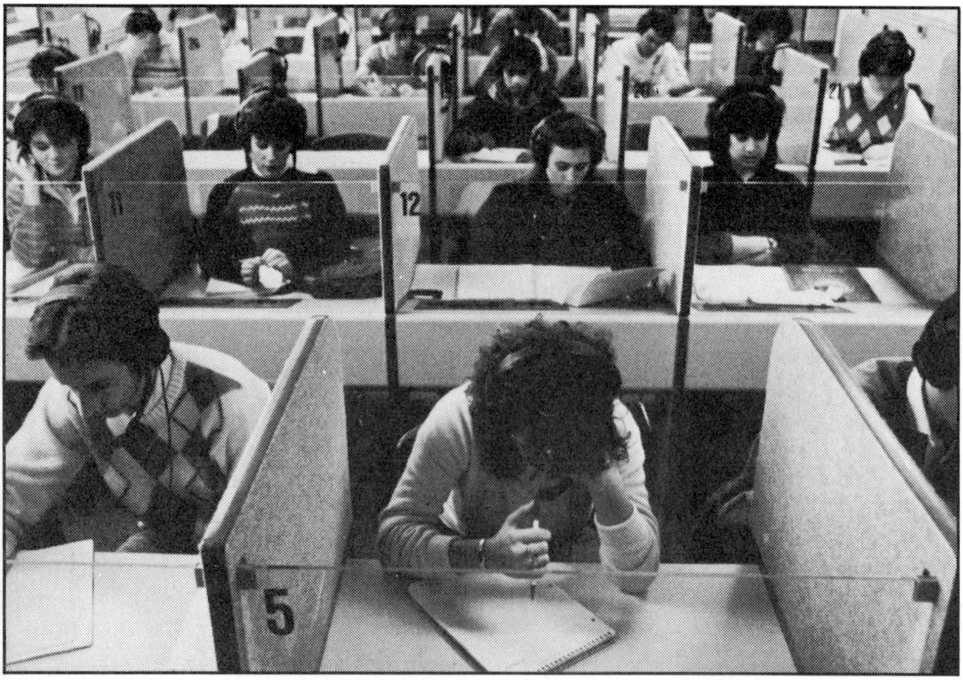

12
5

# CHAPTER 7

T HE POWER an individual can exercise is not simply a matter of personality characteristics. Rather, as we argued in Chapter 6, it is dependent on the *positions* the person occupies in society, as determined by her or his achieved and ascribed statuses. In this chapter we will extend this argument to include the person's positions in the bureaucratic organizations which to a large extent control daily interactions, such as those in the institutions of education and work.

In calling attention to the organizational nature of social life we are focusing on one of the central dimensions of modern existence, the extent to which behaviors are shaped by **bureaucracy** and the bureaucratic form of organization. You were probably born in a bureaucratically organized medical setting called a hospital, for example. Your parents paid for your arrival into the world with medical charge cards from bureaucracies like Blue Cross/Blue Shield. As a child you entered society through bureaucratic institutions such as the public schools, which grouped you into grades composed of children of a similar age. You moved through this organization in steps, passing from the lowest grades up to the final year of high school. Because you have chosen to continue your schooling in a college or university, you again are experiencing the progression from new student to senior.

## ■ THE PERVASIVE EFFECTS OF BUREAUCRACY

For most American adults, even the smallest daily experiences are shaped by large-scale bureaucratic organizations. Waking up in the morning, we turn on the radio or television and listen to the news presented by a local station owned by a national corporation such as NBC. The network gets its information from a worldwide news source such as the Associated Press. Our breakfast foods are provided by multinational corporations such as General Foods. Then we get in our mass-produced cars and drive to work on highways built and maintained with funds allocated by state and federal agencies. We are likely to work for a bureaucratically organized firm which employs large numbers of people with officially designated job titles. We encounter bureaucracies if we pay taxes or purchase licenses, seek medical services at a hospital or clinic, have a question about a bill at a department store, try to make a change in a utility service, and in numerous everyday activities.

Arriving home at the end of the day, we read our mail, which has been delivered by another government bureaucracy, the U.S. Postal Service. At certain times of the month the mail includes a large number of computerized bills from utility companies, banks, credit card agencies, and department stores—organizations which maintain a keen interest in our prospects and locations as long as we occupy a numbered niche in their computer systems.

Our encounters with strangers are also often influenced by the presence of a third party in the form of bureaucratic agencies such as insurance companies and the courts. Suppose, for example, you are driving down a highway and notice an injured person lying on the side of the road. Your humanitarian impulses urge you to stop and offer aid, but you also are aware of problems that could result if you do so. In moving the injured person into your car for a trip to the hospital, for example, you could aggravate an injury. Under the law in many states you could be held liable for such injuries and sued in court for damages. To deal with this dilemma, California and Minnesota have passed Good Samaritan laws which provide protection from legal suits for those who aid another person. They have in fact gone to the other extreme; in these states you may be sued if you do *not* render aid in a situation where you could have done so.

Dilemmas similar to those faced in encounters between strangers are also faced by people on more intimate terms, such as neighbors (see box). In modern American society people are continually confronted with problems which cannot be resolved informally and must be referred to government agencies, business organizations, insurance companies, or the courts. Because the society is composed of hundreds of millions of persons of diverse backgrounds, it is almost impossible to establish policies which would be sensitive to all the subtle meanings of individual behaviors. The bureaucratic solution is to set standardized procedures

## Caught in the Bureaucratic Net

The safety net of social services which is supposed to catch and support needy persons can also ensnare them, even if they require such services only because they had good intentions. This was the case with a Detroit resident, Todd Fruehauf, who saved his neighbor's two little children from their burning home. Fruehauf later developed a cough and began to have difficulty breathing. When, about a month after the rescue, he suffered a respiratory attack at work, his doctor ordered him not to work until his lungs improved. As a result of smoke inhalation, the doctor said, Fruehauf's lungs were in the condition of a 70-year-old man who had smoked all his life, even though he was a nonsmoker and only 31 years old.

Fruehauf also encountered financial difficulties as a result of his good deed. His sick pay ran out, he was denied worker's compensation, and he could not collect unemployment compensation because he hadn't been fired. His company continued to pay his medical insurance for a time, but it could be stopped at any time on the company doctor's recommendation. Fruehauf faced loss of his own house when he could no longer make the mortgage payments.

Fruehauf's admirable actions brought him into collision with his company's medical policies because his illness resulted from the fire and not from his job. Since it was not work-related, the company was not legally obligated to continue making medical insurance payments on his behalf. The rescue effort also brought him into conflict with his own and his neighbor's insurance companies. His neighbor's house was covered by a fire insurance policy, but it only protected the neighbor's family and possessions. There were no provisions for Good Samaritans. Fruehauf's own homeowners' insurance would only cover damage to his house and possessions, which were not involved in the fire.

According to Fruehauf, when he asked for help from his neighbor's insurance company, a representative told him his neighbor's fire was none of his business, and if necessary he should have just stood by and let the house burn and the children perish. Would Fruehauf do the same thing again, a reporter asked? He replied that after what he had been through, he would have to think about it if a similar situation arose again. And then, he said, it could be too late to act.

*Source:* "Hero in House Fire Says He's Paying the Price Now," *Detroit Free Press*, August 31, 1983.

and rely on elaborate systems of rules and regulations for interactions between individuals in specific situations. Society seems to have reached a point where individual behaviors are to a large extent controlled and directed by the policies of large-scale public and private organizations.

## ■ THE BUREAUCRATIZATION OF MODERN LIFE

Noted sociologists such as Emile Durkheim and Max Weber have traced the origins of modern society to the processes of urbanization and industrialization which began in the late 18th century. The rise of the industrial city was accompanied by such developments as the capitalist economy, technological advances, and new social categories like the working class (or **proletariat,** in Karl Marx's term) to supply the needs for workers in the factory system.

### From Mass Society to Organizational Society

The development of industrial technology and the factory system of production and labor attracted newcomers of varied social origins to the cities. Peasants prevented from farming by agricultural reforms or "enclosure acts" were forced to seek their livelihoods in the urban factories. The most dramatic effect of these processes on social life was the separation of work from the home, however. As Peter Laslett puts it, the result was a **mass society:**

> The factory won its victory by outproducing the working family, taking away the market for products of hand-labour and cutting prices to the point where the craftsman had either to starve or take a job under factory discipline himself. ... [W]e can say that the removal of the economic functions from the patriarchal family at the point of industrialization created a mass society. It turned the people who worked into a mass of undifferentiated equals, working in a factory or scattered between the factories and mines, bereft forever of the feeling that work was a family affair, done within the family. (1971:18–19)

The factory system brought the introduction of labor for wages and mechanized methods of production marked by repetition and standardization. Workers did the same tasks all day, day after day, wherever they could get the highest wage, and at a pace determined by the employer (Schwartz, Schuldenfrei, and Lacey, 1978:242). For women, mechanization had both liberating and enslaving consequences. It began to free them from the restricted confines of the home and a male-dominated social order, while it imposed on them "the chains of wage labor" (Ehrenreich and English, 1979:14). The effects of industrialization on the lives of workers led to various reform movements which attempted to improve conditions (Jacoby, 1976).

Efforts to make workers as efficient as machines led in the early 20th century to the development of administrative techniques called **scientific management.** An industrial engineer, Frederick Taylor, developed ideas for a factory workplace in which the division of labor was highly specialized and individual work tasks were minutely scrutinized and reduced to their most basic elements. Managers sought to take over control of the production process from the hands of the workers, in line with a distinctive characteristic of bureaucratic functioning—**control from the top down.** As Ralph Hummel observed, in an industrial society "People's work is divided not only to make them expert and more efficient but also to make them dependent on managerial control" (1982:29).

Taylor's ideas reflected social processes which were even then laying the foundation for the current model of control by big business, big labor, and big government (Braverman, 1974; Clawson, 1980). Beginning about 1875, social, economic, and political trends in the United States prepared the way for what Robert Presthus (1978) calls the **organizational society,** characterized by large-scale bureaucratic institutions in virtually every area of social life.

## The Rise of the White-Collar Worker

One of the most significant changes has been in the types of work done by the majority of adults in American society. The data in Table 7.1 on major occupational groups in the United States show a substantial increase in the proportion of the work force in **white-collar occupations,** from 18 percent in 1900 to 55 percent in 1982. The percentage of workers employed in all **blue-collar occupations** fluctuated only moderately during this period, but the proportion working as nonfarm laborers declined sharply, from 13 to 5 percent of the labor force. Skilled blue-collar craft workers and operatives, who make up the membership of the large national labor unions such as the United Automobile Workers, about held their share of the labor force until the early-1980s recession. During the same period the character of **service occupations** changed dramatically, from almost all domestic service to predominantly work outside private households.

White-collar occupations supply the clerical, managerial, and financial support for agricultural and industrial production. As first agriculture and then factory work began to wane in the 20th century, support and service occupations grew accordingly. In the 10 years from 1972 to 1982

Table 7.1
Percentage of Labor Force in Types of Occupations, United States, 1900–1982

| Type of Occupation | Years | | | | |
|---|---|---|---|---|---|
| | 1900 | 1920 | 1940 | 1970 | 1982 |
| White-Collar Occupations | 18% | 25% | 32% | 48% | 55% |
| Professional and technical | 4 | 5 | 8 | 14 | 17 |
| Managers, officials, and proprietors | 6 | 7 | 7 | 11 | 12 |
| Clerical | 3 | 8 | 10 | 17 | 19 |
| Sales | 5 | 5 | 7 | 6 | 7 |
| Blue-Collar Occupations | 37% | 41% | 39% | 36% | 30% |
| Craft and kindred workers | 11 | 13 | 12 | 13 | 12 |
| Operatives | 13 | 16 | 18 | 18 | 13 |
| Nonfarm laborers | 13 | 12 | 9 | 5 | 5 |
| Service Occupations | 10% | 8% | 12% | 12%* | 14%* |
| Service workers, except private households | 4 | 5 | 7 | | |
| Private household workers | 6 | 3 | 5 | | |
| Farm Occupations | 38% | 27% | 17% | 4%* | 3%* |
| Farmers and farm managers | 20 | 15 | 10 | | |
| Farm workers | 18 | 12 | 7 | | |

*Total number of workers in category.

Sources: U.S. Bureau of the Census, *Historical Statistics of the United States: Colonial Times to 1957* (Washington, D.C.: U.S. Government Printing Office, 1960), Table Series D 72–122; and *Statistical Abstract of the United States, 1984* (Washington, D.C.: Government Printing Office, 1983), Table 693.

alone, the labor force grew by nearly 22 percent, but employment in agriculture, forestry, and fishing declined by 5.1 percent, and in manufacturing it grew by only 2.1 percent. The big increases were all in white-collar occupations: 44.9 percent in finance, insurance, and real estate; 44.5 percent in service occupations in health, education, and business; and 42 percent in state government (Robey and Russell, 1984).

## *Effects on Society*

By 1970, according to Presthus, white-collar workers were employed in large-scale organizations where the conditions of work included standardization, impersonality, specialization, a hierarchy of authority, and dependence. Such organizations, moreover, could provide the research and management skills which intensified these conditions (1978:58). The growth of white-collar work was the force behind the emergence of a new social category: the **new middle class** of corporate managers, salaried white-collar professionals, salespeople, and office workers. By contrast, the old middle class which had dominated American society was composed of farmers, self-employed businessmen, and independent professionals (Mills, 1956).

## ■ THINKING ABOUT BUREAUCRACY

Nineteenth-century social scientists, living through the monumental social changes which accompanied industrialization and urbanization, sought to comprehend their effects on both individual behaviors and society. Max Weber (1922/1946) was among the first to identify the characteristics of bureaucratic organizations, which he considered to be the most efficient means of managing or controlling large groups of people. Numerous social scientists have advanced different ideas on the nature and consequences of this organizational form and have debated the issue of its dehumanizing effects. The symbolic interaction perspective is that bureaucratic organizations are not separate entities with a life of their own but are created by the daily interactions of their members.

### Weber's Model of Bureaucratic Organizations

A bureaucracy, according to Weber, has certain readily identifiable characteristics, such as a clear-cut specialized **division of labor,** a **hierarchy of authority,** and an elaborate system of rules and regulations. Bureaucracies are organized in a pyramidal fashion, with power concentrated in the hands of a few officials in the higher positions. Employees at one level are responsible to those immediately above them and exercise authority over those immediately below them. The division of labor is carefully specified by formal descriptions of job content and the range of authority entailed in the various positions. In the name of efficiency and to eliminate needless motion and time from the production process, tasks are divided into their most basic operations. In working situations, however, as many observers have pointed out, bureaucracies can generate a good deal of excess paperwork and encourage buck-passing and other procedures which actually are counterproductive.

In most bureaucracies employees are listed by job title in a personnel department, which has an administrative staff to perform the necessary specialized record-keeping. The emphasis on files and record-keeping is not simply an internal personnel matter but rather reflects a much deeper quality of organizational life—the tendency to reduce relationships with customers and clients to definable categories of behavior. Individuals are dealt with in terms of the category into which they fall. Universities, to choose an example close to home, have separate files for students in good standing, students on probation, students who lack the necessary courses for admission. Should a student wish to appeal a grade received in a course, it is necessary to file a formal grievance which is then referred to the appropriate grievance file.

Table 7.2
Tongue-in-Cheek Guide to Employee Performance Appraisal

Performance Degrees

| Performance Factors | Far Exceeds Job Requirements | Exceeds Job Requirements | Meets Job Requirements | Needs Some Improvement | Does Not Meet Minimum Requirements |
|---|---|---|---|---|---|
| Quality | Leaps tall buildings with a single bound. | Must take running start to leap over tall buildings. | Can only leap over a short building or medium with no spires. | Crashes into buildings when attempting to jump over them. | Cannot recognize buildings at all, much less jump. |
| Timeliness | Is faster than a speeding bullet. | Is as fast as a speeding bullet. | Not quite as fast as a speeding bullet. | Would you believe a slow bullet? | Wounds self with bullet when attempting to shoot gun. |
| Initiative | Is stronger than a locomotive. | Is stronger than a bull elephant. | Is stronger than a bull. | Shoots the bull. | Smells like a bull. |
| Adaptability | Walks on water | Walks on water in emergencies. | Washes with water. | Drinks water. | Passes water in emergencies. |
| Communication | Talks with God. | Talks with the Angels. | Talks to himself. | Argues with himself. | Loses these arguments. |

Source: Alan Dundes and Carl Pagter, Work Hard and You Shall Be Rewarded (Bloomington, IN: Indiana University Press, 1978), p. 80.

Weber's model of bureaucracy emphasizes the **meritocracy** inherent in such organizations. Employees are supposed to be hired on the basis of their personal merit or individual abilities, independent of political considerations, family ties, or personal favoritism. Career movements within the organizations also are supposed to reflect meritocratic principles, with the most competent employees rising to the highest positions. In practice, however, the system often fails to work this way (see Table 7.2). Observing this, Lawrence J. Peter and Raymond Hull (1969) proposed the **Peter principle,** based on the idea that employees in a hierarchy tend to rise to their individual levels of *incompetence*—and remain there. It suggests that individuals who are doing their work competently are singled out for promotion, until they are given a job in which their incompetence becomes apparent. Then the promotions stop and the employees remain in their highest positions, where they continue to perform incompetently.

For Weber, bureaucratic organizations exemplified a principle which he termed **rationalization:** the systematic and logical application of formal rules and procedures to every aspect of modern life. In his writings, Weber demonstrated how this principle came to permeate all spheres of life, ranging from economic activities to art and classical music. In the final analysis, Weber remained deeply pessimistic about the prospects for a fully human life in a world in which bureaucratic policies continually reduce persons to files in anonymous record-keeping systems. An example of the extremes such policies can produce was visualized as the experiences of the character Joseph K. in Franz Kafka's haunting novel, *The Trial.*

## Perrow's View: Organizations as a Means of Power

Contemporary analysts of bureaucratic life have suggested a number of changes in Weber's model which would allow a less critical view of such organizations. Charles Perrow, for example, considers organizations as "tools for shaping the world as one wishes it to be shaped" (1978:13). Those who control organizations can use the power they represent to impose their own view of reality on others. In Perrow's view, "The power of the rich lies not in their ability to buy goods and services, but in their capacity to control the ends toward which the vast resources of large organizations are directed" (p. 13).

Perrow takes the position that what are commonly viewed as the "sins" of bureaucracy would have a different effect if they were viewed from a less moralistic perspective. The charge of favoritism in hiring practices, for example, should be viewed in relation to the "real" goals of the organization. If the goal is to land a defense contract, for example, hiring only employees with high-level contacts in the Pentagon would be reasonable, since doing so furthers the organization's goals. Such employees may not be the most qualified and competent managers, but that's not why they are being hired. The larger issue is not whether the company is acting in terms of meritocratic principles, but whether the public interest is jeopardized by the conflicting loyalties of government employees. They may be tempted to forget their commitment to the public by the possible rewards for helping associates in the private business sector.

In response to the charge that career tenure in bureaucracies promotes incompetence, Perrow argues that tenure is a trade-off for employees who have invested a great deal of their skills, time, and energies in the service of the organization. In his terms, they would be unwilling "to master sets of skills through long technical training or experience in an organization if they knew that they could not perpetually draw upon the capital of their investment" (p. 10).

After reviewing numerous theories about bureaucracy as well as several case studies of specific organizations, Perrow concludes that we may be fooling ourselves if we attribute all the ills of society to bureaucracy and large-scale organizations. He suggests we are not talking about bureaucracy but about

> . . . the uses to which the power generated by organizations is put. The presence of hierarchy, rules, division of labor, tenure provisions, and so on can hardly be blamed for maladministration or abuses of social power. Indeed, the bureaucratic model provides a greater check upon these problems than do nonbureaucratic or traditional alternatives once you have managerial capitalism. Critics, then, of our organizational society . . . *had best turn to the key issue of who controls the varied forms of power* generated by organizations rather than flail away at the windmills of bureaucracy. (Italics added; 1978:55–56)

## The Symbolic Interaction Perspective on Organizations

Another sociological tradition, the symbolic interaction perspective which is taken in this book, stresses that organizations are humanly created phenonema. They owe their origin, maintenance, and eventual change to the daily interactions and communications that take place among their members.

The symbolic interaction view is that people transform their social organizations as well as themselves through their interactions with one another. Organizational life therefore is not preordained but is shaped by fluid processes. Humans live in a world of socially constructed meanings which can always be changed through dialogues such as the civil rights activists of the 1960s engaged in to redefine the meaning of the work *black*. In the face of life's uncertainties, individuals create social organizations such as bureaucracies to serve both as tools to achieve various goals and, in the broadest sense, as avenues to make the world meaningful and thereby manageable. By imposing some sense of social structure, organizations make the terrors occasioned by life's imponderable mysteries more bearable and predictable.

While bureaucracies embody the formal characteristics Weber identified, such as a hierarchy of authority and the division of labor, there is also a great deal of leeway in any organizational environment. To use Karl Weick's (1976) phrase, in all organizations there are enough "loose couplings," or situations marked by uncertainty or ambiguity, so individuals must supply their own definitions of reality.

## The Construction of Organizations by Their Members

As organizational members respond to and redefine the formal rules of bureaucratic settings, they construct **informal subcultures** within the organization. Stuart Clegg (1975:130) is referring to these in his statement that "The organization is what members make of uncertainty and the formal organization." Factory workers, for example, establish quotas restricting their own productivity in an effort to exercise some control over their work situations (Pfeffer, 1979). Similarly, college students in classroom settings may adopt a posture of "civil attention" and restrict their participation in discussions so they do not appear too eager to please the professor (Karp and Yoels, 1976). Such subcultures provide different experiences to organizational members, according to their positions in the hierarchy. In effect, organizations are thickly populated by multiple realities. The meanings which constitute these realities define what the organization is in terms of human behaviors.

The interactionist approach to the study of bureaucracy emphasizes the ongoing, interpretive communication process by which members construct their own organizational realities. It suggests that organizations should be viewed as the result of a process of **negotiated order,** rather than as fixed in granite or completely regulated by an organizational chart of official positions (Maines, 1977). Researchers such as Anselm Strauss argue that the social order reflects ongoing negotiations between participants as they deal with each other in order to get things done. In his view, negotiation is not just a specific human activity or process which appears in particular relationships such as diplomacy and labor relations. Rather, it is "of such major importance in human affairs that its study brings us to the heart of studying social orders . . . a given social order, even the most repressive, would be inconceivable without some forms of negotiation" (Strauss, 1978:234–235).

In thinking about bureaucracies, the interactionist perspective is principally concerned with how people respond to formal rules and procedures. New meanings are created by those at the top and the bottom of the hierarchy, despite official patterns of authority and control. Efforts at spontaneity and innovation continually occur, even though the "higher-ups" attempt to mold the behaviors of the "lower-downs" into highly predictable forms. Life in a bureaucracy, then, is determined more by the informal interactions of individuals than by the formal rules and procedures of the organization.

## ■ WORK IN BUREAUCRACIES

From the interactionists' view that bureaucracies have no life of their own but are constructed by the interactions of members, it follows that the way to study life in bureaucracies is to examine the experiences of the members. In contemporary American society, the need or desire to work leads most adults to become involved in corporate organizations.

### The Social Ethic: Getting Along as the Key to Getting Ahead

If the Protestant work ethic, with its emphasis on hard work, thrift, and competition, was the driving force behind the industrialization of American society, the social ethic, with its emphasis on cooperation and management, has been the impetus for the spread of bureaucratization. To illustrate how the social ethic became the rationale for organizing work as a group effort under the corporate form, William H. Whyte, Jr., contrasted the training programs for new executives which were being offered college graduates of the 1950s by two major national corporations—Vick Chemical Company and General Electric. The title of his study, *The Organization Man* (1956), reflected a corporate ideology which regarded man (literally; woman was only peripherally involved in the corporate world) as existing as a unit of society; "Of himself, he is isolated, meaningless; only as he collaborates with others does he become worthwhile, for by sublimating himself in the group, he helps produce a whole that is greater than the sum of its parts" (pp. 7–8).

Social scientists have studied the conditions of corporate life by identifying a new social ethic and examining leadership in relation to the employee's position in the organizational hierarchy. They have explored the multiple realities of corporate life, including the psychological isolation of top-level executives, the frustrating status of secretaries, and the routine, predictable, powerless jobs of unskilled blue-collar workers.

## The Protestant Ethic (Work) versus the Social Ethic (Managing)

William H. Whyte's controversial study *The Organization Man* (1956) called attention to a fundamental change in the nature of American society: the transformation of the **Protestant work ethic** into the **social ethic.** Earlier generations of Americans had believed that work is service to God and respectability goes hand in hand with the accumulation of wealth through hard work, competition, and individual effort. In the 1950s, Whyte argued, a new ethic oriented to cooperation and managing others' work was emerging. This social ethic was ideally suited for life in a world of large, bureaucratically administered corporations (see box).

---

The Vick Company training program exemplified the traditional Protestant ethic approach. Executive trainees were hired for specific jobs and given a short orientation program. Any additional training they received was geared toward improving their performance in their particular jobs. Trainees were expected to excel in competition with other trainees before they would be considered for advancement. In short, they would have to prove they were competent managers in a specific job before they would be considered for any additional responsibilities.

General Electric's management trainee program reflected a commitment to the emerging social ethic. Men were hired as potential managers and were encouraged from the outset to see themselves in that role. Rather than being assigned to specific jobs, GE trainees were put into a central pool and moved along as a group through a series of simulated job exercises which exposed them to the company's managerial view. The schooling lasted for two years or more.

The trend toward bureaucratization was clearly evident in General Electric's program. Additional evidence of the change in emphasis from the actual process of production to the management of work was provided by the growing reliance on personality tests as screening devices for the selection of managers. Corporations began to insist that managers demonstrate the skills of getting along before they were allowed to get ahead. GE's trainees were not taught work skills so much as they were taught the skills of managing other people's work. They came to view the manager as "a man in charge of people getting along together, and his *expertise* is relatively independent of who or what is being managed. Or why" (p. 135).

The organization man continues to be the dominant model of the corporate manager in the 1980s, though Michael Maccoby (1976) has identified a more competitive, technologically trained entrepreneur ver-

---

The social ethic was based on three major premises: "a belief in the group as the source of creativity; a belief in 'belongingness' as the ultimate need of the individual; and a belief in the application of science [to human relations] to achieve the belongingness" (Whyte, 1956, p. 7). Such beliefs encouraged loyalty and total commitment to the organization. A person's private life and innermost desires were considered secondary to smooth organizational functioning.

Whyte concluded his study with a plea for the accommodation of individualism within the corporate social ethic. He was not pining for a nostalgic return to the wide-open frontier of the 19th century or the rugged individualism of "robber barons" like John D. Rockefeller and Andrew Carnegie. Rather, he was urging corporate leaders to act more flexibly in the creation of job tasks and to pay more respect to the unique differences in individuals' skills and talents. In short, he was arguing that "the individual is more creative than the group" (p. 445) and that corporate policies should not obscure this fact by their unquestioning standardization and compartmentalization of behaviors.

## Leadership and Organizational Position

Whyte's work had a significant role in sensitizing social scientists to the critical issue of leadership in large, complex organizations. Since that time numerous studies have examined such organizational behaviors in a wide range of contexts (Baron, 1983; Hall, 1977). The leadership issue illuminates the concept of multiple realities in organizations, as determined by the individual's position within the organizational hierarchy.

sion. This model includes four ideal character types: the craftsman, who honors the work ethic; the jungle fighter, who lusts for power; the company man, who values cooperation and the human side of the corporation; and the gamesman, who sees business in terms of options and contests. The training program for this model of manager could consist of *terminal jobs*. College graduates are hired to fill such jobs at the entry level for definite periods of about two years, after which nearly all of them return to business schools for graduate study. The program gives companies and graduates a chance to size each other up without making any permanent commitments (Williams, 1985).

Strong support for this idea was found in a survey of corporate managers conducted by the American Management Association (AMA) (Pearce, 1977). Responses from more than 1,000 managers who returned questionnaires revealed striking contrasts in the views of top-level and mid-level managers. Top-level managers were much more likely to report that their careers had exceeded their personal expectations and to feel in control of their own professional destinies. This is certainly understandable, since their positions were themselves evidence of the company's regard for their value and worth. Top managers also generally believed that results and ability to lead are what count in terms of career advancement. (The idea of occupational careers as a moving perspective on life is discussed in Chapter 9.)

By contrast, mid-level personnel were much more skeptical that personal leadership qualities would lead to success in the organization. Many middle managers saw loyalty, conformity, and office politics as the major avenues by which organizational careers are advanced. They were much less likely to believe that individual managers can control their own careers. This is also readily understandable, since their performances are constantly being monitored by top-level managers.

Top-level and middle-level managers about equally acknowledged the importance of managerial talents and communicative skills as factors in career advancement. Mid-level managers were much more inclined to see factors beyond their own control as impediments to their careers, however.

The views of mid-level managers surveyed in this study were reinforced by data from a later AMA survey report (Breen, 1983). The major conclusion was that the middle managers surveyed collectively cast

... a strong vote of "no confidence" in their current corporate leadership, both in its ability to guide their organizations through the troubled eighties and in its efforts to prepare them for individual career advancement. These findings may indeed startle top managers, who also score well below par on their basic "honesty and straightforwardness." In fact, only 33 percent of the respondents agreed with the statement "Middle managers in my organization respect the honesty and straightforwardness of top management." (p. 12)

Surveys like the 1977 and 1983 AMA reports give a good idea of what many people are experiencing in organizational environments. Other studies of a qualitative sort, including first-hand accounts by social scientists, have provided deeper, richer data on organizational life, however.

## The Lonely Manager

The top levels of the organizational hierarchy provide managers with satisfying opportunities to exercise leadership and advance their careers. A feeling of loneliness and isolation in these positions has been reported to be a significant drawback, however. Social scientists have studied various aspects of life at the top in bureaucratic organizations.

### Psychological Isolation

A first-hand account of the psychological isolation of top-level administrators in large organizations was offered by Philip Jackson, director of the University of Chicago's Laboratory School from 1970 to 1975. Jackson's experiences as an administrator in an academic setting were similar to those of managers in other bureaucratic settings. In dealing with the isolation issue, Jackson (1977) calls attention to the heightened self-consciousness of top officials who find themselves constantly in the public spotlight. He found that his presence was gradually accepted by both teachers and students, but the feeling of being perceived as "someone special, a shade apart from the others," never disappeared (p. 428).

Administrative tasks produce an almost obsessive concern with time, which must be parceled out to visitors. Jackson found the lack of accessibility to those at the top helped make him a "distant figure shielded by a secretary, a closed office door, and a cramped schedule." He had to learn to give visitors the impression that he had plenty of time to listen to their concerns when, in truth, his "inner eye" was on the clock (p. 431).

When the administrator must make decisions which affect the lives of others, such as dismissing personnel or allocating budgets, the sense of isolation intensifies. The access of top-level managers to a great deal of confidential information about their associates and subordinates is another source of power which can produce a feeling of being both close and distant to other employees. Jackson was unprepared for this:

> I was unaware until I assumed my administrative role how many secret things I would come to know—information about the private lives of teachers and students, knowledge about the financial status of families and the emotional well-being of their members. Much of this was privileged information of a highly personal sort, in degree of intimacy much like the kind of confidential information entrusted to doctors, lawyers, and priests. . . . The funny thing about this knowledge, I discovered, is that it brings you closer to the few while separating you further from the many. (1977:429)

The manager may respond to such pressures and criticism from associates by creating a "public front" or trying to present an impression of infallibility. Jackson found this "psychological padding" was necessary when he was forced to adopt a pose of confidence while he was internally plagued by doubts and hesitation.

### *Physical and Social Isolation*

Jackson's personal account of isolation at the top of the organizational hierarchy was supported in a study of employees of a major national corporation conducted by a Yale sociologist, Rosabeth Moss Kanter (1977). Using interviews, survey questionnaires, and observational techniques, as well as numerous sources of data, she collected information over a five-year period while working as a consultant to a major American corporation which she called Industrial Supply Corporation (Indsco). In an article on upper-echelon managers based on this study, titled "How the Top Is Different," Kanter (1979) echoes Jackson's observations about administrative isolation and points out some important symbolic dimensions of organizational life. Higher-ups were, in fact, literally higher up; that is, their offices were on the top floors of the building, providing ample testimony to the manner in which, at Indsco, "Physical height corresponded to social height" (p. 23). Office sizes varied directly with status in the organization, and the types of office furnishings carefully mirrored subtle distinctions. Higher-ups were entitled, for example, to marble-top desks, while lower-downs worked on desks with wood tops and steel frames. Secretaries also functioned as significant status symbols. A woman working at a desk in front of a manager's office reflected his image and status. As Kanter was told, "She's the sign of how important he is" (p. 23).

Upper-level managers, situated alone in a huge office on the top floor, with a secretary in front to run interference, as it were, were well along the road to social as well as physical isolation from those entrusted with the day-to-day tasks of running the organization. This isolation bred uncertainties as to how the corporation should be run. In response, top managers sought security by hiring subordinates they could trust, men who were like themselves in terms of background, values, and interests. Social homogeneity (similarity) thus is a crucial filtering device for entry into upper management circles, and conformity to established policies is the standard operating procedure for those seeking such entry. As Kanter notes, the process has all the earmarks of a self-fulfilling prophecy:

The more closed the circle, the more difficult it is for "outsiders" to break in. Their very difficulty in entering may be taken as a sign of incompetence, a sign that insiders were right to close their ranks. The more closed the circle, the more difficult it is to share power when the time comes, as it inevitably must, that others challenge the control by just one kind. (1979:29)

Women recently have presented a serious challenge to the privileged position of men in corporate life. They have made some progress in entering the world of executives, but, as statistics on the U.S. labor force indicate, they continue to face difficulties in trying to pierce the impenetrable wall so eloquently described by Kanter. According to the U.S. Census Bureau, the number of women in managerial and administrative positions increased from 1.1 million in 1960 to 3.2 million in 1982, when they represented 7.4 percent of all women's jobs. During that same period, the number of men in administrative and managerial positions increased from 6 million to 8.3 million, or 14.7 percent of all men's jobs (U.S. Bureau of the Census, 1983, Table 693). In 1982, men outnumbered women in upper-level positions by better than 2.5 to 1. While over two-thirds of women's jobs in 1982 were classified as white-collar work, half of those were in lower-level clerical positions (U.S. Bureau of the Census, 1983, Table 693). Kanter described what life is like at the bottom of the bureaucratic white-collar world by examining the secretary-boss relationship (see box).

The secretary's subordinate role in the corporate world and the ways it is handled provide a good illustration of the symbolic interaction perspective on bureaucracy. Within the organization there is a male-dominated subculture which defines the "rules of the game" to the bosses' advantage. The social realities that these more powerful members construct are different from the realities perceived by the secretaries. Within their own subculture they develop negotiating skills to reconcile their realities with those of the bosses and to accommodate to the rules and

## The Organization Man Meets the Organization Woman

Rosabeth Moss Kanter filled in some of the big blanks left in William F. Whyte's study *The Organization Man* (1956) with a study titled *Men and Women of the Corporation* (1977). In Whyte's study of a corporate world dominated by the social ethic, only men were considered for managerial positions. The role of women, as far as the organization was concerned, was as "company wives" who would support the growing domination of the family by the corporation (Whyte, 1956, pp. 287–291). Some 20 years later, Kanter recognized that women had a place in corporate society, but it was limited to clerical and secretarial positions. In the male-dominated subculture of the organization, even the few women who had achieved "token" managerial status were regarded as essentially female secretaries (Kanter, 1977:206–238).

According to Kanter, the secretary-boss relationship illustrates the presence of feudal remnants in a supposedly rationalized work order. Secretaries at Indsco (the fictionalized name of the major national corporation she studied) functioned much like personal appendages and servants of their male bosses. In return for demonstrating absolute loyalty, they received what were considered appropriate "rewards," not necessarily in monetary form. Like personal possessions, they were usually taken along when their bosses moved up the organizational hierarchy. The power of secretaries varied directly with the status of their bosses, from whom they acquired privileges or "perks" such as "freedom to come and go, to set their own office hours; office status symbols such as drapes, outside offices with windows, special ashtrays, and steel file trays." Secretaries of top executives got special gifts and were invited to parties for projects even though they did no actual work on the task. The lower-level employees who did the work were seldom invited (p. 75).

The secretary was expected to be a specialist (although a very poorly paid one) in the management of the office's emotional climate. Whatever success the secretary achieved at work had far more to do with her skills in "reading" her boss's moods and emotional states than her clerical and administrative skills. Secretaries at Indsco soon recognized the need to "learn the *boss* rather than the organization." As lower-downs, they had to demonstrate greater skills and sensitivity in role-taking than their bosses, the higher-ups (see Chapter 6). Such role-taking skills were reflected in the extent to which bosses expected their secretaries to "anticipate their needs, to respond to their requests, and to know exactly what the boss would do in any situation" (p. 92).

The bosses in Kantor's study tended to believe that the secretaries were quite content with their jobs, content enough, they thought, so that there was little reason for a secretary to want to work for any other boss. Since secretaries were rewarded for putting on a convincing emotional front, the boss was unlikely to probe more deeply. The fact that many of Indsco's secretaries did have reservations about the unrewarding, unchallenging, boring nature of their jobs generally went unrecognized. Since the boss expected total loyalty, he believed his secretary would be pleased and satisfied with emotional rather than material rewards. This discrepancy in their views was captured in an incident reported to Kanter by a woman who had had an offer from another department which would give her better pay and more challenge. The woman said her department heads tried to keep her by saying: " 'We love you. We want you to stay.' They didn't say, 'We'll pay you more.' I couldn't get that from them. Just, 'We love you.' I wanted to say to them, 'I get the love from my husband. I work for other reasons' " (pp. 86–87).

---

regulations of the organization, both formal and informal. Their **autonomy** or ability to control the corporate world in which they work depends upon their ability to negotiate within an arena where the rules are set by the official power and authority of the bosses.

### The Blue-Collar Worker's Search for Autonomy

The issue of autonomy in the workplace also is central to the lives of blue-collar workers, whose daily activities are likely to be as unchallenging and unrewarding as those of women white-collar workers (Miller, 1981; Tausky, 1984). Industrial plants in the United States are typically still organized in terms of ideas formulated in the early 1900s by Frederick Taylor. Work tasks are bureaucratized and structured to provide management with maximum control over workers' jobs. By the process of **deskilling,** the skilled components of production jobs are replaced by tasks which require repetitive actions rather than talents developed on the job by experienced craftsmen. As a result, unskilled blue-collar workers can exert very little control over their work.

Lack of autonomy makes blue-collar workers among the least satisfied in American society, according to social scientists who have devised mea-

Because of the great power disparity between the secretaries and their bosses, the secretaries had to use negotiating skills, creativity, and imagination to tailor their jobs to their own talents and interests. One secretary was able to transform her position into that of an assistant. She added her own comments to the performance appraisals she was given to type and began writing as well as typing the monthly newsletter. When she was asked to take notes at a committee meeting, she wrote the report and asked to be made a member of the team. For most secretaries, however, such negotiations were confined to the more subtle tasks of getting things accomplished by accurately reading the office's emotional climate. This was a safer route for the lower-downs because it avoided a direct and open challenge to the authority of the higher-ups. As a former secretary told Kanter:

> Women, like men, learned what the rules of the game are. A secretary goes in to see her boss and quivers and cries. Not because she's so emotional, but because she knows the rules. She gets the raise because he can't stand to see her cry. . . . We have to use the rules we have available to us. Women in business use what they can. . . . (p. 96)

---

sures of **job satisfaction.** One such measure is whether workers would choose similar jobs again if they had an opportunity to change. Results of a survey conducted by the U.S. Department of Health, Education, and Welfare, published under the title *Work in America* (1973), indicated that "Dull, repetitive, seemingly meaningless tasks, offering little challenge or autonomy, are causing discontent among workers at all occupational levels" (p. xv). The discontent was strongest among blue-collar workers, however. Only 24 percent of a cross-section of blue-collar workers said they would take the same jobs again, compared to 43 percent of a cross-section of white-collar workers. Job satisfaction varied directly with the degree of skill; satisfaction with their present jobs was indicated by only 16 percent of unskilled automakers but 41 percent of skilled automakers. Among professionals, in contrast, an average of 84 percent said they would choose the same work again (p. 16).

### Getting Around Top-Down Control

Since the working conditions of unskilled workers are largely dictated by management, they face the constant problem of trying to achieve some degree of control over their own jobs without being reprimanded,

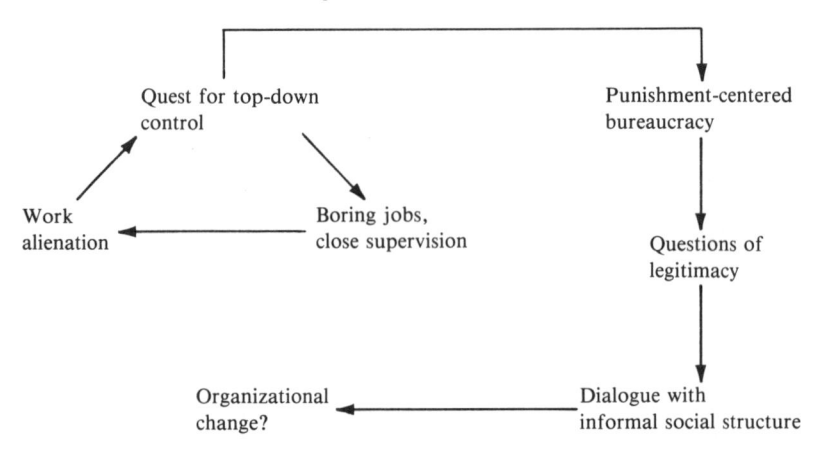

Figure 7.1
Flowchart of Control-Alienation Spiral in Bureaucracies

```
                Quest for top-down                Punishment-centered
                     control                          bureaucracy

    Work                        Boring jobs,
    alienation                  close supervision    Questions of
                                                     legitimacy


                Organizational                   Dialogue with
                    change?                      informal social structure
```

*Source:* Reprinted with the permission of The Free Press, a Division of Macmillan, Inc., from *Introduction to Sociology* by Jack D. Douglas. Copyright © 1973 by The Free Press.

laid off, or fired by management. A useful way to think about this dialectic between managerial control and workers' efforts at autonomy is shown in Figure 7.1 which illustrates the consequences of management's efforts to control workers from the top down. As the left side suggests, top-down control leads to the creation of boring jobs with close monitoring by supervisors. This has the consequence of alienating workers from their work and the company, which in turn leads management to intensify its efforts at control. As the right side suggests, top-down control, plus punishment, can lead to questions of legitimacy by workers which may force management to acknowledge the existence of informal work groups. If the grievances of these groups merit consideration, the process may result in official changes in organizational policies. The unionization of production workers reflects the process illustrated on the right.

Given their opposite positions in the corporation's hierarchy of authority, it is not at all surprising that blue-collar workers and management have different conceptions of the reality of the work situation. Their ideas about break times are an example of how multiple realities exist within an organizational setting. Donald Roy's (1959/1982) study of machine operators found that the workers divided their workday with break times which they heavily invested with their own meanings (see Figure 7.2). While management saw the workday as composed of distinct units

Figure 7.2
Workers' and Management's Conceptions of the Workday

| Time | Management's Terms | Workers' Terms |
|---|---|---|
| 8 a.m. | Official check-in | Coffee time<br>Peach time<br>Banana time<br>Window time |
| 12 N.–12:30 p.m. | Lunch break | Lunch break |
| 12:30 p.m. | | Pickup time<br>Fish time<br>Coke time |
| 5:30 p.m. | Check out | Quitting time for Sammy and Ike |

*Source: Human Organization* (Winter, 1959–60) vol. 18, 4, pp. 158–168. Adapted from Donald Roy, "Banana Time: Job Satisfaction and Informal Interaction," in R. Luhman (ed.), *The Sociological Outlook* (Belmont, Cal.: Wadsworth Publishing Co., 1982).

of clock time marked by check-in, lunch, and check-out, the workers created intermediate periods which they referred to with such terms as coffee time, peach time, banana time, and fish time. Other planned interruptions were called window time and pickup time, and the staggered hours of two co-workers were called "quitting time for Sammy and Ike."

The workers in Roy's study endowed these interruptions with a variety of meanings which made a boring day endurable and, at times, enjoyable for them. The breaks were events that stood out from the rest of the day and could be looked forward to as times when joking, socializing, and good-humored heckling might reaffirm the humanity and personal identity of the workers. In banana time, for example, Ike would "steal" a banana from Sammy's lunchbox every day, while crying out "Banana time!" In response, Sammy would appear to make a fuss. All the actors played their parts in this little scenario with such skill and verve that it became an event which all eagerly awaited. These created "times" had the effect of stimulating group interactions which "not only marked off the time . . . but gave it content and hurried it along" (p. 246).

## *Negotiating a More Satisfactory Order*

A study of workers in an English factory producing electrical components also highlights the efforts of workers to negotiate some degree of control over their daily jobs. In this plant, management allowed the workers a lunch break and two 10-minute tea breaks, one in the morning and one in the afternoon. D. H. J. Morgan (1975) skillfully describes how the workers transformed the meaning of these breaks to include a number of activities prior to the actual break, such as visiting the toilets and washing cups and teapots. As a result, the two breaks were considerably longer than the officially allowed 10 minutes. As in Roy's study of banana time, workers in Morgan's plant also took various undesignated work breaks during the day for tea, conversation, and pre-leaving activities called "getting ready for the off." These workers, it appears, engaged in such actions without incurring serious reprimands from management.

In terms of the negotiated-order aspect of bureaucracies, Morgan's study demonstrates the critical issue of power within large-scale organizations. Management cast an apparently forgiving eye on the break practices because it had its attention on a much larger, more significant issue, namely, workers' salaries. By overlooking these practices, it could keep salaries low by arguing that production suffered as a result of all those extended break times. Morgan's study suggests that negotiation is ". . . something which is constantly open to change, modification, rediscovery, use, and denial. It is not something which is 'just there' or even 'given,' but something which is used, bargained about, enjoyed in private or flouted in public, taken and accepted" (p. 224).

## ■ CONCLUSION

The emergence of large-scale bureaucratic organizations can be linked to the processes of urbanization, industrialization, and the development of capitalism and technology. Factories and corporations were organized to ensure maximum managerial control over workers' activities. Bureaucracies also were organized to control government functions. Now bureaucracy is shaping a wide variety of everyday behaviors. Contacts between intimates and strangers are mediated by the intervention of third-party agencies such as insurance companies, government bureaus, and the courts.

Scholars, beginning with Max Weber, have used various approaches in thinking about bureaucracy. The interactionist view is that organizations are created, maintained, and changed through the daily interactions of their members, using the process of negotiated order. They therefore include multiple realities which vary with the individual's position in the organization's hierarchy of authority. Informal subcultures define the organization in terms of human behaviors rather than rules and regulations.

In the world of work, individuals' locations in the hierarchy—executives, secretaries, and blue-collar workers—shape their conceptions of the job and the organization. Workers with little autonomy in their jobs strive to achieve some degree of control over their work lives. Their efforts to make their jobs meaningful often involve deviation from official rules and procedures. In the next chapter we will elaborate on the concept of deviance by illustrating its central position in numerous aspects of everyday life.

## Definitions

**Bureaucracy.** A principle of organization utilizing a hierarchical structure of authority, the clear specification of work tasks, and an elaborate system of rules and regulations. The goal of a bureaucratic organization is to maximize efficiency.

**Proletariat.** The working class. Karl Marx applied the term to industrial workers who were prevented from owning the means of production, that is, the factories where they worked.

**Mass society.** A large-scale society in which the status distinctions between various groups have been blurred.

**Scientific management.** An effort to organize work, particularly in the factory, in terms of the principles of science. The idea was developed by Frederick Taylor to promote task specialization and control of workers' activities by management.

**Control from the top down.** A system of authority which is characteristic of bureaucracies. The orders are issued by upper management, and those lower down in the hierarchy of authority are expected to comply without resistance.

**Organizational society.** An urban-industrial society characterized by the presence of large-scale bureaucratic organizations.

**White-collar occupations.** Work which is primarily mental in character. White-collar workers provide the support services needed for industrial production.

**Blue-collar occupations.** Work in which people use their hands as well as their minds to make a product or supply a service.

**Service occupations.** Work in which people perform various services for others rather than producing a product.

**New middle class.** A social category composed of corporate managers, salaried white-collar professionals, salespeople, and office workers.

**Division of labor.** The assignment of different functions as tasks in the workplace to accomplish a group goal.

**Hierarchy of authority.** The chain of command in an organization which specifies who can issue orders to whom.

**Meritocracy.** A principle of organizational functioning which would allocate rewards on the basis of the quality of a person's performance. Hiring and promotion are supposed to be done solely on the basis of personal merit or ability.

**Peter principle.** The idea that employees in an organization tend to rise to their individual levels of incompetence—and then remain there. The idea was suggested by Lawrence Peter and Raymond Hull.

**Rationalization.** The systematic and logical application of formal rules and procedures to every aspect of modern life. According to Max Weber, bureaucracy exemplifies this principle.

**Informal subcultures.** The unique ways of doing things developed by members of various subgroups in an organization. These subcultures, which often have no formal structure, form an *informal organization* which sets the norms for behaviors within the formal organization.

**Negotiated order.** The process by which members construct organizations. Negotiation by individuals also is the process by which social order is constructed.

**Protestant work ethic.** The notion that the ultimate value and meaning of life are to be found in hard work and industrious labor. Work was regarded as service to God and a mark of respectability.

**Social ethic.** The notion that the ultimate value and meaning in life are to be found in one's acceptance by others.

**Autonomy.** Ability to control one's own daily activities. Autonomy is particularly sought in the workplace.

**Deskilling.** The process by which the skilled components of production jobs are replaced by tasks requiring little skill or talent.

**Job satisfaction.** The extent to which people find their work enjoyable and meaningful.

# Discussion Questions

1. Have you ever had a dispute concerning a bill with a bureaucratic organization—a credit union, hospital, or department store, for example? What kinds of frustrations, if any, did you experience in trying to rectify the situation?

2. How have your experiences in college supported the notion of the university as a bureaucratic organization? What strategies have you developed to "get around" the official bureaucratic rules? Which ones have been the most successful?

3. Fifty years ago your grandmother probably would never have imagined suing her neighbor because she fell on ice in front of the neighbor's house. Nowadays such actions are commonplace. What kinds of situations do you think might be brought into the courts in the future as bases for suing another person?

4. Think of an incident in which you had an argument or disagreement with a stranger. Is there anything about that incident that led you to think about going to court to settle the issue? What does such an incident reveal about everyday life in a bureaucratic society?

5. In the past workers formed labor unions as a collective response to the alienating conditions in bureaucratic factory settings. Do you think white-collar workers will form organizations to make their jobs more meaningful in the face of increasing bureaucratization? What kinds of organizations would these be?

6. If you have ever worked in a bureaucratic setting—an office or factory, for example—describe how your place in the organization's hierarchy influenced your view of how the organization functioned. How do you think your boss and colleagues viewed the organization?

7. Numerous critics have noted how bureaucracies make individuals "faceless" by reducing them to particles in a mass of particles. This allows individuals to blend into the mass and not have to take personal responsibility for their actions. What might be the political consequences of this process?

# References

Baron, R. 1983. *Behavior in Organizations.* Newton, Mass.: Allyn & Bacon.

Braverman, H. 1974. *Labor and Monopoly Capital.* New York: Monthly Review Press.

Breen, G. 1983. *Middle Management in the '80s.* New York: American Management Association.

Clawson, D. 1980. *Bureaucracy and the Labor Process.* New York: Monthly Review Press.

Clegg, S. 1975. *Power, Rule, and Domination.* London: Routledge & Kegan Paul.

Ehrenreich, B., and D. English. 1979. *For Her Own Good: 150 Years of the Experts' Advice to Women.* New York: Doubleday Anchor Books.

Hall, R. 1977. *Organizations, Structure, and Process.* Englewood Cliffs, N.J.: Prentice-Hall.

Hummel, R. 1982. *The Bureaucratic Experience.* New York: St. Martin's Press.

Jackson, P. 1977. "Lonely at the top: Observations on the genesis of administrative isolation." *School Review* (May):425–432.

Jacoby, H. 1976. *The Bureaucratization of the World.* Berkeley: University of California Press.

Kanter, R. 1977. *Men and Women of the Corporation.* New York: Harper & Row.

Kanter, R. 1979. "How the top is different." In *Life in Organizations,* ed. R. Kanter and B. Stein. New York: Basic Books.

Karp, D., and W. Yoels. 1976. "The college classroom." *Sociology and Social Research* 60 (July):421–439.

Laslett, P. 1971. *The World We Have Lost.* New York: Charles Scribner's Sons.

Maccoby, M. 1976. *The Gamesman.* New York: Simon & Schuster.

Maines, D. 1977. "Social organization and social structure in symbolic interactionist thought." *Annual Review of Sociology* 3:235–259.

Miller, G. 1981. *It's a Living.* New York: St. Martin's Press.

Mills, C. W. 1956. *White Collar.* New York: Oxford University Press.

Morgan, D. H. J. 1975. "Autonomy and negotiation in an industrial setting." *Sociology of Work and Occupations* 2 (August):203–226.

Pearce, R. 1977. *Manager to Manager II.* New York: American Management Association.

Perrow, C. 1978. *Complex Organizations.* Glenview, Ill.: Scott Foresman.

Peter, L., and R. Hull. 1969. *The Peter Principle: Why Things Always Go Wrong.* New York: William Morrow.

Pfeffer, R. 1979. *Working for Capitalism.* New York: Columbia University Press.

Presthus, R. 1978. *The Organizational Society.* New York: St. Martin's Press.

Robey, B., and C. Russell. 1984. "A portrait of the American worker." *American Demographics* 6 (March):17–21.

Roy, D. 1982. "Banana time: Job satisfaction and informal interaction." In *The Sociological Outlook,* ed. R. Luhman. Belmont, Cal.: Wadsworth. Originally published in *Human Organization* 18 (Winter 1959–60):158–164.

Schwartz, B., R. Schuldenfrei, and H. Lacey. 1978. "Operation psychology as factory psychology." *Behaviorism* 6:229–254.

Strauss, A. 1978. *Negotiations.* San Francisco: Jossey-Bass.

Tausky, C. 1984. *Work and Society.* Itasca, Ill.: F. E. Peacock.

U.S. Bureau of the Census. 1983. *Statistical Abstract of the United States, 1984.* Washington, D.C.: Government Printing Office.

U.S. Department of Health, Education, and Welfare. 1973. *Work in America: Report of a Special Task Force to the Secretary of Health, Education, and Welfare.* Cambridge, Mass.: M.I.T. Press.

Weber, M. 1922/1946. "Bureaucracy." In *From Max Weber: Essays in Sociology,* ed. H. Gerth and C. W. Mills. New York: Oxford University Press (originally published 1922).

Weick, K. 1976. "Educational organizations as loosely coupled systems." *Administrative Science Quarterly* 21 (March):1–19.

Whyte, W. H. 1956. *The Organization Man.* New York: Simon & Schuster (Doubleday Anchor).

Williams, M. J. 1985. "The baby bust hits the job market." *Fortune* (May 27):122–135.

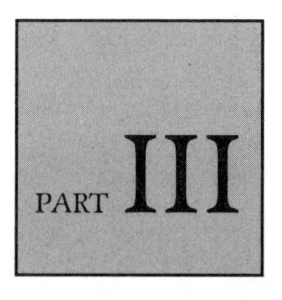

# PART III — Disorder and Change in Everyday Life

CHAPTER 8      DEVIANCE IN EVERYDAY INTERACTIONS   221
- Everyday Deviances and Deviant Careers   224
- Embarrassment as a Fractured Transaction   225
- Restoring Identities Damaged by Deviance   231
- Labeling Theory and Lifestyle Deviance   236

CHAPTER 9      AGING AND THE LIFE CYCLE   249
- Age Categories in American Society   252
- The Meanings of Age   261
- Effects of Aging on Work and Careers   265
- Gender Differences in the Aging Process   269

CHAPTER 10     SOCIAL CHANGE AND THE SEARCH FOR SELF   277
- Symbols, Selves, and Society   279
- Social Movements and Conceptions of Injustice   283
- The Contemporary Concern with Self   286
- Future Selves   294

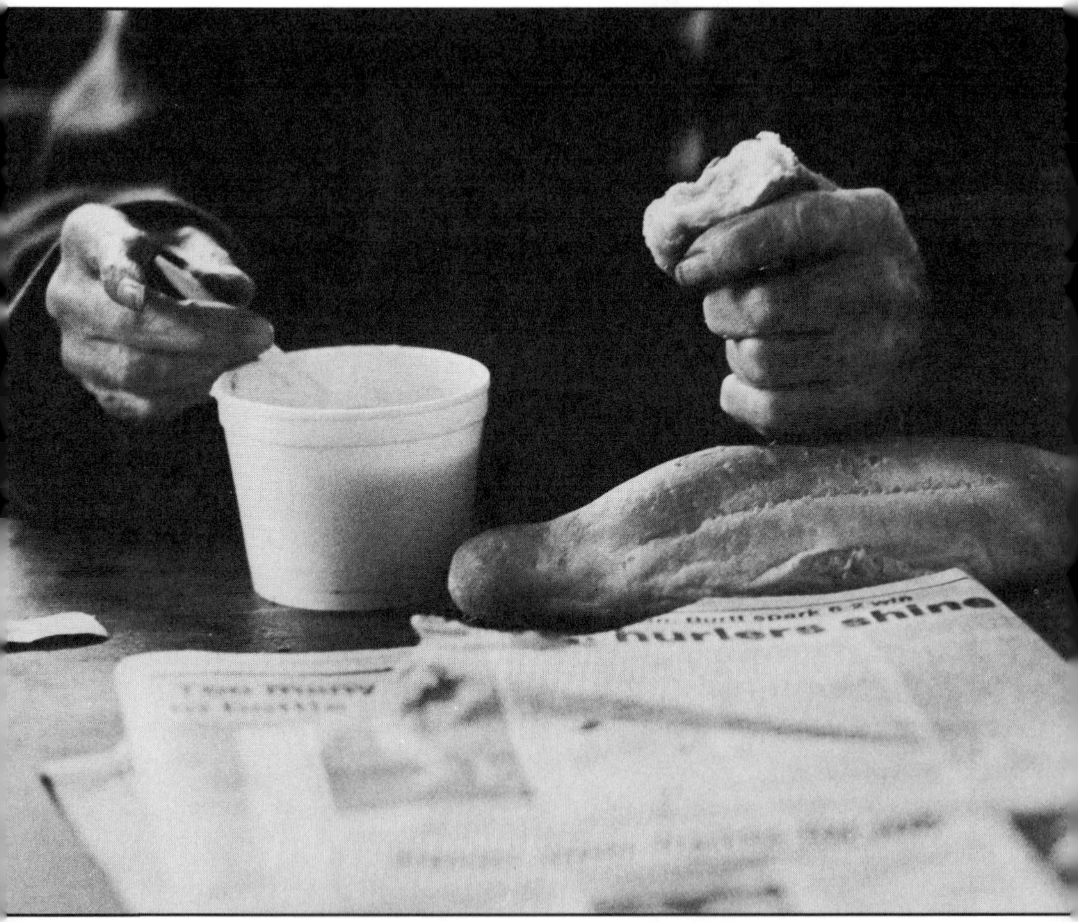
hurlers shine

# PART III

PERHAPS THE MOST FUNDAMENTAL sociological question is how order is possible in society—how society hangs together as an ongoing concern. So far in this book, we have focused on those features of social life that give it stability, predictability, and order. We would be theoretically shortsighted if we neglected the study of change and disorder in social life, however. While we have stressed the idea that human beings are symbolic animals who collectively give meaning to their worlds, it is also true that everyone does not abide by the same set of social rules or share the same significant symbols and social realities. Moreover, human beings and society are constantly changing. In Part III it will become clear to you that the symbols and meanings which make a life coherent in certain circumstances may not "work" in others.

One source of disorder in social life is the fact that people break rules. Individuals who accidentally fail to follow social norms may experience embarrassment as the structure of social interaction is momentarily threatened, and their identities are called into question. As a result, they are likely to experience discomfort, *dis*-ease, and personal *dis*-order. In Chapter 8 we analyze how social encounters sometimes go awry and how people try to fix such fractured interactions.

Transgressions of cultural expectations also can have more serious consequences for individuals and society. Some people so consistently break the conventional rules of society that they are labeled and treated as deviant throughout their lives. Those who are labeled as criminals or mentally ill, for example, may seem to threaten social order to the extent that they are removed from society altogether. Chapter 8 will give you an understanding of how both everyday deviances and those that envelop a person's whole life can threaten the social order.

The social order is also continually subject to change, which is characteristic of the entire life cycle, from birth to death. Each significant point in the life cycle, such as childhood, adolescence, middle age, and old age, requires the adoption of new roles, statuses, and identities. Chapter 9 explores the meanings people confer on the process of aging throughout the course of their lives.

In the analysis of aging, we examine processes of change at two levels. Not only do people change as they move from one age status to another, but aging must also be understood within the context of broader cultural, structural, and historical changes. For example, the meanings given to different age categories (such as middle or old age) certainly are not the same now as they were at the turn of the century. Purely from a statistical point of view, the significance attached to age categories varies with such demographic factors as the number of people falling into each age category and changes in life expectancy. Structural changes such as these result in changing interpretations of specific phases of the life cycle. The theoretical perspective of symbolic interaction also emphasizes how persons occupying different locations in society experience aging differently. Chapter 9 will help you see, for example, how occupational careers structure the way people think about aging and how the power positions of women compared to men influence the social process of aging.

Discussions of both deviance and aging should lead you to think about how individuals deal with disorder and change in their lives. Both involve the analysis of identity change. The most powerful kind of personal dislocation, however, results when people become uncertain of their identities, when they have trouble answering the question, "Who am I?"

Questions of personal identity are linked to broad historical changes in society. In simpler preurban societies, the question of identity raised no problems. People had little difficulty knowing who they were, and battalions of psychiatric experts did not exist to help them find themselves. Numerous social scientists have observed that one of the most dramatic consequences of industrialization has been the rapid, widespread increase in geographical and social mobility for large segments of the population. The sense of rootlessness which often accompanies industrialization has led to enormous concern with questions of identity, self-worth, alienation, and the larger significance of life. In the final chapter of this book you will learn how the issue of personal identity has been brought to the forefront of contemporary consciousness in the Western world.

# CHAPTER 8
# Deviance in Everyday Interactions

I. Everyday Deviances and Deviant Careers
   A. Everyday Deviances in the Social Order
II. Embarrassment as a Fractured Transaction
   A. The Social Contours of Embarrassment
   B. Efforts to Avoid Embarrassment: Maintaining Identity and Poise
      1. Control of space
      2. Control of props
      3. Control of bodies
III. Restoring Identities Damaged by Deviance
   A. Assessing Motives and Offering Accounts
      1. Excuses and justifications
   B. Making Disclaimers
   C. Disavowing Deviance
      1. Deviances of varying visibility
IV. Labeling Theory and Lifestyle Deviance
   A. Ways of Thinking about Deviance
   B. The Medicalization of Deviance
      1. The politics of the medical model
   C. Deviant Careers
      1. Development of a deviant identity
      2. Institutional definitions
V. Conclusion

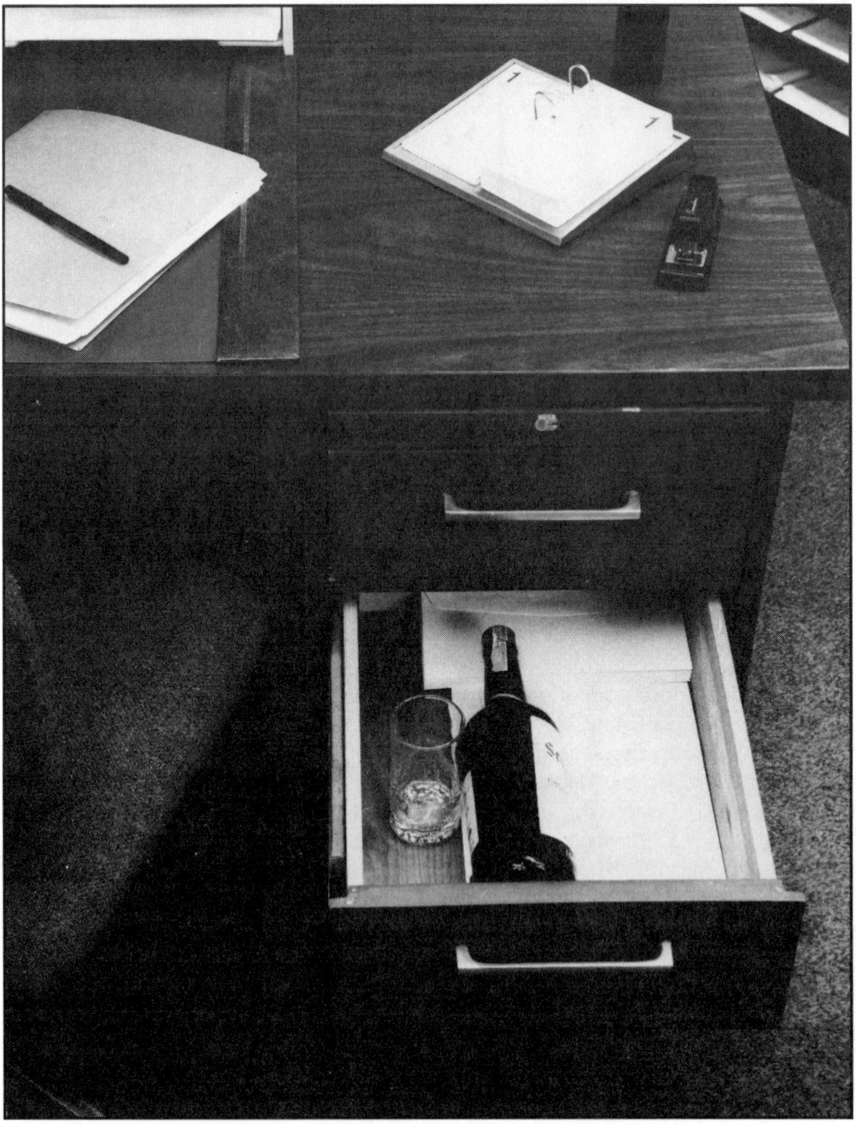

# CHAPTER 8

IMAGINE THAT you have made an appointment with your sociology teacher to discuss a term paper. Because your meeting extends through the lunch hour, the professor takes out a brown-bag lunch and, shortly after, a smear of ketchup adorns the professor's cheek. Now you have a bit of a problem on your hands. How should you deal with this situation? A little thought suggests that the choices open to you all pose difficulties. You could immediately interrupt the conversation and inform the professor of the smear, but such communications are typically reserved for intimates, such as a wife or husband. Your second alternative is to pretend that there is nothing wrong about the situation and hope that the professor will wipe off the smear in the normal course of things. This strategy also involves some risk, however. The situation might be punctured by the appearance of a colleague who would immediately remark on the professor's social blunder. Then the professor would realize that you had known about it for some time and had pretended not to see it. The professor's discovery of the smear under this circumstance could heighten the discomfort felt by everyone in the room.

Social life abounds with similar situations in which people's behaviors or presentations of self somehow harm or compromise the identities they are trying to present. These situations may make them appear to be wrong, incorrect, improper, or possibly even immoral, and they may feel awkward, uneasy, or embarrassed as a result. In some situations a person's presented self or identity becomes so compromised or tainted that the result is a fractured interaction (see Chapter 3). The social situation may even completely break down. In this sense everyday life is risky because of the ever-present possibility that events will make a person "look bad." Even in the most routine encounters we may be defined by others as improper, nonsocial, or deviant.

## ■ EVERYDAY DEVIANCES AND DEVIANT CAREERS

In this chapter we are departing momentarily from conventional discussions of deviance, which typically address such issues as various kinds of crime, delinquency, drug use, prostitution, rape, and mental illness. These are broad, **lifestyle deviances,** which effectively involve people in lifelong deviant careers. The causes and solutions of many of these types of behavior, the extent of the harm they do, and what can be done about them are controversial (Little, 1983, p. 7). Individuals who behave in these ways are considered deviant when they are labeled as such by those in positions of power in the society.

There is another aspect of deviance which we will consider first. This is concerned with **everyday deviances,** occasional improprieties which temporarily mark certain individuals as somehow nonconforming, awkward, or difficult. Regardless of the degree of involvement by an individual, in either lifestyle or everyday deviances, according to Jown Hewitt, "deviance is a phenomenon in which the social identity and self-conception of the deviant are thoroughly implicated. A deviant act reflects negatively on the *identity* of the one who engages in it" (italics in original; 1976:207). The principal characteristic of most everyday deviances is that they may be unsettling or embarrassing, but they mar a person's identity only momentarily. Embarrassment may cause only limited discomfort or be so intense it disrupts an interaction, however.

### Everyday Deviances in the Social Order

Everyday deviances are far less dramatic than those that envelop a person's whole life. After all, we are not thrown in jail for embarrassing ourselves. Nevertheless, it is important to study everyday deviances in order to understand how society hangs together. While in a statistical sense very few people are involved in lifelong deviant careers, everyone must continually create, sustain, and repair the social interactions that comprise everyday life. A key assumption of this book is that any theoretical conception of how a society operates must begin with an understanding of how the everyday, face-to-face encounters of its members are ordered.

Our interactions are inherently fragile things, easily disrupted by inappropriate remarks, improper displays of emotionalism, lack of bodily control, and the like. Further, there is a deep morality in everyday life which requires efforts to protect both our own and others' identities in our interactions. In those instances where our selves—and thus our social situations—are somehow tarnished, we are charged with the responsibility of setting things right. People who have been properly socialized know how to improve situations when there is the perception that they have done something embarrassing or somehow wrong. To shed some light on how and why encounters sometimes go awry and how people try to fix fractured interactions, we will consider the nature of embarrassment and its relation to roles, identities, and social organization.

## ■ EMBARRASSMENT AS A FRACTURED TRANSACTION

If a social scientist wants to know what normally keeps a social system in balance, or in **social equilibrium,** it is a good strategy to examine what happens when that equilibrium is disturbed. **Embarrassment,** one such disturbance, arises out of individuals' knowledge that others are evaluating them negatively. This knowledge can produce feelings of social discomfort great enough to impede a person's thought, speech, and action, so it is difficult or impossible to continue an interaction. By showing what happens in these circumstances, studies of embarrassment can reveal a good deal about the social order and the basic requirements of successful role performance.

The study of embarrassment and role requirements by Edward Gross and Gregory P. Stone (1964), for example, was equivalent to putting the concept under a microscope to magnify its basic features. In their view, poise as well as identity must be established in transactions. Once established, they must be continuously reaffirmed and maintained, and provisions must be made for their repair if they break down. Their study was designed to clarify "the structure of transactions where identities have been misplaced or forgotten, where poise has been lost or destroyed, or where, for any reason, confidence that identities and poise will be maintained has been undermined" (p. 2).

### The Social Contours of Embarrassment

The effects of embarrassing events on individuals and social situations vary by degrees. At one extreme, embarrassment may be mild, causing limited discomfort; a slight blush, a fixed smile, a nervous laugh, or downcast eyes. At the other extreme are instances in which embarrassment is sustained throughout the encounter, perhaps becoming severe enough to demand that the individual leave the situation. In either case, it is the person's honor that is at stake. It may be called into question, compromised, or lost altogether.

It is sometimes said that embarrassed persons have "lost their cool." **Coolness** is poise under pressure; it is "the capacity to execute physical acts, including conversation, in a concerted, smooth, self-controlled fashion in risky situations" (Lyman and Scott, 1968b:95). The kind of risk under consideration, of course, is social risk. We make claims about our value as persons in every social situation, but there is always the possibility that such claims will not be validated by others. Every interaction is to some degree risky, because events may occur that will compromise the identities we are presenting. According to Stanford Lyman and Marvin Scott, "Any encounter is likely to be suddenly punctured by a potentially embarrassing event—a gaffe, a boner, or uncontrollable motor response—that casts new and unfavorable light upon the actor's performance" (1968b:95). Embarrassment provides a good example of how our feelings about ourselves derive from our interpretations of how some audience views and evaluates our behaviors (see Chapter 1).

Embarrassment is not only costly to the individual whose identity, honor, or coolness has been compromised. It also is contagious and has the potential of enveloping the whole situation in which it occurs. All interactions are joint ventures, joint actions. People become embarrassed within some social context which involves other people who recognize the embarrassment and must somehow deal with it. Embarrassment thus is lodged in social situations as well as in individuals. It not only affects the person who is embarrassed; it is shared by all of those who are parties to the encounter.

We share the embarrassment felt by others; we blush at their blushing and we feel embarrassed for their embarrassment. When the self of any one person in a situation is threatened or discredited, the selves of all those involved become implicated. Further, if others who observe an embarrassing act do not handle it well—in a tactful fashion—they may increase the discomfort felt by all. According to Erving Goffman, each participant in an interaction must honor the selves presented by all the other participants. If a participant is discredited, he says:

> By the standards of the wider society, perhaps only the discredited individual ought to feel ashamed; but, by the standards of the little social system maintained through interaction, the discreditor is just as guilty as the person he discredits. . . . This is why embarrassment seems to be contagious, spreading, once started, in ever-widening circles of discomfiture. (1967:106)

Embarrassment also can have positive functions as a form of **social**

**control.** A person may be deliberately embarrassed in order to socialize or train her or him to put on a poised performance. One form of this training is the practical jokes children play on one another and their other attempts to cause their friends to "lose face." Teenagers, too, frequently engage in competitive testing encounters designed to assert their own superiority and skillfulness in maintaining personal honor. Deliberate embarrassment also can keep group members in line. Even the *threat* of embarrassment may be used to stop behaviors that could be disruptive or harmful to a group. A good example of this social control function is the possibility of public reprimands faced by government officials who embarrass their superiors or the administration.

## Efforts to Avoid Embarrassment: Maintaining Identity and Poise

Order and disorder, deviance and conformity, effective and disrupted role performances each represent flip sides of the same coins. In order to sustain our proper identities in any social encounter, we need to arrange and control the space surrounding the interaction, the props we use in our self presentations, and our bodies, which must be held ready for interaction. Control of these components of self and situations in the environment is critical if interactions are to come off without a hitch.

### *Control of Space*

One source of embarrassment is the attempts of individuals to occupy spaces or territories where they do not belong. An obvious example would be a man accidentally entering a women's restroom, or vice versa. In American society there are clear norms governing who should be doing what and *where.* The where is critical, since roles performed properly in one context may injure a person's identity when performed in a different one. A father may play on the floor with his children in their bedroom, for example, but in the living room, in the company of adults, he is expected to sit on a chair and converse. The boundaries of space, or areas within which interactions take place, may be more or less sharply defined. When the bounds are overstepped, embarrassment, signalling a loss of poise, is likely to result, according to Gross and Stone (1964:8).

The meaning and significance of role performance are defined by the context in which they take place, as we noted in Chapter 1. It is impossible to know the meaning of behavior or acts apart from the situations in which they occur. Some actions are restricted to particular settings. People are expected to act on their sexuality in private spaces, for example. Indeed, the bedroom has symbolic significance in American society because it is recognized as a place where persons put on performances which reveal "deep" aspects of themselves. The bathroom, similarly, has been institutionalized as a "back region." Bedrooms and bathrooms are among the few places in American society where you can legitimately lock yourself in. In these two contexts people engage in behaviors which, if they could be seen, might not be in accord with the impressions of themselves they normally try to present.

The adequacy of a role performance may be determined by who controls the space or the situation. Because teachers control classroom spaces, students often experience a heightened sense of self-awareness in this context. Those who are late coming to class may be profusely apologetic about the impropriety they think they have committed. They feel embarrassed even though the teacher attaches little significance to the event. People may lose their poise when they act out of place or accidentally invade spaces where they feel they do not belong.

## Control of Props

The props used in carrying off interactions are a second component of self and situation which must be controlled in order to protect identity and maintain poise. Spaces are filled with objects that frame interactions. Rooms are filled with furniture, rugs, paintings, mirrors, room dividers, stairways, and the like. Normally, these props stand unobtrusively in the shadows of interactions, but they can affect the chances that an interaction will be successful. Furniture may be rearranged to improve communication at a party, for example, and grocery store displays are artfully constructed to prompt impulse buying.

While most props facilitate transactions, a prop failure can also stop an interaction in its tracks, casting doubt on the intentions, motives, or capacities of the participants. The lights, pillows, and soft music props in a single's place may be so overdone that they provoke a date to laughter, rather than inspiring the intended mood of sensuality. Props cause embarrassment most often when people lose control over them, as when someone stumbles over a rug or trips on a flight of steps.

Often, through no fault of our own, objects or pieces of equipment cause disruptions that prove embarrassing. Bowling balls are unceremoniously dropped, cars become stalled in dense traffic, food accidentally spills in laps, silverware and dishes appear on the table with spots on them. Much slapstick humor, like that in the Marx Brothers, Charlie Chaplin, or Three Stooges movies, is built around the awkwardness created by prop failures. The humor works because it exaggerates the misadventures that could befall anyone, as the following incident illustrates:

> ... at a formal dinner, a speaker was discovered with his fly zipper undone. On being informed of this embarrassing oversight after he was reseated, he proceeded to make the requisite adjustment, unknowingly catching the tablecloth in his trousers. When obliged to rise again at the close of the proceedings, he took the stage props with him and of course scattered the dinner tools about the setting in such a way that others were forced to doubt his control. His poise was lost in the situation. (Gross and Stone, 1964:10)

Clothing, another prop, was described in Chapter 3 as a significant feature of the selves we present. This prop must be carefully maintained, controlled, and arranged. An example of the importance attached to it is the television commercials for a detergent in which the woman expressed acute embarrassment upon learning that the shirts she had washed gave her husband "ring around the collar." As a prop, clothing is a direct extension of a person's body. Countercultural groups from the Bohemians of the fifties to the hippies of the sixties and the punkers of the eighties have adopted unconventional clothing as a way of communicating that their selves are far different from those the conventional world would like to see presented.

Members of such alternate lifestyle groups have found support within their own subcultures for wearing clothes that others considered outlandish, though their parents have probably been greatly embarrassed by such behavior. The fact that the dress of such groups can elicit very strong emotional responses—even hostility—is evidence of the potent symbolism of clothing.

## *Control of Bodies*

Whether or not we will be regarded as proper persons depends in large measure on the appearance of our bodies and the control we can exercise over them. Our bodies are monitored by others as a check on our internal feelings. Trembling hands, profuse sweating, dilated pupils, blushing, stuttering, turning white, and involuntary breaks in the voice are among the body gestures that may belie our efforts to appear in charge of ourselves and situations. In extreme cases, complete loss of body control incapacitates further interaction, as when a person gives way to emotionalism, "floods out," or expresses violent anger or fear. Flatulence, drooling, involuntary urination and other losses of visceral control can cause deep embarrassment.

A fascinating study that considered the importance of both clothing and the body is Martin Weinberg's analysis of modesty in nudist camps. He provides persuasive evidence that nudists behave in accordance with social norms that sustain modesty despite their total disregard for body covering, a situation where modesty might seem highly unlikely. The embarrassment that ordinarily accompanies such exposure is prevented by rules that desexualize it. There are taboos against staring or otherwise showing overinvolvement with another person's body, any form of bodily contact, attempts to cover areas of the body, and unnecessary accentuation of the body. Weinberg's study is a potent reminder that the meanings of acts are always connected with the norms governing particular settings. The strictly enforced rules of the nudist camp prevented "rampant sexual interest, promiscuity, embarrassment, jealousy, and shame," according to Weinberg (1965:318).

Bodies that either do not work correctly or are somehow incapacitated or disfigured have the greatest potential for disrupting social situations. People who are physically handicapped or who have permanent disfigurements or disabilities face unique contingencies in interaction with "normals." Unlike others whose settings, props, and bodies might only infrequently fail them and cause embarrassment, those with permanent body impairments must adopt strategies to convince others they should not be defined as deviant in every social encounter. We will discuss efforts to restore such identities in a later section of this chapter.

## ■ RESTORING IDENTITIES DAMAGED BY DEVIANCE

Any interaction is inherently risky because everyday deviances can threaten a person's identity and poise and can paralyze role performance efforts. The embarrassment that results when this happens and a fractured interaction results is hardly a trivial outcome. In order to maintain the integrity and order of society, there is a moral imperative which calls for efforts to salvage identities under assault and to save situations which are threatening to break apart. These efforts are part of the unwritten social contract which underlies social life. Lyn Lofland puts it this way: "All social life may be viewed as a kind of social bargain, a whispered enjoinder to let us all protect each other so that we can carry on the business of living" (1971:226).

The protection of identities is a major concern in everyday encounters. Participants maneuver to achieve a valued identity for themselves but also try to conduct themselves so that others' identities are protected. When events occur that openly damage the identity of one or more of the persons involved in an interaction, it signals the need for what might be termed **face games.** The purpose of such transactions is to save face, or repair identities that have gone wrong. A face game can restore a situation to what it was before the intrusion of an unwelcome event or normalize a situation that has become abnormal.

Sometimes the events disrupting a situation are relatively slight, and the situation can be normalized easily and quickly. As an example, suppose you inadvertently belch loudly at a lecture. The process of identity restoration begins when others acknowledge the impropriety, perhaps by glancing at you momentarily. You then try to remedy the situation immediately by offering an apology, bowing your head slightly, covering your mouth with a hand, and uttering a quick "Excuse me." With these gestures you are in effect communicating: "I know that I did something wrong and I am acknowledging it. I am trying to show you that I am, in fact, a proper person who wishes to abide by the rules. Having done this I expect that you will readmit me to this situation as a person with an identity that is once more intact." It is necessary to go through this brief social ritual in order to avoid being considered a boor.

Identity restoration efforts involve communication and a display of motives. Efforts to "clear" identities that are temporarily under a cloud call for satisfactory answers to such actual or implied questions as: "Why did you do that? What motivated you to behave as you did? Explain what was in your head that made you break the rules." Unless individuals can offer satisfactory reasons for their behavior when others have defined it as improper, their identities remain suspect, and their status in good standing remains in doubt.

## Assessing Motives and Offering Accounts

Ascertaining others' motives and explaining our own are necessary parts of all ongoing interactions. In the broadest sense, human conduct is grounded in a continuous assessment of motives. We feel compelled to explain our own behavior, and we cannot formulate our behavior toward others without also assessing the motives underlying theirs.

C. Wright Mills says such assessments constitute a **vocabulary of motives.** He defines a *motive* as "a complex of meaning, which appears to the actor himself or to the observer to be an adequate ground for his conduct. A satisfactory or adequate motive is one that satisfies the questioners of the act . . ." (1972:396). To Mills, "motive talk" is a central feature of everyday experience. It provides one of the organizing techniques of social interaction, determining how acts are interpreted, including the moral evaluations attached to them.

To explain our motives when our actions are seen as deviant or damaging to our identity, we use linguistic devices called *accounts*. Lyman and Scott define an account as a verbal statement made to explain "unanticipated or untoward behavior" (1968a:33). Accounts can take the form of excuses or justifications.

### Excuses and Justifications

**Excuses** are verbal accounts people offer to acknowledge that their behaviors have been undesirable or wrong, but also to indicate why they should not be held accountable for those behaviors. They are intended to indicate why admittedly incorrect behaviors could not have been avoided. Everyday deviances may be explained away as resulting from:

An accident: "We had a flat tire and couldn't get home on time."

Events outside a person's will: "I have family troubles and have been feeling depressed."

Factors rooted in biology: "If only I could control my drinking, it wouldn't have happened."

The behaviors of others: "I am doing poorly because he doesn't give me enough encouragement."

Such excuses offer an appeal to the charge of deviance by citing events beyond the person's control.

Like excuses, **justifications** also are accounts people offer to acknowledge that they have committed acts which are being questioned. These accounts, however, are also designed to indicate why the acts should not be interpreted as deviant. Justifying an act asserts its positive value, despite claims to the contrary.

According to Gresham Sykes and David Matza (1957), justifications are used to attempt to neutralize possible definitions of acts as illegitimate by providing nondeviant interpretations of them. Techniques of neutralization include efforts to:

Deny that any real harm has come from an act: "I know that I took your car out for a joy ride, but I was only borrowing it and did not hurt it."

Suggest that those who were injured deserved what they got: "It's true we harassed them, but they are, after all, communists."

Argue that in the large scheme of things an act is not too awful: "The amount of income I withheld from the IRS is nothing compared to the ripoffs of big business."

Indicate that an act is permissible and even proper because it was done out of loyalty. "After all the times he's saved my skin, I just couldn't refuse to do what the lieutenant asked."

Both excuses and justifications lubricate interactions by explaining personal motives in such a way that charges of deviance are quickly defused. In this way, momentarily troubled encounters are allowed to resume a smooth course quickly. Sometimes, however, accounts are not honored, and efforts to restore identities fail. For a variety of reasons, motive explanations may be deemed unacceptable.

Some accounts have been so overused they may not be accepted even when true ("Not tonight, dear, I have a headache"). Others will succeed with some people and not others. For example, explanations for recreational drug use may be accepted by other drugusers but are likely to be rejected by "straights." Accounts also may be deemed unreasonable if they do not conform to commonly held cultural expectations. Suppose you go home and find your wife or roommate with her head in the oven. You would probably ask, "What are you doing?" If she responds, "I'm cleaning the oven" that would probably be a satisfactory explanation. But if she claims that she heard voices telling her to put her head in the oven, you would make quite a different interpretation of her action. People who continually offer culturally unacceptable motives for their behaviors run the risk of being labeled mentally ill.

## Making Disclaimers

Accounts are a form of motive talk which *follows* a questionable action. Other verbal strategies are used *in advance* to counter doubts and negative evaluations which could result from intended conduct. We rehearse our future acts in our minds, trying to anticipate the responses others will make to them. When we determine that what we plan to do could be interpreted negatively, we preface our actions with **disclaimers** to provide a nondeviant frame of reference within which our behavior can be interpreted (Hewitt and Stokes, 1975).

Everyday talk is filled with disclaimers, including expressions of the following sort:

"I'm no expert, of course, but. . . ."
"Don't get me wrong, I like your work, but. . . ."
"I'm not prejudiced—some of my best friends are Jews, but. . . ."
"I know this is against the rules, but. . . ."
"This may seem strange to you, but. . . ."

Such disclaimers protect individuals by indicating that despite the way their present behaviors might appear, they really are people who abide by prevailing norms and cultural constraints.

## Disavowing Deviance

Everyday deviances usually cause individuals' selves or identities to fall into disrepute only momentarily. In most instances they are not ruined beyond repair, and the situation can be saved. Some people, however, have attributes which are so stigmatized by others that their behavior is considered "wrong" in virtually every situation. Highly visible attributes such as physical handicaps, disfigurements, and mental retardation immediately tag people who have them as different in their interactions with "normals." Others, such as homosexuals and those with a history of mental illness, may be able to hide their negative attributes, but discovery of them would complicate their everyday interactions and could cause them great social harm. Still others are marked by attributes which characterize them as members of devalued members in a society, including certain racial, ethnic, religious, and occupational groups.

Persons with any of these kinds of attributes are faced with the task

### Breaking Through: How the Handicapped Handle Interactions

People with obvious physical disabilities, such as those who are blind or confined to wheelchairs, are at a disadvantage in everyday interactions. Unless they work at minimizing their differences from "normal" persons, the reactions of others to their disabilities can complicate any type of encounter.

Fred Davis has studied the strategies handicapped persons adopt to manage their interactions and try to normalize their daily encounters. In the strict sense of the word, the handicapped are considered deviant because they are commonly perceived as different, as odd, as "estranged from the common run of humanity." Their dealings with others are apt to be stiff or awkward and uncomfortable. From the handicapped person's perspective, the signs of others' discomfort are clear and predictable. Davis describes these signs as "the guarded references, the common everyday words suddenly made taboo, the fixed stare elsewhere, the artificial levity, the compulsive loquaciousness, the awkward solemnity" (1965:123).

Such reactions make it difficult to maintain the concern for both self

of managing identities that some others regard as deviant or undesirable. In our everyday interactions we willingly provide some pieces of identity information about ourselves, while we conceal others (see Chapter 3). We play information games, with stakes that are higher for those whose identities have been negatively evaluated. To participate in interactions comfortably, such persons must give a great deal of attention to information management and control.

## Deviances of Varying Visibility

The mode of information management used by those with damaged identities varies with the visibility of the status being questioned. In some cases, negative identities are highly visible and cannot be hidden. Physical handicaps, for example, are obvious attributes which cannot be missed. For those with such disabilities, information is less important than minimizing the inevitable problems and discomforts that are part of nearly every encounter (see box).

---

and others which characterizes successful interactions. In interactions with handicapped persons, it is not easy to discount the obvious differences between the participants. The "normal's" efforts to disguise awareness of the other person's handicap may require so much effort and be so transparent and painful that the handicapped person must try to disguise her or his awareness of the normal's disguise, and so on and so on.

The handicapped person usually takes the lead in redefining the situation, at least initially, so that the handicap eventually fades insignificantly into the background. Davis describes a handicapped person's experience of a feeling of "breaking through" when the other person can see beyond the handicap, so it ceases to influence the course of the interaction:

The first reaction a normal individual or goodlegger has is, "Oh gee, there's a fellow in a wheelchair," or "there's a fellow with a brace." And they don't say, "Oh gee, there is so-and-so, he's handsome" or "he's intelligent," or "he's a boor," or what have you. And then as the relationship develops they don't see the handicap. It doesn't exist any more. And that's the point that you as a handicapped individual become sensitive to. You know after talking with someone for a while when they don't see the handicap any more. That's when you've broken through. (p. 123)

In other cases there may be attempts to disavow troublesome identities, as when criminals assume aliases, or nicknames are used in deviant subcultures to conceal participants' identities from outsiders. People who know that their attributes will be discrediting in particular situations may try to conceal them temporarily. Many homosexuals, for example, go to great lengths to appear straight at work and in the presence of heterosexual friends, but not otherwise. In such situations, control and management of identity information can become quite complex.

**Passing** is a strategy which can be employed by those with negatively evaluated attributes that are not immediately apparent. A person who passes tries to achieve the status of a normal member of some group and must continually contend with the stress of possible detection. An example is light-skinned blacks who can, if they wish, sustain an identification of themselves as whites. Passing is basically a dangerous strategy because once begun it cannot be stopped. Harold Garfinkel (1968) gives the example of a transsexual who, as she acted our her new status as a woman, felt that she knew something others did not, and the disclosure of her secret would ruin her: "punishment, degradation, loss of reputation, and loss of material advantages were the matters at risk should the change be detected" (p. 136). Garfinkel says it would be more accurate to say that she was continually engaged in the work of passing, rather than to say that she had passed.

The possibility that an individual will be called on to disavow deviance or repair a damaged identity depends on how deviance is determined in the first place. A powerful way to think about how deviance is created and how some persons (but not others) come to follow deviant careers is provided by labeling theory, the topic of the next section. This discussion brings the chapter full circle: from our earlier consideration of the daily improprieties that momentarily spoil a person's identity, to analysis of those deviances that can thoroughly envelop a person's whole life.

## ■ LABELING THEORY AND LIFESTYLE DEVIANCE

Since the early 1960s, many social scientists have emphasized the idea that conceptions of morality, respectability, and deviance are social constructions, reflecting the symbolic meanings which have been adopted by individuals or groups (see Chapter 5). In this view morality is a relative notion, and there are no behaviors that are intrinsically immoral or deviant. The behavior of an individual or group can be identified as wrong, evil, immoral, or threateningly different only in terms of the current, commonly held construction of reality that has been adopted by a dominant group in a given setting. Immoral behavior is immoral only because it has been so defined in terms of some prevailing notion of social reality.

This relativistic view of deviance is expressed in **labeling theory.** The central idea is that powerful persons and groups are able to impose their definitions of morality on others by labeling certain activities and the individuals who engage in them as deviant. These labels are very "sticky." Once they have been applied by powerful persons, they have tremendous, long-lasting consequences for those who are so labeled.

## Ways of Thinking about Deviance

Labeling theory is only one of several social science theories expressing ways to think about deviance. Other theorists attempt to explain it in terms of a learning process based on association with established deviants (Edwin H. Sutherland) or the blockage of legitimate avenues of success for certain groups (Robert K. Merton). Deviance may also be related to social class values (Walter B. Miller) or the inequities created within capitalist societies (Richard Quinney). These theorists diverge on certain points, but the theories need not be viewed as in competition with one another. Because of the complex and varied nature of deviance, each has explanatory power. We have chosen to emphasize labeling theory in this chapter because it fits the interactionist perspective and because of the special capacities it provides for thinking about deviance in everyday life.

An important conceptual shift from earlier thinking on deviance is reflected in labeling theory. Theorizing about the causes of deviant behavior formerly focused on the type of person committing the behavior. Labeling theory suggests that such an emphasis is misplaced. Rather than putting the spotlight on rule breakers, as do most theories of deviance, it focuses on the activities of rule makers. Howard Becker, a proponent of labeling theory, makes this point clearly: "Whether a given act is deviant or not depends in part on the nature of the act (that is, whether or not it violates some rule) and in part on what other people do about it" (1963:14).

Labeling theory thus shifts attention from the individual actor to the audience that evaluates the act. According to Kai Erikson, "deviance is not inherent in certain forms of behavior; it is a property conferred on these forms by the audience which directly or indirectly witnesses them" (1962:11). Becker voices the argument this way:

Social groups create deviance by making the rules whose infraction constitutes deviance, and by applying those rules to particular people and labelling them as outsiders. From this point of view, deviance is not a quality of the act the person commits, but rather a consequence of the application by others of rules and sanctions to an offender. (1963:9)

Just who makes the rules? On one level, we all have investments in our own version of reality, and to some degree we force our private rules onto others. The rules that govern our personal lives are the product of prior negotiations, however. Becker suggests that some individuals, who he terms **moral entrepreneurs,** are on crusades to establish rules, to implement them, and then to label others who do not accept the rules as offenders. Members of certain religious groups, for example, may battle fiercely to control definitions of deviance, as the pro-choice and right-to-life arguments about abortion illustrate. Over time some groups become especially powerful in a society and particularly influential in creating the rules. The role of the institution of medicine in defining deviance is a case in point. It provides a compelling example of how a powerful group controls the fate of individuals through labeling—in this case, by being able to define certain behaviors as illnesses.

## The Medicalization of Deviance

In the history of medicine, the number of behaviors which fit the medical model explanation has steadily increased (Conrad and Schneider, 1980). Under the medical model, behavioral problems that used to be regarded as misbehavior subject to punishment are considered instead as medical problems subject to medical intervention, often with the use of drugs. Craig Little (1983:95) cites the examples of stimulants such as Ritalin for hyperactive children, amphetamines for overeating, Antabuse for alcoholism, and methadone for heroin abuse. Potent psychotropic agents like Thorazine are used to control intractable behaviors in mental hospitals, prisons, or even nursing homes.

Acceptance of the medical model has led to the **medicalization of deviance,** or reliance on medical professionals to provide conditions which are considered both normal and healthy. The medical model is based on the easily accepted assertions that normalcy is preferable to abnormalcy, and normalcy can be considered a synonym for health and abnormalcy a synonym for pathology. Health and pathology are defined in terms of experience and laboratory research, which are presumed to be based on scientific, objective, unbiased standards.

Because it is better to be healthy than to be sick, the medical model insists that physicians' decisions, whether they are requested or not, are necessary to ensure health and determine what is healthy. No other profession provides for the extensive access to a person's body and self that physical and psychiatric medicine do. By defining certain aspects of the human condition as illnesses to be cured, physicians give themselves the right to explore every part of the human anatomy, to prescribe a myriad of curative agents, and even to compel treatment.

The term *healthy*, as used in the medical model, also can be equated with the term *conforming*, as Thomas Szasz, Ronald Laing, and Erving Goffman, among others, have pointed out. In societies where this model predominates, it is often used instead of the law or religious commandments to regulate behavior. "Peculiar" individuals who were once viewed as "possessed" or as agents of the devil are classified as emotionally ill under the medical model. In the name of science, the advice of medical experts is used in the courts to determine whether certain actions should be defined as crimes. Medicine is used to "treat" those whose behaviors do not conform to the expectations of others or impinge on their moral sensitivities. Even children are affected by the medicalization of deviance, which embraces such problems as hyperactivity (Conrad, 1976) and child abuse (Pfohl, 1977).

## The Politics of the Medical Model

The medical model is supported by the political reality created by a coalition of physicians, teachers, judges, and other health professionals. Peter Berger and Thomas Luckman (1967) refer to the members of this coalition as "universe maintenance specialists" from different disciplines who set the norms defining the behaviors that are proper or improper, deviant or conforming, normal or pathological, and sick or healthy. The social control role of psychotherapy ensures that actual or potential deviants stay within the official, institutionalized definitions of reality.

Moral and scientific judgments become entangled in the medical model, which not only defines behaviors as troublesome but also attempts to explain their causes. The redefinition of a behavior as sick rather than bad is not merely a semantic issue. These labels have critical implications for the treatment accorded those who have been so labeled. A society's treatment of homosexuals, for example, depends on whether it views homosexuality as an evil state, as a sickness condition, or as a legitimate sexual lifestyle. Medical interventions to "cure" violent persons can be traced to the medical model's idea that violent behaviors are products of disease. With funding from the National Institute of Mental Health, psychosurgery for violence-prone individuals was seriously proposed as a measure to prevent ghetto riots, and California authorities have used it to control noncompliant prisoners (Chavkin, 1978). The labeling of behavior as illness is very much a political process with policy and moral implications.

## Deviant Careers

Labeling theorists are concerned with the politics of deviance, or how powerful groups create rules and then oversee their enforcement. The labels employed by groups such as physicians influence how the society responds to those to whom the labels are applied. But labels have an even deeper impact on individuals, because ultimately they influence how those who have been labeled *respond to themselves.* Labels can, in fact, alter people's identities, affecting not only what they do but who they become.

Charles Horton Cooley, a turn-of-the-century sociologist, coined the term **the looking-glass self** to convey the idea that others serve as mirrors in which we see ourselves reflected. Through these reflections, we adopt subjective definitions of ourselves. Labels applied by powerful persons or **significant others** in our lives (for example, parents, teachers, and peers) are profoundly influential because they fashion images of self that we may maintain for a lifetime. The proposition that individuals who are consistently responded to as deviant eventually come to define themselves that way is a central idea in labeling theory. Labeling theorists, however, qualify this idea by arguing that deviant identities arise from a *process over time,* and deviant identities lead to deviant careers.

### *Development of a Deviant Identity*

All acts of deviance, even those that are considered to be lifestyle deviances, do not produce deviant identities. Many people commit acts which could land them in jail if they were caught, but most people do not

---

### Living up to Expectations: The Saints and the Roughnecks

Almost every high school has gangs or groups of youths like those studied by William Chambliss (1973/1983). The Saints, the sons of "good, stable, white upper-middle-class families, active in school affairs, good pre-college students," were popular. In their relations with police and school

routinely think of themselves as deviant. To understand the differences between acts of deviance that remain isolated and those that lead to a deviant career, labeling theorists distinguish between primary and secondary deviances.

**Primary deviances** are the initial, usually isolated breaches of rules that nearly everyone has engaged in. Rule violations resulting from accident, peer pressure, or experimentation may elicit negative responses from others, but they remain primary as long as the individuals involved define them as incidental to "who they really are." The violations become **secondary deviances** when, *as a result of consistent responses* from the society to their actions, individuals begin to think of themselves as deviant and to behave accordingly. The distinction between primary and secondary deviances was first made by the sociologist Edwin Lemert. His description of the process whereby secondary deviances are produced is as follows:

. . . (1) primary deviation; (2) social penalties; (3) further primary deviation; (4) stronger penalties and rejections; (5) further deviation, perhaps with hostilities and resentment beginning to focus on those doing the penalizing; (6) crisis reached in the tolerance quotient, expressed in formal action by the community stigmatizing of the deviant; (7) strengthening of the deviant conduct as a reaction to the stigmatizing and penalties; (8) ultimate acceptance of deviant social status and efforts at adjustment on the basis of the associated role. (1951:77)

Studies of deviant subcultures have confirmed the movement from primary to secondary deviance described by Lemert. The process does not apply to every group which supports deviant acts, however. Young people who engage in truancy and vandalism may be perceived by the public, the schools, and the police as good students who are merely sowing a few wild oats or as hooligans and delinquents, depending on the social groups to which they belong (see box).

---

authorities they were polite and respectful. The Roughnecks were lower-class white boys who received average grades in school and were constantly in trouble with the police and the community. A high level of mutual distrust and dislike characterized their relations with authorities.

In the publbic's perception, Chambliss says,

The Saints were good boys who just went in for an occasional prank. After all, they were well dressed, well mannered, and had nice cars. The Roughnecks were a different story. Although the two gangs of boys were the same age, and both groups engaged in an equal amount of wild-oat sowing, everyone agreed that the not-so-well-dressed, not-so-well-mannered, not-so-rich boys were heading for trouble. (1983:288)

In fact, however, Chambliss found that the Saints were almost constantly occupied with truancy, drinking, reckless driving, petty theft, and vandalism. They cheated in class and contrived elaborate schemes to get out of class and off the campus. On weekends they went to a nearby city, where they drank heavily, drove dangerously, and committed acts of vandalism which damaged property and had the potential of seriously injuring others. A favorite prank was to steal lanterns and barricades around construction sites or road repairs, enjoy the plight of those who fell into the traps, and then erect the warning signals where they could cause more confusion.

The Roughnecks' behavior in school was not particularly disruptive, and they generally regarded it as a necessary burden to be borne with the least possible conflict. Their delinquency took three forms, theft, drinking, and fighting. Of these, petty stealing, of both small and expensive items, was the most regular and frequent activity. Their drinking was limited because they lacked the cars and the cash required for ready access to liquor. There were frequent fights between members and others, but they seldom involved the whole group.

After observing the two groups for about two years, Chambliss looked for answers to two questions:

Why did the community, the school, and the police consider the Saints

## *Institutional Definitions*

Studies of deviance have found that public **degradation ceremonies** such as court trials, with the proceedings permanently codified in case records, help solidify deviant identities (Garfinkel, 1956). Confinement in **total institutions,** an environment isolated from the rest of the community which provides for complete control of every aspect of the lives of members or inmates, such as a mental hospital or a prison also has been found to have a dramatic impact on identity (Goffman, 1961). It is extremely difficult for individuals to cling to their definitions of normalcy when they are surrounded by other "inmates" controlled by "experts" with contrary definitions. The extraordinary struggle involved in overcoming institutional definitions is vividly portrayed by the character

to be "good boys" with bright futures, but regard the Roughnecks as delinquents and potential criminals?

Why did the careers of the Roughnecks and the Saints after high school generally live up to these expectations?

Chambliss concluded that the reasons for the different reactions to the behaviors of the groups' members were related to the differences in the visibility of their activities, their demeanor, and the bias of the community, the schools, and the police. Primarily because of their social class position, the members of the two groups received widely different labels, and eventually they came to see themselves in terms of these labels. The Saints never thought of themselves as deviant, while the Roughnecks responded to the community's definition by becoming more involved in deviant activities. Chambliss describes the Roughnecks' progression from primary to secondary deviance this way:

> The community responded to the Roughnecks as boys in trouble, and the boys agreed with that perception. Their pattern of deviancy was reinforced, and breaking away from it became increasingly unlikely. Once the boys acquired an image of themselves as deviants, they selected new friends who affirmed that self-image. As that self-conception became more firmly entrenched, they also became willing to try new and more extreme deviances. With their growing alienation came freer expression of disrespect and hostility for representatives of the legitimate society. This disrespect increased the community's negativism, perpetuating the entire process of commitment to deviance. (1983:296)

Extracts published by permission of Transaction, Inc. from *Society*, vol. 11, no. 1, copyright © 1973 by Transaction, Inc.

---

Randal Patrick McMurphy in Ken Kesey's novel *One Flew Over the Cuckoo's Nest* (1962). Once admitted to the mental hospital, there was nothing McMurphy could do to persuade the authorities, personified by Big Nurse, that he was normal. All his efforts to produce a definition of his self that was different from the institution's definition resulted in reprisals from the staff.

A dramatic experiment which speaks directly to this point is D. L. Rosenhan's study entitled "Being Sane in Insane Places" (1973/1983). To find out whether the sane can be distinguished from the insane, he had eight colleagues pose as "pseudopatients" and apply for admission to 12 different mental hospitals. None of the eight had any history of mental illness, but they were told to present themselves at the hospital admission offices complaining that they had been hearing voices. With the exception of that one lie, they were to tell the truth about all other aspects of their lives. Once admitted, they were to say they were feeling fine and no longer experiencing the symptoms. They were to arrange their own releases by convincing the staff, through their behaviors, that they were sane.

The experimenters were easily and immediately admitted, all but one with the diagnosis of schizophrenia. Their subsequent show of sanity could not convince the staff that these "patients" were fakes, however. The only ones who ever questioned their status as real patients were the other patients on the ward. Once they had been officially diagnosed as schizophrenic, there was nothing the experimenters could do to shake the label. In fact, the staff interpreted everything they did in terms of the label. The social scientists made written notes on what they were seeing and experiencing, for example. After they were discharged, they learned from the nurses' records that their note-taking was considered "obsessive," and "engaging in writing behavior" had been interpreted as evidence of their illness.

After hospitalization periods ranging from 7 to 52 days, the pseudopatients were discharged with a diagnosis of schizophrenia "in remission," but in the institution's view they were not sane and had not been since they applied for admission; Rosenhan concluded that "once a person is designated abnormal all of his other behaviors and characteristics are colored by that label" (1983:371). He offers this conclusion about "the stickiness of psychodiagnostic labels":

A psychiatric label has a life and an influence of its own. Once the impression has been formed that the patient is schizophrenic, the expectation is that he will continue to be schizophrenic. . . . Such labels, conferred by mental health professionals, are as influential on the patient as they are on his relatives and friends, and it should not surprise anyone that the diagnosis acts on all of them as a self-fulfilling prophecy. Eventually, the patient himself accepts the diagnosis, with all its surplus meanings and expectations, and behaves accordingly. (1983:373)

## ■ CONCLUSION

When the word *deviant* is used to describe a person, it normally conjures up an image of someone whose behaviors are against the law or, at the very least, unmistakably different and "odd." In this chapter we have adopted a broader view of deviant behavior to include *any* act that compromises the perception that a person's identity is proper or socially correct. Everyday deviances are occasional improprieties that *everyone* engages in from time to time. They may result only in discomfort or embarrassment.

When individuals somehow "lose face," remedial interactions are necessary to restore the identities of self and others and remedy the situation. Our discussion of the contours of embarrassment and the motive talk which accounts for untoward behaviors pointed out that analysis of everyday deviances is part of a larger theoretical agenda. A close look at circumstances in which interaction is threatened by deviance can shed light on how an ordered daily life is produced, sustained, and protected.

Lifestyle deviances are related to the labeling of individuals and actions as deviant by powerful groups. Labeling theory fits the symbolic interaction perspective because it conceives of deviance as a matter of arbitrary human definition. According to this view, no act is by its very nature deviant.

As the discussion of the medicalization of deviance showed, definitions of deviance are connected to matters of power. The position of persons and groups in the society determines their ability to have their views of deviance become "official" definitions. Labeling theory thus shifts the focus in deviance from rule breakers to rule makers. Labeling also influences the ways individuals think of themselves. Movement from primary to secondary deviance occurs when people accept the negative labels that others put on them. As their own identities shift, they seek out others who have been similarly labeled. Membership in a deviant subculture is a step in embarking upon a deviant career.

Fundamentally, deviance is concerned with the breaking of rules or violations of the social norms that direct behaviors. In the next chapter we will consider how the meaning of the life cycle and people's movement through it are guided by clear age norms. What people do and feel at different ages cannot be interpreted apart from the social context in which they are living. Such age categories as childhood, adolescence, middle age, and old age are social constructions, in the same way deviance is.

# Definitions

**Lifestyle deviances.** Acts of deviance which an individual engages in repeatedly and over a long time. People who engage in lifestyle deviances such as crime or drug addiction can be described as following a *deviant career*. They usually are members of a *deviant subculture* composed of people who engage in the same deviance.

**Everyday deviances.** Acts of deviance which occur during the normal course of everyday interaction and temporarily mark individuals as nonconforming or improper.

**Social equilibrium.** The state which exists when a social system is operating free of conflict or disruption. Sociologists are interested in the conditions that allow social systems to operate trouble-free as well as the forces that create *disequilibrium*.

**Embarrassment.** The feeling of self shame following the commission of an impropriety which arises out of individuals' knowledge that others have negatively evaluated something they have done. Embarrassment may vary in intensity from very mild to so severe that an individual must withdraw entirely from a situation.

**Coolness.** Poise under pressure, or the capacity to execute acts, including conversation, in a smooth and self-controlled fashion, especially when such a performance might be difficult to carry off.

**Social control.** The various techniques and strategies for regulating human behavior in a society and ensuring that individuals conform to social norms. Techniques of social control can range from expressions of dissatisfaction with another's behavior, to ridicule, to outright force.

**Face games.** Ritualized behaviors designed to help individuals "save face" when events occur during interactions which openly damage the identity of participants.

**Vocabulary of motives.** C. Wright Mills's term for the broad explanatory schemas used to explain different categories of behavior. *Motives* are the "whys" of behaviors, the intentions or purposes which explain their direction and persistence. Basic physiological needs such as hunger or thirst, as well as complicated motives such as the needs for love, achievement, belongingness, and esteem, can all motivate behavior.

**Excuses.** A type of verbal *account* offered for behaviors that have been deemed unacceptable or deviant by some audience. Those who offer excuses admit that their behavior has been undesirable or wrong, but they also indicate the extenuating circumstances that required them to behave as they did.

**Justifications.** Accounts which people offer to acknowledge that they have committed acts being questioned but which are designed to indicate why the acts should not be interpreted as deviant.

**Disclaimers.** Statements meant to provide a nondeviant frame of reference within which forthcoming behaviors can be interpreted.

**Passing.** Presenting oneself as having attributes that are different from one's real statuses to avoid being evaluated negatively by others. People who change distinctive ethnic names may try to pass as members of an entirely different ethnic group, for example.

**Labeling theory.** The idea that powerful persons and groups are able to impose their definitions of morality on others by labeling certain activities and the individuals who engage in them as deviant. People who are repeatedly labeled as deviant are said to accept the label eventually and then define themselves as deviant.

**Moral entrepreneurs.** People who are constantly on crusades to establish rules, to implement them, and then to label those who do not follow them as offenders. The term was coined by Howard Becker.

**Medicalization of deviance.** The process through which medical professionals have been allowed to define various deviant behaviors as states of illness requiring treatment. Increasingly, medicine is being used to "treat" those whose behaviors do not conform to societal expectations.

**The looking-glass self.** The idea, suggested by Charles Horton Cooley, that others serve as mirrors in which we see ourselves reflected, and through those reflections we adopt subjective definitions of ourselves.

**Significant others.** Those other people with whom we have strong emotional attachments and whose judgments are most important in determining our behaviors.

**Primary deviances.** The initial, usually isolated breaches of rules that nearly everyone has engaged in. Rule violations remain primary as long as the individuals involved define them as incidental to "who they really are."

**Secondary deviances.** Norm violations that result from individuals' self-definitions as deviant. Violations become secondary deviances when, as a result of consistent negative responses from others, individuals begin to think of themselves as deviant and to behave accordingly.

**Degradation ceremonies.** Proceedings such as court trials in which individuals are publicly labeled as deviant. Harold Garfinkel suggests that the acquisition of a deviant identity is hastened by such labeling.

**Total institutions.** A place of residence and work where the participants or inmates are physically and socially insulated from the outside world, as in prisons, mental hospitals, and the military.

# Discussion Questions

1. Think about three instances in which you have felt embarrassed. For each one analyze the aspects of role performance that were disrupted. What did you do to "correct" your identity in each case? What did others do to decrease or increase your embarrassment?

2. What is "coolness?" How do you recognize coolness when you see it? What do you lose when you lose your cool?

3. Think of a time when you have interacted with a person who has a visible physical handicap. How did the person's handicapped status alter the interaction? Was there a point when it ceased to influence the encounter? If so, when did this happen, and why?

4. Throughout a one-day period take note of every instance in which you or others explain motives for behaviors. How would you categorize these specimens of motive talk—as excuses, justifications, or disclaimers? Were there any cases when the audience did not honor the motive explanation? If not, why not?

5. Describe a time when you were labeled by some authority figure or person significant to you. (Labels, of course, can be positive as well as negative.) How powerful was the label? Did it significantly affect the ways others responded to you? Did the label influence your view of yourself?

6. Have you ever committed an act which would have landed you in a courtroom were you caught? Was this a case of primary deviance? If so, did it lead to any secondary deviances? Why or why not?

# References

Becker, H. 1963. *Outsiders.* New York: Free Press.

Berger, P., and T. Luckman. 1967. *The Social Construction of Reality.* New York: Doubleday Anchor Books.

Chambliss, W. J. 1973/1983. "The saints and the roughnecks." *Society* 11 (November–December):24–31. Reprinted in *Social Interaction: Readings in Sociology,* ed. H. Robboy and C. Clark. New York: St. Martin's Press.

Chavkin, S. 1978. *The Mind Stealers: Psycho-Surgery and Mind Control.* Boston: Houghton Mifflin.

Conrad, P. 1976. *Identifying Hyperactive Children.* Lexington, Mass.: D. C. Heath.

Conrad, P., and J. Schneider. 1980. *Deviance and Medicalization.* St. Louis: C. V. Mosby.

Davis, F. 1965. "Deviance disavowal: The management of strained interactions by the visibly handicapped." In *The Substance of Social Deviance,* ed. V. Swigert and R. Farrell. Sherman Oaks, Cal.: Alfred.

Erikson, K. 1962. "Notes on the sociology of deviance." *Social Problems* 9:247–257.

Garfinkel, H. 1956. "Conditions of successful degradation ceremonies." *American Journal of Sociology* 61:420–424.

Garfinkel, H. 1968. *Studies in Ethnomethodology*. Englewood Cliffs, N.J.: Prentice-Hall.

Goffman, E. 1961. *Asylums*. New York: Doubleday Anchor Books.

Goffman, E. 1967. *Interaction Ritual*. New York: Doubleday.

Gross, E., and G. Stone. 1964. "Embarrassment and the analysis of role requirements." *American Journal of Sociology* 70 (July):1–15.

Hewitt, J. 1976. *Self and Society*. Boston: Allyn and Bacon.

Hewitt, J., and R. Stokes. 1975. "Disclaimers." *American Sociological Review* 40:1–11.

Kesey, K. 1962. *One Flew Over the Cuckoo's Nest*. New York: Signet.

Lemert, E. 1951. *Social Pathology*. New York: McGraw-Hill.

Little, C. B. 1983. *Understanding Deviance and Control: Theory, Research and Social Policy*. Itasca, Ill.: F. E. Peacock.

Lofland, L. 1971. *A World of Strangers*. New York: Basic Books.

Lyman, S., and M. Scott. 1968a. "Accounts." *American Sociological Review* 33 (December):46–62.

Lyman, S., and M. Scott. 1968b. "Coolness in everyday life." In *Sociology and Everyday Life*, ed. M. Truzzi. Englewood Cliffs, N.J.: Prentice-Hall.

Mills, C. W. 1972. "Situated actions and vocabularies of motive." In *Symbolic Interaction*, ed. J. Manis and B. Metzer. Boston: Allyn & Bacon.

Pfohl, S. 1977. "The discovery of child abuse." *Social Problems* 24:310–323.

Rosenhan, D. L. 1973/1983. "On being sane in insane places." *Science*, 179:250–258. Reprinted in *Social Interaction: Readings in Sociology*, ed. H. Robboy and C. Clark. New York: St. Martin's Press.

Sykes, G., and D. Matza. 1957. "Techniques of neutralization: A theory of delinquency." *American Sociological Review* 22:664–670.

Weinberg, M. 1965. "Sexual modesty, social meanings, and the nudist camp." *Social Problems* 12:311–318.

# CHAPTER 9: Aging and the Life Cycle

I. Age Categories in American Society
   A. The Aging of the U.S. Population
   B. Age Categories as Social Constructions
      1. The social invention of childhood
      2. Adolescence: Between childhood and adult status
      3. Crisis and rebirth in middle age
      4. How old is old age?
II. The Meanings of Age
   A. Age Norms in Everyday Life
   B. Chronological Age and Experiential Age
   C. A Symbolic Interaction Approach to Aging
III. Effects of Aging on Work and Careers
   A. Age Consciousness and Career Structure
   B. Imbalance in Age Positions
      1. Women's rocky career road
IV. Gender Differences in the Aging Process
   A. The Double Standard of Aging
V. Conclusion

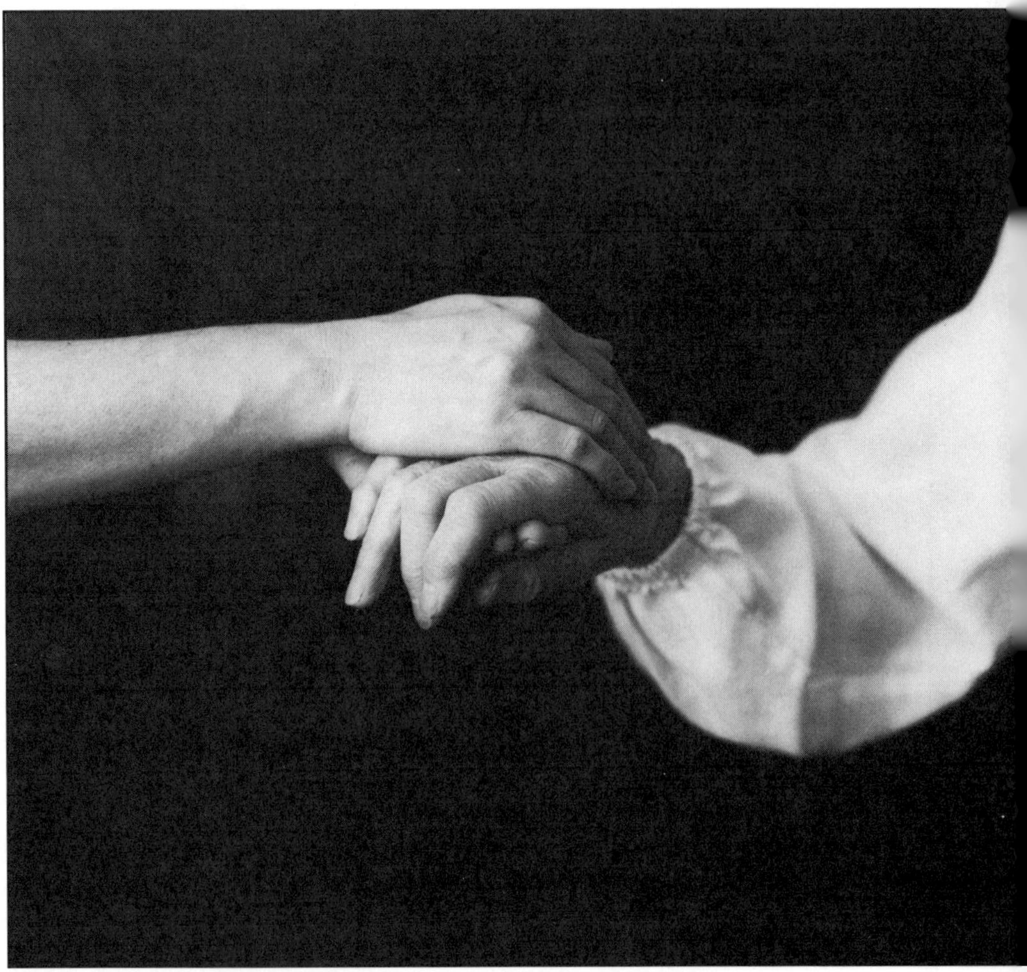

# CHAPTER 9

At age 88, Colonel Sanders, the original fried chicken fast food expert, told a reporter: "I'm real interested in old folks because I guess maybe someday I'll be old myself." Baseball players become "grand old men" after age 40. Indeed, sports figures may be considered young and old at the same time. At age 36, Dave Cowens, former player-coach of the Celtics basketball team, was described as the "boy" coach and the "middle-aged" player. Executives and managers, on the other hand, are viewed as in their prime in their mid 30s but approaching retirement in their mid 50s. There is a clear connection between general cultural values, the values particular to specific social contexts, and the meanings attached to chronological age.

The **meanings of age** are contextual; that is, they are tied to the societies and situations in which individuals find themselves. As we move from situation to situation in our daily lives, we are defined differently by those around us at various times and are required to behave in accordance with quite different age conventions. Your classmates may consider you one age, your professors another, and the members of your family a quite different one. Within each of these contexts you have to be responsive to a number of age definitions. Your parents may define you throughout your life as their little boy or girl, a definition you may seek to avoid. Your children may eventually define you as too old to understand their problems, while your brothers, sisters, friends, and cou-

*Note:* This chapter is adapted in part from David Karp and William Yoels, *Experiencing the Life Cycle*, 1982. Courtesy of Charles C Thomas, Publisher, Springfield, Illinois.

sins will think of one another as still "the boys" or "the girls." In some contexts a person's age requires adopting a subordinate position, in other situations the same age merits a dominant position. Different situations call forth varying expectations about age-appropriate behaviors. What you can say, the attitudes you can safely express, the respect you believe is due you, and the responses you predict others will make to you, all relate to their expectations of someone your age. In short, age is a critical factor in determining how others define us and how we define ourselves. In dramaturgical terms, age helps determine the performances we put on in front of a given audience.

In this chapter we take the position that age, as such, has no intrinsic meaning. In every society meanings which often are quite arbitrary are assigned to different ages in the life cycle. In this view there are many definitions of the aging process, and aging is a social construction built on age norms. The age structure of a society, however, is produced by demographic changes and historical processes. Before we examine the meanings attached to age, we will describe the present age structure in American society and consider how various age categories have developed over time.

## ■ AGE CATEGORIES IN AMERICAN SOCIETY

While social scientists have traditionally been interested in documenting stages of childhood development, in recent years they have begun to consider the regular stages of development throughout the **life cycle** as well (Erikson, 1968; Levinson, 1978). In *The Human Cycle* (1983), Colin Turnbull makes the interesting argument that each life stage reflects a different art of living. He describes childhood as the art of becoming, adolescence as the art of transformation, youth as the art of reason, adulthood as the art of doing, and old age as the art of being.

As interactionists we find such theories of adult development intriguing, but we suggest that theories which claim to identify *universal* stages of human development should be approached with caution. Although people may well move through regular stages in their lives, we question whether such movement applies equally to all segments of society. For example, we are hard-pressed to imagine that people from upper-class social circles in the United States move through the same life stages as those whose income is below the poverty level. One's **age status** in a society is determined by social and cultural as well as biological factors. The meanings attached to different age categories are influenced, for example, by the **age structure** of a society, or the number of people in different age categories.

## The Aging of the U.S. Population

Each day approximately 4,000 Americans turn 65, and approximately 3,000 persons over 65 die. There is thus a net increase of 1,000 persons older than 65 each day in the U.S. population, and there is an absolute increase of 365,000 persons per year in that age category (Davis, 1979). The median age of the population, which was 30 in 1980, is expected to rise to 35 by the turn of the century. For the first time in history, the population over 65 is increasing in size while the population under 35 is decreasing.

One of the consequences of this changing age structure is that as an age category increases in size, its political importance as a voting block whose collective interests must be considered also increases. Table 9.1, which shows actual and projected changes in the age distribution of the population from 1960 to 2000, indicates the shifting balance of political power held by different age groups in the United States. While the age group 18–44 remains the largest category of the voting-age population, the percentage of the population in this group will actually decline by the year 2000. The percentage between 45 and 64 has remained fairly stable since 1960. At the same time, the over-65 age group, which represented only 9.2 percent of the population in 1960, has been rising steadily and should reach 13 percent by the year 2000. Moreover, if the birth rate continues at its current low rate (nearly zero population growth), and if mortality rates continue their slight decline, 24.2 percent of the voting age population (nearly one-fourth of those eligible to vote) will be 65 or older by the year 2030 (U.S. Bureau of the Census, 1977).

The potential power generated by the large numbers of elderly people in American society could stimulate major changes in governmental health and economic policies. The likelihood of such changes, of course, depends on whether the elderly can achieve a unity of purpose through effective political organization. Their political clout could also improve younger persons' conceptions of the aged, which often inspire substantial discrimination and prejudice. Robert Butler (1975:11) has coined the

Table 9.1
Percentage of Population in Age Groups, United States, 1960–2000

| Age Group | 1960 | 1970 | 1980 | 1990 | 2000 |
|---|---|---|---|---|---|
| Under 18 | 35.7% | 34.1% | 27.7% | 26.4% | 26.6% |
| 18–44 | 35.0 | 35.7 | 41.2 | 42.7 | 38.4 |
| 45–64 | 20.0 | 20.5 | 19.6 | 18.3 | 22.0 |
| 65 and older | 9.2 | 9.8 | 11.3 | 12.6 | 13.0 |

*Source:* U.S. Bureau of the Census, *Statistical Abstract of the United States, 1984* (Washington, D.C.: Government Printing Office, 1983), Tables 30 and 31.

term **ageism** to describe "the deep and profound prejudice against the elderly which is found to some degree in all of us" (see box). In American society ageism is connected to the high value placed on youth, and it has increased as the number of older people making demands on the nation's resources has grown.

## Age Categories as Social Constructions

Terms such as *infant, child, teenager,* and *adult* are very much a part of our social reality. They are used to describe such everyday interactions as babies being nurtured by their parents, children playing in parks, teenagers mingling at school dances, and young adults meeting in singles' bars. The use of **age categories** to identify individuals of varying chronological ages appears natural and to be taken for granted. Surely

### Old Age: Everyone's Own Future

The fundamental existential question for the elderly in American society, according to Robert Butler, is "Why survive?" Medical science can ensure a longer life, but the quality of that life may fall far below the generally affluent standards of the society.

To some extent Americans idealize old age. The retirement years are supposed to be the "golden years." Advertisements portray the elderly as carefree, well-dressed, and well-fed. If they no longer live in their family homes, they are pictured as happy members of retirement communities with names like Sun City or Leisure World. But a more sinister side to Americans' image of the elderly is betrayed by our language. According to Butler, we may say those who are growing old are "fading fast," "over the hill," "out to pasture," an "old crock," a "fogey," or a "geezer."

In reality large numbers of elderly people must bear economic, physical, and emotional burdens. Those on fixed incomes can easily fall into poverty, and they may be denied work even if they are able. They are discriminated against when seeking housing. They suffer the indignities encouraged by others' incorrect stereotypes about what it is to be old. Political leaders are often insensitive to the needs of the elderly in the

there have always been and always will be infants, children, teenagers, and young adults. But is that really the case? Have such age categories always existed throughout history, or do the definitions of what constitutes appropriate behavior for an age category vary from one period or culture to another?

The answers to such questions become apparent when age categories are considered as arbitrary social constructions rather than fixed biological or chronological divisions. The behaviors underlying such categories ultimately derive their meanings from the social contexts in which they occur. In this section we will focus on the historical origins of four contemporary age categories: childhood, adolescence, middle age, and old age. We will be concerned with how changes in the organization of society have created the context in which people's sense of aging, or experience of the passage of time, has undergone changes as well.

---

policies they create. Eventually the old may suffer technologized deaths in impersonal institutions.

According to Butler, the truth is that there can be no promise of a decent existence for the elderly. There are few provisions in American society to house, employ, and or even feed them adequately. While their previous work helped make possible the present generally affluent standard of living, now they are considered economic burdens. In Butler's words:

In America, childhood is romanticized, youth is idolized, middle age does the work, wields the power and pays the bills, and old age, its days empty of purpose, gets little or nothing for what it has already done. The old are in the way, an ironic example of public-health progress and medical technology creating a huge group of people for whom survival is possible but satisfaction in living elusive. (1975:xi–xii)

Butler's book *Why Survive? Being Old in America* (1975) is an eloquent plea to Americans to change their cultural sensibilities toward the old. He outlines a national policy on aging which would create practical solutions to the problems of the elderly. He also presents the compelling argument that "When we talk about old age, each of us is talking about his or her own future. We must ask ourselves if we are willing to settle for mere survival when so much more is possible" (p. xiii).

### The Social Invention of Childhood

As a distinct age grouping, childhood has a fairly short history. It did not exist in the Middle Ages, when the life cycle proceeded directly from infancy to little adulthood and adulthood. Those in the age groups that we call children today were then considered to be adults on a smaller scale (Aries, 1962).

Prior to the 17th century, adults and "little adults" participated in virtually the same activities. They worked and played together, in continual physical contact with each other. Adults and children played exactly the same games with the same degree of involvement, enthusiasm, and, most importantly, seriousness. Children played games of chance for money, and adults played games such as leapfrog. We could just as well say that the children of the time played *adultishly* as that the adults played *childishly*.

Life was never all fun and games for the young, of course. Lloyd DeMause considers the history of childhood "a nightmare from which we have only recently begun to awake" (1975:85). In the 19th century children were routinely beaten, beginning at an early age and continuing regularly throughout childhood. DeMause gives a dramatic example of how parents enforced discipline:

> A common moral lesson involved taking children to visit the bigget, where they were forced to inspect rotting corpses hanging there as an example of what happens to bad children when they grow up. Whole classes were taken out of school to witness hangings, and parents would often whip their children afterwards to make them remember what they had seen. (1975:86)

A far cry indeed from modern parental punishments, such as suspending TV privileges or allowances or "grounding" the child in the house for several days!

The emergence of childhood as an age category has been associated with the development of the modern family as a particular type of social and emotional arrangement (see Chapter 5). This was related to the growth of the new middle class as the effects of industrialization and urbanization intensified, changing the character of American society in the late 19th century (see Chapter 7). The middle class cultivated a new sensibility about children which was based on the idea that they should be protected from contacts with various kinds of "dangerous persons." Children were required to attend schools where they were processed bureaucratically into distinct age-grade groupings, for example.

As childhood came to be viewed as a bona fide age category, a new set of attitudes and values about relations between parents and young children was ushered in. The accepted view is that parents should not physically abuse their children or treat them in cold, emotionally distant ways. Children generally are to be protected from the ugly and often brutal realities of what life is "really like."

### Adolescence: Between Childhood and Adult Status

Having experienced the agonies and ecstasies of adolescence, you may assume that this phase of the life cycle, like childhood, has a certain timelessness and universality to it. But rather than being an inevitable passage between childhood and adulthood in the lives of all human beings, the adolescent stage is also a fairly recent idea.

The construction of adolescence as an age category in American society can be linked to three social movements in the late 19th and early 20th centuries: compulsory public education, child labor legislation, and separate legal procedures for the treatment of juveniles (Bakan, 1971). These movements were designed to protect children for increasingly longer periods of their lives. By establishing age regulations in the areas of schooling, work, and criminal violations, social reformers helped mark out precise age categories. Adolescence became recognized as the period between puberty, a biological event, and the ages specified by the law for the end of compulsory education, the beginning of employment, and the limits of special treatment in criminal procedures.

These social movements were a response to the urbanization and industrialization of the United States. Cities came to be seen as places where the young easily fell prey to the vices of sexual immorality, crime, and alcohol abuse. Urban life was considered a "pathological" corruptor of innocent, defenseless youths who were urgently in need of the state's protection. The evils of long hours and hard work for children became more apparent as the need for their services declined.

During the colonial period parents were largely responsible for their own children's education, although there was some community involvement (Demos, 1970). Compulsory education for everyone between the ages of 6 and 16 was mandated in the late 19th century, under laws stimulated by reformers' desire to "bundle every child warmly in the garment of education, to make school a veritable asylum for the preservation and culture of childhood" (Kett, 1977:123). Previously the rhythms of the school year were dictated by the agricultural seasons, with school attendance linked to the needs for young laborers on the farm. Now attendance was required, and truancy became defined as a deviant act punishable by law.

The movement to regulate working conditions and set a minimum age at which children were allowed to work outside their own families also helped segregate teenagers from the rest of society and prolong their dependency on their parents. A labor surplus in the post-Civil War period prompted the campaign for child labor laws, which limit the hours, wages, and types of work permissible for youths under a certain age.

The increasing technical sophistication of industrial production called for skilled and disciplined workers. Michael Katz (1968) suggests that many employers favored both the child labor laws and compulsory education because they needed a labor force suited to the capitalistic industrial society that was taking shape. Required school attendance and minimum age restrictions kept unskilled labor out of the factory and produced better disciplined and more manageable workers who knew how to follow a supervisor's orders. The relationship between work and education in the early 20th century was recognized in teacher training textbooks which suggested that the habits learned by marching between the playground and class and in classroom drills and routines would prepare students for industrial work. According to Joel Spring, these arguments "were primarily directed toward increasing industrial efficiency by increasing managerial control" (1976:88).

The creation of a special category of deviance for youthful offenders, juvenile delinquency, furthered the processing of youths as members of a separate category. According to Gerald Platt, "the invention of adolescence went hand in hand with the 'invention of delinquency' " (1969). The first Juvenile Court Act, passed by the Illinois legislature in 1899, defined behaviors as juvenile delinquency only when they applied to adolescents, including "immoral conduct around schools, association with vicious or immoral persons, patronizing public poolrooms, wandering about railroad yards, truancy, incorrigibility, absenting self from home without consent, smoking cigarettes in public places, begging or receiving alms." The goal was to protect youthful offenders by treating them differently from hardened criminals, but the result was another thread in the tapestry of adolescence as a separate age category, distinguished from both childhood and the adult stage.

### Crisis and Rebirth in Middle Age

In popular culture, middle age is often portrayed as a time of crisis or trauma in the life cycle. This stage is generally viewed as the period between the ages of 40 and 60, but the social construction of middle age has indefinite boundaries. As Gail Sheehy points out in her best-selling book *Passages: Predictable Crises of Adult Life* (1977):

> How to put an age label on true middle age is a hot potato. Working-class men describe themselves as middle-aged at 40 and old by 60. Business executives and

professionals, by contrast, do not see themselves as reaching middle age until 50, and old age means 70 to them. (p. 375)

The middle years are often a time of crisis because it is then that most people begin to face the reality of their own aging and pending death. It is a time of major change in interactions in the areas of work and the family, as John Connally laments in the country-western tune "On the Back Side of 30." But the problems of middle age can be transformed into a blessing, as Eda LeShan argues in *The Wonderful Crisis of Middle Age* (1973)—a book whose cover proclaims, "Over 40? The best is yet to come!" Sheehy says the midlife passage prepares people of age 45 and older to "accept entry to middle age and enjoy its many prerogatives" (p. 375). According to Bernice Neugarten (1968), middle-aged men and women are the norm bearers and decision makers who control the society.

Social science literature on the subject of aging also raises serious questions about the extent to which the middle-aged experience this stage of life as a trauma. Demographers and historians have produced a fascinating body of data on the transformations of American family life which sheds light on aging as a socially defined process and middle age as a distinct age category.

Studies of change in American family life cycles in the 20th century by Paul Glick (1977) found that women in the 1970s were having their last child about three years earlier and were having fewer children than women in the early 1900s. Women were also older when their spouses died (a median age of 65.2 years in the 1970s, compared to 57.0 years in 1900). The period called the **empty nest**—the time couples spend alone after their last child has left home—was extended from 1.6 years in the early 1900s to 12.9 years in the 1970s, an increase of over 11 years. Where previously the death of a spouse usually occurred less than two years after the last child had left home, couples could anticipate spending about 13 more years alone together. Tamara Haravan (1978) notes that in the 19th century the major transition a woman faced was the decision to marry, whereas now it is a "transition out of parental role."

Other demographic developments have had a considerable impact on both family structure and people's sense of their own aging. In 1920 life expectancy was only 54.1 years (U.S. Bureau of the Census, 1983, Table 101), so many couples spent their entire married lives raising their children. When the last child was ready to leave home and establish a household, the parents had few years of life left. In 1982 life expectancy was 74.5 years. Couples who stay together now have a considerable portion of their lives to spend only in each other's company.

With retirement at age 65 set as the original standard for benefits in the social security system, many workers put in another 20 years or more on the job after the need to support a family ends. For men who have followed continuous careers, the meanings attached to work earlier in the life cycle take on a different cast, prompting a good deal of mind work about its values and significance. For women who begin their careers later in life, after family demands diminish, work is something to be approached in middle age with high involvement and intensity (Karp, 1985). In general, though, one of the ways a person's sense of being middle-aged is formed is related to the period of life between the completion of child rearing and retirement from work. Earlier generations experienced no such clearly identified age category.

### How Old is Old Age?

The age categories of childhood, adolescence, and middle age do not exist naturally but are social constructions created by humans. Members of all societies do seem to make some kind of distinction between the old and other age groups, but the meanings of old age also vary depending on the historical period and the cultural setting.

The definition of old age in industrialized nations is closely related to developments in the laws concerning pensions and retirement. In England and the United States, the ages of 60 and 65 have been linked to specific governmental actions defining old age. But before official retirement and pension ages were set, the meaning of old age was subject to much discretion and individual judgment. People were considered to be old when they were getting on in years and unable to support themselves. The label of *aged and infirm* could be applied to people aged anywhere from their late 40s to 80 and older, since ability to support oneself varies with individuals and their occupations (Roebuck, 1979).

Inevitably, government finances dictate the "proper" point at which old age and pensions are to begin. The Social Security Act of 1935 established a distinct legal age status for the elderly in American society. The choice of age 65 for retirement was heavily influenced by political and economic considerations. Wilbur Cohen, former secretary of the Department of Health, Education, and Welfare, noted that "It was understood that a reduction in the age below 65 would substantially increase costs and, therefore, might impair the possibility of . . . acceptance of the plan by Congress. A higher retirement age, of say 68 or 70, was never considered because of the belief that public and congressional opposition would develop against such a provision in view of the widespread unemployment that existed" (quoted in Cain, 1974:169–170).

In recent years efforts to keep the social security system financially sound have led to attempts to curtail a trend to early retirement and to prolong the working years. The 1983 amendments to the social security act provide for gradually increasing the retirement age at which full benefits are payable from 65 to 67 by the year 2027. The age of **mandatory retirement,** at which employees can be forced to retire, was raised to 70 in 1978.

Definitions of old age may have little to do with the inherent condition of the elderly. Rather, such definitions are a product of competing ideologies, political bartering, and economic conditions. Neugarten (1974) suggests that, rather than automatically giving benefits to everyone over 65, the social security system could serve the needs of the elderly best by providing separate programs for the **young-old,** those 65 to 74, who generally have good health, adequate financial resources, and support from family members, and the **old-old,** those over 75, who are more likely to have health and economic problems and to be isolated from others.

## ■ THE MEANINGS OF AGE

When age categories are viewed as social constructions, their meanings are derived from changing human interpretations of various phases of the biological life cycle. The behaviors expected of those in these age categories also are products of an ongoing interpretive process and people's continuing attempts to make sense of their interactions. In some instances chronological age has a significant effect on the ways people relate to one another, and in others it is far less important. Individuals also hear different messages about the meanings of various age categories, and they respond to these messages in different ways, depending on their social attributes and position in the social order.

### Age Norms in Everyday Life

Many of our daily activities and experiences are prescribed and regulated by **age norms** or social conventions. Older men are expected to marry younger women, for example, but the reverse situation may inspire comment or criticism. The distinctions are often finely grained, such as the expectations we have of a three-year-old and a five-year-old.

Even a few years in age can make a large difference in age attributes and our judgments about what a person can and cannot do or ought and ought not to do, as we noted in Chapter 3. In some social circles

18 or 19 years is thought to be too young to marry, but remaining unmarried once one reaches the late 20s is regarded by parents, relatives, and friends as a cause for concern. Some age norms have been incorporated into law. The social security system was based on mandatory retirement at age 65, and 21 has been federally endorsed as the minimum age for drinking alcoholic beverages. Surveys have found substantial agreement on the ages at which people are expected to engage in specific activities. The early to mid 20s are thought to be the best times for Americans to marry; by age 24 to 26, men, especially, are expected to be settled in careers; and for most people the early 20s marks a time when schooling should end and work should start (Neugarten, Moore, and Lowe, 1965).

The norms of aging are deeply embedded in our consciousness and seem to exist "naturally." Nevertheless, like all social conventions, they are arbitrary social constructions which are derived from societal values and the more specific values of the groups and persons with whom an individual interacts. The requirements attached to specific ages therefore may be quite different in various societies and historical eras. Evidence of the socially constructed nature of age norms can be found in a society's laws and proposed legislation. In New Jersey, for example, there were recent attempts to reduce the age of consent for sexual relationships to 13. The lowering of the legal age for marriage in Iran following the takeover of the government by the Ayatollah Khomeini in 1979 was in keeping with Islamic tradition and also reflects that society's religious values.

There is a clear relationship between cultural norms, biological processes, and the social context of aging experiences. In some cases even biological processes do not occur independently of social forces and age limitations, as might be expected, but are regulated by the messages people hear from society. Research has found a substantial decrease in sexual activity among the elderly, for example, though it has failed to identify any biological factors that would prevent a vigorous and active sex life into old age (Masters and Johnson, 1966; Pfeiffer, Verwoerdt, and Davis, 1972). Negative opinions about older people who remain sexually active may cause others among the elderly to curtail their own sexual activity, and they may believe that the decline is the inevitable result of biological changes. Many Americans past 50 now admit to having a rich sex life, however, according to the results of a five-year Consumers' Union survey of over 4,000 men and women aged 50 to 93 (Brecher et al., 1984). The authors of this survey suggest that the reason this finding might be considered astonishing was that older people had never been asked frank sexual questions before.

The age norms in American society number well into the thousands and are constantly changing. An almost endless number and variety of cultural prescriptions about appropriate age affect the daily encounters and interactions of people of all ages.

## Chronological Age and Experiential Age

Because age norms are social constructions, there are differences between chronological age and **experiential age,** or age as subjectively measured by an individual's range of life experiences. Age norms are closely tied to specific social contexts.

Consider the meanings children attach to slight chronological age differences, for example, and the sharp distinctions they make concerning who may be friends with them. During their early years, children are flooded with new experiences, rights, and obligations. Because of their short biographies and limited life experiences, children are constantly learning and experiencing new things. Age differences of even a few months mean substantial differences in their knowledge. Six-year-olds think they are infinitely wiser than five-year-olds and in a class separate from anyone younger than that. This is in some measure appropriate, since during the early ages children who are separated by only one chronological year do inhabit quite different social, experiential, and symbolic worlds, and a difference of only one year assumes significance.

Parents are constantly setting rules to limit behavior of their children. Largely on the basis of communications with other parents like themselves, they define the rights, expectations, duties, and freedoms appropriate to their different-aged children. Often these judgments are made in terms of the parents' perceptions of their children's physical and emotional readiness to assume certain tasks or engage in certain behaviors. In that sense there is a correspondence between the stages of childhood in the life cycle and the norms for children's behaviors. But parents' decisions about age-related behaviors for their children also emerge from the situation and are made on an individual basis.

Children are not the only ones who attach great value to small chronological age differences in choosing appropriate friends and acquaintances. A one-year age difference also is given considerable significance by college sophomores, who typically have few freshmen among their close friends. At this point in the students' lives, the slight one-year difference corresponds to a very large status difference. The sophomores already know their way around and are wise to the customs, mores, and norms of college life. Because sophomores have experienced events that sharply discriminate them from freshmen, they think of themselves as being much older.

Another example of how chronological age is related to experiential age is the friendships struck up by women of quite different ages who meet while watching their children in parks and playgrounds. In this case the women's ages are generally irrelevant to the interaction, but the age of the women's children is critical. Two women aged 22 and 35, both with three-year-old children, will respond to each other as equals, for example. The two women are experiencing a similar point in their family life cycles, despite a 13-year age gap. In such a context chronological age has far less bearing than experiential age.

## A Symbolic Interaction Approach to Aging

As we noted in Chapter 2, the ability to evaluate one's own behaviors objectively from the perspective of others is necessary in order to become a "normal" member of society. A person who acquires that ability possesses the essential components of what George Herbert Mead called *the self*.

Definitions of self incorporate a personal sense of aging. A woman's awareness of reaching middle age, for example, comes about through her recognition of others' definitions of her as middle-aged. Neugarten notes that one way men perceive the onset of middle age is by the way others treat them in the work setting: "One man described the first time a younger associate held open a door for him; another, being called by his official title by a newcomer in the company; another, the first time he was ceremoniously asked for advice by a younger man" (1968:96). It is as though others become mirrors in which we see ourselves reflected, and through these reflections we come to have certain subjective definitions of ourselves. A woman in Neugarten's survey used exactly this metaphor to describe the origins of her own sense of age:

It is as if there are two mirrors before me, each held at a partial angle. I see part of myself in my mother who is growing old, and part of her in me. In the other mirror, I see part of myself in my daughter. I have had some dramatic insights, just from looking in those mirrors. . . . It is a set of revelations that I suppose can only come when you are in the middle of three generations. (1968:98)

The symbolic interaction approach to aging suggests that the adage "You are as young as you feel" should be amended. More precisely, it should say that "You are as young or old as *others* make you feel." Like any other symbol, age can have a multiplicity of meanings which emerge out of our interactions with others. These meanings are likely to be modified and reinterpreted in the course of interactions, depending upon our own and others' definitions of the situations in which we find ourselves.

The interactionist approach also is attentive to other broad dimensions of the aging process. While the process involves regular, predictable biological changes and chronological stages, it cannot be understood without considering its various social and cultural definitions. The meanings given to chronological age categories vary from context to context and with different individuals. In interactionist terminology, different groups respond to age in terms of different inventories of symbols and create among their members different aging selves. The meanings attached to age vary with individuals' place in history and the historical times in which they live. Social attributes, such as gender, race, ethnic affiliation, occupation, social class, and marital status, also influence the meaning of a particular age for a particular person. The meaning of being 35 years old is quite different for a baseball player whose career is nearly over than for a corporate manager, for example.

Two specific life contexts which affect our notions of aging and our views of self over the course of the humanly constructed life cycle are work and gender. These contexts will be examined in the following sections.

## ■ EFFECTS OF AGING ON WORK AND CAREERS

Our involvement with work helps determine how we experience the passage of time. Because work structures the ways we think about the present and how we anticipate the future, it is a primary source of our sense of aging (Sarason, 1977). Those who pursue different work lives or careers hear different messages about the meaning of age. Ability to do the work may or may not be affected by age, and different career patterns involve varying conceptions of what it means to be on schedule, ahead of schedule, or too late. The ways individuals measure and evaluate their own life progress and their experiences of growing older are a function of where society expects them to be in their occupations at a given point in their lives.

In his voluminous and influential writings on work, Everett Hughes demonstrated the value of conceptualizing a **career** as "the moving perspective in which the person sees his life as a whole and interprets the meanings of his various attitudes, actions, and the things which happen to him" (1958:63). This definition of career accords well with the interactionist position. Hughes certainly recognized that, in an objective sense, various occupational careers are established within work organizations, but his definition also directs attention to another aspect of the career process. Based on communications with others in their work situations, people arrive at subjective, evaluative meanings for the various stages in their own career patterns.

The notion of career is not just a conceptual tool social scientists use to look at the nature of work. We can also use it as a frame for interpreting where we are in the life cycle and how the things happening to us at any point in our lives make sense. Whatever the occupational role we choose, the career pattern associated with it helps us to evaluate our performance to a certain point and to preview our likely future.

## Age Consciousness and Career Structure

Success in a career is closely connected with age. Most careers are age-graded; that is, we ride an escalator of sorts which travels up the career ladder and are expected to be at a certain point by a certain age. Our careers are considered satisfactory if we "make the grade" at the appropriate age. If we get there earlier we have reason to be pleased and proud, and if we get there late we experience first anxiety and then relief (Sofer, 1970:53).

As well as being the measure of success in a career, age is the variable along which career lines are established. The roles available (and unavailable) to those in a work organization, and the workers' construction and meaning of their work commitments, are defined in terms of age. Robert Faulkner has studied how individuals come to terms with organizations that are youth oriented and structured along very rigid career paths. To illustrate the connection between career demands and a personal sense of aging, Faulkner (1974) draws on two occupations: professional hockey players and orchestra musicians. Careers in these occupations involve special contingencies and force a direct **age consciousness** on participants. Both hockey players and orchestra members recognize the decreased probability of making it to the "majors" beyond a certain age. The hockey player laments, "This is a business and they go with youth. I'd say that after 28, the odds are against you. My wife and I say we'll give it till 26 or 27 maybe, then I'll know if I'll be in the NHL. After that they give up on you" (p. 156). The orchestra member is also concerned with making it to the majors, or getting a job with one of only a select few city orchestras. As in any occupation, musicians who reach a certain age take stock of their occupational position with the idea that they might not make it:

Look, let's not kid ourselves. I'm nearly 40 years old. I make a good living here. I do some recording work on the side, I'm not going to be first in the New York Philharmonic anyway, not at my age . . . (but) things could be worse, like being stuck in some bush league place with little money and no musical satisfaction. (p. 154)

These examples suggest that every occupation generates its own distinctive career path and consequently its own set of symbols and meanings of age. In most occupations people are required to engage in a continual process of interpretation and reinterpretation about their current occupational position and its meaning. Periodically they must assess their success, whether or not they are currently making it, and their chances for eventually doing so. Questions about career success and failure constantly call attention to age. Faulkner calls age consciousness "an aspect of occupational and organizational life whose centrality . . . has a paramount reality in experience" (1974:167).

To a significant degree, it is the structure of occupational life that injects meaning into the phrase "growing older." Studies of such diverse occupations as fashion models, boxers, lawyers, scientists, and strippers have affirmed the relationship between the ways individuals experience the world of work and their self-conceptions of aging.

## Imbalance in Age Positions

An imbalance may exist when an individual's age status in one organization or institution does not fit well with his or her position and obligations in other institutions. A lawyer who begins his legal career in his late forties may have followed a very conventional family life cycle, for example, so that he has children about to enter college as he begins his practice. This would be an example of what Leonard Cain (1964) terms **age-status asynchronization.** Normally workers approach the peak of their earning capacity in their midlife years. Here there would be a discrepancy or an imbalance between the low starting income of the lawyer and the demands imposed on him by his family life cycle status.

Cyril Sofer sums up the need for balance between age and career status this way:

A man is in a socially "appropriate" and personally reassuring situation when he is in the "right" career phase for his age. He is in an embarrassing and discomforting situation when he is "too old" for his current career phase or where the career phase is discordant with his status elsewhere. (1970:55)

### Women's Rocky Career Road

The career paths of women often reflect such imbalances. Social scientists have only recently begun to pay attention to women's careers. Many married women delay entry into the labor market until after their children have reached school age. They may have to continue their own schooling and enter an occupation when they are in their mid 30s or early 40s and beyond, ages well past those at which men typically take entry-level jobs. Such women may be regarded as violating both career and gender-role cultural expectations, and in this sense they may be defined as deviant. A government article on age and discrimination put it this way:

> Midlife women are limited by what is perceived to be appropriate behavior for their age and sex; they are expected to be in step with the "social clocks." To be off time is to be "age deviant." For a 55-year-old woman to start work on a graduate degree or a 42-year-old woman to have a first child is considered to be "age deviant." (Troll and Turner, 1978:16)

For the woman who has invested her energies until midlife in the rearing of a family and who discovers at that point just how limited her career options are, the response is often bewilderment and anger. The following quotation expresses a typical woman's reaction:

> It's unbelievable when I think of it now. I never really saw past about age 42, where I am now. I mean I never thought about what happens to the rest of life. Pretty much the whole adult life was supposed to be around your husband and raising children. Dammit, what a betrayal! Nobody ever tells you that there's many years of life after children are raised. Now what? (Rubin, 1979:123).

There are many questions to be raised about the increasing numbers of women in such an age-career position: What kinds of age-graded career expectations can these women have? What kind of status inconsistencies do they experience when they relate to younger male colleagues higher up in the organizational hierarchy? Do women think about careers and evaluate job success differently than men do? To what extent do the different career patterns of men and women contribute to the different aging experiences they have? These are among the questions for which social scientists have little current data. The changing career options for women are only beginning to indicate how women can reshape the work world and how they might be reshaped themselves. The next section of this chapter suggests some of the critical differences in the ways men and women age.

## ■ GENDER DIFFERENCES IN THE AGING PROCESS

A frequent guest on television talk shows, projecting an image of glamour and feminine allure, used to be a Hollywood personality called Zsa Zsa Gabor. Like many other such creations, she always refused to reveal her "real" age, and we all laughed when she said, "But, dahling, I'm just going on 29!" George Burns, another frequent guest who was well into his 80s, was never reluctant to admit his age on television. In fact, when he announced it, the audience cheered and clapped with approval. But we understand Zsa Zsa's reluctance to tell her age and George's pride in his. The reason is that the aging process has affected the lives of men and women in American society in different ways.

Powerful differences between men and women have run through the entire life cycle, from birth to old age. A woman's reluctance to reveal her age and society's good-humored response to this strategy testify to the position women have held and the social evaluations men have made of women in American society. Such evaluations have imposed standards of acceptable social performance and physical appearance on women that women themselves have been forced to acknowledge if they wanted to achieve a position of value in a male-dominated society.

### The Double Standard of Aging

From childhood on, females are socialized to place a great deal of emphasis on their physical appearance. The warehouse of cosmetics that women use to maintain their looks certainly indicates the significance of physical attractiveness for them. Men, by contrast, are expected to minimize their concern with appearance.

The response society makes to men's and women's physical attributes is not simply a result of biological functioning but rather a product of cultural, historical, and sociological conditions. Susan Sontag draws the following picture of these differences:

Women do not simply have faces, as men do; they are identified with their faces. . . . A man's face is defined as something he basically doesn't need to tamper with; all he has to do is keep it clean. He can avail himself of the options for ornament supplied by nature: a beard, a mustache, longer or shorter hair. But he is not supposed to disguise himself. What he is "really" like is supposed to show. A man lives through his face; it records the progressive stages of his life. . . . By contrast, a woman's face is potentially separate from her body. She does not treat it naturalistically. A woman's face is the canvas upon which she paints a revised, corrected portrait of herself. One of the rules of the creation is that the face not show what she doesn't want it to show. Her face is an emblem, an icon, a flag. How she arranges her hair, the type of make-up she uses, the quality of her complexion—all these are signs not of what she is "really" like, but of how she asks to be treated by others, especially men. They establish her status as an "object." (1972:34)

In growing up, males are judged by two sets of physical standards—one appropriate to boys, and another for men. Sontag notes that the beauty standards for boys are similar to those for girls: "In both sexes it is a fragile kind of beauty and flourishes only in the early part of the life-cycle" (1972:36). As boys are socially transformed into men, society allows them to be judged by another set of beauty standards—those relating to maturity, such as "character lines" around the eyes and the effects of daily shaving. Females, however, are judged throughout their lives by one standard of physical beauty—that appropriate to *young girls*. The loss of girlishness, and society's response to it, pressures some women to try to fight the natural ravages of time by a frantic concern with appearance and the use of nose jobs, breast enlargements, face lifts, bottom lifts, and any other conceivable means of enhancement. These women try to disguise, conceal, or lie about their real age. Such behaviors are tragic testimony to the double standard of aging in our society.

For women, beauty is an important physical attribute with significant effects on how others perceive and value them. As the passage of time takes its toll on physical appearance, the homemaker with no real occupational career may be confronted with a very real question of social worth. Males, who from their early years are evaluated in terms of what

## The Principle of Least Interest and Family Politics

In the traditional family pattern, a woman marries in her teens or early 20s, begins to have children shortly thereafter, and has no job skills or experience to assure her place in the work world. Her husband has a well-defined occupational career. This basic difference carries the seed for many women's discontent with their traditional adult gender roles, which grows as they age.

The wife's role becomes firmly entrenched inside the home during the early years of child rearing. The husband meanwhile is typically moving up the career ladder and achieving some success in the work world. The wife may work in order to contribute to the family income, but the jobs she can take are necessarily unskilled, part time, or temporary, to ac-

they are and do, may also experience a sense of deterioration as time attacks physical appearance. But the males' response is likely to be much less devastating, since they have a standing in the occupational world to draw upon as a source of social worth and self-respect. These differences in the power positions of men and women are growing smaller as increasing numbers of women enter the labor force (see Chapter 5), but they continue to be troublesome in the marriage relationship.

In his studies of courtship and dating, the sociologist Willard Waller (1938) coined the phrase **the principle of least interest** to express the idea that whoever has the least interest in maintaining a relationship also has the most power in it. The other person is required to work harder and demonstrate more involvement in the relationship in order to keep it going. You may recall situations in which you were apathetic or indifferent about seeing a person who was very intent on seeing you. Did you feel a certain sense of power in that relationship? And, by the same token, you have surely been involved with a person who was less interested than you were in keeping up your social ties. Did you feel frustrated and powerless in that relationship? Such situations involve the matter of who has access to certain highly prized resources such as attractiveness, status, money, family background, or friends. Much-sought-after men and women can afford to "hang loose" and "play it cool" in their relations with others, since they have numerous possibilities from which to choose. In a marriage, the principle of least interest has operated to favor the male member (see box).

---

commodate the demands on her time for domestic tasks and child care. The husband's occupational career comes first if job transfers are involved or the wife should be offered more demanding or time-consuming job responsibilities.

By the time the family cycle has entered the stage referred to as the empty nest, the wife is confronted with three simultaneous problems: her fragmented work history has limited career progress and opportunities, or she has little training for any work other than housework; her physical appearance requires increasing efforts to maintain; and she may be faced with a crisis in the meaning of her life now that she no longer takes the mother role with her own grown children. The woman who most fervently accepts the traditional role of mother-wife finds herself in a void when her children are grown. She not only is deprived of her role, but her children may seem unappreciative and resentful of her efforts in their behalf. She suffers from what Pauline Bart (1970) called "Mother Portnoy's complaint."

In effect, over time, the husband's position in the marriage becomes much more advantageous than the wife's because he has the least interest in it. As he gets older he is evaluated less in terms of physical attractiveness and more in terms of occupational success. His socially rewarding role-taking is not restricted until some time in his 60s, when he may consider retirement from work. As the marriage continues, the husband's options are increasing while the wife's are being further restricted.

In American society it is considered "natural" and "normal" for an older man to have an affair with or marry a much younger woman, but

---

Like any other physical or social attribute, age acquires its meaning through interaction. To fully understand the aging process, we need to know how people tune in to, interpret, and respond to repeated social messages about the meanings of age. Men and women hear quite different messages about the aging process. At the root of the differing life courses of men and women lies a power differential which operates to age women considerably faster than men, according to the definitions of aging in American society. Jessie Bernard (1972) suggests that there is a "his" and "her" marriage. We suggest there is also a "his" and "her" aging.

## ■ CONCLUSION

Our experience of the aging process depends on where we stand in society, particularly our age, our gender, and the work we do. We oversimplify the aging process if we think of it only in chronological or biological terms. Age carries no intrinsic meaning. Rather, human beings in communication with one another attach meanings to age. Our feelings about growing up, older, and old are formed by the values of the society at large and by those of the particular groups to which we belong.

Because human beings are not simply objects in nature, or passive receptacles for biological processes associated with the passage of time, they shape the aging process by thinking about it, interpreting it, defining it, categorizing it, labeling it, and attaching values to it. These mental

the same does not hold for a woman. If the couple have children and decide to divorce, the wife is assumed by society and the courts to be the natural caretaker of the children. She continues to bear the emotional burden of child care, and often the financial burden as well. This is one reason why the likelihood of women finding a mate decreases dramatically after age 25. A study of the demography of the marriage market in the United States found that the outlook for marriage is especially poor for more educated, older women: "At ages 40–49, for example, there are fewer than three suitable men available for every ten college-educated women" (Golman, Westoff, and Hammerslough, 1984:20).

The facts that women prefer older men and they live longer than men produce a very unbalanced marriage market situation in the United States. In a market with insufficient male partners, the principle of least interest clearly operates to favor men.

---

activities have critical consequences for actual behaviors. Chronological age is a symbol which is subject to continuous human definition and redefinition, and age categories are social constructions which cannot be understood outside the context in which they are defined. The norms regulating the behaviors expected of people of various ages are also shaped and defined by their own interactions and communications.

Throughout this chapter we have explored how aging identities are formed. Age is certainly one of our most meaningful identity pegs or markers. We think of ourselves in terms of the age categories into which we fit at different points in our life. Age, however, is only one dimension by which individuals define who they are to themselves and others. The last chapter of this book examines the issues of identity more broadly. It will consider some of the features of the modern world that make it increasingly difficult for individuals to answer the question, "Who am I?"

## Definitions

**Meanings of age.** The varied meanings attached to a particular chronological age according to the individual, the situations in which interactions take place, and the age conventions of the society. Because age categories are social constructions, the meaning of an age varies with the social, cultural, and historical context in which it is defined.

**Life cycle.** The pattern of broad developmental stages through which all human

273

beings are said to pass as they move through life.

**Age status.** The roles, duties, obligations, and responsibilities expected of individuals of a certain age. Some age-related cultural expectations are codified into law, such as the voting age and the drinking age.

**Age structure.** The number of people in different age categories in a society. A society's age structure is determined primarily by birth rates and rates of mortality, and it changes over time.

**Ageism.** Prejudice and discrimination directed toward older people. Ageism is comparable to sexism (prejudice directed at women or men) and racism (prejudice directed at racial and ethnic minority groups).

**Age categories.** Broad designations used to describe persons of different chronological ages. The meanings attached to age categories such as childhood and adolescence have varied cross-culturally and in different historical eras.

**Empty nest.** The period in the family life cycle after the last child leaves home and child care and support needs diminish. The lengthening of the empty nest period in recent years has created new life tasks for both women and men.

**Mandatory retirement.** The age at which employees can be forced to retire. In the United States, the mandatory retirement age was raised to 70 in 1978.

**Young-old and old-old.** Two segments of the elderly population, consisting of those between the ages of 65 and 74 and those older than 75. Bernice Neugarten argues that because of the growing numbers of the elderly and their increased life span, policymakers should make this distinction. The old-old are more likely to have health and economic problems and to be isolated from social contact with others.

**Age norms.** Cultural prescriptions or regulations for appropriate behaviors at particular ages. Chronological age is an important basis for determining how persons ought to behave in all societies, but age norms vary across cultures and in different historical periods.

**Experiential age.** A subjective measure of where individuals are in the life cycle according to their life experiences rather than their chronological age.

**Career.** The perspective individuals have of their lives as a whole and their interpretation of the meanings of their various attitudes and actions and the things that happen to them. An occupational career is one frame within which people understand and interpret their movement through the life cycle.

**Age consciousness.** Awareness of being a certain age at certain life events, such as women who reach the age of 40 and approach the end of the child-bearing years without have borne the children they want.

**Age-status asynchronization.** A situation in which one's various age statuses are not synchronized or in balance. An individual's age status in one organization or institution may not fit well with his or her other positions and obligations.

**Principle of least interest.** A term coined by Willard Waller to express the idea that whoever has the least interest in maintaining a relationship also has the most power in it.

# Discussion Questions

1. How old are you? Whatever your age, try to describe as many norms as you can that influence what people your age can or cannot do. Think of such categories of norms as proper dress, drinking behavior, involvement in work, and sexual behavior.

2. Into what age category (for example, middle age, late middle age, old age, early adulthood) would you place your parents? Why have you placed them into that age category? Explain the meaning you are giving to that category. How will you know when your parents are no longer in that category?

3. There is an old saying that goes, "You are as young as you feel." Explain why a symbolic interactionist might want to amend this piece of folk wisdom to say, "You are as young or as old as *other* people make you feel."

4. Suppose you knew three men, all in their late 30s, who hold quite different jobs. Imagine that one is a professional athlete, the second a lawyer, and the third a machine operator in a factory. How would their respective occupations influence the way they are experiencing the same chronological point in the life cycle? More generally, how might jobs at different points in the class structure produce a different sense of age?

5. We have argued in this chapter that gender critically influences how individuals experience aging. There is a double standard of aging that places women at a greater disadvantage than men as they grow older. Based on your observation of social life, what evidence would you submit to argue that such a double standard does, in fact, exist?

6. In earlier times people on average died in their early 40s rather than their mid 70s, as is the case today. How do you think this demographic fact of life has influenced family and work life? What if the average age span were to become, say, 100? How would such a change influence the structure of family and work life?

7. Describe any relationship familiar to you in which one of the persons had a deeper commitment than the other. How would you use Waller's principle of least interest to explain the behaviors of each of the persons involved?

# References

Aries, P. 1962. *Centuries of Childhood.* New York: Vintage Books.
Bakan, D. 1971. "Adolescence in America: From idea to social fact." *Daedalus* 100 (Fall):979–995.
Bart, P. 1970. "Mother Portnoy's complaint." *Transaction* 8 (November–December):69–74.
Bernard, J. 1972. *The Future of Marriage.* New York: Basic Books.
Brecher, E. M., et al. 1984. *Love, Sex, and Aging: A Consumer's Union Report.* Mt. Vernon, N.Y.: Consumer's Union.
Butler, R. 1975. *Why Survive? Being Old in America.* New York: Harper & Row.
Cain, L. 1964. "Life course and social structure." In *Handbook of Modern Sociology.* Chicago: Rand McNally.
Cain, L. 1974. "The growing importance of legal age in determining the status of the elderly." *The Gerontologist* 14:167–174.
Davis, R. 1979. "Aging: Prospects and issues." In *Aging: Prospects and Issues,* ed. R. Davis. Berkeley, Cal.: University of California Press.
DeMause, L. 1975. "Our forebears made childhood a nightmare." *Psychology Today* (April):85–88.
Demos, J. 1970. *A Little Commonwealth.* New York: Oxford University Press.
Erikson, E. 1968. *Identity: Youth and Crisis.* New York: W. W. Norton.
Faulkner, R. 1974. "Coming of age in organizations." *Sociology of Work and Occupations* 1:131–174.
Glick, P. 1977. "Updating the life cycle of the family." *Journal of Marriage and the Family* 39:5–13.
Golman, N., C. Westoff, and C. Hammerslough. 1984. "Demography of the marriage market." *Population Index* 50:5–25.
Haravan, T. 1978. "Family time and historical time." In *The Family,* ed. A. Rossi, J. Kagan, and T. Haravan. New York: W. W. Norton.
Hughes, E. 1958. *Men and Their Work.* New York: Free Press.
Karp, D. 1985. "Gender, academic careers, and the social psychology of aging." *Qualitative Sociology* 8:9–28.

Karp, D., and W. Yoels. 1982. *Experiencing the Life Cycle: A Social Psychology of Aging*. Springfield, Ill.: Charles C Thomas.

Katz, M. 1968. *The Irony of Early School Reform*. Cambridge, Mass.: Harvard University Press.

Kett, J. 1977. *Rites of Passage*. New York: Basic Books.

LeShan, R. E. 1973. *The Wonderful Crisis of Middle Age*. New York: Warner Books.

Levinson, D. 1978. *The Seasons of a Man's Life*. New York: Alfred A. Knopf.

Masters, W. H., and V. E. Johnson. 1966. *Human Sexual Response*. Boston: Little, Brown.

Neugarten, B. L. 1968. "The awareness of middle age." In *Middle Age and Aging*, ed. B. Neugarten. Chicago: University of Chicago Press.

Neugarten, B. L. 1974. "Age groups in American society and the rise of the young-old." *Annals of the American Academy of Political and Social Science* 415 (September):187–198.

Neugarten, B., J. Moore, and J. Lowe. 1965. "Age norms, age constraints and adult socialization." *American Journal of Sociology* 70:710–717.

Pfeiffer, E., A. Verwoerdt, and G. Davis. 1972. "Sexual behavior in middle life." *American Journal of Psychiatry* 128:1262–1267.

Platt, G. 1969. *The Child Savers*. Chicago: University of Chicago Press.

Roebuck, J. 1979. "When does 'old age' begin: The evolution of the English definition." *Journal of Social History* 12:416–428.

Rubin, L. 1979. *Women of a Certain Age*. New York: Harper & Row.

Sarason, S. 1977. *Work, Aging, and Social Change*. New York: Free Press.

Sheehy, G. 1977. *Passages*. New York: Bantam Books.

Sofer, C. 1970. *Men in Mid Career: A Study of British Managers and Technical Specialists*. Cambridge, England: Cambridge University Press.

Sontag, S. 1972. "The double standard of aging." *Saturday Review* (September):29–38.

Spring, J. 1976. *The Sorting Machine: National Educational Policy Since 1945*. New York: David McKay.

Troll, L., and J. Turner. 1978. "Overcoming age-sex discrimination." In *Women in Mid Life: Security and Fulfillment*. Washington, D.C.: Government Printing Office.

Turnbull, C. 1983. *The Human Cycle*. New York: Simon & Schuster.

U.S. Bureau of the Census. 1977. "Projections of the population of the United States: 1977 to 2050." *Current Population Reports*, Series P25, no. 704. Washington, D.C.: Government Printing Office.

U.S. Bureau of the Census. 1983. *Statistical Abstract of the United States, 1984*. Washington, D.C.: Government Printing Office.

Waller, W. 1938. *The Family: A Dynamic Interpretation*. New York: Gordon.

# CHAPTER 10  Social Change and the Search for Self

 I. Symbols, Selves, and Society
    A. Life Problems in Traditional and Contemporary Societies
 II. Social Movements and Conceptions of Injustice
    A. The Liberal Humanitarian Movement
    B. The Socialist Movement
    C. The Contemporary Movement
 III. The Contemporary Concern with Self
    A. The Consumption Ethic
    B. Buyers and Sellers in the Identity Marketplace
    C. The New Religions
       1. Significance and social consequences
       2. The appeal of Oriental religions for Westerners
    D. The Journey Inward
 IV. Future Selves
    A. Measuring Self-Concepts
    B. The Adaptable, Mutable Self
    C. The Tricky Business of Predicting the Future
 V. Conclusion

SCIENCE & INTUITIVE WISDOM
BRUNO BETTELHEIM
FREUD
MAN'S SOUL
Lifelong Lover
The New Way to Lasting Sexual Intimacy
WHAT EVERY WOMAN OUGHT TO KNOW ABOUT LOVE & MARRIAGE
Dr. Joyce Brothers
What Every Woman Should Know
LOVE
LEO BUSCAGLIA
Leo Buscaglia, Ph.D.
YOUR ERRONEOUS ZONES
GANDHI'S TRUTH
OVERCOMING THE FEAR OF
THE ART OF LOVING
Erich Fromm
L. RON HUBBARD
Love Is Letting Go of Fear

# CHAPTER 10

SIDDHARTHA, son of a high-caste Brahmin in India, was the central character in a widely read novel of the 1950s by Hermann Hesse which movingly portrayed a difficult quest for a meaningful life. While Hesse's novel (1951) was written in the 1930s and is set in Asia, Siddhartha's **search for self** has come to represent a central life problem for millions of persons in the present urban-industrial nations of Western Europe and North America (the West). This search has led many Westerners to seek membership in organizations such as encounter groups and Asian or neo-Christian religious sects. The emergence of such organizations in Western societies has been a response to what Orrin Klapp (1969) aptly calls a "collective search for identity."

## ■ SYMBOLS, SELVES, AND SOCIETY

In this concluding chapter we examine how the matters of personal identity and self-worth have been brought to the forefront of contemporary consciousness in the Western world. Before dealing directly with that issue, however, we will briefly consider the present situation by highlighting some of the main points of the preceding chapters.

Throughout this book we have repeatedly made the point that the selves individuals present to one another are not bestowed by nature. Human selves do not exist as independent entities but emerge, are sustained, and are transformed as a consequence of the symbolic dialogues, both verbal and nonverbal, which individuals constantly engage in with others. Clothes, for example, as well as words are symbolic announcements to others of how an individual wants to be viewed.

Central to the interactionist perspective on human life is the notion that people are sensitive to the impressions they make on each other. They go to great lengths to withhold discrediting information about themselves from others in order to appear proper in their eyes. In our discussions of stranger and intimate relationships in Chapters 4 and 5 we stressed the connection between the information people have about others and their ability to role-take with them. We analyzed behavior in public places in terms of the relative scarcity of information strangers have about each other. The measure of trust, risk, uncertainty, and commitment people invest in their relationships is calculated in terms of their faith that others' performances reflect their real intentions and identities.

Sensitivity to others is not distributed equally throughout the social order, as our treatment of the politics of interaction in Chapter 6 demonstrated. Those in positions of power can afford to be insensitive to the feelings of the less powerful. Because the ability to role-take is inversely related to power, disadvantaged ascribed-status characteristics such as female gender, lower- and working-class status, and minority group membership are conducive to superior role-taking ability. The faces power presents, short of sheer physical force or other forms of coercion, are primarily symbolic. Through facial expressions and the techniques of interrupting, crowding others' space, pointing, and staring, the powerful affirm their status while keeping others under their scrutiny.

Not only are symbols crucial in the communication of power differentials, but, in a larger sense, human social life itself is symbolic, or a social construction. Objects and things have no inherent meaning, only the meanings people confer on them. These meanings are, in the final analysis, arbitrary, since there are always several possible meanings that could be given to them. Whatever the meaning attributed to it, a thing can only be understood within the context in which it is situated.

As we suggested in Chapter 2, the symbol-using capacity of human beings makes possible a kind of liberation. Freed from the animal's dependence on instinctual biological impulses and signs, humans can use symbols to bring into reality virtually anything they can imagine. The ability to transcend the world of the here and now through symbolic processes is not without its costs, however. It also heightens humans' awareness that they are destined to die (see box).

# Small Gods and Worms: The Paradox of Human Existence

There is one issue we all must face alone, sooner or later, though we all have an urgent need and desire to avoid it. We must conceive of the reality of our own death and accept it. Elizabeth Kübler-Ross, who has studied attitudes toward death of dying patients and their families, acknowledges that human knowledge has actually increased the fear of dying:

> We would think that our great emancipation, our knowledge of science and of man, has given us better ways and means to prepare ourselves and our families for this inevitable happening. Instead the days are gone when a man was allowed to die in peace and dignity in his own home. The more we are making advancements in science, the more we seem to fear and deny the reality of death. (1970:7)

While Kübler-Ross considers the topic of death in relation to treatment of the dying and medical science, the fear and denial of death have a basis in more fundamental societal attitudes. The essential paradox of human existence is that humans transcend nature but also are a part of it, and death is a natural consequence. Ernest Becker has written some eloquent words to explain this twofold dilemma:

> Man has a symbolic identity that brings him sharply out of nature. He is a symbolic self, a creature with a name, a life history. He is a creator with a mind that soars out to speculate about atoms and infinity, who can place himself imaginatively at a point in space and contemplate bemusedly his own planet. This immense expansion, this dexterity, this ethereality, this self-consciousness gives to man literally the status of a small god in nature, as the Renaissance thinkers knew.
>
> Yet, at the same time, as the Eastern sages also knew, man is a worm and food for worms. This is the paradox: he is out of nature and hopelessly in it; he is dual, up in the stars and yet housed in a heart-pumping, breath-gasping body that once belonged to a fish and still carries the gill-marks to prove it. His body is a material fleshy casing that is alien to him in many ways—the strangest and most repugnant way being that it aches and bleeds and will decay and die. Man is literally split in two: he has an awareness of his own splendid uniqueness in that he sticks out of nature with a towering majesty, and yet he goes back into the ground a few feet in order blindly and dumbly to rot and disappear forever. It is a terrifying dilemma to be in and to have to live with. The lower animals are, of course, spared this painful contradiction, as they lack a symbolic identity and the self-consciousness that goes with it. They merely act and move reflectively

as they are driven by their instincts. If they pause at all, it is only a physical pause; inside they are anonymous, and even their faces have no name. They live in a world without time, pulsating, as it were, in a state of dumb being. This is what has made it so simple to shoot down whole herds of buffalo or elephants. The animals don't know that death is happening and continue grazing placidly while others drop alongside them. The knowledge of death is reflective and conceptual, and animals are spared it.

## Life Problems in Traditional and Contemporary Societies

The awareness of death has been present among members of all societies throughout human history. In preindustrial, tradition-oriented societies, however, people are somewhat shielded or insulated from the trauma of death consciousness. Their religious ideology helps explain life's mysteries for them. Individuals may know that they are going to die, but they also believe that they know *why* they are destined to die and *where* their death will take them. Members of such societies are also fairly secure in the knowledge of *who* they are. The anxiety occasioned by identity questions is siphoned off by the importance accorded to ascribed-status characteristics. In such societies, an individual's family status dictates nearly all life experiences, and, as Peter Berger and Thomas Luckman put it,

> ... everyone pretty much *is* what he is supposed to be. In such a society identities are easily recognizable, objectively and subjectively. Everybody knows who everybody else is and who he is himself. A knight *is* a knight and a peasant *is* a peasant, to others as well as to themselves. There is, therefore, no *problem* of identity. The question "who am I?" is unlikely to arise in consciousness, since the socially defined answer is massively real subjectively and consistently confirmed in all significant social interaction. (Italics in original; 1967:164)

In contemporary urban-industrial societies, people are confronted with a very different set of life problems. Social scientists have observed that one of the most dramatic consequences of urbanization and industrialization is the rapid increase in geographic and social mobility for large segments of the population. The resulting sense of rootlessness and personal **alienation** has increased concern with questions of identity, self-worth, and the larger significance of life.

They live and they disappear with the same thoughtlessness: a few minutes of fear, a few seconds of anguish, and it is over. But to live a whole lifetime with the fate of death haunting one's dreams and even the most sun-filled days—that's something else. (1973:26)

Reprinted with permission of The Free Press, a Division of Macmillan, Inc. from *The Denial of Death* by Ernest Becker. Copyright © 1973 by the Free Press.

## ■ SOCIAL MOVEMENTS AND CONCEPTIONS OF INJUSTICE

Before urbanization and industrialization, when a framework of religious explanations dominated American society and other parts of the Western world, human suffering and restrictions on life-chances were accepted as natural and inevitable, as "God's way." In the modern world, the influence of democratic ideologies, technology, and science has acted to make many things which were previously accepted as natural and inevitable now seem subject to human will and action. For example, the needy no longer passively plead for charity; they expect it and demand that governments engage in social welfare activities. If the governments did not comply, large segments of their populations would view it as an *injustice*.

When people come together and collectively act on their definitions of injustice, a **social movement** is born. In Ralph Turner's words: "A movement becomes possible when groups of people cease to petition the good will of others for relief of their misery and demand as their right that others ensure the correction of their condition" (1969:491).

In the Western world, social movements have varied in their social bases, their ultimate aims, and the solutions to injustice they have proposed. Turner identifies two former major social movements, the liberal humanitarian and socialist movements, and the contemporary movement, whose dominant theme is that advanced industrial societies damage their members' identity and deny them a **sense of self-worth** (see Table 10.1). The distinctive new feature is "the phenomenon of a man crying out with indignation because his society has not supplied him with a sense of personal worth and identity." Turner concludes that "The idea that a man who does not feel worthy and who cannot find his proper place in life is to be pitied is an old one. The notion that he is indeed a victim of injustice is the new idea" (p. 395).

Table 10.1
The Concept of Injustice in Past and Present Social Movements

| Social Movement | Historical Era | Social Base | Definition of Injustice | Proposed Solutions |
|---|---|---|---|---|
| Liberal humanitarian | Late 18th and early 19th century | Emerging middle class (bourgeoisie) | Denial of voting rights, free speech, free press, freedom of assembly | Reform the political arena to allow populace full participation |
| Socialist | Mid 19th to mid 20th century | Working class (proletariat) | Existence of poverty and material want | Reform the economy to redistribute the wealth |
| Contemporary | 1960s to present | Primarily adolescents and young adults | Society's denial of persons' self-worth and sense of identity | No one solution for the problem of psychological alienation |

*Source:* Adapted from Ralph Turner, "The Theme of Contemporary Social Movements," *British Journal of Sociology* 20 (1969):390–405.

## The Liberal Humanitarian Movement

To understand how the denial of a person's sense of self-worth by society has come to be viewed as an injustice, we must look at the social movements characterizing earlier periods. The emergence of a democratic ideology in the Western world was intimately associated with the American and French revolutions. These revolutions were products of the Enlightenment philosophy which dominated 18th-century Western thought. Philosophers such as Jean Jacques Rousseau in France and John Locke in Great Britain emphasized the rational powers of the human mind. They believed that social institutions should be changed to conform with rational human nature in order to ensure the fullest possible development of the individual. Injustices were defined in terms of full participation in the political process. If the people were allowed to choose their own destinies freely, it was argued, human misery would be alleviated.

Rousseau's faith in the "general will" of the populace represents this philosophy, as do the freedoms incorporated in our Declaration of Independence. Borrowing from the thought of Karl Mannheim, a 20th-century German social theorist, Turner refers to the social movement organized around this philosophy as the **liberal humanitarian movement.**

The launching pad for this movement was the emerging middle class, or **bourgeoisie,** which was striving to throw off the power of the aristocratic gentry. The gentry had held the dominant position in society for centuries on the basis of their family lineage and possession of land. Members of the middle class valued instead freedom of movement and pursuit of economic gain and regarded anything which hindered them as an injustice. Since they found it possible to amass wealth themselves, they saw no need to reform the economy other than to broaden the opportunities to conduct business. The "solutions" to injustice they proposed focused on demands for full participation in the political arena.

## The Socialist Movement

The liberal humanitarian movement was followed by the **socialist movement,** which began to take shape in Western Europe and the United States during the latter part of the 19th century. The social base of this movement was the working class, or proletariat (see Chapter 7), and the new definition of injustice focused on living conditions in an industrial, capitalistic economy. The working class, organized in labor unions, began to demand that the government recognize poverty and material want as an injustice. The proposed solution was economic and social reforms to redistribute the wealth. These demands peaked in the 1930s, when they were instrumental in the formulation of Franklin D. Roosevelt's New Deal programs. Many present U.S. social welfare policies grew out of the legislation passed in this period.

## The Contemporary Movement

The social movement characterized by the contemporary period's definition of injustice has a much broader goal than the earlier demands for full political participation or freedom from poverty. This movement takes the form of demands from various segments of the population that entire societies should be reformed in order to ensure every person's sense of self-worth. Unlike the two preceding movements, which had their base in specific social classes, the **contemporary movement** cuts across class lines. It primarily takes its membership from adolescents and young adults, however.

In contemporary Western societies, alienation, which was previously seen only as a work-related phenomenon, has a much broader connotation. The term used to be associated with such issues as the manager's feelings of loneliness and isolation, the secretary's sense of frustration at being limited to support roles, and the blue-collar worker's lack of job satisfaction (see Chapter 7). Now it is defined as a life problem or central injustice, and alienation designates a psychological state or psychiatric condition. The situation of contemporary youth in relation to technology is a critical factor in the broader meaning of alienation. Turner says young people are in a "nonperson status":

> The problem of alienation and the sense of worth is most poignantly the problem of a youthful generation with unparalleled freedom and capability but without an institutional structure in which this capability can be appropriately realized. Adolescence is peculiarly a "non-person" status in life. And yet this is just the period in which the technical skills and the new freedom are being markedly increased. The sense of alienation is distinctively the sense of a person who realizes great expectations for himself yet must live in a non-status. (1969:396)

## ■ THE CONTEMPORARY CONCERN WITH SELF

As the more personalized conception of alienation has been accepted in American society, popular writings by psychiatrists, psychologists, and advice columnists have taken on an influential role. Television appearances have made "mind-tinkerers" such as Leo Buscaglia and Ruth Westheimer instant celebrities. Their appeal attests to the pervasive anxiety about questions of identity and psychological well-being in the society. Such "experts" are constantly dispensing prescriptions for happiness, sexual fulfillment, or mental health. A quick glance at such publications as the *National Enquirer* gives an immediate feel for today's concern with events that threaten "normalcy" and a sense of well-being.

The movement toward this all-embracing concern with psychological health and personal identity has been accompanied by a corresponding transformation in our vocabulary of motives, or explanatory schemas of human behavior (see Chapter 8). When people act in a manner that we consider deviant, our first impulse is to question their mental health and probe their psychological make-up. Are they normal persons? Why are they doing that? Because of the medicalization of deviance (described in Chapter 8), behaviors such as alcoholism which would have been viewed years ago as evidence of sinfulness or moral degeneracy are now explained as illness. We use a "sickness vocabulary" rather than a "sin vocabulary." Watching the greasy man with the waxed mustache tie up the beautiful blond on the railroad tracks as the train approaches, we now ask, "What would make a person do something as sick as that?" Our grandparents would have had little difficulty in understanding such behavior. For them the man was simply *evil!*

## The Consumption Ethic

The change to medical explanations of deviant behaviors has been accompanied by a corresponding change in the activities that mobilize our attention and involvement. In the age of the sin vocabulary, society was primarily organized around the world of work. A person who did not work, for any reason other than physical disability, was defined as immoral, lazy, and worthless. This perspective on work was beautifully captured in Max Weber's notion of the Protestant ethic, or the work ethic (see Chapter 7). Guided by this ethic, as Gregory P. Stone has noted, "We used to work—at least ideally and Protestantly—because work was our life. By our works we were known" (1968:319).

For sizable segments of the middle class, the work ethic and its moral restraints have been replaced by a **consumption ethic.** Whereas people used to consume so they could work, now they seem to work to live and live to consume. In recent years a new word has entered the American vocabulary to describe the young people who have embraced this ethic. *Yuppies*, or young urban professionals, are characterized by the communications media as oriented toward the consumption of such goods as expensive clothing, sportscars, and innovative products of modern technology.

The current emphasis on consumption has led to a paradox, according to George Albee. The capitalist system which developed along with the morality of the Protestant ethic required workers who would postpone immediate gratification and who would work at unpleasant tasks for the sake of future rewards. Sex had to be foregone and marriage postponed in the interests of industrial efficiency. As the industrial system became more and more technologically sophisticated and productive, the dilemma of what to do with the endless stream of goods, few of which satisfied any genuine needs, grew. A solution was found in the growth of advertising (Ewen, 1976) and the transformation of the pleasure-denying work ethic into a self-indulgent society of consumers. As Albee aptly states:

To encourage consumption in the absence of real need and to associate status and self-esteem with wasteful consumption, it has been necessary to encourage relatively mindless impulse buying and self-gratification. By now, we have raised several generations of people on endless and repetitive exhortations that it is all right to yield to impulse, to buy without guilt, and to consume without shame. Installment buying may have been the fatal blow to the self-denial of the Protestant ethic. (1977:150)

This shift toward the social production of consumer-oriented selves has had far-reaching consequences. Albee relates the consumer ethic to "the decline of traditional religion, the rise of the new hedonism, and the beatification of the pleasure principle." In his view, "With nothing left to believe in but *Peter Pan Peanut Butter*, it is little wonder that there is a growing and pervasive sense of meaninglessness, nihilism, and purposelessness" (p. 159).

Since material possessions alone cannot ensure feelings of meaningfulness and satisfaction, many people today find themselves caught up in an endless quest for a sense of significance in their lives. This quest is made even more illusive by the built-in obsolescence of the products produced. There must always be a "better" product in the works, and the flames of advertising are always available to heat the cauldron of contemporary anxiety.

## Buyers and Sellers in the Identity Marketplace

A number of recent social developments have been related to the psychological alienation created by life in a mobile, affluent, secularized society subject to rapid change. The development of a distinctive drug subculture beginning in the early 1960s, for example, seems to have been a product of alienation among young people. Many commentators, most notably Kenneth Kenniston, have identified a youth generation which felt deprived of real involvement, saw no opportunity for commitment, and believed their lives had been robbed of personal meaning. These alienated youths became involved in attempts to explain the meaning of their lives, or what Kenniston refers to as a **search for sentience:**

> Here the self is defined not by action, but by perception; and meaning is created by heightened receptivity and openness. Experience is defined as subtlety, sensitivity, and awareness; the purpose of existence is not to alter the world so as to create new experiences, but to alter the self so as to receive new perceptions from what is already there. (1960:181)

It is not hard to see how LSD, especially, became a source of sentience and provided a release from the numbing boredom of a life without commitment among such young people (Davis and Muñoz, 1967).

Many new forms of social organization have been devised to provide "services" to those who are trying to increase their self-awareness or are searching for their "real selves." One of the first was the **sensitivity training** technique which originated in California and was adopted so widely it became recognized as a cultural force in the late 1960s (Back, 1972). Another development was the rural communes modeled along the lines of 19th-century utopian communities, which found some favor among young people in the 1970s. Today, those who are interested in personal growth experiences or consciousness raising can choose from a wide array of group and individual therapies, ranging from weekend marathons at expensive resorts to years of in-depth analysis. An extraordinary variety of religious and quasi-religious groups also is taking on new forms to provide guidance of another sort in the individual's search for self.

The range and variety of offerings in the identity marketplace are great. Our examination of the contemporary search for self therefore will focus on the recent proliferation of religions and religious-oriented groups in the United States which have come to be called the **new religions.** We will examine this phenomenon in terms of its meaning to those involved in it as well as its significance as a reflection of change in the society.

## The New Religions

Groups of shaven-headed, incense-bearing, tambourine-playing young people in yellow tunics chant "Hare Krishna, Hare Krishna" as they persistently press flowers or literature on passers-by in exchange for donations. Clean-cut, intense, middle-class young people engage in a variety of business enterprises to support Reverend Sun Myung Moon's Unification Church. Prayer sessions sponsored by the Campus Crusade for Christ proceed next door to assemblies of the Jews for Jesus proclaiming the approaching coming of the Messiah. Far Eastern religious sects with histories that may go back several thousand years enlist the support of young, well-educated Americans, many of them from affluent homes.

There is ample evidence of the fervor and intensity of religious-oriented activities among certain groups of young people in American society. Very little hard data are available on the extent of participation in them, however. One sociological study by Robert Wuthnow (1976) which did address this issue used a sample of 1,000 persons age 16 and over living in the San Francisco Bay area. Participants in the survey were asked questions about 13 religious and quasi-religious groups divided into three categories. **Countercultural movements,** offshoots of distinctly non-Western or non-Christian traditions, reject established cultural mores and norms and call into question the social, political, economic, and moral bases of conventional society. **Personal growth movements** are of Western origin but are essentially neutral to the Christian tradition. Groups in this category propose different methods for helping individuals achieve greater happiness by improving their self-awareness and insight into their own motives and behaviors. **Neo-Christian movements** are relatively new Christian groups which are offshoots of traditional Chris-

Table 10.2
Examples of Current Religious and Quasi-Religious Groups

| Countercultural | Personal Growth | Neo-Christian |
|---|---|---|
| Zen Buddhism | Erhard Seminar Training (est) | Christian World Liberation Front |
| Yoga groups | Scientology | Children of God |
| Hare Krishna | Synanon | Jews for Jesus |
| Satanism |  | Campus Crusade for Christ |
| Transcendental meditation |  | Groups that speak in tongues |

*Source:* Robert Wuthnow, "The New Religions in Social Context," in *The New Religious Consciousness*, ed. C. Y. Glock and R. Bellah (Berkeley: University of California Press, 1976).

tianity. Examples of groups in each category are listed in Table 10.2.

Wuthnow's data indicate that few people in his sample knew very much about any of these groups. About half knew something about Synanon, the drug treatment program, and Yoga groups, and about one-third knew something about the countercultural groups in general. Nevertheless, Wuthnow argues that these 13 groups have had a substantial and widespread impact. Nearly four out of every five persons claimed to know a little bit about at least one of the movements. Actual participation was less common, but one out of every five persons said they had taken part in at least one group (p. 274).

A later study conducted in Montreal echoes Wuthnow's findings for the San Francisco Bay area. Frederick Bird and Bill Riemer (1982) found that "a surprisingly high proportion of the adult population" (somewhere between one-fifth and one-fourth) had participated in new religious and para-religious movements. Most persons who did participate became involved only for a while and then dropped out, however.

### Significance and Social Consequences

Wuthnow (1976) suggests that the significance of such groups goes far beyond the limited number who actually participate in them. One reason is that "those who take part in them tend to be among the better educated and, as a result, are the kind of people whose influence will probably become greater in the future" (p. 288). But this is only one possible interpretation. The social base from which these movements recruit their members also affects their likely significance. According to Wuthnow, these groups appeal to young people who *(a)* have never been married, *(b)* are looking for a job, *(c)* have moved twice or more in the last two years, *(d)* are bothered about work or work plans, and *(e)* are bothered about their sex lives.

Wuthnow proposes two contrasting predictions about the future of these groups:

> On the one hand, they have garnered most of their support from the better educated and more intellectually aware. If there is something about these movements that is more compatible with the modern intellectual climate than traditional religion has been, they may prosper well into the future, especially as more and more people become educated. On the other hand, they seem to appeal most to young people who are still at an unsettled stage in their lives. As these young people mature and become more settled, they may abandon these groups. (1976:292–293)

The latter interpretation raises the intriguing possibility that membership in such groups may eventually become an *institutionalized* part of the life cycle, something each generation of middle-class persons will be socialized to participate in and then leave at the appointed time. If this happens, such movements might assume the role of **identity markers** symbolizing the transition from youth to adult status.

## *The Appeal of Oriental Religions for Westerners*

To probe why such groups appeal to some people, Harvey Cox, a noted theologian, and some of his students at the Harvard Divinity School spent three years informally studying dozens of Oriental religious groups as they had taken form in Cambridge, Massachusetts. The researchers took part in the affairs of these groups, using a research strategy called participant observation. Their participation led them to sense a discrepancy between the personal reasons members gave for joining the movement and the official teaching of the movement's leaders.

The appeal of these groups, Cox (1977) argues, lies less in the actual content of their teaching and more in the opportunities they provide for: *(a)* friendship; *(b)* "a way to experience life directly without the intervention of ideas and concepts"; *(c)* an authoritative version of "the Truth"; and *(d)* a return to nature, spontaneity, and feeling. One member told Cox:

> All I got at any church I ever went to were sermons or homilies about God, about "the peace that passes understanding." Words, words, words. It was all in the head. I never really felt it. It was all abstract, never direct, always somebody else's account of it. It was dull and boring. I'd sit or kneel or stand. I'd listen to or read prayers. But it seemed lifeless. It was like reading the label instead of eating the contents. But here it really happened to me. I experienced it myself. I don't have to take someone else's word for it. (1977:39)

Other observers of the new religions do not share Cox's judgment that young people turn to Eastern religions only to gain a sense of authority, human companionship, or "far out" experiences, or his view that as Oriental religions are practiced in this country, they are consumer oriented. Jacob Needleman, a philosopher at San Francisco State University, provides a much more sympathetic analysis of these religions. He views their emergence as an indication that the philosophical traditions of Western civilization have reached a dead end for many Americans, and the concepts of reality, self, and mind elaborated in Oriental religions pose severe challenges to Western conceptions. The difference between these conceptions, he says, is that:

> . . . the central thrust of Eastern religion is toward the *transformation of desire*, not satisfaction of desires. At its purest, it is a radical and constant movement inward into the "self." Thus, the contemporary idea of "relevance"—which by and large has to do with the satisfaction of certain desires, or the allaying of certain fears—is antagonistic to the sense of Eastern religion. (1970:198)

In the broadest sense, Needleman sees the appeal of these movements in their expansion of the intuitive mode of being. Many young people turn to Eastern religions as a reaction to the penetration of science and bureaucratic rationality into every aspect of our everyday lives (see Chapter 7). They seek an opportunity to get back in touch with their feelings, an unarticulated dimension of their selves. In a world in which science and technology have portrayed the universe as barren and bereft of meaning, with humans like pebbles on a vast beach, a need is created in some persons for an infusion of personal life-forces such as astrology, for example, provides. Such ideas can give many a sense of cosmic sig-

## The Dangers of the Awareness Trap

The search for the real self and meaningful intimate relationships occupies a good deal of the attention and energies of many young people in American society. They believe that by increasing their own self-awareness and accepting responsibility for themselves, they will secure the benefits of "the good life." The trouble with this idea is that people may become so involved in their own search for self that they fail to take into account the built-in sources of inequality and injustice in the social structure which make it more difficult for some people to achieve this goal than others. There are situations in which no amount of self-

nificance that is otherwise lacking in their lives. To Needleman the interest in astrology represents "a rebellion against the idea of an un-alive cosmos which modern science has given us, a cosmos in which man is at best a lonely anomaly" (p. 198).

## The Journey Inward

Involvement with new religions is only one route persons can take on their journey inward—a journey aimed at rekindling previously ignored and unexpressed feelings. The constant movement into the self has been the keynote of many contemporary ideas and groups. Increased self-awareness is the goal of the various forms of psychotherapy which have emerged in the United States, for example. To uncover the intuitive, emotional aspects of the self, these therapeutic activities attempt to harness the methodologies and perspectives of behavioral science rather than the teachings of religions.

Regardless of how increased self-awareness is achieved, it is not always a wholly positive development. There is a danger that the raising of personal consciousness could result in a diminished sense of **social consciousness** in American society (see box). Nevertheless, the new religions do reflect an effort by contemporary Americans to find urgently needed alternative solutions to the problems that confront them (Kilbourne and Richardson, 1984). Seen in that light, such movements may be viewed more as agents of social change than as reinforcements of the status quo.

---

awareness will suffice to solve social problems, as Edwin Schur points out in *The Awareness Trap* (1976).

Schur's basic thesis is that the self-awareness movement has consequences which pose obstacles to the goal of social justice. It encourages the perception that "we cannot expect other people to solve our problems for us . . . and by the same token we cannot solve theirs" (p. 4). The political consequence of such a position is that people who "make it" feel complacent and not obliged to help shoulder the responsibility for those who fail, for whatever reason.

Promoters of self-awareness argue that the various aspects of people's everyday lives—health, family life, and jobs, for example—would all be significantly improved if they became more sensitive both to their own real selves and those of the others they encounter. Schur shows how this idea has taken form in a variety of developments within the self-awareness movement, including open marriage, encounter groups, "positive thinking," primal therapy, and transcendental meditation, to name a few. Participants in these phenomena are linked in their belief that the good life and meaningful personal relationships can be achieved through self-development or some sort of consciousness-raising.

Schur maintains that such people ignore a very important fact about the nature of their social words: the structured, institutionalized sources

## ■ FUTURE SELVES

Who am I? How am I unique from other people? What is the meaning and significance of my life? Today we encounter difficult problems in looking for answers to such questions. We are caught in the midst of a major historical transformation with dramatic implications for our psychological well-being.

Western culture has passed through two central historical epochs, characterized first by agricultural, preurban society and then by urban-industrial society. The postindustrial society we are now entering relies on technological knowledge and is a time of rapid, often confusing social change. Alvin Toffler describes the acceleration of change as "a concrete force that reaches deep into our personal lives, compels us to act out new roles, and confronts us with the danger of a new and powerfully upsetting psychological disease" which he calls **future shock** (1971:10). Disorientation, irrationality, malaise, and "free-floating violence" on a mass scale are attributed to people's inability to adapt to change. But Toffler (1980) also perceives a "third wave" of civilization following the thousands of years of agricultural society and the mere 300 years of urbanization and industrialization. In his view, the present upheavals of technology form a clearly discernible pattern which is producing a giant transformation in the ways Americans live, work, play, and think.

In the wake of such transformations, social scientists have raised troubling questions about the future. Does a modern society, with its emphasis on technical information, services, and consumption, require a different conception of self than the one that fit in the eras of agricultural and industrial production? Will individuals be able to make the self-adaptations required in a complex, rapidly evolving society?

of inequality in the society. To change things for the better, it is not enough for individuals to behave in more loving, more liberated ways. Oppression, he says,

> . . . is systematic, socially structured, and culturally reinforced. To understand and change it, we usually will need to focus on a great many sociocultural factors—ranging from economic structure to the mass media, from status hierarchies to the legal system, from unemployment opportunities to child-rearing attitudes. *When problems transcend the personal or interpersonal levels, so too must the solutions.* (Italics added; pp. 4–5)

## Measuring Self-Concepts

In confronting such issues, Louis Zurcher used a technique called the Twenty Statements Test (TST) to measure self-concepts. The TST is compatible with the assumptions of symbolic interaction theory because it taps individuals' self-perceptions, or how they view themselves. To complete this test, participants are asked to make 20 responses to the question "Who am I?" by completing the sentence "I am ____" 20 different ways. They are instructed to write their statements quickly, in the order they come to mind, and without worrying about the logic or importance of their responses.

The TST is scored by classifying the responses into categories or modes. Repeated samplings of responses led Zurcher (1977) to conclude that the test reveals four central conceptions of self:

The A mode, or the physical self.
The B mode, or the social self.
The C mode, or the reflective self.
The D mode, or the oceanic self.

The **physical self** is indicated by responses that refer to actual physical attributes as well as other attributes that involve no interaction with others. A person's residential address would be an example of the latter. The **social self** refers to positions and statuses which clearly locate persons in a social structure or social circle. Examples of responses in this mode would include statements like "I am a college student," or "I am an electrical engineer." **The reflective self** is indicated by abstract statements which transcend specific social situations. These responses indicate the behaviors that respondents attribute to themselves. Examples would include such statements as "I am a moody person," or "I am a spendthrift." The **oceanic self** is reflected in statements that are "so vague that they lead us to no reliable expectations about behavior" (p. 46). Statements such as "I am a loving individual" or "I am a person who wants the best for everyone" would be placed in the oceanic-self category.

## The Adaptable, Mutable Self

When Zurcher administered the TST in 1969 he found that the most frequent mode of response was the C mode, or the reflective-self category. In fact, 68 percent of his respondents fell into this category. This finding was in dramatic contrast to the results of an earlier administration of the TST by Wynona Hartley in 1957. Hartley's study yielded the following results: A/physical mode = 2 percent; B/social mode = 51 percent; C/reflective mode = 31 percent; and D/oceanic mode = 16 percent. What sense could be made of such significant differences over time? Zurcher reasoned that perhaps the proliferation of C-mode self-definitions in his own 1969 sample was a response to the rapid rate of cultural and technological change in advanced industrial nations. He formulated a social change hypothesis to suggest that if C-mode self-definitions are associated with conditions of sociocultural change, then people who are caught in "dramatic examples" of such change ought to display C-mode self-definitions (p. 52).

To test this hypothesis, Zurcher administered the TST to individuals who were subject to especially rapid sociocultural change, a group of dissident priests and a group of paroled ex-felons. Zurcher chose these groups because "they had taken a step back (priests) or been forced back (ex-felons) from previous identification with a social structure. They had turned away from self as object, looked inward for a sense of identity, and had moved toward self-as-process" (p. 55). The priests were in conflict with the church, and the parolees had recently left the prison institutional setting. Zurcher found strong support for his hypothesis—83 percent of the priests and 77 percent of the ex-felons fell into the reflective category of response.

His data led Zurcher to adopt a positive view of humans' capacity for adaptation to social change. He suggests that we may be witnessing a transition from the B mode (social self) to the C mode (reflective self) which is part of the development of what Zurcher terms the **mutable self.** As Figure 10.1 shows, the mutable self integrates the physical, social, reflective, and oceanic conceptions of self. Rather than fixating on one of the four components of self to the exclusion of others, the mut-

Figure 10.1
Central Conceptions of Self

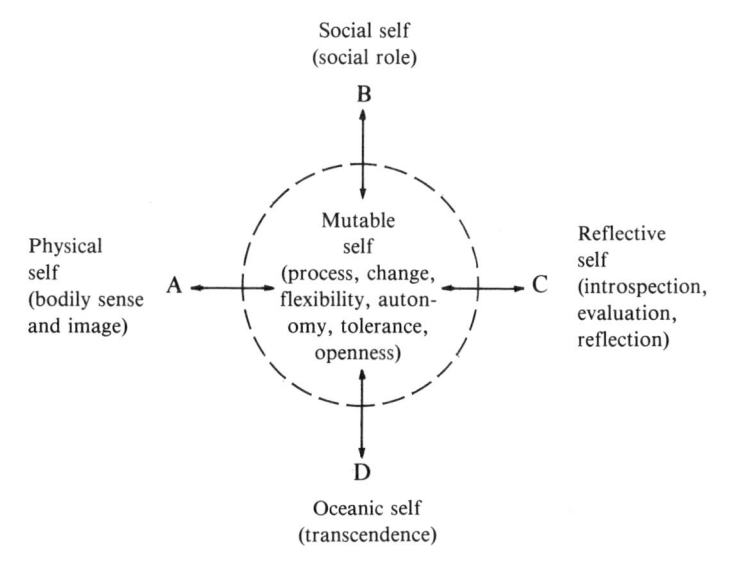

```
                    Social self
                   (social role)
                        B
                        ↑
                   ╱ ─ ┼ ─ ╲
                 ╱   Mutable    ╲
   Physical    ╱      self        ╲    Reflective
   self       │  (process, change, │   self
   (bodily sense A ─┼ flexibility, auton- ┼─ C  (introspection,
   and image)   │   omy, tolerance,   │   evaluation,
                 ╲    openness)     ╱    reflection)
                   ╲ ─ ┼ ─ ╱
                        ↓
                        D
                   Oceanic self
                  (transcendence)
```

*Source:* Louis A. Zurcher, Jr., *The Mutable Self,* p. 217. Copyright © 1977 by Sage Publications, Inc. Reprinted by permission of Sage Publications, Inc.

able-self person is able to assume a particular self to fit the various situations encountered in everyday life. Zurcher suggests that the persons most suited for living under conditions of rapid social change are those whose self-concepts are complete, open, and flexible enough to permit a process of alternation among A, B, C, and D-mode self-concepts as the situation requires:

Since the Mutable Self person has a process orientation and relates to the world through all four components of self, he or she is not traumatized or rendered ineffective by rapid sociocultural change. Transition, ambiguity, or uncertainty can be tolerated. Those factors can be lived with, accepted, accommodated, evaluated, resisted, modified, or controlled as the person sees fit. (1977:224)

A test of Zurcher's argument which utilized the responses to the TST of more than 1,000 college students from 1976 to 1979 found a dramatic shift in the locus of self in contemporary American society. In various social and demographic groupings, the idea of a self anchored in institutions was being replaced by a self anchored in impulse. Among college students, the shift appeared to be "a fairly pervasive social psychological phenomenon" (Snow and Phillips, 1982:471).

## The Tricky Business of Predicting the Future

Even though analyses like Zurcher's are grounded in carefully collected, valid data, prediction about the future remains a tricky, highly uncertain endeavor. Social scientists cannot make *absolute* predictions about future forms of social life easily. Few of them accurately forecast the civil rights activities of the early 1960s, the urban riots of the mid 1960s, the women's rights activities of the 1970s, or the international terrorist attacks of the 1980s. The failure to anticipate such social movements does not signal some technical or theoretical flaw in sociological work. It is, instead, affirmation of one of the central messages of this book: human beings are continually in the process of rearranging their social worlds in ways that they themselves cannot fully predict in advance.

What, then, can we say about the future? The data presented in this chapter, and throughout this book, justify optimistic judgments about our capacity for adapting to a rapidly changing society. The creation of the expressive, self-awareness, and consciousness-raising groups described in the preceding section illustrates a fundamental aspect of social life. When individuals find their lives becoming too impersonal and too rational, they will inject into them some sentiment, some passion. When social life becomes too routinized, people will collectively find ways to experience novelty. Similarly, when they find their lives becoming too unpredictable, they will introduce some routine into their daily activity. Individuals who feel uncertain of their personal identities and are bothered by a diminished sense of self-worth will respond collectively by trying to alter their environments to meet their needs.

In this book we have tried to convey the value of sociology—more specifically of a sociological focus on everyday life—for understanding the mutual transformations in the relationships of situations and selves. In doing so we have stressed certain themes: the balance between social order and freedom; the interplay of individuals and social structures; the interpenetration of macro and micro social worlds. As boundaries for human interaction, these themes are critical if we are to obtain insight into the organization of our daily lives and the likely shapes of our individual and collective futures.

## ■ CONCLUSION

In nearly all the chapters of this book, we have stressed the ways in which individuals' identities are fashioned by the particular social circumstances of their lives. Certainly your sense of self is related to the socialization you have experienced, your family's values and attitudes, your social class, your race, and your gender. We have also argued from time to time throughout this volume that people's consciousness about themselves and the world cannot be understood apart from the particular historical period in which they live. In this last chapter the argument has been that we are now living through a period of history that makes it uniquely difficult to answer the question "Who am I?"

Today's American society is more complicated, more bureaucratized, more impersonal, and more fast-paced than any other in the history of humankind. As a result there are widespread feelings of anxiety, personal malaise, psychological alienation, and rootlessness. Preoccupied with their *dis*-ease, many people in today's society purchase the time and expertise of professionals in order to discover more about themselves. The helping professions (among them psychiatrists, psychologists, therapists, and social workers) have emerged as a major cultural force in the last few decades. For an increasing proportion of the population, professional help is needed to feel better, "to get their acts together," "to get their heads together." It seems a fair characterization that contemporary Americans, in contrast to members of other cultures and historical eras, are uniquely concerned with themselves.

One vehicle for the contemporary search for self is fundamentalist and Eastern religions which have been around for thousands of years but have achieved significant appeal only recently in American society. We think that their popularity is due in large measure to the efforts of young people to understand their place in the world. These "new" religions are a reaction to the growing rationalization of modern life. The memberships of such religious movements are relatively small compared to the population as a whole, but their significance should not be dismissed. They are among the most visible "pilgrims" involved in a journey into themselves.

Some observers of the American cultural scene are pessimistic about our collective future. They wonder whether the rate of social change will outrun our ability to cope with it. Studies suggest a more optimistic image of the future, however. Louis Zurcher, for example, indicates that human selves are remarkably adaptable. His data, confirmed by others, offer support for the notion of a mutable self which is open and flexible enough to accommodate to situations of rapid social and cultural change. Such a view is, of course, consistent with the symbolic interactionist perspective that has guided this whole enterprise. Human beings are not merely passive products of culture. Because they are symbolic animals, they have the potential to create cultures that meet their needs.

# Definitions

**Search for self.** Individuals' attempts to define their personal identity. Organizations such as encounter groups and neo-Christian religious sects and psychotherapy suggest different answers to the question, "Who am I?"

**Alienation.** Individuals' feelings of disassociation from the surrounding society. Alienation may express itself as feelings of powerlessness, normlessness, meaninglessness, depersonalization, or isolation.

**Social movement.** Attempts to change society by a group of people which collectively perceives that some aspect of society affects them negatively or results in an injustice to them. They may involve millions of people and have a broad societal focus or be organized around specific issues such as Mothers Against Drunk Driving (MADD).

**Sense of self-worth.** The feeling that one fits well into society and is performing roles the society values. Fundamentally, people feel a sense of self-worth when the roles they perform provide a source of meaning in their lives.

**Liberal humanitarian movement.** A broad social movement during the late 18th and 19th centuries which was organized around the theme that individuals have a right to democratic participation in political processes. The social base was the bourgeoisie.

**Bourgeoisie.** The term used by Karl Marx to refer to the middle class.

**Socialist movement.** A broad social movement with a social base in the proletariat or working class which proposed economic and social reforms to redistribute wealth in society. It arose in the late 19th century and peaked in the Great Depression of the 1930s.

**Contemporary movement.** A current social movement identified by Ralph Turner in which various segments of the population demand that entire societies be reformed in order to ensure every person's sense of self-worth. This movement appeals to young people and cuts across class lines.

**Consumption ethic.** Belief that one's sense of identity and self-worth can be enhanced through consumption of material things. The value of work is regarded as enabling people to pay for the myriad goods and services available in urban-industrial societies.

**Search for sentience.** Attempts to increase personal sensitivity and awareness through a variety of experiences. The term, coined by Kenneth Kenniston, describes the search of many young people for avenues such as the use of drugs through which they can perceive and experience the world differently.

**Sensitivity training.** Group activities designed to increase interpersonal awareness and improve understanding of self and others. Sessions encourage participants to express their feelings about each other openly and to be aware of others' reactions.

**New religions.** Religious groups which may be based on principles that are thousands of years old but which have only recently been introduced in their present form in the United States. Youthful persons especially have been drawn to them in large numbers.

**Countercultural movements.** Groups which reject certain norms and values of the prevailing culture. Members may question the social, political, economic, or moral basis of conventional society.

**Personal growth movements.** Groups devoted to helping individuals gain greater self-awareness and insight into their own motives, behaviors, and life choices. The ultimate goal of members is to increase their personal happiness.

**Neo-Christian movements.** Relatively new religious groups which are offshoots of traditional Christianity.

**Identity markers.** Events occurring throughout life which plainly mark off, define, or indicate one's current identity. Every society has rituals that mark the transition into adulthood, for example, such as obtaining a driver's license or graduating from high school in American society.

**Social consciousness.** A deep interest in and concern for the problems facing society. People with a strong social consciousness typically seek to remedy inequality and injustice.

**Future shock.** A term coined by Alvin Toffler to describe the negative consequences of the rapid social change which is typical of contemporary society. Toffler attributes disorientation, irrationality, malaise, and violence to people's inability to adapt to change.

**Physical self.** Conceptions of self that are related to individuals' physical attributes and attributes that involve no interactions with others, such as place of residence.

**Social self.** Positions and statuses such as education or occupation which clearly locate individuals in a social structure or social circle.

**Reflective self.** Conceptions of self which are abstract enough to transcend specific social situations.

**Oceanic self.** Conceptions of self which are so vague and general that they lead to no reliable expectations about a person's behavior.

**Mutable self.** Louis Zurcher's term for a conception of self which would integrate the physical, social, reflective, and oceanic selves. The mutable-self person would assume any of the selves which fit the situations encountered in everyday life.

motives from a sin vocabulary to a sickness vocabulary. Do you agree with the sin-to-sickness change in explanations of deviant behavior?

3. How do you think about the place of work in contemporary society? Do you consider work as an end in itself or as the means to other ends? Has there been a transformation from a work ethic to a consumption ethic? What part does advertising play in the way people think about work and leisure?

4. Robert Wuthnow divides recent movements into three categories: countercultural, personal growth, and neo-Christian. Are you personally familiar with any of the 13 groups mentioned? Do you know anyone who is involved in any of these groups? What kinds of persons do you think are most likely to join such groups? What functions do you feel these groups perform for their members?

5. Do you see any dangers to society created by the self-awareness, personal growth movement? How might the promise of better and more meaningful lives create an "awareness trap"?

6. Are you optimistic about our capacity to adapt to today's rapidly changing society? What form might such adaptations take? How would you speculate about likely changes in individuals' conceptions of self?

# Discussion Questions

1. Which features of contemporary urban-industrial society seem to you most responsible for creating questions of personal identity and self-worth? Name some specific aspects of modern institutions that heighten the problem of alienation.

2. Cite some recent examples illustrating the transformation in our vocabularies of

# References

Albee, G. 1977. "The Protestant ethic, sex and psychotherapy." *American Psychologist* 32:150–162.

Back, K. 1972. *Beyond Words: The Story of Sensitivity Training and the Encounter Movement.* New York: Russell Sage.

Becker, E. 1973. *The Denial of Death.* New York: Free Press.

Berger, P., and T. Luckman. *The Social Construction of Reality.* New York: Doubleday Anchor Books.

Bird, F., and B. Riemer. 1982. "Participation rates in new religious and para-religious movements." *Journal for the Scientific Study of Religion* 21:1–14.

Cox, H. 1977. "Eastern cults and Western culture: Why young Americans are buying Oriental religions." *Psychology Today* 11:36–42.

Davis, F., and L. Muñoz. 1967. "Heads and freaks: Patterns and meanings of drug use among hippies." *Journal of Health and Social Behavior* 9:156–164.

Ewen, S. 1976. *Captains of Consciousness: Advertising and the Social Roots of the Consumer Culture.* New York: McGraw-Hill.

Hesse, H. 1951. *Siddhartha.* New York: New Directions.

Kenniston, K. 1960. *The Uncommitted.* New York: Dell.

Kilbourne, B., and J. Richardson. 1984. "Psychotherapy and new religions in a pluralistic society." *American Psychologist* 39:237–251.

Klapp, O. 1969. *The Collective Search for Identity.* New York: Holt, Rinehart & Winston.

Kübler-Ross, E. 1970. *On Death and Dying.* New York: Macmillan Paperbacks.

Needleman, J. 1980. *The New Religions.* New York: Doubleday.

Schur, E. 1976. *The Awareness Trap.* New York: McGraw-Hill.

Snow, D., and C. Phillips. 1982. "The changing self orientations of college students: From institution to impulse." *Social Science Quarterly* 63:462–476.

Stone, G. P. 1968. "Halloween and the mass child." In *The Sociological Perspective,* ed. S. McNall. Boston: Little, Brown.

Toffler, A. 1971. *Future Shock.* New York: Bantam Books.

Toffler, A. 1980. *The Third Wave.* New York: Bantam Books.

Turner, R. 1969. "The theme of contemporary social movements." *British Journal of Sociology* 20:390–405.

Wuthnow, R. 1976. "The new religions in social context." In *The New Religious Consciousness,* ed. C. Y. Glock and R. Bellah. Berkeley: University of California Press.

Zurcher, L. 1977. *The Mutable Self.* Beverly Hills, Cal.: Sage Publications.

# INDEXES

# Name

Abbott, Ward, 52
Albee, George, 287
Allon, Natalie, 72, 75
Andreski, Stanislav, 29
Arafat, I., 149, 151
Aries, P., 134, 256

Bach, George, 143
Back, K., 75, 288
Bakan, D., 257
Baron, R., 202
Bart, Pauline, 272
Becker, E., 39, 281, 283
Becker, Howard, 114, 237, 238
Bell, Wendell, 24
Bellah, R., 290
Berger, B., 49, 164, 165
Berger, P., 48, 49, 53, 84, 98, 100, 164, 165, 229, 281
Bergman, Ingrid, 14
Bernard, Jessie, 272
Berscheid, E., 71
Bickman, Leonard, 75, 76, 77
Bird, Frederick, 290
Birdwhistell, R., 16, 73
Black, H., 176
Blumer, Herbert, 19, 37, 44
Bogart, Humphrey, 14
Bohrnstedt, G. W., 71
Boss, D., 179
Brannon, Robert, 135
Braroe, Niels, 176
Braudel, Ferdinand, 62
Braverman, H., 193
Brecher, E. M., 262
Breen, G., 203
Bridge, Willamette, 172
Brislin, R. W., 71

Brodsky, Josip, 52
Brown, Roger, 178
Burns, George, 269
Buscaglia, Leo, 286
Butler, Robert, 253, 254, 255
Byrne, Don, 142

Cahnman, W., 75
Cain, L., 260, 267
Calanico, James, 171, 174
Carnegie, Andrew, 202
Carns, Donald, 155, 156
Cavan, S., 132
Chafetz, J. S., 139
Chambliss, William, 240, 241, 242, 243
Chavkin, S., 240
Clawson, D., 193
Clegg, Stuart, 199
Cobb, Jonathon, 169
Cohen, Wilbur, 260
Connally, John, 259
Conrad, P., 238, 239
Cook, M., 73
Cooley, Charles Horton, 240
Cowens, Dave, 251
Cox, Harvey, 291
Cuber, John, 148

Darley, John, 111, 112, 113
David, Deborah, 135
Davis, Fred, 234, 235, 288
Davis, G., 262
Davis, Murray, 144
Davis, R., 253
DeMause, Lloyd, 256
Demos, J., 257
Deutsch, Ronald, 143
Domhoff, G. William, 166

*303*

*304 Index*

Douglas, J., 23
Douglas, Jack, 210
Dundes, Alan, 196
Durkheim, Emile, 22, 138, 192

Ehrenreich, B., 192
Einstein, Albert, 13
Ekman, P., 73
English, D., 192
Erikson, E., 252
Erikson, Kai, 237
Eshleman, J. Ross, 150, 152
Ewen, S., 287

Farberman, H., 15
Fasteau, M., 135
Faulkner, Robert, 266, 267
Feinbloom, Deborah, 68
Feldman, S. D., 71
Fine, G., 15
Fischel, Joan, 72
Fischer, C., 128
Fleming, J., 40
Fox, M., 177
Franks, David, 171, 174
Freud, Sigmund, 85
Friesen, W., 73
Fruehauf, Todd, 191

Gabor, Zsa Zsa, 269
Gagnon, John, 132, 148
Gardiner, Allen, 40, 41
Gardiner, Beatrice, 40, 41
Garfinkel, Harold, 8, 25, 236, 242
Garson, Barbara, 169, 170
Gaudier-Brezke, Henri, 52
Gellner, E., 7
Genovese, Kitty, 110, 113
Gillen, F., 8
Gitter, G. A., 176
Glick, Paul, 259
Glock, C. Y., 290
Goffman, Erving, 14, 17, 54, 68, 72, 79, 80, 81, 82, 84, 85, 104, 117, 171, 176, 226, 239, 242
Golman, N., 273
Gordon, Suzanne, 154–55
Gouldner, A., 82
Griffin, Donald, 41
Gross, Edward, 225, 227, 228
Gross, Harriet Engel, 138

Haley, Alex, 176
Hall, Edward, 10, 11, 12
Hall, R., 202
Hammerslough, C., 273

Handel, W. H., 84
Haravan, Tamara, 259
Hartley, Wynona, 296
Hartung, F., 39
Henley, N., 17, 172, 177, 179, 180, 181
Henslin, J., 46, 100, 101
Heslin, R., 179
Hess, E. H., 16
Hesse, Hermann, 279
Hesse-Biber, S., 177
Hewitt, J., 224, 233
Hill, Charles, 146
Hochschild, Arlie Russell, 83
Hofferth, S., 136
Horowitz, Irving, 114
Howe, Florence, 136
Hughes, Everett, 265
Hull, Raymond, 197
Hummel, Ralph, 193
Humphreys, Laud, 106

Iliffe, A. H., 73

Jackson, Philip, 204, 205
Jacoby, H., 193
James, William, 44
Jedlicka, D., 147
Johnson, V. E., 262

Kafka, Franz, 197
Kando, T., 68
Kanter, Rosabeth Moss, 205, 206, 207, 208, 209
Karlen, A., 153
Karp, D. A., 15, 19, 51n, 62, 102, 105, 109n, 128, 199, 251, 260
Kasarda, John, 181
Katz, Michael, 258
Kellner, Hansfried, 98, 100
Kenniston, Kenneth, 288
Kesey, Ken, 242
Kett, J., 257
Keyes, R., 155
Khomeini, Ayatollah, 262
Kilbourne, B., 293
Klapp, Orrin, 279
Knafl, Katherine, 147
Koch, K., 7
Kohler, Wolfgang, 42
Kübler-Ross, Elizabeth, 281

Lacey, H., 192
LaFrance, M., 9
LaGory, M., 115
Laing, Ronald, 239
Laslett, Peter, 192

## Index

Latané, Bibb, 111, 112, 113
Lauer, R. H., 84
Lemert, Edwin, 241
LeShan, Eda, 259
Lever, Janet, 72
Levine, J., 104
Levinson, D., 252
Lewis, J., 99
Lewis, S. A., 71
Liebow, Eliot, 168, 169
Liederman, V. R., 75
Lipman-Blumen, Jean, 177
Little, C. B., 224, 238
Locke, John, 284
Lofland, Lyn, 104, 107, 108, 109, 181, 230
Love, Ruth, 115
Lowe, J., 262
Luckman, Thomas, 48, 53, 84, 239, 282
Luhman, R., 211
Lyman, S., 10, 120, 226, 231

Maccoby, Michael, 202
Macklin, Eleanor, 149, 151, 152
Maddox, G. L., 75
Maines, D., 199
Mann, Brenda, 67
Mannheim, Karl, 53, 284
Marx, Karl, 22, 163, 192
Maslow, Abraham, 85
Masters, W. H., 262
Matza, David, 232
Mayo, C., 9
Mead, George Herbert, 44, 45, 46, 47, 48, 49, 50, 56, 84, 264
Merton, Robert K., 237
Milgram, Stanley, 77, 110, 112
Miller, A. G., 71
Miller, G., 208
Miller, Walter B., 237
Millman, M., 75
Mills, C. Wright, 231
Molloy, J. T., 75
Moon, Sun Myung, 289
Moore, J., 262
Moore, K., 136
Morgan, D. H. J., 212
Morris, J., 68
Mostofsky, D., 176
Muñoz, L., 288

Nash, Jeffrey, 15
Needleman, Jacob, 292
Neugarten, Bernice, 259, 261, 262, 264
Newton, Isaac, 27
Nixon, Richard, 74

Oakley, A., 46

Packard, Vance, 138
Pagter, Carl, 196
Park, Robert, 98, 114
Pearce, R., 203
Peplau, Letitia, 146
Perrow, Charles, 197, 198
Persell, C., 167
Peter, Lawrence J., 197
Pfeffer, R., 199
Pfeiffer, E., 262
Pfohl, S., 239
Phillips, C., 297
Pipkin, J., 115
Platt, Gerald, 258
Pleck, J., 136
Polt, J. M., 16
Presthus, Robert, 193, 194

Quinney, Richard, 237

Razran, G., 73
Reagan, Ronald, 74
Reiss, Ira, 141
Reusch, H., 7
Richardson, J., 293
Riemer, Bill, 290
Riesman, David, 129
Robboy, Robert, 136
Robey, B., 194
Robinson, I., 147
Rockefeller, John D., 262
Roebuck, J., 260
Roosevelt, Franklin D., 285
Rosenhan, D. L., 243, 244
Rosenthal, Robert, 175
Rossner, Judith, 20
Rousseau, Jean Jacques, 284
Roy, Donald, 210, 211
Rubin, Lillian, 135, 138
Rubin, Zick, 146, 178
Rush, F., 180
Russell, Bertrand, 142
Russell, C., 194

Sarason, S., 265
Sanders, Colonel, 251
Sartre, Jean Paul, 52
Schacter, S., 128
Schneider, J., 238
Schuldenfrei, R., 192
Schur, Edwin, 293, 294
Schutz, Alfred, 98
Schwartz, B., 15, 16, 192
Schwartz, Pepper, 72

Scott, M., 10, 120, 226, 231
Sennet, Richard, 169
Sheehy, Gail, 258
Shoshid, N., 80
Siegal, B., 74
Simmel, Georg, 22–23, 28, 97, 110
Simon, William, 132, 148
Sofer, Cyril, 266, 267
Sommer, Robert, 9
Sontag, Susan, 269, 270
Smith, B., 166
Snow, D., 297
Spencer, B., 8
Spradley, James, 67
Spring, Jack, 258
Starr, Joyce, 155, 156
Stein, Peter, 153, 154
Stokes, R., 233
Stone, G. P., 15, 63, 77, 102, 109n, 128, 225, 227, 228, 287
Stonequist, Everett, 98
Strauss, Anselm, 199, 200
Stryker, S., 37
Sullivan, Harry Stack, 85
Sumner, William Graham, 23
Sutherland, Edwin H., 237
Suttles, Gerald, 63
Sykes, Gresham, 232
Szasz, Thomas, 239

Tausky, C., 208
Tawney, R. H., 171
Taylor, Frederick, 193, 208
Thomas, Darwin, 171, 173, 174
Thorman, G., 151
Toffler, Alvin, 294

Tönnies, Ferdinand, 23, 128
Troll, L., 208
Turnbull, Colin, 252
Turner, J., 268
Turner, R., 80, 283, 284, 286
Tyree, A., 166

Verwoerdt, A., 262
Vinson, A., 104

Waller, Willard, 140, 271
Weber, Max, 23, 192, 195, 199, 212, 287
Weick, Karl, 199
Weigert, A., 15, 99
Weinberg, Martin, 229, 230
Weiss, R., 129
Weitz, Shirley, 174
Wells, W., 74
West, C., 180
Westheimer, Ruth, 286
Westoff, C., 273
White, Leslie, 39
Whyte, William Foote, 137
Whyte, William H., Jr., 137, 200, 201, 202, 207
Williams, M. J., 203
Wolff, Michael, 102, 104, 182
Wood, D., 104
Wrong, Dennis, 51n
Wuthnow, Robert, 289, 290, 291

Yoels, W. C., 15, 19, 51n, 62, 102, 109n, 128, 199, 251
Yorburg, B., 149, 151
Zimmerman, D. D., 180
Zurcher, Louis A., Jr., 295, 296, 297, 299

# Subject

Accounts, 231–33
　defined, 231–32
　excuses and justifications, 232–33
Achieved status, 65
　definition, 86
　distinguished from ascribed status, 164
Acting situation, 19
　definition, 31
Adolescence, 257–58, 286
　working conditions regulated, 257–58
Advertising, 287, 288
Affection for subordinates, 178–79
Affiliation, 128
Age as definition of individual, 65, 68

Age categories, 252–62
　adolescence, 257–58
　childhood, 256–57
　definition, 274
　middle age, 258–60
　old age, 260–61
　social constructions, 254–55
Age consciousness, 266, 267
　definition, 274
Ageism, 254, 274
Age norms, 261–63
　definition, 274
Age status, 252
　definition, 274

Age-status synchronization, 267
  definition, 274
Age structure, 252
  definition, 274
Aging
  chronological and experiential age, 263-64
  effects on work and career, 265-70
  government policies, 253
  life expectancy, 259
  meanings of age, 251
  norms of, 261-63
  retirement, 260, 261-62
  sexual activity, 262
  symbolic interaction approach to, 264-65
  traditional role in family, 270-71
  U.S. population, 253-54
Alienation, 282, 285, 286, 288
  definition, 300
Alternate lifestyle groups, 113, 121, 229
American Management Association, 203
Animal communication, 40-43
Animal thinking, 41
Anonymity, 102, 104
Appearance, 71-73, 81
  attraction, 71-73
  character assessment, 73-75
  clothing, 75-77
Arabs, 10-13
Areas of conversation, 98
  definition, 121
Arunta tribe (Australia), 7
Ascribed status, 65
  characteristics embedded in institutions, 166
  definition, 86
  distinguished from achieved status, 164
  role-taking, 174-76
Authority in bureaucracy, 195
Authority and obedience (Milgram's experiment), 77
Autonomy
  blue-collar workers, 208-12
  definition, 214
  women in organization, 208
Avoidance as form of social interaction, 17, 108-9, 121
  perceptual objects, 103
Awareness, *see* Self-awareness
*The Awareness Trap* (Schur), 293

Background expectancies, 8
Backstage, 176
  definition, 184

Behavior, 18, 22
  formulating, 19-21
  produced by interpretation, 19
  relationship between social structure and individual, 22, 24-25
"Being Sane in Insane Places" (Rosenhan), 243-44
Biographical strangers, 98-99
  definition, 121
Blacks, 52
  income comparison with whites, 167-68
  passing, 236
  social class, 168
Blue-collar occupations, 193-94
  definition, 213
  search for autonomy, 208-12
Boredom, 15
Boston Women's Health Book Collective, 148
Bourgeoisie, 285
  definition, 300
Bureaucracy, 15, 23-24
  career tenure, 198
  construction by members of, 199-200
  definition, 213
  leadership, 202-6
  means of power, 197-98
  models of organizations, 195, 197-98
  negotiated order, 211-12
  pervasive effects of, 189-92
  symbolic interaction perspective, 195, 198-200
  urbanization and industrialization, 192
  work in, 200-212
Bystander apathy, 111-12

Cabdriver's assessment of strangers, 100-102
Career, 265-67
  age consciousness, 266-67
  age-status synchronization, 267
  definition, 274
  women, 136, 166-67, 170, 192, 206, 207-8, 268
Childhood
  industrialization and urbanization affecting, 256
  Middle Ages, 256
  relations between parents and children, 256-57
Child labor laws, 258
Chronological age, 263
*Cinderella*, 144
Civil inattention, 104, 121

Clothing
  assessment of individual, 75-76, 279
  control of props, 229
Cohabitation, 149-53
  definition, 149
Collective search for identity, 279
Commitment crisis, 145
Communes, 288-89
Communication, 61
  failed, 62
  information, 63-85
    controlling, 79-85
    gathering and processing, 64-79
    importance of, 63
  role-taking, 61-64
  symbolic, 38-44
Compulsory public education, 257-58
Computer dating, 127
Configuration of attributes, 68-69
  definition, 86
Conformity, 82
Conning strategies, 176
  definition, 184
Consumption ethic, 287
  definition, 300
Contemporary social movement, 283, 285-86
  definition, 300
"Corner boys", 136-37
Control from the top down, 193, 209-11
  definition, 213
Controlled contact, 115, 121
Coolness, 226
  definition, 246
Counterculture movements, 289, 290
  definition, 300
Crowding another's space, 180-81
Cultural expectations, 8, 9
  definition, 31
Cultural strangers, 98-99, 117
  definition, 121
Culture, 8
  definition, 31
  language, 42
Cynicism in role-taking, 82-84


Dating
  bars, 20
  computer, 127
Death and dying, 280-82
Degradation ceremonies, 242
  definition, 247
Delay strategies as power exercise, 15
Deskilling, 208
  definition, 214

Detouring pattern of pedestrian
  behavior, 103
Deviance, 51, 286
  development of deviant identity, 240-41
  everyday, 224-36
  institutional definitions, 242-44
  labeling theory, 237-38, 241
  lifestyle, 224, 236, 240-44
  medicalization, 238-40, 286, 287
  politics of, 240
  primary, 241
  secondary, 241
  subcultures, 240-42
*Diagnostic and Statistical Manual of Mental Disorders*, 53
Differential access to resources, 164
  definition, 183
Diffusion of responsibility, 111
  definition, 121
Disclaimers, 233
  definition, 246
Discourse as information, 76-79
  verbal, 78
Disorder in society, 219
Distrust, 100-101
Division of labor, 195
  definition, 213
Dramaturgical view of human
    interaction, 79-80, 170
  conformity, 82
  defined, 82, 87
  situational view of self, 84-85
Drug subculture, 288

Eastern religions, 291-93
Ectomorph, 74
  definition, 87
Embarrassment, 225-30
  body control, 229-30
  definition, 246
  poise, 226-28
  prop control, 228-29
  social control, 226-27
  space control, 227-28
  varying effects of, 225-26
Empty nest period, 259, 271
  definition, 274
Endomorph, 74
  definition, 87
Eskimos, 7
Ethnic groups, *see* Racial and ethnic groups
Everyday deviance, 224-36
  definition, 245
  embarrassment, *see* Embarrassment

restoring identities
  assessing motives, 231–32
  disavowals, 234–35
  disclaimers, 233
  information management, 235–36
  offering accounts, 231–33
Everyday interactions, 8–9
  definition, 31
  *see also* Symbolic interaction
Excuses, 232
  definition, 246
Experiential age, 263
  definition, 274
Extended family, 134
Eye contact, 10, 17

Face games, 230–31
  definition, 246
Face information, 70, 73–74, 100
  definition, 86
Facial expressions, 73
Factory system, 192
Failed communication, 62
  definition, 86
Family, 133–34
Forms of address, 177–78
Fractured interaction, 63, 223
  embarrassment, 225
Friendships, 134–35
  organization men, 137–38
  social class affecting, 136–39
  working class men, 136–37, 138
Frontstage, 176
  definition, 184
Frowning, 181–82
Future shock, 294
  definition, 301

Game stage of socialization, 47–48
  definition, 57
Gender roles, 52
  ascribed status differences, in role-taking, 174–76
  as definition of individual, 65–68
  intimacy, 134–36
  masculine core requirements, 138
  transexualism, 66–68
General Electric Company, 200–201
Generalized other, 48
  definition, 57
Generation, 54
  definition, 57
Generational differences as sources of nonconformity, 54–55
Gesture conventions, 16–18

*Gone With the Wind*, 133
*The Graduate*, 132

Handicapped persons, 234–35
Hare Krishna, 289
*Harold and Maude*, 132
Head-over-the-shoulder pattern of pedestrian accommodation, 103
*The Hidden Injuries of Class* (Sennett and Cobb), 169
Hierarchy of authority, 195
  definition, 213
*The Higher Circles* (Domhoff), 166
Homosexuals, 106, 113, 236, 239
*Human Cycle* (Turnbull), 252

The I aspect of the self, 49
  definition, 57
Identification with others, 63
Identity, 223
  collective search for, 279
  personal, 279
Identity markers, 291
  definition, 300
Identity pegs, 67
Identity protection, 227–38
Identity restoration after everyday deviance, 230–36
  assessing motives, 231–32
  disavowals, 234–35
  disclaimers, 233
  information management, 235–36
  offering accounts, 231–33
Immigrants, 98, 117
Impression management, 79–82, 106–7
  definition, 87
  interactionist perspective, 280
  love relationship, 142–44
  single lifestyle, 155
Income distribution in U.S., 165
Indian-white relations, 176
Individual-society relationship, 22–25
Industrialization, 192, 195, 282
  childhood, 256
  rootlessness, 220
Inferiors, 164
  definition, 183
Informal subcultures, 199
  definition, 213
Information
  controlling, 79–85
  mutual protection, 81–82
  importance in role-taking, 63–64
  inferences about people dependent on, 69
  physical attributes, 70–79

provided by social attributes, 64–69
restoring identities in everyday
  deviances, 235–36
stranger interaction, 117–18
Inner-directed personality, 129
Insanity, 243
Insubordination, 179
Interaction, *see* Symbolic interaction
Interpretation, 18
  in acting situation, 19
  definition, 31
  of social life, 24
Interrupting as power exercise, 180
Intimacy, 127
  cohabitation,. 149–53
  definitions, 133
  gender differences, 134
  historical changes in meaning, 133
  interactionist perspective, 130–39
  love relationships, 139–47
  marriage, 147
  parent-child relationship, 133–34
  premarital sex, 148
  relationship in contemporary society, 128–30
  single lifestyle, 154–56
  social construction, 131–33
  sexuality, 132–33
  social status, 134–39
Intimacy process, 139
Intimate distance, 11
  definition, 31
Involved indifference, 108
  definition, 121
Involvement shield, 17, 81

Jalé tribe (New Guinea), 7
Job satisfaction, 209, 214
Justifications, 232
  definition, 246
Juvenile delinquency, 258

Kinesics, 16
  definition, 31

Labeling theory, 237–38
  definition, 246
Language, 42–44
Latent function of institutions, 155
Leadership, 202–6
Least interest, principle of, 270–71
  definition, 274
Liberal humanitarian social movement, 283, 284–85
  definition, 300

Life-chances, 163
  definition, 183
Life cycle, 252
  definition, 273
Life expectancy, 259
Lifestyle deviance, 224, 236, 240–44
  definition, 245
  institutional definitions, 242–44
  subcultures, 240–42
*The Lonely Crowd* (Riesman), 129
*Looking for Mr. Goodbar* (Rossner), 20
Looking-glass self, 240
  definition, 246
Love relationship, 139–47
  breaking up, 146
  mutual dependence and commitment, 144–47
  physical attraction, 142
  romantic ideal, 139–40
  wheel theory, 141
Lower and working classes
  friendships, 136–37, 138
  occupational achievement, 169
  self-conceptions, 168
  values, 168–69

Macrosociological investigations, 25, 165
  definition, 32
Macro world, 164, 181
  definition, 183
*The Managed Heart* (Hochschild), 83
Managers, 203
  isolation, 204–6
Mandatory retirement, 261, 262, 274
Manifest functions of an institution, 155
Marginal man, 98, 121
Marital relationships, 136
Mass society, 192–93
  definition, 213
Master attributes, 65
  age, 68–69
  definition, 86
  gender, 68–69
  processing, 68–70
  race, 68–69
Meanings of age, 251, 261–65
  definition, 273
  norms in everyday life, 261–63
The me aspect of the self, 49, 84
  definition, 57
Medicalization of deviance, 238–40, 286, 287
  definition, 246
  politics of, 237–40
*Men and Women of the Corporation* (Kanter), 207

Meritocracy, 197, 198
  definition, 213
Mesomorph, 74
  definition, 87
Microsociological investigation, 25, 165
  definition, 32
Micro world, 164, 181
  definition, 183
Middle age, 258-60
Middle class, 194, 285
Minority groups, 114
Monitoring as pedestrian accommodation, 103
Moral entrepreneurs, 238
  definition, 246
Morality, 236
"Mother Portnoy's Complaint," 272
Motives, 231
Motive talk, 231
  accounts, 233
Multiple identities, 81
  definition, 87
Mutable self, 296-97
  definition, 301

*National Enquirer*, 286
National Institute of Mental Health, 239
*A Nation of Strangers* (Packard), 138
Need for affiliation, 128
Negotiated order, 199, 211-12
  definition, 214
Neo-Christian movements, 289, 290
  definition, 300
New Deal programs, 285
New middle class, 194
  definition, 213
New religions, 289-92
  appeal of Oriental religions, 291-92
  definition, 300
  significance and social consequences, 290-91
Nonconformity, 50
  definition, 56
Non-person status, 286
Nonverbal communication
  definition, 31
  role-taking, 174-75
  stranger interaction, 119
Norm, 9
  definition, 31
  laws, 31
  *see also* Social conventions
Norm of noninvolvement, 111, 112, 119
  definition, 121
Norm of trust, 99
  definition, 121

Nuclear family, 134
Nudist camps, 229-30

Obedience to authority (Milgram's experiment), 77
Obesity, 74-75
Oceanic self, 296
  definition, 301
Old age, 260-61
  definition, 261
Old-old age group, 261
  definition, 274
Operation Match, 127
Oppression, 294
Organization, *see* Bureaucracy
Organizational position, 202-6
  definition, 213
*The Organization Man* (W. H. Whyte), 137, 200, 207
Organization men, 137-38
Oriental religions, 291-93
Other-directed personality, 129
*Our Bodies-Our Selves*, 148

*Pairing: How to Achieve Genuine Intimacy* (Bach and Deutch), 143
Parent-child relationships, 133-34
Participant observation, 291
*Passages: Predictable Crises of Adult Life* (Sheehy), 258
Passing, 236
  definition, 246
Pedestrian behavior, 102-3
Personal distance, 11
  definition, 31
Personal growth movement, 289, 290
  definition, 300
Personal space, 10-12
  definition, 31
  Middle East crisis, 10-13
Peter principle, 197
  definition, 213
Physical attractiveness as factor in love relationship, 142
Physical attributes, 70-79
  appearance and attraction, 71-73
  appearance and character assessment, 73-74
  definition, 87
Physical contact, 17-18
Physical self, 295, 296
  definition, 301
Pink-collar ghetto, 136
Play stage of socialization, 46-47
  definition, 56
Pluralistic ignorance, 113

Pointing, 181–82
Poise, 226–28, 230
Politics of interaction, 164
Postindustrial society, 294
Posture conventions, 16–18
Power, defined, 171, 184
Power relations, 164
  ascribed status differences, 174–75
  conning strategies of powerless, 176–77
  everyday interactions, 177–82
  family income and wealth, 165–68
  organizations as means to, 197–98
  role-taking, 170–77
  social class, 168–70
  symbols, 280
  within family, 173
Premarital sex, 148–49
Presentation of self, 80, 223
  definition, 87
Primary deviances, 241
  definition, 246
Principle of least interest, 271
  definition, 274
Private space, 181
Process of interpretation, 18
  definition, 31
Profile of Nonverbal Sensitivity (PONS), 175
Proletariat, 192
  definition, 213
Protestant work ethic, 201, 287
  definition, 214
Proxemics, 9
  definition, 31
Psychiatrists, 53
Public behaviors, 102–9
Public definition of love relationship, 144
Public distance, 11
  definition, 31
Public privacy, 105
  definition, 121
Punctuality, 13, 15

*Queuing and Waiting* (Schwartz), 15
Race as master attribute, 65, 68
Racial groups
  blacks, 52, 167–68, 236
  conning strategies of powerless, 176–77
  discrimination, 113
  social reality, 53
*Rape Culture*, 133
Rationalization, 197
  definition, 213

Reality. *see* Social reality
Reference groups, 52
  definition, 57
Reflective self, 295, 296,
  definition, 301
Reification, 23, 37
  definition, 32
Relationship filters, 144
Religions, new forms of, 289–92
Respect for superiors, 178–79
Retirement, 260
  mandatory, 261
Role-making, 80
  cohabitation, 153
  definition, 87
Role performance, 227–28
Role-taking, 45–46
  ascribed status differences, 174
  communication, 61–64
  cynicism and sincerity, 82–84
  definition, 56
  information, 63–85
  nonverbal communication, 174–75
  power in society, 170–77, 280
  symbolic interaction perspective, 45
  women in organizations, 207–8
Romantic love ideal, 139–40
*Roots* (Haley), 176
Rural personality types, 112

Scientific inquiry, 26
Scientific management, 193
  definition, 213
Search for self, 279–98
  definition, 300
Search for sentience, 288
  definition, 300
Secondary deviances, 241
  definition, 247
Self, 44
  aging, 264
  definitions of, 56, 264
  development through interaction, 44–50
    components of, 48–50
    interdependence with society, 50
    role taking, 45–46
    socialization process, 46–48
  existence as independent agencies, 279
  future adaptations, 294–98
  the I aspect, 49
  the me aspect, 49, 84
  presentation of, 80, 223
  search for, 279–98
  situational view of, 84–85

313 Index

Self-awareness, 292–94
  obstacles to social justice, 293
Self conceptions, 168, 178, 295–96
Self-management techniques, 106–8
  definition, 121
Self-worth, 279, 283
  denial as injustice, 284
  sense of, definition, 300
Sensitivity training, 288
  definition, 300
Sentience, search for, 288
  definition, 300
Service occupations, 193, 194
  definition, 213
Sexual abuse of children, 180
Sexuality, 132–33
Shared meaning structures, 23
  definition, 32
Sign, 39
  definition, 56
Significant others, 240
  definition, 246
Sincerity in role-taking, 82–84
Single lifestyle, 154–56
  bars, 20
  computer dating, 127
  impression management, 155
Sin vocabulary, 286, 287
Situational view of self, 84–85
Smiling, 174, 182
Social attributes, 64, 66
  definition, 86
Social bonds, 22
  definition, 31
Social class, 168
  definition, 184
Social consciousness, 298
  definition, 301
*The Social Construction of Reality*
  (P. Berger and Luckman), 48
Social constructions, 131
Social contracts among groups, 114–115
Social control, 226–27
  definition, 246
Social conventions, 9, 37
  definition, 31
  failing to follow, 219
  guides to social order, 9
  physical contact, 17–18
  posture and gesture, 16–18
  spatial, 9–12
  time, 12–16
Social distance, 11
  definition, 31
Social equilibrium, 225
  definition, 246

Social ethic, 200, 201–2
  definition, 214
Socialist movement, 283, 285
  definition, 300
Socialization, 46–48
  definition, 56
  game stage, 47–48
  play stage, 46–47
Social mobility, 136
Social movement, 283
  definition, 300
Social norms, *see* Social conventions
Social order, 219–20
  everyday deviances, 224–25
Social reality, 50
  assumption of common sharing, 51
  definition, 56
  fluidity of, 54
  multiple, 53–54
  power to impose definition, 53
  racial groups, 53
Social Security Act of 1935, 260, 261
Social security system, 262
Social self, 295, 296
  definition, 301
Social settings for stranger interaction, 116–17
Social status, 65
  definition, 86
  intimacy, 134
Social stratification, 163
  definition, 183
Social structure, 22
  definition, 31
  lower animals, 42
  reification, 23
Social worlds, 9
  definition, 31
  people's definition of, 37
Sociological skepticism, 28
Sociology
  everyday life, 25–29
  symbolic interaction approach, 22
Spatial conventions, 9–12
Spatial ordering, 115–16, 121
  avoiding embarrassment, 227–28
Spread effect of pedestrian behavior, 103
Staring, 179
Step and slide pattern of pedestrian accommodation, 102
Stimulus overload, 110, 121
Strangers
  biographical, 98–99
  cabdriver's assessment of, 100–102
  cultural, 98–99

## 314 Index

definition, 97–98
establishing relations with, 116–19
   information, 117–18
   initiating, 118–19
   social settings and situations, 116–19
interaction in cities, 109–16
structure of public behavior, 102–9
trust, 99–102
Street Corner Society (W. F. Whyte), 137
Subversion, 53, 54
Superiors, 164
   definition, 183
Symbol, 38, 280
   awareness of death, 280–83
   differences among groups, 62–63
   definition, 56
   distinguished from signs, 38–39
   meaning, 38–39
   power, 280
Symbolic communication, 38–44
   animals, 40–43
   definition, 56
   formation of society, 52
   liberating effects, 43–44
   requirements of an audience, 44
Symbolic interaction, 9
   approach to aging, 264–65
   bureaucracies, 195, 198–200
   central premises, 37
   conception of self, 44
   definition, 31
   every day interactions, 8–9
   impression management, 280
   intimacy, 130–39
   performance aspects, 82–84
   power, 177–82
   relationship between individual and society, 22
   role-taking, 45
   scientific neglect of, 26
   sociology, 22

Tearoom Trade (Humphreys), 106
Temporal conventions, see Time conventions
Terminal jobs, 203
Territoriality, 10
   definition, 31
Time conventions, 12–16
   American society, 13
   influence on behavior, 14
   power to make others wait, 15–16
   urbanization and industrialization, 14–15
Tolerance for alternate lifestyles, 113–16

social contracts among groups, 114–15
spatial ordering of urban activities, 115–116
Top down control, 193, 209–11
   definition, 213
Total institutions, 242
   definition, 247
Touching, 18
   as power exercise, 179–80
Transexualism, 66–68, 236
The Trial (Kafka), 197
Trust, 51, 99–102, 121
Twenty Statements Test (TST), 295

Unification Church, 289
Unionization, 210
The Unresponsive Bystander: Why Doesn't He Help? (Darley and Latané), 111
Upper class, 165–66
   friendship, 137
Urban personality types, 112
Urbanization, 109, 282
   bureaucracy, 192
   childhood, 256
   crowding, 181

Verbal contact, 10
Verbal discourse, 78
Vick Chemical Company, 200–201
Vocabulary of motives, 231
   definition, 246

Waiting time, 15–16
Wheel theory of love, 141
White-collar occupations, 193, 194
   definition, 213
   women, 206
Why Survive? Being Old in America (Butler), 255
Women
   age and career discrimination, 268
   ascribed status differences in role taking, 174–76
   autonomy in organizations, 208
   careers, 136, 166–67, 170, 192, 206, 207–8, 268
   employment patterns, 136
   friendships, 138–39
   gender differences in aging process, 268–72
   love relationship, 142
   management positions, 206, 207–8
   nonverbal communication, 174–75, 182
   occupational opportunities, 166–67, 170, 192

Women's movement, 53 (cont.)
  PONS test, 175
  social class, 169
Women's movement, 53
*The Wonderful Crisis of Middle Age* (LeShan), 259
Work
  defined, 169
  lower and working class men, 169
*Work in America*, 209
Working class, *see* Lower and working classes

Yoga groups, 290
Young-old age group, 261
  definition, 274
Yuppies, 287

Zen Buddhism, 290
Zoning ordinances, 181

THE BOOK'S MANUFACTURE

*Sociology and Everyday Life* was typeset at Auto-Graphics, Inc., Monterey Park, California. The typefaces are ITC Zapf light and demibold. Printing and binding was by Kingsport Press, Inc., Kingsport, Tennessee. Cover design, internal design, and page layouts were by Design & Production Services Co., Chicago.